LINCOLN
IN THE TIMES

ALSO BY DAVID HERBERT DONALD

Lincoln
We Are Lincoln Men
Lincoln Reconsidered
Lincoln at Home
Why the North Won the Civil War
With My Face to the Enemy
Look Homeward

ALSO BY HAROLD HOLZER

Lincoln at Cooper Union
Lincoln Seen and Heard
Lincoln As I Knew Him
The Lincoln Family Album
The Lincoln Image
Dear Mr. Lincoln: Letters to the President

LINCOLN
IN THE TIMES

THE LIFE OF
ABRAHAM LINCOLN
AS ORIGINALLY REPORTED IN

The New York Times

EDITED BY

DAVID HERBERT DONALD AND HAROLD HOLZER

ST. MARTIN'S PRESS | NEW YORK

www.stmartins.com

Frontispiece: Abraham Lincoln, flanked by detective Allan Pinkerton (left) and Gen. John A. McClernand, pose for photographer Alexander Gardner near Sharpsburg, Maryland, on October 3, 1862, during the president's visit to the Army of the Potomac two weeks after its victory at the Battle of Antietam. (See "Lincoln at the Front" on page 151.)

Unless credited, all photos courtesy of The New York Times Photo Archives

Designed by Paula Russell Szafranski

Library of Congress Cataloging-in-Publication Data

Lincoln in the times : the life of Abraham Lincoln as originally reported in the New York
    times / edited by David Herbert Donald and Harold Holzer.—1st ed.
        p. cm.
    Includes index (page 403).
    ISBN 0-312-34919-X
    EAN 978-0-312-34919-6
    1. Lincoln, Abraham, 1809–1865. 2. Lincoln, Abraham, 1809–1865—Relations with journalists. 3. Presidents—United States—Biography. 4. Presidents—Press coverage—United States. 5. United States—Politics and government—1861–1865—Sources. 6. United States—History—Civil War, 1861–1865—Sources. 7. United States—History—Civil War, 1861–1865—Press coverage. I. Donald, David Herbert, 1920– II. Holzer, Harold. III. New York times.

E457.15.L535 2005
973.7'092—dc22
[B]   2005044293

First Edition: November 2005

10   9   8   7   6   5   4   3   2   1

CONTENTS

A Note on the Texts   ix

Introductions

  Sixteenth President Wrote His Own Book on Leadership   1

  Lincoln and the Press: A Wary, Sometimes Testy,
    Relationship   9

Part One: The Rise to Power 1858–1861

  The Lincoln-Douglas Debates   15

  Cooper Union Spotlight   18

  Underdog Wins!   35

  The Making of a President   46

  Victory Lap, with Potholes   48

  Assassination Fears   65

  First Inaugural   73

  "Wanted—A Policy!"   89

Part Two: The Early War Years 1861–1862

  Fort Sumter Falls   95

  South Blockaded   106

  Looking for Leadership   109

  Presidential Prerogatives   117

  First Income Tax   129

  Lincoln Curbs Frémont   133

  Cabinet Shakeup   135

  Death of Willie   137

Gradual Emancipation   138
Lincoln vs. McClellan   141
Planning the Proclamation   145

Part Three: Commander-in-Chief 1862–1864
Lincoln at the Front   151
General Walks the Plank   153
Signing the Proclamation   155
Revolutionizing Banking   158
The Draft and the Dodgers   161
Education for All   166
War Tests Civil Liberties   168
New York Draft Riots   176
Blacks in the Military   181
Gettysburg Address   186
When War Ends   191
Grant Takes Command   198
The Great Forgery Uproar   199

Part Four: The Martyred President 1864–1865
The Business of Politics   207
Beating the Odds, Again   211
Peace Nears, Slavery Ends   213
Rebels Rejected   217
Even the Sun Came Out   221
Lincoln Inspects Richmond   226
Surrender at Appomattox   229
Assassin Marks His Man   235
Ford's Theatre, April 14, 1865   240
"Our Great Loss"   247

Part Five: A Nation in Mourning 1865–1867
Mind of an Assassin   289
Mrs. Surratt Captured   297
Booth's Letter   307
United in Mourning   311
Lingering Questions   340
Long Journey Home   367
Swift Justice   371
"Oh Captain! My Captain!"   397

Index   403

A NOTE ON THE TEXTS

Back then, as now, *The New York Times* customarily provided its readers with complete texts of the most important speeches of the day. Thus, many of Abraham Lincoln's best-known public documents appear on the following pages just as they first appeared in *The Times* from 1860 through 1865: his Cooper Union and Gettysburg addresses, his annual and special messages to Congress, and his preliminary and final Emancipation Proclamations, to name a few.

Lincoln was a stickler for accuracy in the publication of his speeches (after an exhausting performance and a sumptuous banquet, he proofread his Cooper Union address at a New York newspaper office late into the night of February 27, 1860). But once elected, the president had little time for such hands-on review, and *The Times* and other papers relied on wire dispatches, shorthand accounts, and imperfect texts marred by errors in the hasty transmission from Lincoln's pen to newspaper composing room to printed page. These speeches are presented here just as they first appeared in *The Times*, in texts that invariably differ, especially as to punctuation and paragraphing, from the canonical transcripts in Lincoln's own hand, as republished in the 1950's in *The Collected Works of Abraham Lincoln*.

The text also includes the ordinary run of original typographical and punctuation errors, as well as two errors that readers may well notice: the spelling of "Fort Sumpter" and, on pages 255 and 267, Lincoln's date of birth. For this book, only in cases of confusing errors have the editors inserted a cautionary *sic*, or an explanatory note, to make certain that Lincoln's original meaning is accurately preserved.

—*The Editors*

LINCOLN
IN THE TIMES

INTRODUCTIONS

Sixteenth President Wrote His
Own Book on Leadership

by David Herbert Donald

On April 25, 1861, the lead editorial in *The New York Times* began: "Wanted—a Leader!" It continued: "In every great crisis, the human heart demands a leader that incarnates its ideas, its emotions and its aims. Till such a leader appears, everything is disorder, disaster and defeat. The moment he takes the helm, order, promptitude, and confidence follows as the necessary result. . . . No such hero at present directs affairs. The experience of our Government for months past has been a series of defeats. It has been one continued retreat. . . . Well may the great heart of the North turn away sickened at such a spectacle."

Wounded by this and other similar attacks in *The Times,* President Abraham Lincoln clipped the offending editorials for his files, labeling them "Villainous articles." He was hurt not merely by the tone of the criticism but by the idea behind them. "Leadership" was not a word in Abraham Lincoln's vocabulary. It occurs nowhere in his public papers, in his many speeches, or in his hundreds of private letters. This was not a concept with which he felt comfortable. Indeed, he never referred to himself as a leader and only infrequently applied that term to others.

He was reluctant to think in terms of leadership because he had no model to emulate. He certainly had no intention of patterning his presidency after the ineffectual terms of James Buchanan, Franklin Pierce, Millard Fillmore or Martin Van Buren. Indeed, he had to reach back to the Revolutionary era to find a chief executive whom he could respect. Lincoln called these Founding Fathers "iron men," for whom he felt veneration approaching awe. George Washington bore the "mightiest name of earth," and Thomas Jefferson enunciated "the definitions and axioms of free society." But these great figures were too remote to be envied or copied.

When Lincoln and his contemporaries thought of leadership their minds turned to Napoleon Bonaparte. To some, like Ralph Waldo Emerson, Napoleon was one of the great "representative men," who embodied the will of the people, but other Americans saw him as a dictator who reversed the democratic gains of the French Revolution and swept his country, and the world, into never-ending wars. Lincoln thought of Napoleon as a darkly ambiguous figure, often referring to him as a dangerous leader. Though not given to literary quotations, Lincoln memorized (while slightly misquoting) the characterization of Napoleon by Charles Phillips, the famous British orator, as a figure "grand, gloomy and peculiar . . . wrapped in the solitude of his own originality . . . the man without a model, and without a shadow."

This was the kind of leader that Lincoln feared might emerge in America. In an 1838 address before the Young Men's Lyceum of Springfield, he warned that the day-to-day administration of the government would not long satisfy "an Alexander, a Caesar, or a Napoleon." Such "men of ambition and talents," who belonged "to the family of the lion or the tribe of the eagle" would try to pull down the republican temple so carefully constructed by the Founding Fathers.

To Lincoln, and to many others of his generation, Andrew Jackson represented such a threat, and they feared that Jackson and his Democratic followers were moving toward "a total change of the pure republican character of our government, and to the concentration of all powers in the hands of one man." These critics saw in Jackson's reliance on his military reputation, his formation of an informal "kitchen cabinet" of advisers, and, especially, his high-handed decision to kill the Second Bank of the United States, a real danger of Bonapartism in America. Jackson's "executive usurpation" of power revealed his critics that he was a "detestable, ignorant, reckless, vain and malignant tyrant."

To counteract this peril, Jackson's opponents formed the Whig Party, to which Lincoln belonged for twenty years, and he shared Whig fears of bold leadership. In the 1840's, when Jackson's protégé, President James K. Polk, led the country into war with Mexico without congressional authorization, Lincoln feared the danger of executive tyranny. As an Illinois member of the House of Representatives, he attacked Polk for setting a precedent that would allow presidents "to make war at pleasure" and would place a future chief executive in the place "where kings have always stood."

Whigs maintained that leadership in government should not come from the president but from the senators and representatives, who more accurately understood the wishes of the people. According to Zachary Taylor, one of the two Whigs elected president, "the Executive has authority to recommend (not to dictate) measures to Congress" and "cannot rightfully control the decision of Congress on any subject of legislation."

Lincoln agreed with these views. What he called his "political education" taught him that Congress should make policy and the president should execute it. He opposed even the threat of a presidential veto of legislature, on the ground that "Congress should originate, as well as perfect its measures, without external bias." Consequently, as president, he had little to do with the most important nonmilitary legislation of the Civil War years, such as the acts that authorized the transcontinental railroad, established land-grant colleges and created the Department of Agriculture. During his whole term in office he vetoed only two bills, both for technical flaws.

To some extent Lincoln also shared the traditional Whig view on the role of the cabinet. Whigs thought of the president as a chief administrator, who presided over the board of equal associates. According to the great Massachusetts Whig leader, Daniel Webster, all measures of an administration should be brought before the cabinet, where "their settlement was to be decided by the majority of votes, each member of the cabinet and the president having but one vote." Lincoln was too independent to accept Webster's theory but he avoided challenging it by holding infrequent cabinet meetings, at which only minor matters were discussed.

Even the decision to issue the Emancipation Proclamation did not come before the cabinet for a vote. Before making it public, Lincoln read the documents to the heads of departments and invited their stylistic criticisms, but he announced bluntly: "I do not wish your advice about the main matter—for that I have determined for myself."

After a time Salmon P. Chase, the Secretary of the Treasury, refused to attend sessions of the "so-called cabinet," because they were a waste of time. We . . . are called members of the cabinet," he protested, "but are in reality only separate heads of departments, meeting now and then for talk on whatever happens to come uppermost, not for grave consultation on matters concerning the salvation of the country." When Judge David Davis, a long-time political ally, asked Lincoln how frequently he sought the opinion of the department heads, he replied, according to Davis, that "he never consulted his cabinet; they all disagreed so much he would not ask them."

To most of the cabinet members Lincoln gave a free hand in running their departments. He was not much interested in the Department of the Interior, which was badly and corruptly managed, and he cared little for the very efficient work of his postmaster general. Even the centrally important Treasury Department came only occasionally under his personal scrutiny. Because he had what he called a "special interest" in banking legislation from his days in the Illinois legislature, he did confer with Chase, the treasury secretary, on setting up the new national banking system, but on other vital financial questions he allowed Chase to make all the decisions, telling him: "You understand these things. I do not." In foreign affairs, he intervened occasionally to curb his bellicose Secretary of State, William H. Seward, but allowed Seward to manage routine diplomatic correspondence.

Practical considerations reinforced Lincoln's reluctance to assume the role of leader. He came to office woefully lacking in personal authority. The Republican Party that elected him in 1860 was new and untried. It was composed, as Lincoln himself said, of "strange, discordant and even hostile elements," which banded together to defeat the Democrats.

In most of the states that voted for him in 1860 he received considerably fewer votes than the Republican candidates for governor or for Congress. There were at least half a dozen other Republican leaders—among them Charles Sumner of Massachusetts, Seward of New York, Simon Cameron of Pennsylvania, Chase of Ohio, Zachariah Chandler of Michigan, Lyman Trumbull of Illinois and James H. Grimes of Iowa—who had given longer service to the party, which Lincoln had joined belatedly, and who had wider experience in the national government than Lincoln, who had served only a single term in the House of Representatives back in the 1840's. Lincoln was painfully aware that he was a minority president, without a popular mandate, who had received less than 40 percent of the popular vote in 1860. In eight of the states that seceded to form the Confederacy not a single vote was cast for Lincoln.

Though constrained by ideology and practicality, Lincoln was too strong-minded to become a do-nothing president, like his predecessors, James Buchanan and Franklin Pierce. Indeed, at times he was tempted to make a Napoleonic gesture, boldly asserting leadership. More than once, frustrated by the tardiness and incompetence of his generals, he thought of assuming his constitutional role as commander-in-chief and taking to the field himself as the head of the army. After the battle of Gettysburg, when Gen. George Gordon Meade allowed Robert E. Lee and his Confederate army to slip unscathed back across the Potomac River, the president was deeply grieved and told his son Robert: "If I had gone up there I could have whipped them myself." But with tight self-control he did not permit action to follow impulse.

In one area he felt free to act. From the outset of his administration he accepted a basic premise of Whig thought, forcefully enunciated by John Quincy Adams, that the president, though constrained in many areas, had a free hand when the war power was involved. Acting on this assumption, he took a firm hand in closely supervising the work of the War Department, whether under the incompetent Simon Cameron or, later, under the highly efficient Edwin M. Stanton.

At times he even undertook detailed planning of military operations. Facing a crisis over Fort Sumter immediately after his inaugural, he invoked "the power in me vested by the Constitution and the laws" and called up 75,000 members of the states' militias to put down the rebellion. Without congressional authorization he also ordered the expansion of the regular army and navy and advanced $2 million to a New York committee to pay emergency defense expenses. In a series of proclamations he suspended the privilege of the writ of habeas corpus, so that Federal commanders could arrest and imprison without charges people they suspected of disloyalty. "Whether strictly legal or not," he explained, these measures "were ventured upon, under what appeared to be a popular demand and a public necessity; trusting . . . that Congress would readily ratify them."

Such actions proved that Lincoln did not lack daring but they did not demonstrate leadership. Lincoln himself recognized that these emergency measures did little in a loosely organized, invertebrate society like the United States to build a consensus favoring his goals. From his years of experience in local and state politics he had learned that public opinion was "the great moving principle of free government." Or, as he said more succinctly the year before he was elected president, "Public opinion in this country is everything."

But the task of shaping public opinion was not easy, and Lincoln's view of the proprieties of his office did not make it easier. He followed his predecessors in refraining from making public addresses while in the White House. "In my present position," he told a crowd in 1862, eager to hear his plans and hopes, "it is hardly proper for me to make speeches." He did, of course, make his policies known in his annual messages to Congress, but tradition prevented him from delivering them in person. Instead, these long documents were read aloud, by a bored clerk, to the inattentive legislators.

Even had he wished to do so, there was no way, in these days long before radio or television, for a president to communicate to all the people. Only through the newspapers could he reach anything approaching a very large audience, but most editors were partisan and had limited vision. The only newspaper with anything approaching a national circulation was *The New York Tribune,* whose editor, Horace Greeley, was so erratic and untrustworthy that Lincoln could not count on his support. He did receive staunch backing from a few newspapers, like *The Springfield* (Mass.) *Republican.* Initially highly critical, Henry J. Raymond, the editor of *The New York Times,* came to understand the difficulties the president faced and became one of Lincoln's most loyal supporters, but *The Times* was still essentially a local paper.

As a result, Lincoln was obliged to resort to retail, rather than wholesale, tactics to shape public opinion. He early made a practice of allowing any and all visitors to come to his office on the second floor of the White House. Day after day hundreds of candidates for office, applicants for military appointments, supplicants who wanted favors and visitors who simply wanted to shake hands with the president flooded his rooms. Again and again his friends and his overworked private secretaries urged him to limit access, but the president insisted on seeing everybody who wanted to see him. He claimed that he learned a great deal from these "public opinion baths," and no doubt that was the case. But he also realized that nearly all these visitors left his office charmed by his candor and warmth and eager to urge their neighbors to support a president who was so humane and so deeply concerned for the public welfare.

Equally important was the rapport Lincoln established with the Union soldiers. In the early days of the war he often took carriage rides out to the encampments that encircled Washington, accompanied by Secretary Seward or another member of his cabinet, in order to see for himself how the soldiers were faring. Later he made frequent visits to the army in northern Virginia, sometimes staying for several days, conferring with his commanders, conducting reviews of the troops and visiting the wounded in the hospitals.

The ostensible purpose of these trips was to coordinate military plans with his generals, and they had the secondary goal of affording the president relief from the unending pressure of business in Washington. But they also served as an immense boost to the morale of the troops. To them the president was not a remote authority figure but a friend who shared their lodgings, who ate hardtack with them at meals and who at least on one occasion was himself exposed to enemy fire. He chatted and joked with the common soldiers, and once he demonstrated he could still split rails as efficiently as he had done as a young man in Illinois. He made a point of visiting the field hospitals.

Late in the war, at City Point, he greeted and shook hands with 7,000 soldiers wounded in General Grant's final campaign. Though some of the officers were unimpressed, most common soldiers adored "Father Abraham," and it is hardly surprising that in 1864 he received an overwhelming majority of the soldiers' votes.

But Lincoln recognized that such personal ties of loyalty, important as they were, did not form a firm base for his leadership. For that, a change of tone and of ideas was required. Neither prohibition of slavery in the national territories—as promised in the platform on which he was elected president—nor opposition to secession was a stirring enough issue to unite the North behind a long and bloody war effort.

In the bitter summer of 1862, as the Union armies seemed stalled, he came under increasing pressure to make a daring exhibition of leadership by ordering the emancipation of the slaves. Though he offered numerous practical reasons for not acting, he clearly was tempted. When a delegation of Chicago Christians of all denominations urged him to strike down slavery, they reminded him: "If the leader will but utter a trumpet call the nation will respond with patriotic ardor. No one can tell the power of the right word from the right man to develop the latent fire and enthusiasm of the masses." Deeply moved, the president exclaimed: "I know it."

The Emancipation Proclamation he issued in September 1862, after much hesitation and debate, was not such a trumpet call; applying only to slaves in areas that were not under the control of the Union armies, it seemed to many a hesitant halfway step. It reflected Lincoln's tacit recognition that his leadership was limited so long as the objective of the war was narrowly conceived as the preservation of the Union. He came to see that he and his fellow countrymen had to redirect their thinking toward broader war aims.

In his December 1862 message to Congress he gave an indication of the direction in which his ideas were moving: "The dogmas of the quiet past are inadequate to the stormy present. The occasion is piled high with difficulty, and we must rise with the occasion. As our case is new, we must think anew, and act anew. We must disenthrall ourselves, and then we shall save our country."

His call, buried at the end of a long and tedious annual message, was little noted, but in the following year he found a way of reaching out to the American people. In a series of magnificent public letters, which were carried in nearly every important newspaper in the country, he made it clear that he had become not merely a president who presided over the usual transactions of government but a transforming leader, who was changing the very nature of discourse about the war, about slavery and about postwar reconstruction.

In one letter, written in June 1863, in reply to the protests of New York Democratic politicians over the suspension of habeas corpus and, in particular, over the arrest of Congressman Clement L. Vallandigham for inciting resistance to the draft, he offered a carefully reasoned defense of his decision to invoke the war power to act for the public good. Then he asked, in a language that any reader could understand: "Must I shoot a simple-minded soldier boy who deserts, while I must not touch the hair of a wiley agitator who induces him to desert?"

In August, he wrote another widely publicized letter to his old Illinois friend, James C. Conkling, proudly pointing to Union victories at Antietam, Murfreesboro and Gettysburg and rejoicing, now that Grant had taken Vicksburg, that "the Father of Waters again goes unvexed to the sea." Along with celebration he offered a pointed defense of his administration's decision to enlist African-Americans in the army, where they had proved their valor. When peace came, he predicted, "there will be some black men who can remember that, with silent tongue, and clenched teeth, and steady eye, and well-pointed bayonet, they have helped mankind on to this great consummation; while, I fear, there will be some white ones, unable to forget that, with malignant heart, and deceitful speech, they have strove to hinder it."

Important as popular accessibility and lofty rhetoric were, Lincoln knew that it was also necessary to create an efficient and hard-working political machine that would mobilize the nation behind his war aims. This was a task for which he was superbly fitted. His years in the Illinois legislature had taught him just how politics worked, for, operating largely behind the scenes, he had been the principal organizer for the Whig party and then the Republican party in his home state.

As president, he applied these skills more broadly. He carefully scrutinized all appointments to make sure that jobs went to the Republican faithful. Proudly he claimed that his administration had "distributed to its party friends as nearly all the civil patronage as any administration ever did."

At the same time he made sure that the Republicans who received appointments were supporters of his policies and of his re-election in 1864. Congressmen who favored his Republican rivals, Chase and John C. Frémont, found their requests filed away unanswered in the White House, and job holders who did not work for Lincoln's re-election were frozen out.

Astute political management, idealistic public appeals and broad popular support were the three essential elements that guaranteed that Lincoln would be the first president to win a second term since Andrew Jackson was re-elected in 1832. Slowly and unobtrusively Lincoln had created a distinctive American pattern of leadership—without once using the word.

DAVID HERBERT DONALD *has twice won the Pulitzer Prize in biography and his* Lincoln *won the prestigious Lincoln Prize. He is Charles Warren Professor of American History and American Civilization Emeritus at Harvard University and recently published* We Are Lincoln Men: Abraham Lincoln and His Friends *(Simon & Schuster).*

Lincoln and the Press: A Wary, Sometimes Testy, Relationship

by Harold Holzer

Public sentiment is everything," Abraham Lincoln declared at the first of his famous campaign debates with Stephen A. Douglas in 1858. "With public sentiment, nothing can fail; without it nothing can succeed. Consequently he who molds public sentiment goes deeper than he who enacts statutes and pronounces decisions." And as a foreign visitor noted a few years later: "Amid the noisy confusion of discordant voices which always arises in a free country at moments of crisis," Lincoln always managed to "distinguish with marvelous acuteness the true voice of public opinion."

To understand Lincoln's long, complex relationship with the press as an essential instrument in molding public opinion requires an appreciation of the vastly different political and journalistic culture of the 19th century. In an age before newsreels, radio or television, America's daily newspapers provided eager readers with constant access to candidates and issues—and plenty of what would be called today biased copy. These journals openly aligned themselves with political parties, producing partisan coverage that stimulated the public's passion for politics. Newspaper editors often sought and served in public office themselves. Within this competitive, bare-knuckled tradition, most cities had at east two rival newspapers, one Democratic and one Whig (later Republican). Lincoln's hometown was no exception: Springfield's *Illinois State Journal* favored Lincoln's Whigs and the *State Register* favored the Democrats of Lincoln's archrival, Douglas.

The relationship between politician and newspaper was symbiotic. In his earliest political address, the twenty-three-year-old Lincoln conceded,

"I am young and unknown to many of you." He immediately found a way to remedy the situation. His speech was printed in the pro-Whig *Journal,* effectively introducing him to his constituents. Though he lost his first race for the State Legislature, Lincoln learned a vital lesson about using the press to his advantage.

From then until his election to the presidency, the *Journal* remained—in Lincoln's own words—"always my friend." More than once Lincoln himself wrote articles for the paper, usually without attribution. On one embarrassing occasion, this practice might have killed him. Abetted by his future wife, Mary Todd, Lincoln pseudonymously published articles ridiculing a local Democrat, James Shields. Infuriated, Shields challenged him to a duel. The fight was called off only after the long-limbed Lincoln chose broadswords for weapons, giving him an insurmountable advantage.

Lincoln continued to use the Whig press during his single term in Congress. He saw to it that his House speeches were routinely printed in the hometown party newspaper—perhaps, ironically, dooming his slim chance of renomination by publicizing his controversial stand against the Mexican War.

Years later, a journalistic revolution helped propel Lincoln into wider prominence. When he and Senator Douglas agreed to debate in 1858, Chicago's Republican and Democratic papers each, for the first time, assigned "phonographic reporters" to record the candidates' speeches in shorthand. Their transcriptions were republished throughout the country. Flawed as they were—both candidates complained that careless or conspiratorial stenographers mangled their orations—the newspaper reprints were later issued as an influential best-selling book.

Although Lincoln lost the 1858 race for the United States Senate, newspaper coverage helped make him a national figure, and less than two years later, he was aspiring to the presidency. For that, Lincoln first needed the endorsement of the all-powerful Republican *Chicago Press and Tribune,* so he campaigned for the paper's blessing more aggressively than he campaigned for the presidency itself. His reward was a February 16, 1860, editorial predicting that he "would lead the Republican party on to a glorious victory." Traveling to New York a few days later to deliver his Cooper Union address, Lincoln did not rest on his laurels as favorite son or visiting orator. That night he went to the *New York Tribune* press room to proofread personally the typeset version of his speech. Its publication the next day, showing that the Westerner had triumphed before a discerning Eastern audience, helped propel him to the White House.

Once nominated, following the custom of the day, Lincoln withdrew form the public eye, gave no speeches and limited press access. He did, however, pose for artists and photographers whose work was engraved for the illustrated weeklies. He engineered publication of his campaign biography for the Eastern press. ("Of course it must not appear to have been written by myself," he cautioned, though in fact he did write it.) And he hired as private secretary a sympathetic Illinois newspaper editor, John G. Nicolay. Though he maintained his public silence as president-elect, Lincoln no doubt had foreknowledge—and perhaps advance approval—of a number of friendly articles appearing during this waiting period, and into his White House term, by Nicolay's assistant, John Hay.

Lincoln installed Nicolay as White House chief of staff, but his presence did not change the political culture that inhibited direct contact between the president and the press. Lincoln held no news conferences and granted few interviews during the Civil War, and sometimes regretted an exception. When Nathaniel Hawthorne wrote frankly for the *Atlantic Monthly* about his rare visit to the executive mansion, editors were so horrified by the author's description of the "lengthy awkwardness" of the man he called "Uncle Abe" that they insisted that Hawthorne delete all personal references to the president.

The president got a far more sympathetic hearing from Noah Brooks, Washington correspondent for the *Sacramento Daily Union,* who praised Lincoln throughout the war. The president would probably have named Brooks chief of staff for his second term, but Lincoln died too soon. Earlier Lincoln had cemented his alliance with the pro-Republican press in time for his re-election when the Republican National Committee named as its new chairman Henry J. Raymond, editor of *The New York Times.*

Claiming extraordinary wartime powers to limit civil protest and combat "disloyalty," such as suspending the right of habeas corpus and curbing free speech, the military shut down two Democratic Party–affiliated newspapers for disloyalty and imprisoned their editors and publishers. The president eventually revoked the orders, but never apologized. Interestingly, the crackdown did little to chill critical press coverage. Reporting on the 1864 re-election campaign proved robust and at times, viciously partisan. The most Lincoln ever said on the subject was in jest. "The Secretary of War, you know, holds a pretty tight rein on the press, so that they shall not tell more than they ought to," he told an audience in Jersey City, New Jersey, in 1862, "and I'm afraid that if I blab too much he might draw a tight rein on me."

Lincoln remained reluctant to "blab," but had he attempted to curry press favor more directly, he might have received laudatory coverage more often, including praise for what is now considered his greatest speech. Instead, the Gettysburg Address probably ranks as the biggest missed press opportunity of the Civil War. Although pro-Republican journals praised it, and pro-Democratic papers predictably assailed it, few understood its importance, and most gave it little space. Lincoln had no press secretary or speechwriter on his staff to promote his public image. The president handled such matters himself and for the most part he did so brilliantly.

During the war he wrote a number of "state papers" intended to carry his arguments directly to the people through the newspapers. When, for example, a convention of New York State Democrats scathingly condemned the administration's record on civil liberties, Lincoln wrote a passionate defense and encouraged friendly newspapers around the country—many of which depended upon paid Republican party advertising—to print it.

Disinclined to travel while the war raged, Lincoln found that he could write public letters in lieu of speeches, which newspapers would publish as if he had delivered them on the scene. In this way, he managed a "homecoming" in Springfield, Illinois, in 1863 without setting foot outside Washington. His speech there was read aloud by a stand-in, but this made little difference to newspaper subscribers around the country, who were soon reading Lincoln's rousing vow that Union victory would show "there can be no successful appeal from the ballot to the bullet."

When it came to Emancipation, Lincoln tried manipulating the press audaciously while preparing white America for the society-altering order. When *The New York Tribune*'s Horace Greeley editorialized that Lincoln was "strangely and disastrously remiss" on the issue, Lincoln replied with a widely reprinted letter that declared his "paramount object" was to save the Union, not to end slavery. To cloud the issue further, in 1862, he received a delegation of free African-Americans at the White House, making sure a journalist was on hand to record his remarks, and bluntly urged blacks to emigrate to Africa or the Caribbean. In both cases the president was being disingenuous, or at lest too clever for his own good, because he failed to disclose that he had already written the Emancipation Proclamation and was merely awaiting a Union battlefield triumph before issuing it. Lincoln's spin doctoring came back to haunt him in history, forever making him appear insensitive and indecisive on the issue of black freedom.

Though one of the most vilified American presidents, Lincoln remained sensitive to newspaper reaction. Critical journalists he saw as "villainous reporters" who "persistently garbled" his words. But "commendation in newspapers," he admitted in 1862, was ". . . all that a vain man could wish." Lincoln was not a particularly vain man. But when he dressed for the last time before going to Ford's Theatre on April 14, 1865, he put in his pockets nine newspaper clippings he thought worthy of saving. Not surprisingly, several praised him lavishly.

HAROLD HOLZER *is co-chairman of the 2009 Abraham Lincoln Bicentennial Commission and senior vice president for external affairs at the Metropolitan Museum of Art, and author and coauthor of twenty-three books on Lincoln and the Civil War, most recently the award-winning* Lincoln at Cooper Union, *which earned a 2005 Lincoln Prize.*

PART ONE

THE RISE TO POWER
1858–1861

The Lincoln-Douglas Debates

A braham Lincoln and Stephen Douglas were already political rivals, and veterans of previous debates, by the time Illinois Republicans nominated the former Congressman in June 1858 to challenge Democrat Douglas's bid for re-election to the U.S. Senate. Lincoln accepted the nod with his ringing "House Divided" address, famously declaring: "I believe this government cannot endure, permanently half slave and half free."

Douglas believes otherwise. As father of the doctrine of "popular sovereignty," he argued that citizens of new federal territories had the right to vote to welcome or ban slavery for themselves. Just as adamantly, Lincoln insisted that the federal government must prevent the spread of slavery in order to place it "on the course of ultimate extinction."

Lincoln knew from the start that he faced an uphill battle. The Douglas campaign was well organized and better financed. The foes went at each other twice in July in separate appearances before they agreed on new ground rules for seven joint appearances from mid-August through October.

The New York Times paid belated, but extensive, attention to the growing contest predicting (accurately as it turned out) that Douglas would ultimately win. It was evident that the Lincoln-Douglas campaign debates had become not just a local phenomenon, but a national one.

On July 22, the pro-Democratic Chicago Daily Times suggested: "Let Mr. Douglas and Mr. Lincoln agree to canvass the state together, in the old western style." Weary of shadowing his opponent, Lincoln seized on the idea, issuing a formal challenge two days later: "Will it be agreeable to you to make an arrangement for you and myself to divide time, and address the same audience during the present canvass?" Douglas had little

15

to gain and much to lose by appearing alongside his lesser-known foe. But to decline would have been unmanly.

On August 3, still apparently viewing Lincoln as an upstart, The Times reprinted Douglas's acceptance letter, and a pro-Douglas article from Chicago that described Lincoln's "desperate attempt" to reply there to the senator. Two weeks later, the candidates met for their first debate at Ottawa. "The fire flew some," Lincoln confided after a less-than-inspired performance, "and I am glad to know I am still alive." By the second debate at Freeport on August 26, Lincoln had gained the offensive.

On through October, Lincoln and Douglas attracted enthusiastic crowds throughout Illinois. Except for personal attacks, they debated no subject other than slavery. Douglas insisted that Lincoln was an abolitionist plotting to introduce racial equality; Lincoln retorted that the Declaration of Independence declared "all men were created equal," including men of color.

Republican candidates outpolled Democrats that November, a triumph for Lincoln. But, as expected, the Legislature remained solidly Democratic thanks to holdovers and because under the political system at the time a U.S. senator was chosen by legislators, not by popular vote— assuring Douglas's return to Washington. Lincoln, however, won by losing. He made up for the lack of national coverage by publishing a scrapbook edition of the debates—just in time for the 1860 national convention.

—HAROLD HOLZER

POLITICAL INTELLIGENCE.

Senator Douglas's Reply to Mr. Lincoln's Challenge.

The Hon. ABRAHAM LINCOLN having challenged Senator DOUGLAS to stump the State of Illinois with him, during the present canvass, Mr. DOUGLAS accepts the offer in part, under certain conditions, set forth in the following letter:

CHICAGO, Saturday, July 24, 1858,

HON. A. LINCOLN—*Dear Sir*: Your note of this date, in which you inquire if it would be agreeable to me to make arrangement to divide the time and address the same audience during the present canvass, was handed me by Mr. JUDD. Recent events have interposed difficulties in the way of such an arrangement.

I went to Springfield last week for the purpose of conferring with the Democratic State Central Committee upon the mode of conducting the canvass, and with them, and under their advice, made a list of appointments covering the entire period until late in October. The people of the several localities have been notified of the times and places of the meetings. Those appointments have all been made for Democratic meetings, and arrangements have been made by which the Democratic candidates for Congress, for the Legislature, and other offices will be present and address the people. It is evident, therefore, that these various candidates, in connection with myself, will occupy the whole time of the day and evening, and have no opportunity for other speeches.

Besides, there is another consideration which should be kept in mind. It has been suggested recently that an arrangement had been made to bring out a third candidate for the United States Senate, who, with yourself, should canvass the State in opposition to me, with no other purpose than to insure my defeat, by dividing the Democratic Party for your benefit. If I should make this arrangement with you, it is more than probable that this other candidate, who has a common object with you, would desire to become a party to it, and claim the right to speak from the same stand; so that he and you in concert might be able to take the opening and closing speech in every case.

I cannot refrain from expressing my surprise, if it was your original intention to invite such an arrangement, that you should have waited until after I had made my appointments, inasmuch as we were both here in Chicago together for several days after my arrival, and again at Bloomington, Atlanta, Lincoln, and Springfield, where it was well known I went for the purpose of consulting with the State Central Committee, and agreeing upon the plan of the campaign.

While, under these circumstances, I do not feel at liberty to make any arrangement which would deprive the Democratic candidates for Congress, State officers, and the Legislature from participating in the discussion at the various meetings designated by the Democratic State Central Committee, I will, in order to accommodate you as far as it is in my power to do so, take the responsibility of making an arrangement with you for discussion between us at one prominent point in each Congressional District in the State, except the second and sixth districts, where we have both spoken, and in each of which cases you had the concluding speech. If agreeable to you, I will indicate the following places as those most suitable in the several Congressional Districts at which we should speak, to wit: Freeport, Ottawa, Gatesbury, Quincy, Alton, Jonesboro, and Charleston. I will confer with you at the earliest convenient opportunity in regard to the mode of conducting the debate, the times of meeting at the several places, subject to the condition, that where appointments have already been made by the Democratic State Central

Committee at any of those places, I must insist upon you meeting me at the times specified.

Very respectfully,
Your most ob'dt servant,
S. A. DOUGLAS.

———

Cooper Union Spotlight

When Lincoln left Springfield for New York and what he recognized as the most important speaking engagement of his career, Lincoln did not even know that he would be appearing in Manhattan. Invited to lecture at Henry Ward Beecher's Plymouth Church in Brooklyn, he did not learn until his arrival that his talk had been moved to Cooper Union, the new free college on the Bowery.

The more prominent change of venue was subtle, but significant. Lincoln now found himself a pawn in a campaign by some local Republicans to find Western alternatives to the overwhelming favorite for the presidential nomination—their own U.S. Senator, William H. Seward. Lincoln would follow other westerners to Cooper Union to audition as giant killers and even more acutely than before, he sensed the critical importance of his opportunity—and the near-fatal risk of failure.

Lincoln rose to the occasion. Though his ill-fitting clothes, unkempt hair, awkward gestures and odd accent at first startled his audience, the crowd quickly warmed to him, astonished that the debater was capable of producing the legalistic, history-suffused, precisely argued antislavery oration he flawlessly delivered that night to about 1,200 people.

But Lincoln's greatest triumph came the following day, when four daily newspapers, including The Times, *reprinted the entire speech in what was to become his first front-page article. The paper reported that Lincoln was given "three rousing cheers" when he concluded his two-hour oration with this ringing call for solidarity in the fight to prevent the expansion of slavery:*

"Neither let us be slandered from our duty by false accusations against us, nor frightened from it by menaces of destruction of the Government nor of dungeons to ourselves. Let us have faith that right makes might, and in that faith, let us, to the end, dare to do our duty, as we understand it."

—H. H.

REPUBLICANS AT COOPER INSTITUTE.

Address by Hon. Abraham Lincoln, of Illinois.

Remarks of Messrs. Wm. Cullen Bryant, Horace Greeley, Gen. Nye and J. A. Briggs.

The announcement that Hon. ABRAHAM LINCOLN, of Illinois, would deliver an address in Cooper Institute, last evening, drew thither a large and
enthusiastic assemblage. Soon after the appointed hour for commencing the
proceedings, DAVID DUDLEY FIELD, Esq., arose and nominated as Chairman of the meeting Mr. WILLIAM CULLEN BRYANT. The nomination was
received with prolonged applause, and was unanimously approved. . . .

Mr. LINCOLN advanced to the desk, and smiling graciously upon his
audience, complacently awaited the termination of the cheering and then
proceeded with his address as follows:

SPEECH OF MR. LINCOLN.

MR. PRESIDENT AND FELLOW-CITIZENS OF NEW-YORK:
The facts with which I shall deal this evening are mainly old and familiar; nor is there anything new in the general use I shall make of them.
If there shall be any novelty, it will be in the mode of presenting the facts,
and the inferences and observations following that presentation.

In his speech last Autumn, at Columbus, Ohio, as reported in the NEW-
YORK TIMES, Senator DOUGLAS said:

"Our fathers, when they framed the Government under which we live,
understood this question just as well, and even better, than we do now."

I fully indorse this, and I adopt it as a text for this discourse. I so adopt
it because it furnishes a precise and agreed starting point for a discussion
between Republicans and that wing of the Democracy headed by Senator
DOUGLAS. It simply leaves the inquiry: "What was the understanding
those fathers had of the question mentioned?"

What is the frame of the Government under which we live?

The answer must be: "The Constitution of the United States." The
Constitution consists of the original, framed in 1787 (and under which the
present Government first went into operation,) and twelve subsequently
framed amendments, the first ten of which were framed in 1789.

Who were our fathers that framed the Constitution? I suppose the
"thirty-nine," who signed the original instrument may be fairly called our
fathers who framed that part of the present Government. It is almost

exactly true to say they framed it, and it is altogether true to say they fairly represented the opinion and sentiment of the whole nation at that time. Their names, being familiar to nearly all, and accessible to quite all, need not now be repeated.

I take these "thirty-nine," for the present, as being "our fathers who framed the Government under which we live."

What is the question which, according to the text, those fathers understood as well, and even better than we do now?

It is this: Does the proper division of local from Federal authority, or anything in the Constitution, forbid our Federal Government to control as to Slavery in our Federal Territories?

Upon this, DOUGLAS holds the affirmative, and Republicans the negative. This affirmation and denial form an issue; and this issue—this question—is precisely what the text declares our fathers understood better than we.

Let us now inquire whether the "thirty-nine" or any of them, ever acted upon this question; and if they did, how they acted upon it—how they expressed that better understanding.

In 1784—three years before the Constitution—the United States then owning the Northwestern Territory, and no other—the Congress of the Confederation had before them the question of prohibiting Slavery in that Territory; and four of the "thirty-nine" who afterward framed the Constitution were in that Congress, and voted on that question. Of these, ROGER SHERMAN, THOMAS MIFFLIN and HUGH WILLIAMSON voted for the prohibition—thus showing that, in their understanding, no line dividing local from Federal authority, nor anything else, properly forbade the Federal Government to control as to Slavery in Federal territory. The other of the four—JAMES MCHENRY—voted against the prohibition, showing that, for some cause, he thought it improper to vote for it.

In 1787, still before the Constitution, but while the Convention was in session framing it, and while the Northwestern Territory still was the only Territory owned by the United States—the same question of Slavery in the Territory again came before the Congress of the Confederation; and three more of the "thirty-nine" who afterward signed the Constitution were in that Congress, and voted on the question. They were WILLIAM BLOUNT, WILLIAM FEW and ABRAHAM BALDWIN; and they all voted for the prohibition—thus showing that, in their understanding, no line dividing local from Federal authority, nor anything else, properly forbade the Federal Government to control as to Slavery in Federal territory. This time the prohibition became a law, being a part of what is now well known as the Ordinance of '87.

The question of Federal control of Slavery in the Territories seems not to have been directly before the Convention which framed the original Constitution; and hence it is not recorded that the "thirty-nine," or any of them, while engaged on that instrument, expressed any opinion on that precise question.

In 1789, by the first Congress which sat under the Constitution, an act was passed to enforce the Ordinance of '87, including the prohibition of Slavery in the Northwestern Territory. The bill for this act was reported by one of the "thirty-nine," THOMAS FITZSIMMONS, then a member of the House of Representatives from Pennsylvania. It went through all its stages without a word of opposition, and finally passed both branches without Yeas and Nays, which is equivalent to a unanimous passage. In this Congress there were sixteen of the "thirty-nine" fathers who framed the original Constitution. They were:

John Langdon,	Thos. Fitzsimmons,	Richard Bassett,
Nicholas Gilman,	William Few,	George Read,
Wm. S. Johnson,	Abraham Baldwin,	Pierce Butler,
Roger Sherman,	Rufus King,	Daniel Carroll,
Robert Morris,	William Paterson,	James Madison,
	George Clymer.	

This shows that, in their understanding, no line dividing local from Federal authority, nor anything in the Constitution, properly forbade Congress to prohibit Slavery in the Federal territory; else both their fidelity to correct principle, and their oath to support the Constitution, would have constrained them to oppose the prohibition.

Again, GEORGE WASHINGTON, another of the "thirty-nine," was then President of the United States, and as such approved and signed the bill, thus completing its validity as a law, and thus showing that, in his understanding, no line dividing local from Federal authority, nor anything in the Constitution, forbade the Federal Government to control as to Slavery in Federal territory.

No great while after the adoption of the original Constitution, North Carolina ceded to the Federal Government the country now constituting the State of Tennessee; and a few years later Georgia ceded that which now constitutes the States of Mississippi and Alabama. In both deeds of cession it was made a condition by the ceding States that the Federal Government should not prohibit Slavery in the ceded country. Beside this, Slavery was then actually in the ceded country. Under these circumstances, Congress, on taking charge of these countries, did not absolutely prohibit Slavery within them. But they did interfere with it—take control of it—even there, to a certain extent. In 1798, Congress organized the Territory of Mississippi. In the act of organization, they prohibited the bringing of slaves into the Territory, from any place without the United States, by fine, and giving freedom to slaves so brought. This act passed both branches of Congress without Yeas and Nays. In that Congress were three of the "thirty-nine" who framed the original Constitution. They were, JOHN LANGDON, GEORGE READ and ABRAHAM BALDWIN. They all, probably, voted for it. Certainly they would have placed their opposition to it upon record, if, in their understanding, any line dividing local from Federal authority, or anything in the Constitution, properly forbade the Federal Government to control as to Slavery in Federal authority [*sic*; should be "territory"—eds.].

In 1803, the Federal Government purchased the Louisiana country. Our former territorial acquisitions came from certain of our own States; but this Louisiana country was acquired from a foreign nation. In 1804, Congress gave a Territorial organization to that part of it which now constitutes the State of Louisiana. New-Orleans, lying within that part, was an old and comparatively large city. There were other considerable towns and settlements, and Slavery was extensively and thoroughly intermingled with the people. Congress did not, in the Territorial act, prohibit Slavery; but they did interfere with it—in a more marked and extensive way than they did in the case of Mississippi. The substance of the provision therein made, in relation to slaves, was:

First—That no slave should be imported into the Territory from foreign parts.

Second—That no slave should be carried into it who had been imported into the United States since the first day of May, 1798.

Third: That no slave should be carried into it, except by the owner, and for his own use as a settler; the penalty in all the cases being a fine upon the violation of the law, and freedom to the slave.

This act also was passed without yeas and nays. In the Congress which passed it, there were two of the "thirty-nine." They were ABRAHAM BALDWIN and JONATHAN DAYTON. As stated in the case of Mississippi, it is probable they both voted for it. They would not have allowed it to pass without recording their opposition to it, if, in their understanding, it violated either the line properly dividing local from Federal authority, or any provision under the Constitution.

In 1819–20, came, and passed, the Missouri question. Many votes were taken, by Yeas and Nays, in both branches of Congress, upon the various phases of the general question. Two of the "thirty-nine"—RUFUS KING and CHARLES PINCKNEY—were members of that Congress. Mr. KING steadily voted for Slavery prohibition and against all compromises, while Mr. PINCKNEY as steadily voted against Slavery prohibition, and against all compromises. By this Mr. KING showed that, in his understanding, no line dividing local from Federal authority, nor anything in the Constitution, was violated by Congress prohibiting Slavery in the Federal territory; while Mr. PINCKNEY, by his votes, showed that in his understanding there was some sufficient reason for opposing such prohibition in that case.

The cases I have mentioned are the only acts of the "thirty-nine," or of any of them, upon the direct issue, which I have been able to discover.

To enumerate the persons who thus acted, as being four in 1784, three in 1787, seventeen in 1789, three in 1798, two in 1804, and two in 1819–20; there would be thirty-one of them. But this would be counting JOHN LANGDON, ROGER SHERMAN, WM. FEW, RUFUS KING, and GEORGE READ, each twice, and ABRAHAM BALDWIN four times. The true number of those of the "thirty-nine" whom I have shown to have acted upon the question, which, by the text, they understood better than we, is twenty-three, leaving sixteen not shown to have acted upon it in any way.

Here, then, we have twenty-three of our "thirty-nine" fathers, who framed the Government under which we live, who have, upon their official responsibility and their corporal oaths, acted upon the very question which the text affirms they "understood just as well and even better than we do now," and twenty-one of them—a clear majority of the whole "thirty-nine"—so acting upon it as to make them guilty of gross political impropriety, and willful perjury, if, in their understanding, any proper division between local and Federal authority, or anything in the Constitution they had made themselves, and sworn to support, forbade the Federal Government to control as to Slavery in the Federal Territories. Thus the twenty-one acted; and as actions speak louder than words, so actions under such responsibility speak still louder.

Two of the twenty-three voted against Congressional prohibition of Slavery in the Federal Territories, in the instances in which they acted upon the question. But for what reasons they so voted is not known. They may have done so because they thought a proper division of local from Federal authority, or some provision or principle of the Constitution, stood in the way; or they may, without any such question, have voted against the prohibition on what appeared to them to be sufficient grounds of expediency. No one who has sworn to support the Constitution, can conscientiously vote for what he understands to be an unconstitutional measure, however expedient he may think it; but one may and ought to vote against a measure which he deems constitutional, if, at the same time, he deems it inexpedient. It, therefore, would be unsafe to set down even the two who voted against the prohibition, as having done so because, in their understanding, any proper division of local from Federal authority, or anything in the Constitution, forbade the Federal Government to control as to Slavery in the Federal Territory.

The remaining sixteen of the "thirty-nine," so far as I have discovered, have left no record of their understanding upon the direct question of Federal control of Slavery in the Federal Territories. But there is much reason to believe that their understanding upon that question would not have appeared different from that of their twenty-three compeers, had it been manifested at all.

For the purpose of adhering rigidly to the text, I have purposely omitted whatever understanding may have been manifested, by any person, however distinguished, other than the thirty-nine fathers who framed the original Constitution; and, for the same reason, I have also omitted whatever understanding may have been manifested by any of the "thirty-nine" even, on any other phase of the general question of Slavery. If we should look into their acts and declarations on those other phases, as the foreign Slave-trade, and the morality and policy of Slavery generally, it would appear to us that on the direct question of Federal control of Slavery in Federal Territories, the sixteen, if they had acted at all, would probably have acted just as the twenty-three did. Among that sixteen were several of the most noted Anti-Slavery men of those times—Dr. FRANKLIN ALEXANDER HAMILTON and GOUVERNEUR MORRIS—while there was not one now known to have been otherwise, unless it may be JOHN RUTLEDGE, of South Carolina.

The sum of the whole is, that of our "thirty-nine" fathers who framed the original Constitution, twenty-one—a clear majority of the whole—certainly understood that no proper division of local from Federal authority, nor any part of the Constitution, forbade the Federal Government to control Slavery in the Federal Territories; while all the rest probably had the same understanding. Such, unquestionably, was the understanding of our fathers who framed the original Constitution; and the text affirms that they understood the text better than we.

But, so far I have been considering the understanding of the question manifested by the framers of the original Constitution. In, and by, the original instrument, a mode was provided for amending it; and, as I have already stated, the present frame of Government under which we live consists of that original, and twelve amendatory articles framed and adopted since. Those who now insist that Federal control of Slavery in Federal Territories violates the Constitution, point us to the provisions which they suppose it thus violates; and, as I understand, they all fix upon provisions in these amendatory articles, and not in the original instrument. The Supreme Court, in the Dred Scott case, plant themselves upon the fifth amendment, which provides that "no person shall be deprived of property without due process of law;" while Senator Douglas and his peculiar adherents plant themselves upon the tenth amendment, providing that "the powers not granted by the Constitution, are reserved to the States respectively, and to the people."

Now, it so happens that these amendments were framed by the first Congress which sat under the Constitution—the identical Congress which passed the act already mentioned, enforcing the prohibition of Slavery in the Northwestern Territory. Not only was it the same Congress, but they were the identical, same individual men who, at the same session, and at the same time within the session, had under consideration, and in progress toward maturity, these Constitutional amendments and this act prohibiting Slavery in all the territory the nation then owned. The Constitutional amendments were introduced before and passed after the act enforcing the Ordinance of '87; so that during the whole pendency of the act to enforce the Ordinance, the Constitutional amendments were also pending.

That Congress, consisting in all of seventy-six members, including sixteen of the framers of the original Constitution, as before stated, were preeminently our fathers who framed that part of the Government under which we live which is now claimed as forbidding the Federal Government to control Slavery in the Federal Territories.

Is it not a little presumptuous in any one at this day to affirm that the two things which that Congress deliberately framed, and carried to maturity at the same time, are absolutely inconsistent with each other? And does not such affirmation become impudently absurd when coupled with the other affirmation, from the same mouth, that those who did the two things alleged to be inconsistent, understood whether they really were inconsistent better than we—better than he who affirms that they are inconsistent?

It is surely safe to assume that the "thirty-nine" framers of the original Constitution, and the seventy-six members of the Congress which framed the amendments thereto, taken together, do certainly include those who may be fairly called "our fathers who framed the Government under which we live." And so assuming, I defy any man to show that any one of them ever in his whole life declared that, in his understanding, any proper division of local from Federal authority, or any part of the Constitution, forbade the Federal Government to control as to Slavery in the Federal Territories. I go a step further. I defy any one to show that any living man in the whole world ever did, prior to the beginning of the present century, (and I might almost say, prior to the beginning of the last half of the present century,) declare that, in his understanding any proper division of local from Federal authority, or any part of the Constitution, forbade the Federal Government to control as to Slavery in the Federal Territories. To those who now so declare, I give, not only "our fathers who framed the Government under which we live," but with them all the other living men within the century in which it was framed, among whom to search, and they shall not be able to find the evidence of a single man agreeing with them.

Now, and here, let me guard a little against being misunderstood. I do not mean to say we are bound to follow implicitly in whatever our fathers did. To do so would be to discard all the lights of current experience—to reject all progress—all improvement. What I do say is, that if we would supplant the opinions and policy of our fathers in any case, we should do so upon evidence so conclusive, and argument so clear, that even their great authority, fairly considered and weighed, cannot stand; and most surely not in a case whereof we ourselves declare they understood the question better than we.

If any man, at this day, sincerely believes that a proper division of local from Federal authority, or any part of the Constitution, forbids the Federal Government to control as to Slavery in the Federal Territories, he is right to say so, but to enforce his position by all truthful evidence and fair argument which he can. But he has no right to mislead others, who have less access to history and less leisure to study it, into the false belief that "our fathers, who framed the Government under which we live," were of the same opinion—thus substituting falsehood and deception for truthful evidence and fair argument. If any man at this day sincerely believes "our fathers, who framed the Government under which we live," used and applied principles, in other cases, which ought to have led them to understand that a proper division of local from Federal authority, or some part of the Constitution, forbids the Federal Government to control as to Slavery in the Federal Territories, he is right to say so. But he should, at the same time, brave the responsibility of declaring that, in his opinion, he understands their principles better than they did themselves, and especially should he not shirk that responsibility by asserting that they "understood the question just as well, and even better, than we do now."

But enough. Let all who believe that "our fathers, who framed the Government under which we live, understood this question just as well, and even better than we do now," speak as they spoke, and act as they acted upon it. This is all Republicans ask—all Republicans desire—in relation to Slavery. As those fathers marked it, so let it be again marked, as an evil not to be extended, but to be tolerated and protected only because of and so far as its actual presence among us makes that toleration and protection a necessity. Let all the guarantees those fathers gave it be, not grudgingly, but fully and fairly, maintained. For this Republicans contend, and with this, so far as I know or believe, they will be content.

And now, if they would listen—as I supposed they will not—I would address a few words to the Southern people.

I would say to them: You consider yourselves a reasonable and a just people; and I consider that in the general qualities of reason and justice you are not inferior to any other people. Still, when you speak of us Republicans, you do so only to denounce us as reptiles, or, at best, as no better than outlaws. You will grant a hearing to pirates or murderers, but nothing like it to "Black Republicans." In all your contentions with one another, each of you deems an unconditional condemnation of "Black Republicans" as the first thing to be attended to. Indeed, such condemnation of us seems to be an indispensable prerequisite—license, so to speak—among you to be admitted or permitted to speak at all.

Now, can you, or nor, be prevailed upon to pause, and to consider whether this is quite just to us, or even to yourselves?

Bring forward your charges and specifications, and then be patient long enough to hear us deny or justify.

You say we are sectional. We deny it. That makes an issue, and the burden of proof is upon you. You produce your proof, and what is it? Why, that our party has no existence in your section—gets no votes in your section. The fact is substantially true; but does it prove the issue? If it does, then, in case we should, without change of principle, begin to get votes in your section, we should thereby cease to be sectional. You cannot escape this conclusion; and yet, are you willing to abide by it? If you are, you will probably soon find that we have ceased to be sectional, for we shall get votes in your section this very year. You will then begin to discover, as the truth plainly is, that your proof does not touch the issue. The fact that we get no votes in your section is a fact of your making, and not of ours. And if there be fault in that fact, that fault is primarily yours, and remains so until you show that we repel you by some wrong principle or practice. If we do repel you by any wrong principle or practice, the fault is ours; but this brings you to where you ought to have started—to a discussion of the right or wrong of our principle. If our principle, put in practice, would wrong your section for the benefit of ours, or for any other object, then our principle, and we with it, are sectional, and are justly opposed and denounced as such. Meet us, then, on the question of whether our principle, put in practice, would wrong your section; and so meet it as if it were possible that something may be said on our side. Do you accept the challenge? No? Then you really believe that the principles which our fathers who framed the Government under which we live, thought so clearly right as to adopt it, and indorse it again and again, upon their official oaths, is, in fact, so clearly wrong as to demand your condemnation without a moment's consideration.

Some of you delight to flaunt in our faces the warning against sectional parties given by WASHINGTON in his Farewell Address. Less than eight years before WASHINGTON gave that warning, he had, as President of the United States, approved and signed an act of Congress, inforcing the prohibition of Slavery in the Northwestern Territory, which act embodied the policy of the Government upon that subject, up to and at the very moment he penned that warning; and about one year after he penned it he wrote LA FAYETTE that he considered that prohibition a wise measure, expressing in the same connection his hope that we should some time have a confederacy of Free States.

Bearing this in mind, and seeing that sectionalism has since arisen from this same subject, is that warning a weapon in your hands against us, or in our hands against you? Could WASHINGTON himself speak, would he cast the blame of that sectionalism upon us, who sustain his policy, or upon you who repudiate it? We respect that warning of WASHINGTON, and we commend it to you, together with his example pointing to the right application of it.

But you say you are conservative—eminently conservative—while we are revolutionary, destructive, or something of the sort. What is conservatism? Is it not adherence to the old and tried, against the new and untried? We stick to, contend for the identical old policy on the point in controversy which was adopted by our fathers who framed the Government under which we live; while you with one accord reject, and scout, and spit upon that old policy, and insist upon submitting something new. True, you disagree among yourselves as to what that substitute shall be. You have considerable variety of new propositions and plans, but you are unanimous in rejecting and denouncing the old policy of the fathers. Some of you are for reviving the foreign Slave-trade; some for a Congressional Slave Code for the Territories; some for Congress forbidding the Territories to prohibit Slavery within their limits; some for maintaining Slavery in the Territories through the Judiciary; some for the "gur-reat pur-rinciple" that "if one man would enslave another, no third man should object," fantastically called "Popular Sovereignty;" but never a man among you in favor of Federal prohibition in Federal Territories, according to the practice of our fathers who framed the Government under which we live. Not one of all your various plans can show a precedent or an advocate in the century within which our Government originated. Consider, then, whether your claim of conservatism for yourselves, and your charge of destructiveness against us, are based on the most clear and stable foundations.

Again, you say we have made the Slavery question more prominent than it formerly was. We deny it. We admit that it is more prominent, but we deny that we made it so. It was not we, but you, who discarded the old policy of the fathers. We resisted, and still resist, your innovation; and thence comes the greater prominence of the question. Would you have that question reduced to its former proportions? Go back to that old policy. What has been will be again, under the same conditions. If you would have the peace of the old times, readopt the precepts and policy of the old times.

You charge that we stir up insurrections among your slaves. We deny it; and what is your proof? Harper's Ferry! JOHN BROWN! JOHN BROWN was no Republican; and you have failed to implicate a single Republican in the Harper's Ferry enterprise. If any member of our party is guilty in that matter, you know it or you do not know it. If you do know it, you are inexcusable to not designate the man and prove the fact. If you do not know it, you are inexcusable to assert it, and especially to persist in the assertion after you have tried and failed to make the proof. You need not be told that persisting in a charge which one does not know to be true, is simply malicious slander.

Some of you admit that no Republican designedly aided or encouraged the Harper's Ferry affair; but still insist that our doctrines and deliberations necessarily lead to such results. We do not believe it. We know we hold to no doctrines, and make no declarations, which were not held to and made by our fathers who framed the Government under which we live. You never dealt fairly by us in relation to this affair. When it occurred, some important State elections were near at hand, and you were in evident glee with the belief that, by charging the blame upon us, you could get an advantage of us in those elections. The elections came, and your expectations were not quite fulfilled. Every Republican man knew that, as to himself at least, your charge was a slander, and he was not much inclined by it to cast his vote in your favor. Republican doctrines and declarations are accompanied with a continual protest against any interference whatever with your slaves, or with you about your slaves. Surely, this does not encourage them to revolt. True, we do, in common with our fathers, who framed the Government under which we live, declare our belief that Slavery is wrong; but the slaves do not hear us declare even this. For anything we say or do, the slaves would scarcely know there is a Republican Party. I believe they would not, in fact, generally know it but for your misrepresentations of us in their hearing. In your political contests among yourselves, each faction charges the other with sympathy with Black Republicanism; and then, to give point to the charge, defines Black Republicanism to simply be insurrection, blood and thunder among the slaves.

Slave insurrections are no more common now than they were before the Republican Party was organized. What induced the Southampton insurrection, twenty-eight years ago, in which at least three times as many lives were lost as at Harper's Ferry. You can scarcely stretch your very elastic fancy to the conclusion that Southampton was got up by Black Republicanism. In the present state of things in the United States, I do not think a general, or even a very extensive slave insurrection, is possible. The indispensable concert of action cannot be attained. The slaves have no means of rapid communication; nor can incendiary free men, black or white, supply it. The explosive materials are everywhere in parcels; but there neither are, nor can be supplied, the indispensable connecting trains.

Much is said by Southern people about the affection of slaves for their masters or mistresses; and a part of it, at least, is true. A plot for an uprising could scarcely be devised and communicated by twenty individuals before some one of them, to save the life of a favorite master or mistress, would divulge it. This is the rule; and the slave-revolution in Hayti was not an exception to it, but a case occurring under peculiar circumstances. The gunpowder plot of British history, though not connected with slaves, was more in point. In that case, only about twenty were admitted to the secret; and yet one of them, in his anxiety to save a friend, betrayed the plot to that friend, and, by consequences, averted the calamity. Occasional poisonings from the kitchen, and open or stealthy assassinations in the field, and local revolts extending to a score or so, will continue to occur as the natural results of Slavery; but no general insurrection of slaves, as I think, can happen in this country for a long time. Whoever much fears, or much hopes, for such an event, will be alike disappointed.

In the language of Mr. JEFFERSON, uttered many years ago, "It is still in our power to direct the process of emancipation, and deportation, peaceably, and in such slow degrees, as that the evil will wear off insensibly; and their places be, *pari passu*, filled up by free white laborers. If, on the contrary, it is left to force itself on, human nature must shudder at the prospect held up."

Mr. JEFFERSON did not mean to say, nor do I, that the power of emancipation is in the Federal Government. He spoke of Virginia; and, as to the power of emancipation, I speak of the Slaveholding States only.

The Federal Government, however, as we insist, has the power of restraining the extension of the institution—the power to insure that a slave insurrection shall never occur on any American soil which is now free from Slavery.

JOHN BROWN's effort was peculiar. It was not a slave insurrection. It was an attempt by white men to get up a revolt among slaves, in which the slaves refused to participate. In fact, it was so absurd that the slaves, with all their ignorance, saw plainly enough it could [not] succeed. That affair, in its philosophy, corresponds with the many attempts, related in history, at the assassination of kings and emperors. An enthusiast broods over the oppression of a people, till he fancies himself commissioned by Heaven to liberate them. He ventures the attempt, which ends in little else than his own execution. ORSINI's attempt on LOUIS NAPOLEON, and JOHN BROWN's attempt at Harper's Ferry were, in their philosophy, precisely the same. The eagerness to cast blame on old England in the one case, and on New-England in the other, does not disprove the sameness of the two things.

And how much would it avail you, if you could, by the use of JOHN BROWN, HELPER's book, and the like, break up the Republican organization? Human action can be modified to some extent, but human nature cannot be changed. There is a judgment and a feeling against Slavery in this nation, which cast at least a million and a half votes. You cannot destroy that judgment and feeling—that sentiment—by breaking up the political organization which rallies around it. You can scarcely scatter and disperse an army which has been formed into order in the face of your heaviest fire, but if you could, how much would you gain by forcing the sentiment which created it out of the peaceful channel of the ballot-box into some other channel? What would that other channel probably be? Would the number of John Browns be lessened or enlarged by the operation?

But you will break up the Union, rather than submit to a denial of your Constitutional rights.

That has a somewhat reckless sound; but it would be palliated, if not fully justified, were we proposing, by the mere force of numbers, to deprive you of some right, plainly written down in the Constitution. But we are proposing no such thing.

When you make these declarations, you have a specific and well-understood allusion to an assumed Constitutional right of yours, to take slaves into the Federal Territories, and to hold them there as property. But no such right is specifically written in the Constitution. That instrument is literally silent on any such right. We, on the contrary, deny that such a right has any existence in the Constitution, even by implication.

Your purpose, then plainly stated, is, that you will destroy the Government, unless you be allowed to construe the Constitution as you please, on all points of dispute between you and us. You will rule or ruin in all events.

This, plainly stated, is your language to us. Perhaps you will say that the Supreme Court has decided the disputed Constitutional question in your favor. Not quite so. But, waiving the lawyer's distinction between dictum and decision, the Court have decided the question for you in a sort of way. The Court have substantially said, it is your Constitutional right to take Slaves into the Federal Territories, and to hold them there as property.

When I say the decision was made in a sort of way, I mean it was made in a divided Court by a bare majority of the Judges, and they not quite agreeing with one another in the reasons for making it; that it is so made as that its avowed supporters disagree with one another about its meaning; and that it was mainly based upon a mistaken statement of fact—the statement in the opinion that "the right of property in a slave is distinctly and expressly affirmed in the Constitution."

An inspection of the Constitution will show that the right of property in a slave is not distinctly and expressly affirmed in it. Bear in mind the Judges do not pledge their judicial opinion that such right is impliedly affirmed in the Constitution; but they pledge their veracity that it is distinctly and expressly affirmed there—"distinctly"—that is, not mingled with anything else—"expressly"—that is, in words meaning just that, without the aid of any inference, and susceptible to no other meaning.

If they had only pledged their judicial opinion that such right is affirmed in the instrument by implication, it would be open to others to show that neither the word "slave" nor "slavery" is to be found in the Constitution, not the word "property," even, in any connection with language alluding to the things slave, or slavery, and that wherever in that instrument the slave is alluded to, he is called a "person;" and wherever his master's legal right in relation to him is alluded to, it is spoken of as "service or labor due," as a "debt" payable in service or labor. Also, it would be open to show, by contemporaneous history, that this mode of alluding to slaves and Slavery, instead of speaking of them, was employed on purpose to exclude from the Constitution the idea that there could be property in man.

To show all this is easy and certain.

When this obvious mistake of the Judges shall be brought to their notice, is it not reasonable to expect that they will withdraw the mistaken statement, and reconsider the conclusion based upon it?

And then it is to be remembered that "our fathers, who framed the Government under which we live"—the men who made the Constitution—decided this same constitutional question in our favor, long ago—decided it without division among themselves, when making the decision; without division among themselves about the meaning of it after it was made, and so far as any evidence is left without basing it upon any mistaken statement of facts.

Under all these circumstances, do you really feel yourselves justified to break up this Government, unless such a Court decision as yours is shall be at once submitted to as a conclusive and final rule of political action?

But you will not abide the election of a Republican President. In that supposed event, you say, you will destroy the Union; and then you say, the great crime of having destroyed it will be upon us!

That is cool. A highwayman holds a pistol to my ear, and mutters through his teeth, "Stand and deliver, or I shall kill you, and then you will be a murderer!"

To be sure, what the robber demanded of me—my money—was my own; and I had a clear right to keep it; but it was no more my own than my vote is my own; and the threat of death to me, to extort my money, and the threat of destruction to the Union, to extort my vote, can scarcely be distinguished in principle.

A few words now to Republicans. It is exceedingly desirable that all parts of this great Confederacy shall be at peace, and in harmony, one with another. Let us Republicans do our part to have it so. Even though much provoked, let us do nothing through passion and ill temper. Even though the Southern people will not so much as listen to us, let us calmly consider their demands, and yield to them if, in our deliberate view of our duty, we possibly can. Judging by all they say and do, and by the subject and nature of their controversy with us, let us determine, if we can, what will satisfy them.

Will they be satisfied if the Territories unconditionally surrendered to them? We know they will not. In all their present complaints against us, the Territories are scarcely mentioned. Invasions and insurrections are the rage now. Will it satisfy them if, in the future, we have nothing to do with invasions and insurrections? We know it will not. We so know because we know we never had anything to do with invasions and insurrections; and yet this total abstaining does not exempt us from the charge and denunciation.

The question recurs, what will satisfy them? Simply this: We must not only let them alone, but we must, somehow, convince them that we do let them alone. This, we know by experience, is no easy task. We have been so trying to convince them from the very beginning of our organization, but with no success. In all our platforms and speeches, we have constantly protested our purpose to let them alone; but this has had no tendency to convince them. Alike unavailing to convince them is the fact that they have never detected a man of us in any attempt to disturb them.

These natural and apparently adequate means all failing, what will convince them? This, and this only: cease to call Slavery *wrong,* and join them in calling it *right.* All this must be done thoroughly—done in *acts* as well as in *words*. Silence will not be tolerated—we must place ourselves avowedly with them. DOUGLAS' new sedition law must be enacted and enforced, suppressing all declarations that Slavery is wrong, whether made in politics, in presses, in pulpits, or in private. We must arrest and return their fugitive slaves with greedy pleasure. We must pull down our Free-State Constitutions. The whole atmosphere must be disinfected from the taint of opposition to Slavery, before they will cease to believe that all their troubles proceed from us.

I am quite aware they do not state their case precisely in this way. Most of them would probably say to us, "Let us alone, do nothing with us, and say what you please about Slavery." But we do let them alone—have never disturbed them—so that, after all, it is what we say which dissatisfies them. They will continue to accuse us of doing until we cease saying.

I am also aware they have not, as yet, in terms, demanded the overthrow of our Free-State Constitutions. Yet those Constitutions declare the wrong of Slavery, with more solemn emphasis than do all other sayings against it: and when all these other sayings shall have been silenced, the overthrow of these Constitutions will be demanded, and nothing be left to resist the demand. It is nothing to the contrary that they do not demand the whole of this just now. Demanding what they do, and for the reason they do, they can voluntarily stop nowhere short of this consummation. Holding, as they do, that Slavery is morally right, and socially elevating, they cannot cease to demand a full national recognition of it, as a legal right, and a social blessing.

Nor can we justifiably withhold this on any ground save our conviction that Slavery is wrong. If Slavery is right, all words, acts, laws, and Constitutions against it, are themselves wrong, and should be silenced, and swept away. If it is right, we cannot justly object to its nationality—its universality; if it is wrong, they cannot justly insist upon its extension—its enlargement. All they ask, we could readily grant, if we thought Slavery right; all we ask, they could as readily grant, if they thought it wrong. Their thinking is right, and our thinking is wrong, is the precise fact upon which depends the whole controversy. Thinking it right, as they do, they are not to blame for desiring its full recognition, as being right; but thinking it wrong, as we do, can we yield to them? Can we cast our votes with their view, and against our own? In view of our moral, social, and political responsibilities, can we do this?

Wrong as we think Slavery is, we can yet afford to let it alone where it is, because that much is due to the necessity arising from its actual presence in the nation; but can we, while our votes will prevent it, allow it to spread in the National Territories, and to overrun us here in these Free States?

If our sense of duty forbids this, then let us stand by our duty, fearlessly and effectively. Let us be diverted by none of those sophistical contrivances wherewith we are so industriously plied and belabored—contrivances such as groping for some middle ground between the right and the wrong, vain as the search for a man who should be neither a living man nor a dead man—such a policy of "don't care" on a question about which all true men do care—such as Union appeals beseeching true Union men to yield to Disunionists, reversing the Divine rule, and calling, not the sinners, but the righteous to repentance—such as invocations of WASHINGTON, imploring men to unsay what WASHINGTON said, and undo what WASHINGTON did.

Neither let us be slandered from our duty by false accusations against us, nor frightened from it by menaces of destruction to the Government, nor of dungeons to ourselves. Let us have faith that right makes might; and in that faith, let us, to the end, dare to do our duty, as we understand it.

When Mr. LINCOLN had concluded his address, during the delivery of which he was frequently applauded, three rousing cheers were given for the orator and the sentiments to which he had given utterance. There were then loud calls for Mr. GREELEY, who came forward and assured the audience that the orator of the occasion was a specimen of what free labor and free expression of ideas could produce. . . .

Underdog Wins!

New York triumph notwithstanding, few journalists or politicians believed that Senator Seward would be denied the Republican nomination for the White House when the party convened in Chicago in May.

But Lincoln's supporters crafted a brilliant, two-pronged convention strategy to outflank the front-runner. They courted delegates by presenting their candidate as the least objectionable second choice; and they packed the galleries with ardent supporters who would greet Lincoln's name with deafening outpourings of enthusiasm. The strategy worked.

Once Seward failed to amass the necessary majority for nomination on the first roll-call, Lincoln's strength grew swiftly. By the second round of balloting he drew almost even with Seward, and on the third, overtook him. Minutes later, the convention voted to make Lincoln its unanimous choice. The New York senator's supporters were stunned and angry. But inside the Wigwam, the temporary structure built to house the convention, spectators in the balcony showered the delegates with Lincoln pictures, and cheered until they were hoarse. (Lincoln himself, true to the tradition of the day, had remained at home.)

Lincoln would face a familiar rival that fall. The Northern faction of the Democratic party nominated Stephen A. Douglas to oppose him. In sharp contrast to Lincoln, Douglas headed east by train, ostensibly to visit his ailing mother in New England, but managing to stop at cities and towns all along the way to give campaign speeches.

Lincoln's convention strategy remained firmly in place for the entire campaign. The Republican nominee said and wrote nothing new and kept close to his Springfield home. His supporters, meanwhile, organized exuberant torchlight parades and benefited from broadly circulated pamphlets, engravings and lithographs that introduced their standard-bearer to the country. As The Times's *front-page report of his nomination suggested, Lincoln needed all the introductions he could get. The paper reported that day that the nomination had gone to "Abram" Lincoln.*

—H. H.

FROM CHICAGO.

The Republican Ticket for 1860.

Abram Lincoln, of Illinois, Nominated for President.

The Late Senatorial Contest in Illinois to be Re-Fought on a Wider Field.

Hannibal Hamlin, of Maine, the Candidate for Vice-President.

Disappointment of the Friends of Mr. Seward.

Intense Excitement and Enthusiasm

Reception of the Nomination in this City.

How they are Hailed Throughout the North.

Special Dispatch to the New-York Times.

CHICAGO, Friday, May 18.

The work of the Convention is ended. The youngster who, with ragged trousers, used barefoot to drive his father's oxen and spend his days in splitting rails, has risen to high eminence, and ABRAM LINCOLN, of Illinois, is declared its candidate for President by the National Republican Party.

This result was effected by the change of votes in the Pennsylvania, New-Jersey, Vermont, and Massachusetts Delegations.

Mr. SEWARD's friends assert indignantly, and with a great deal of feeling, that they were grossly deceived and betrayed. The recusants endeavored to mollify New-York by offering her the Vice-Presidency, and agreeing to support any man she might name, but they declined the position, though they remain firm in the ranks, having moved to make LINCOLN's nomination unanimous. Mr. SEWARD's friends feel greatly chagrined and disappointed.

Western pride is gratified by this nomination, which plainly indicates the departure of political supremacy from the Atlantic States.

The prominent candidates for Vice-Presidency were Messrs. HICKMAN, BANKS, CLAY and REEDER. Pennsylvania desired HICKMAN. New-York, in order to resent the conduct of Pennsylvania, Massachusetts and Kentucky, favored Mr. HAMLIN, of Maine; and on the second ballot, cast her whole strength for him, and it was owing to this, and the desire to conciliate New-York, that his nomination was so promptly secured.

Immense enthusiasm exists, and everything here would seem to indicate a spirited and a successful canvass. The city is alive with processions, meetings, music and noisy demonstrations. One hundred guns were fired this evening.

The Convention was the most enthusiastic ever known in the country, and if one were to judge from appearances here, the ticket will sweep the country.

Great inquiry has been made this afternoon into the history of Mr. LINCOLN. The only evidence that he has a history as yet discovered, is that he had a stump canvass with Mr. DOUGLAS, in which he was beaten. He is not very strong at the West, but is unassailable in his private character.

Many of the delegates went home this evening by the 5 o'clock train. Others leave in the morning.

A grand excursion is planned to Rock Island and Davenport, and another to Milwaukee and Madison, and still another over the Illinois Central, over the prairies. These will detain a great many of the delegates and the editorial fraternity.

The Wigwam is as full as ever—filled now by thousands of original LINCOLN men, who they "always knew" would be nominated, and who first suggested his name, who are shouting themselves hoarse over the nomination. "What was it Webster said when TAYLOR was nominated?" ask the opponents of LINCOLN. "What was the result of the election?" retort LINCOLN's friends.

Thirty-three guns were fired from the top of the Tremont House.

The dinner referred to in Tuesday evening's dispatch was a private one, and I regret that inaccurate reading of it should have misrepresented the position of the delegation as regards Mr. GREELEY. His right to act as he deemed best politically, was not denied, and consequently there was no defence of his career needed.

Massachusetts delegates, with their brass band, are parading the streets, calling at the various headquarters of the other delegates, serenading and bidding them farewell. "Hurrah for LINCOLN and HAMLIN—Illinois and Maine!" is the universal shout, and sympathy for the bottom dog is the all-pervading sentiment.

The "Wide-Awakes," numbering about two thousand men, accompanied by thousands of citizens, have a grand torchlight procession. The German Republican Club has another. The office of the *Press and Tribune* is brilliantly illuminated, and has a large transparency over the door, saying, "For President, Honest Old ABE." A bonfire thirty feet in circumference burns in front of the Tremont House, and illumines the city for miles around. The city is one blaze of illumination. Hotels, stores and private residences, shining with hundreds of patriotic dips [*sic*]. ENOUGH.

HOWARD.

PROCEEDINGS OF THE CONVENTION.

FROM THE ASSOCIATED PRESS.

CHICAGO, Friday, May 18.

The Wigwam was closely packed for a full hour before the Convention assembled this morning. The interest in the proceedings appears on the increase as the time for balloting approaches. A crowd, numbering by thousands, has been outside the building since 9 o'clock, anxiously awaiting intelligence from the inside. Arrangements have been made for passing the result of the ballots up from the platform to the roof of the building and through the sky-light—men being stationed above to convey speedily the intelligence to the multitude in the streets.

A large procession was formed by the various delegations to march to the Hall, preceded by bands of music, New-York being by far being the most numerous.

As the delegates entered on the platform, the several distinguished men were greeted with rounds of applause by the audience. . . .

After some delay, occasioned by the clearing of the platform and distributing ballots, the Convention proceeded to ballot.

WM. M. EVARTS rose and said: I beg leave to offer the name of WM. H. SEWARD as a candidate before this Convention for the nomination of President of the United States.

This nomination was received with loud and long continued applause.

Mr. JUDD, of Illinois, rose and said: Mr. President, I beg leave to offer as a candidate before this Convention for President of the United States the name of ABRAM LINCOLN, of Illinois.

The crowded audience greeted this nomination with perfectly deafening applause, the shouts swelling into a perfect roar, and being continued for several minutes, the wildest excitement and enthusiasm prevailing. At the close of the applause some hisses were heard, but the pressure for LINCOLN was tremendous. . . .

Mr. SMITH, of Maryland—I am instructed by the State of Indiana to second the motion of ABRAM LINCOLN. [Another outburst of enthusiastic applause from the body of the hall, mingled with some hisses.] . . .

Mr. BLAIR, of Michigan, said on the part of Michigan—I desire to say that the Republicans of that State second the nomination of WM. H. SEWARD for the Presidency.

Tremendous applause followed this speech, thousands of those present rising and waving their hats and handkerchiefs, and swelling the applause to a thunderous roar through several minutes. This was followed by some hisses and loud applause for LINCOLN, when the friends of SEWARD again rallied, determined not to be put down in applause by the friends of LINCOLN. At the second trial of the lungs, however, it was evident that the crowd was more divided than at first appeared, and the Lincoln men apparently had the majority.

TOM CORWIN, of Ohio, nominated JOHN MCLEAN, of Ohio, for the Presidency. [Loud applause.]

CARL SCHURZ, of Wisconsin, on the part of his State, here rose and seconded the nomination of WM. H. SEWARD.

Upon this another scene of the greatest enthusiasm and tumultuous excitement ensued. . . .

Mr. DELANO, of Ohio—On the part of a large number of people of Ohio, I desire to second the nomination of the man who can split rails and maul Democrats, ABRAM LINCOLN. [Rounds of applause by Lincoln men.]

A Delegate from Iowa, also seconded the nomination of Mr. LINCOLN, on the part of that State, amid renewed excitement and applause.

A VOICE—ABE LINCOLN has it by the sound now. Let us ballot.

Cheers and hisses. . . .

The third ballot was taken amidst excitement, and cries of "the ballot." Intense feeling existed during the ballot, each vote being awaited in breathless silence and expectancy.

FOR MR. LINCOLN.

Massachusetts 8	Rhode Island 5	New-Jersey 8
Penn., (appl.) 52	Maryland 9	Kentucky 13
Ohio, (appl.) 29	Oregon 4	

This gave LINCOLN 230½ votes, or within 1½ of a nomination.

Mr. ANDREWS, of Massachusetts, then rose and corrected the vote of Massachusetts, by changing four votes and giving them to LINCOLN, thus nominating him by 2½ majority.

The Convention immediately became wildly excited.

A large portion of the delegates who had kept tally, at once said the struggle was decided, and half the Convention rose cheering, shouting, and waving hats.

The audience took up the cheers, and the confusion became deafening.

State after state rose, striving to change their votes to the winning candidate, but the noise and enthusiasm rendered it impossible for the delegates to make themselves heard.

Mr. McCRILLIS, of Maine, making himself heard, said that the young giant of the West is now of age. Maine now casts for him her 16 votes.

Mr. ANDREWS, of Massachusetts, changed the vote of that State, giving 18 to Mr. LINCOLN and 8 to Mr. SEWARD.

Intelligence of the nomination was now conveyed to the men on the roof of the building, who immediately made the outside multitude aware of the result. The first roar of the cannon soon mingled itself with the cheers of the people, and at the same moment a man appeared in the hall bringing a large painting of Mr. LINCOLN. The scene at this time beggars description—11,000 inside and 20,000 or 30,000 outside were yelling and shouting at once. Two cannon sent forth roar after roar in quick succession. Delegates tore up the sticks and boards bearing the names of the several States and waved them aloft over their heads, and the vast multitude before the platform were waving their hats and handkerchiefs. The whole scene was one of the wildest enthusiasm.

WM. M. EVARTS, of New-York, having obtained a hearing, said: Mr. Chairman, can New-York have the silence of the Convention? [Cries,

"Yes! yes!"] I ask if the vote has yet been announced. [Cries, "Not yet."] Then, Sir, I wait to be in order.

Mr. BROWN, of Missouri, desired to change 18 votes of Missouri for the gallant son of the West, ABRAM LINCOLN. Iowa, Connecticut, Kentucky and Minnesota also changed their votes. The result of the third ballot was then announced:

Whole number of votes cast	466
Necessary to a choice	234
Mr. Abram Lincoln received	354

And was declared duly nominated.

The States still voting for Mr. SEWARD were Massachusetts, 8; New-York, 70; New-Jersey, 5; Pennsylvania, ½; Maryland, 2; Michigan, 12; Wisconsin, 10; California, 3; Total, 110½. . . .

The result was received with renewed applause.

When silence was restored WM. M. EVARTS came forward on the Secretary's table and spoke as follows:

Mr. CHAIRMAN, GENTLEMEN OF THE NATIONAL CONVENTION: The State of New-York, by a full delegation, wishing complete unanimity in purpose at home, came to this Convention and presented its choice—one of its citizens who had served the State from boyhood up, and labored for it and loved it. We came here a great State, with, as we thought, a great statesman, [applause,] and our love for the great Republic from which we are all delegates. The great Republic of the American Union, and our love for the great Republican Party of the Union, and our love of our Statesman and candidate, made us think we did our duty to the country, and the whole country, in expressing our preference and love for him. [Applause.] But, gentlemen, it was from Gov. SEWARD that most of us learned to love Republican principles and the Republican Party. [Cheers.] His fidelity to the country, the Constitution and the laws—his fidelity to the party and the principle that majorities govern—his interest in the advancement of our party to its victory, that our country may rise to its true glory, induce me to declare that I speak his sentiments, as I do the united opinion of our delegation, when I move, Sir, as I do now, that the nomination of ABRAM LINCOLN, of Illinois, as the Republican candidate for the suffrages of the whole country, for the office of Chief Magistrate of the American Union, be made unanimous. [Applause, and three cheers for New-York.]

A life-size portrait of ABRAM LINCOLN was here exhibited from the platform amidst renewed cheers.

Mr. ANDREWS, of Massachusetts, on the part of the united delegation of that State, seconded the motion of the gentleman of New-York, that the nomination be made unanimous. After declaring the devotion of Massachusetts to principles of freedom and equality, he extolled Gov. SEWARD as a statesman and patriot, and pledged the State to roll up over 100,000 majority, and give the 18 (13?) electoral votes to the candidates.

Eloquent speeches, indorsing the nominee, were also made by CARL SCHURZ, F. P. BLAIR, of Missouri, and Mr. BROWNING, of Illinois—all of which breathed a spirit of confidence and enthusiasm.

At the close, three hearty cheers were given for New-York, and the nomination of Mr. LINCOLN was made unanimous.

With loud cheers for LINCOLN, the Convention adjourned till 5 o'clock. . . .

HOW THE NOMINATIONS WERE RECEIVED IN THE CITY.

OPENING OF THE PRESIDENTIAL CAMPAIGN— MEETINGS AT THE REPUBLICAN HEAD-QUARTERS AND IN SEVERAL WARDS—SPEECHES, RESOLUTIONS AND MUSIC—MR. SEWARD'S FRIENDS, THOUGH SORROWING, DO NOT DESPAIR OF THE UNION.

The announcement that the National Republican Convention at Chicago had nominated ABRAM LINCOLN for President, on the third ballot, was published in the City at 1 o'clock, and as it spread, was received by the friends of Senator SEWARD with some show of disappointment. They had been informed by the Republican organ, in the morning, that the opposition to Mr. SEWARD could not be united, and that therefore his prospect of receiving the nomination was very good. Therefore, many of them were unprepared to hear of his defeat soon, if at all, they had not anticipated such a result until after a profound struggle. The result was that the nomination was not received with enthusiasm. During the morning, the only Republicans who seemed pleased with the result, who were inclined to talk, were those of the old friends of HENRY CLAY, who had joined the Republican Party. Some of them showed great delight, not so much because Mr. LINCOLN had received the nomination, as that Mr. SEWARD had been defeated. They claimed that in his defeat he had received full pay for having defeated HENRY CLAY in the very same manner and under similar circumstances. The Democracy seemed jubilant. They said they saw in the action of the Republican Convention the same unfortunate element that destroyed the old Whig Party. The old doctrine of availability had ruled, they said, and it would ruin, as it had done before. They pretended great indignation that the Republicans should have sacrificed their representative man in the present campaign, as the Whigs did in the case of HENRY CLAY and of DANIEL WEBSTER, and resolved to punish them by electing a Democratic President in November next. Later in the day many of the Republicans came to speak of the nomination as a very good one, although they coupled with the remark an expression of regret that Mr. SEWARD had not been made their candidate. At about 4 o'clock one hundred guns were fired in the City Hall Park, and some of the several hundred present spoke cheeringly of the nomination of Mr. LINCOLN. In the evening several meetings were held, which are reported below.

YOUNG MEN'S REPUBLICAN UNION.

A special meeting of this Association was called to assemble at their head-quarters, the Stuyvesant Institute, where at 8 o'clock our reporter found a band of music discoursing favorite national airs to an audience which about half filled the hall. The President and Vice-President of the Association being both absent, Mr. CEPHAS BRAINARD assumed the Chair, and called the meeting to order. They said they had assembled to respond to the nomination which had just been made by the Chicago Convention, and, as he was not much of a speaker himself, he would introduce to the audience Mr. ELLIOT F. SHEPARD, who would favor them with a speech.

Mr. SHEPARD said he could not but be struck with the loyalty of the New-York Republican Union in thus promptly responding to the nomination of their party. The principles of the organization descended from the founders of the Republic, and the character of the member of the Republican Party would compare favorably with that of any other party. It was not strange, that such a party, composed of honest men, should have selected a man for their candidate whose Christian name signified "honest." They knew their candidate and were proud of him. They remembered when he confronted the "Little Giant" of the Democratic party eighteen months ago, and defeated him in his own State on the popular vote. It was only owing to the false apportionment of Representatives that DOUGLAS was elected over him to the Senate of the United States. Mr. LINCOLN had been trying ever since to get an appeal to the Courts from the fraud that cheated him out of the Senatorship without success. But now the people of the United States summon DOUGLAS, or whoever may be the nominee of the opposition, to the supreme tribunal, the people of the country. The speaker continued at considerable length to speak of liberty and the rights of free labor, &c., alluding to the noble platform of the party, and closing by a reference to the enthusiasm that attended the proceedings of the Chicago Convention, and which he hoped would be imitated by the party in this City.

At the close of his speech, the Chairman proposed three cheers for LINCOLN, which were faintly responded to, and the band struck up the

"Star-spangled Banner." Mr. CENTAR was next introduced, and spoke of the good old campaign of 1856, and the part he took in the same. The party was then new, and composed of different elements, while they had a foe to contend with well organized and united. Now, however, the case was different; their foe was divided and broken up—his party was gone, and all the Republicans had to do, was to march on to victory. After referring to the deception practiced by the Democrats in the last Presidential campaign, the final showing of the cloven-foot, and the present demoralized and disunited condition of the party, he asked, "how a party thus divided and disgraced could withstand the onset of us honest Republicans?" "They cannot," said he; "they must be swept down; the country demands it, and you and I will help do it." . . .

THE REPUBLICAN CENTRAL CAMPAIGN CLUB.

Soon after 8 o'clock about one hundred persons met at the rooms of the Republican Campaign Club, and after some conversation, in which regret that WM. H. SEWARD had not received the nomination, was most prominent, a meeting was organized—DANIEL ULLMAN, Esq., President of the Club, in the Chair. Mr. ULLMAN, on taking the Chair, advised all to be of good cheer, and go into the canvass with a determination to be victorious. For himself, he considered the nomination of ABRAM LINCOLN a sure guarantee of the success of the Republican Party in the coming contest. He believed that the Republicans would put aside their preferences for the good of the cause, and rally at the polls in November next. . . .

J. W. WHARTON was the first speaker. He approved of the nomination of ABRAM LINCOLN; he was the man of his choice. He admired him both for his republicanism and for his boldness. He (LINCOLN) had met DOUGLAS face to face in Illinois, and he would meet him again and conquer. He referred to Mr. LINCOLN as a self-made man, a perfectly honest and honorable man, a profound lawyer, and as a statesman, incorruptible—in fact, just the man to honor the Presidential Chair. In conclusion, he expressed his entire confidence in the success of the Presidential ticket.

Mr. A. C. HILLS, of the *Evening Post,* was the next speaker. He said it was enough for him to know that ABRAM LINCOLN had been nominated to make him sure of a great Republican victory. . . . What a contrast there was between the Convention at Chicago and the late Convention at Charleston. In the Republican Convention all was harmony and good feeling, while in the Democratic Convention, the worst passions prevailed. All was discordant, and the result was secession and utter failure.

So it would be on the day of election. The Republicans would march up to the polls in one solid and harmonious phalanx, while the Democracy would be distracted, broken, and utterly routed. [Applause.] . . .

Mr. DITTENHOFF, in an animated speech, gave the views of the German Republicans of the City touching the nomination of Mr. LINCOLN. He knew the Republicans among the Germans would accept the nomination and give it their full support, and he prophesied their entire vote for Mr. LINCOLN.

Mr. E. WEBSTER stated that Gov. BANKS was his first choice for the Presidency, Mr. WADE his next choice, Mr. SEWARD his next, and Mr. LINCOLN the last on the list. Notwithstanding the name of Mr. LINCOLN was the last man on his slate, he should now be the first in receiving his support. [Applause.]

Mr. ULLMANN said a great battle had to be fought and he hoped they would all be fully armed to meet the enemy.

With three times three cheers for ABRAM LINCOLN and HANNIBAL HAMLIN, the meeting adjourned till Monday evening.

THE FEELING IN THE SEVERAL WARDS.

Late in the evening there were gatherings at the Republican Head Quarters in several Wards, for the purpose of talking over the Chicago nominations. Excepting where the gatherings were regularly organized, the conversation was carried on in a very moderate tone of voice. All expressed their astonishment and sore disappointment because of the failure of WILLIAM. H. SEWARD to receive the nomination. With him they were confident they could have carried the State of New York, and, with that, the Union. However, ABRAM LINCOLN was a good Republican, and a strong man. So was HANNIBAL HAMLIN, and with them they would go into the fight, and win if they could. . . .

In the other upper Wards there were no demonstrations of joy. Nearly all the Republicans expressed disappointment and regret freely, though but few of them expressed a determination not to support the ticket. In the lower Wards there was nothing done by way of joyous demonstration except in the City Hall Park, during the afternoon, where one hundred guns were fired, in the presence of several hundred persons.

In Wall-street, when the news of the nomination of Mr. LINCOLN was made known, the Republicans there either declined to talk at all on the subject, or expressed dissatisfaction with the result, nor did they, when the time came for leaving the street, appear to have changed their minds, or to have improved in spirits.

The Making of a President

Historians are still divided on the subject of how Lincoln won the 1860 presidential election.

Some firmly believe that the outcome was decided the moment the Democratic party split into Northern and Southern factions and nominated separate candidates—Stephen A. Douglas and John C. Breckinridge respectively—hopelessly dividing their vote. The addition of a fourth candidate, John Bell of the new Constitutional Union party, further split the anti-Lincoln forces.

But in recent years, scholars have pointed out that even if all his opponents' votes had been lumped together, Lincoln would still have eked out an electoral majority. Nonetheless, when the ballots were counted on November 6, Lincoln could attract no more than 40 percent of the popular vote. His name did not even appear on ballots in ten Southern states, but Lincoln won enough Northern states to earn a decisive victory in the only contest that mattered: the quest for electors.

In New York, despite the acclaim he had received earlier in the year at Cooper Union, Lincoln won only in those areas in which he had never appeared. He carried most of upstate New York, but Manhattan, Brooklyn, and the Bronx voted decisively for the Democrats. New York—a microcosm of the rest of the country—remained bitterly divided. He won the state but not the city. The final national tally was:

Lincoln	**1,866,452**
	(40%; 180 electoral votes)
Douglas	**1,376,957**
	(29%; 12 electoral votes)
Breckinridge	**849,781**
	(18%; 72 electoral votes)
Bell	**588,879**
	(13%; 39 electoral votes)

"At the various hotels on Broadway," one newspaper reported, ". . . the smiling faces of the one side and the elongated countenances of the other at once told which were the victorious party." A more ominous response, quoted later by author Herbert Mitgang, came from the South. "The evil days, so dreaded by our forefathers and the early defenders of the Constitution," one newspaper warned, "are upon us."

—H. H.

THE PRESIDENTIAL ELECTION.

Astounding Triumph of Republicanism.

The North Rising in Indignation at the Menaces of the South.

Abraham Lincoln Probably Elected President by a Majority of the Entire Popular Vote.

Forty Thousand Majority for the Republican Ticket in New-York.

One Hundred Thousand Majority in Pennsylvania.

Seventy Thousand Majority in Massachusetts.

Corresponding Gains in the Western and North-Western States.

Preponderance of John Bell and Conservatism at the South.

Results of the Contest upon Congressional and Local Tickets.

Re-Election of Gov. Morgan.

The canvass for the Presidency of the United States terminated last evening, in all the States of the Union, under the revised regulation of Congress, passed in 1845, and the result, by the vote of New-York, is placed beyond question at once. It elects ABRAHAM LINCOLN of Illinois, President, and HANNIBAL HAMLIN of Maine, Vice-President of the United States, for four years, from the 4th March next, directly by the People. These Republican Candidates having a clear majority of the 303 Electoral votes of the 33 States, over all three of the opposing tickets. They receive, including Mr. LINCOLN's own State, from which the returns have not yet come, in the

New-England States	41
New-York	35
Pennsylvania	27
New-Jersey	7
And the Northwest	61
Total Electoral for LINCOLN	171

Being 19 over the required majority, without wasting the returns from the two Pacific States of Oregon and California.

The election, so far as the City and State of New-York are concerned, will probably stand, hereafter, as one of the most remarkable in the political contest of the country; marked, as it is, by far the heaviest popular vote ever cast in the City, and by the sweeping, and almost uniform, Republican majorities in the country.

The State of Pennsylvania, which virtually decided her preference in October, has again thrown an overwhelming majority for the Republican candidates. And New-Jersey, after a sharp contest has, as usual in nearly all the Presidential elections, taken her place on the same side. The New-England majorities run up by tens of thousands.

The Congressional elections which took place yesterday in this State have probably confirmed the probability of an Anti-Republican preponderance in the next House of Representatives, by displacing several of the present Republican members.

The new House of Assembly for New-York will, as usual, be largely Republican.

Of the reelection of Gov. MORGAN there is little or no question. By the scattering vote thrown for Mr. BRADY in this City, the plurality of Mr. KELLY over Gov. MORGAN is partially reduced, while the heavy Republican majority in the country insures Gov. MORGAN's success. . . .

Victory Lap, with Potholes

As he did so triumphantly during his presidential campaign, Lincoln relied more on image than on substance during his inaugural journey from Springfield to Washington. This time, however, the strategy did not entirely succeed.

The president-elect managed to generate widespread interest—and perhaps, some much-needed reassurance as the secession crisis worsened—by appearing in public with newly grown whiskers. His new look effectively transformed him overnight from "Honest Abe" the rail-splitter into "Father Abraham," the avuncular statesman.

But appearances were not enough. Despite numerous opportunities to offer inspiration and solace at dozens of railroad depots along the route, Lincoln provided little more than homespun jokes and informal appeals to patience and loyalty. "In plain words," he feebly insisted in Pittsburgh, "there is really no crisis except an artificial one." "If anything goes wrong," he blurted at Steubenville, ". . . and you find you made a mistake, elect a better man next time. There are plenty of them."

By the time he arrived in New York City for his first visit since the galvanizing Cooper Union address, Lincoln had done little to soothe angry Southerners, and even less to inspire worried Northerners. To describe the reception he received there as chilly would be an understatement.

According to the enthusiastic New York Times, Lincoln entered his carriage—used by the Prince of Wales earlier in the year—"amid cheers and the waving of handkerchiefs." But Walt Whitman, who witnessed the same scene, remembered "no compliments—no welcome," and "much anxiety conceal'd in that quiet."

Lincoln's New York schedule gave him little opportunity to change course. He met with political and business leaders, spoke from his hotel, joined the mayor for a reception at City Hall, and conferred with the vice president-elect. Press scrutiny was intense. When Lincoln committed a fashion faux pas by wearing black gloves at the opera, tongues wagged merrily.

But Lincoln did make his basic policy absolutely clear during his visit to New York. For the first time during his inaugural journey he gave notice to the South that secession would be resisted. "There is nothing that can ever bring me willingly to consent to the destruction of this Union, under which not only the commercial city of New York, but the whole country has acquired its greatness," he declared firmly at City Hall—in the presence of a mayor who was known to favor the South. "I understand a ship to be made for the carrying and preservation of the cargo, and so long as the ship has been saved, with the cargo, it should never be abandoned."

From then, until the attack on Fort Sumter two months later, there could be little doubt that Lincoln was willing to risk civil war to preserve the Union.

—H. H.

THE INCOMING ADMINISTRATION.

Mr. Lincoln in New-York.

His Reception and Speech at the City Hall.

Entente Cordiale Between the Mayor and the President.

Six Thousand Citizens Welcomed Individually and Six Thousand More Collectively.

How Mr. and Mrs. Lincoln Spent the Day and Evening.

Yesterday morning Mr. LINCOLN breakfasted, by invitation of MOSES H. GRINNELL, Esq., together with a number of representatives of the mercantile wealth of the Metropolis. The party included Messrs. ASPINWALL, MINTURN, Capt. MARSHALL, W. M. EVARTS, Mr. WEBB, Ex-Gov. FISH, Mr. TILESTON, and other gentlemen of equal note.

A VETERAN CONGRATULATOR.

After returning to his hotel, Mr. LINCOLN was called upon by a veteran voter of 94 years of age, who has voted every Presidential Election, and cast his last ballot for "Honest ABE." The interview was pleasing to both parties.

GOING TO THE CITY HALL.

The morning, up to 11 o'clock, was agreeably occupied in receiving the various distinguished gentlemen who called, and at the hour named the Common Council Committee, headed by Alderman CORNELL, made their appearance to escort the President to the Municipal head-quarters. Two carriages were provided for the Presidential party, who were forthwith hurried through the gaping crowd, amid the most enthusiastic cheering, to the entrance of City Hall, whence, through the excellence of the Police arrangements of Mr. KENNEDY, and unobstructed passage was afforded to the Governor's Room. The scene on the line of march was but a repetition of that which has characterized Mr. LINCOLN's every appearance since the commencement of his present journey—only intensified up to the New-York standard.

Meanwhile Mayor WOOD, the Common Council and members of the Press, had been admitted to the Governor's Room, and were eagerly awaiting the arrival which was at length announced by the shouts of the crowd on the stairs, reverberating through the building like a miniature thunder storm.

Escorted by Alderman CORNELL, Mr. LINCOLN entered, hat in hand, and advanced to where Mayor WOOD was posted, behind WASHINGTON's writing desk, and immediately in front of Gov. SEWARD's portrait. The bustle of the Aldermanic and Councilmanic rush for good places having in a measure subsided, Mayor WOOD, in a voice that seemed for a moment slightly tremulous, spoke as follows:

MAYOR WOOD'S SPEECH TO MR. LINCOLN.

Mr. LINCOLN: As mayor of New-York, it becomes my duty to extend to you an official welcome in behalf of the Corporation. In doing so, permit me to say, that this City has never offered hospitality to a man clothed with more exalted powers, or resting under graver responsibilities, than those which circumstances have devolved upon you. Coming into office with a dismembered Government to reconstruct, and a disconnected and hostile people to reconcile, it will require a high patriotism, and an elevated comprehension of the whole country and its varied interests, opinions and prejudices, to so conduct public affairs as to bring it back again to its former harmonious, consolidated and prosperous condition.

If I refer to this topic, Sir, it is because New-York is deeply interested. The present political divisions have sorely afflicted her people. All her material interests are paralyzed. Her commercial greatness is endangered. She is the child of the American Union. She has grown up under its maternal care, and been fostered by its paternal bounty, and we fear that if the Union dies, the present supremacy of New-York may perish with it. To you, therefore, chosen under the forms of the Constitution as the head of the Confederacy, we look for a restoration of fraternal relations between the States—only to be accomplished by peaceful and conciliatory means—aided by the wisdom of Almighty God.

MR. LINCOLN'S REPLY TO MAYOR WOOD.

Mr. LINCOLN, who, during the Mayor's speech, had preserved his characteristically thoughtful look, with that sort of dreamy expression of the eye, as if his thoughts were busily engaged, stepped back a few paces, drew up his tall form to its full height, brightened his face with a pleasant smile, and spoke as follows:

Mr. MAYOR: It is with feelings of deep gratitude that I make my acknowledgements for the reception that has been given me in the great commercial City of New-York. I cannot but remember that it is done by the people, who do not, by a large majority, agree with me in political sentiment. It is the more graceful to me, because in this I see that for the great principles of our Government the people are pretty nearly or quite unanimous. In regard to the difficulties that confront us at this time, and of which you have seen fit to speak of so becomingly, and so justly, as I suppose, I can only say that I agree with the sentiments expressed by the Mayor. In my devotion to the Union, I hope I am behind no man in the nation. As to my wisdom in conducting affairs so as to tend to the preservation of the Union, I fear too great confidence may have been placed in me. I am sure I bring a heart devoted to the work. There is nothing that could ever bring me to consent—willingly to consent—to the destruction of this Union, (in which not only the great City of New-York, but the whole country has acquired its greatness,) unless it would be that thing for which the Union itself was made. I understand that the ship is made for the carrying and preservation of the cargo, and so long as the ship is safe with the cargo it shall not be abandoned. This Union shall never be abandoned unless the possibility of its existence shall cease to exist, without the necessity of throwing passengers and cargo overboard. So long, then, as it is possible that the prosperity and liberties of this people can be preserved within this Union, it shall be my purpose at all times to preserve it. And now, Mr. Mayor, renewing my thanks for this cordial reception, allow me to come to a close. [Applause.]

THE PEOPLE INTRODUCED.

Mayor WOOD then stepped forward and shook hands with Mr. LINCOLN. The gentlemen of the Common Council, Comptroller HAWES and other distinguished personages, were introduced by Mayor WOOD, and then Mr. LINCOLN was requested to take up his position for the reception of the unterrified. He was first placed where the crowd passed him from right to left, but he did not seem to like that position, and said, pointing to the statue of WASHINGTON, "Let me stand with my back to the old General there," which, with sundry jocular remarks, was acceded to, and the desired position assumed. A line of Police was then formed from one door to the other, so that the crowd could pass by Mr. LINCOLN and into the street rapidly.

AN AVALANCHE.

At length the order was given to open the door, and with the aid of a platoon of police that difficult feat was accomplished. It was like turning on the Croton, or tapping a new barrel of ale, or opening a bottle of champagne. The crowd gushed in with an effervescence and a pop somewhat ludicrous to behold, though a very serious matter to undergo. They shouted and crowded and swelted. Now a dozen or so would shoot into the room as if discharged from a piece of ordinance; now they would drip through like lumps from a coagulated mass; now they poured in like an avalanche, to the great discomfiture of the abrased policemen, against whom all who entered were obliged to brush.

Merciless reporters stood by and watched the agony of the occasion, making outrageous puns, such as "They are members of the *Press*" "*Jam satis.*"

Mayor WOOD considerately informed Mr. LINCOLN that he could please himself about shaking hands, and also that the crowd could be stopped at any moment if desired, (as one would shut off the gas or the

Croton) Mr. LINCOLN, however, said he would stand it a little while, and the tide continued to pour in.

It was amusing to see the bewildered look of the injected visitors suddenly emerging as from the compression of a pop gun to the comfortable quarters between lines of police. Some looked wildly about, wondering where was the President; some stopped to pin up sundered garments, smooth their wrinkled attire, recover the equilibrium of their collars or stretch cramped limbs, or cry "Whew!" and feel cool. All were huddled along as rapidly as possible, despite efforts to sidle off among the privileges permanent tenants of the room.

WHAT THE PEOPLE SAID, AND WHAT MR. LINCOLN REPLIED.

Nearly every man had a word for Mr. LINCOLN's ear. "God bless you," "Stand firm," "Glad to see you," &c. were the favorite greetings, but there was an occasional greeting, "How d'ye do, Uncle Abraham," said a frisky youth; "I am glad to see a President who has some reverence for the laws of God," said a gentleman in a white cravat; "It's a hard day's work you have, Mr. LINCOLN," said another. One stout old lady, who had braved the thickest of the crowd and lost her husband in the *melée,* but found him again, took an especial long look, and informed Mr. LINCOLN that her husband was a member of the Legislature.

Ex-Mayor HARPER was introduced by Mr. KENNEDY, and told Mr. LINCOLN that the nation needed his best efforts.

For nearly an hour the crowd poured in at the rate of over three thousand per hour, and still there was no abatement, and at the suggestion of Mayor WOOD and intimate friends, Mr. LINCOLN stopped shaking hands, saying to such as offered, "They won't let me shake hands any more." He still, however, made exceptions in favor of the ladies and the venerable gentlemen.

Thirty of the Veterans of 1812, headed by Col. RAYMOND, came in in a body, and after shaking hands, Presented a series of complimentary resolutions, which Mr. LINCOLN put in his left coat-tail pocket. Shortly afterwards another of the Veterans came along, and said, "We are the old boys, and you must not forget us when you get into your station."

Commodore [BAXTER?—eds.], Capt. FOOTE and Capt. GANSEVOORT received special welcome, the President conversing with them several minutes, and making an appointment to see them again.

To one visitor who announced himself from Canada, Mr. LINCOLN said, "I suppose I must shake hands with the representatives of foreign nations."

A gentleman from Illinois insisted upon shaking hands, but Mayor WOOD said, "we have forbidden the President to shake hands."

A TALL CUSTOMER.

Much merriment was occasioned among all in the room as a remarkably tall man stalked up to pay his respects to the President evidently thinking that he could tower up to the six feet four of the rail-splitter, Mr. LINCOLN good-naturedly turned round to try his stature, back to back, and brought down the house when it was seen that he was at least two inches the taller. Mr. H. DEWEY, the tall gentleman referred to, who is, by the way, a Green Mountain Boy, laughingly said: "Well, I will give in." Mr. LINCOLN subsequently remarked, "I saw he was stretching himself to make the question, so I thought I would try it."

A LONG JOURNEY.

Among the crowd that passed in was one gentleman who did not attempt to shake hands, although he said, "I came forty miles to do it, but never mind." Mr. LINCOLN reached out after him and gave him a cordial grasp.

A NOVEL FLAG.

Among others who came was a well known gentleman who, as he advanced, with his cloak thrown over him, said, "The flag of the country is looking at you." [Laughter.] Mr. LINCOLN said, *sotto voce,* "I hope it will not lose any of its eyes." . . .

MORE OF WHAT THE PEOPLE SAID.

One visitor looking at Mr. LINCOLN, said, "No compromise," but met with no response.

"I hope you will take care of us. I have prayed for you," said another.

"But," said Mr. LINCOLN, "you must take care of me."

"I am a Black Republican lawyer," said another, "and this is my son." Both father and son stood gaping with vacant stare at the President, until made to move on by the Police.

"Is the country safe?" asked another.

"I hope so; but you people must know it, however," said Mr. LINCOLN. And to another he said, "deal honestly."

"May you so satisfy the people that you'll receive the unanimous vote of the electoral college," said another.

"But they won't let me shake hands," replied Mr. LINCOLN.

At 12¾ o'clock it was proposed to close the door, but the crowd was suffered to pour in until precisely 1, when the doors were closed, and no more admitted, although the crowd seemed as great as ever. Toward the last, however, quite a number of ladies, mostly, elderly women, were admitted, and with them Mr. LINCOLN invariably shook hands.

MR. LINCOLN ON THE BALCONY.

In obedience to the general request, Mr. LINCOLN finally showed himself on the balcony. Mr. LINCOLN spoke as follows:

MY FRIENDS: I do not appear for the purpose of making a speech. I design to make no speech. I appear simply to see you and allow you to see me. [Applause.] I have to say to you what I have to say to audiences frequently on the road from my home to this place, that in the sight I have, I suppose, the best of the bargain. I assume that you are all for the Constitution and the Union—["Hip, hip, hurrah!"]—and the perp—["three cheers for LINCOLN!"]—the perpetual liberties of this people. I bid you farewell. [Applause, during which Mr. LINCOLN retired.]

THE POLICE ARRANGEMENTS.

The excellence of the police arrangements, which were under the special care of Superintendent KENNEDY, was beautifully demonstrated, when, at the close of Mr. LINCOLN's speech, it was announced that he was about to leave. The police, who had apparently been gathered in a knot in the crowd like other spectators, suddenly faced outwards, and rapidly cleared a space leading from the City Hall to the carriage-way, and also for the carriages to drive up and pass. Mr. LINCOLN and suite were accompanied to the carriage door by Mayor WOOD and a number of members of the Common Council and despite the vast crowd, the distinguished guests were not in the slightest incommoded. Mr. KENNEDY noticed that the carriages about to drive into the inclosure were followed by a crowd of boys, who were on the point of thus securing excellent places, and gave the word to Deputy CARPENTER to "shot off the boys," which was neatly done, to the great chagrin of the urchins.

A SIGNIFICANT INTERVIEW.

As Mr. LINCOLN was about to step into the carriage door he shook Mayor Wood warmly by the hand, and leaning forward, audibly thanked the Mayor for the kind reception and pleasant attention extended on behalf of the City. On of the City fathers who was near at hand, says "Mr. LINCOLN told Mayor WOOD that, without intending any disparagement of others, he considered his (Mr. WOOD's) speech the most appropriate and statesmanlike yet made on a like occasion, and that he (Mr. LINCOLN) indorsed every word of it."

This is regarded in Aldermanic circles as one of the most significant of Mr. LINCOLN's utterances, and a decided point in favor of the Mayor. The Mayor's speech, it will be remembered, suggests that the restoration of fraternal relations between the States can only be accomplished by *peaceful and conciliatory means,* and as Mr. LINCOLN indorsed the speech both in his public reply and his alleged communication to Mr. WOOD at parting, it is argued that he is committed against a coercion policy, and they give to Mayor WOOD the credit of thus drawing out the policy of the incoming Administration. . . .

THE INCOMING ADMINISTRATION.

Progress of the President Elect Towards Washington.

His Departure from New-York.

Popular Ovation at Jersey City and Speeches of Mr. Lincoln.

The President-Elect nearly Squeezed to Death in the Crowd.

Inefficiency of the Jersey Police.

His Reception at Newark.

Important Speeches Before the Legislature at Trenton.

Arrival and Reception in Philadelphia.

Bright and early yesterday morning Mr. LINCOLN arose, and rapidly disposed of his early callers, his TIMES and his breakfast, for he was to star: *en route* at 8:15. The time of departure was at first fixed for 9 o'clock, but changed to an earlier hour in consequence of the anticipated delay at Jersey City, owing to the reception by the Common Council. It was deemed necessary to depart from the original programme in order to avoid interference. Mrs. LINCOLN and children reached the special train by a private conveyance.

Promptly at the hour named, Mr. VAN RANST was at the door with his stylish carriages, the Presidential party was safely stowed, and without further formality than a cordial shake of the hands to the few personal friends assembled to bid him adieu, Mr. LINCOLN took leave of the City.

At the Jersey City Ferry, in anticipation of his coming, crowds lined the passageways to the boat, the *John P. Jackson,* on which were collected the Mayor and Common Council of Jersey City, and a number of privileged persons. As the carriages were driven on board, DODWORTH's fine band struck up the National airs, congratulatory cannon boomed out a parting salute, and while the boat moved off the multitude sent up their parting cheers, and the shipping in the harbor displayed their national bunting. The Cunard steamers were decorated with the American colors, and at intervals of one minute guns were fired alternately from the two vessels. The steamship *Granada,* passing at the time, also fired a salute. . . .

THE DISEMBARKATION

Arrived at Jersey City, the party left the carriages and marched into the dépôt in procession, Mr. HARDENBERG resigning his charge to Mayor VAN VORST at the gate. The scene in the dépôt was magnificent— presenting, as it did, probably the largest in-door gathering witnessed by the President since his departure. The vast edifice was crowded in every part—the gallery which surrounds the interior, being filled with a bright galaxy of the fair sex. The appearance of Mr. LINCOLN was, of course, the signal for a general outburst of applause, prolonged until long after Mr. LINCOLN had stepped upon the carpeted platform car prepared for him. As he advanced and bowed in acknowledgement, cheer upon cheer broke forth, drowning completely the vain appeals for silence.

Mayor VAN VORST, in the midst of the hubbub, made some unintelligible remarks, welcoming Mr. LINCOLN, probably, and introducing Hon. WM. L. DAYTON, who was to receive him on behalf of the State, rumor says, in the following words:

LADIES AND GENTLEMEN OF NEW-JERSEY: I have the honor to introduce to you, Hon. ABRAHAM LINCOLN, President elect of the United States.

As those on the platform retired and left, Mr. LINCOLN and Mr. DAYTON fronting each other, the crowd took the hint and a general hush-sh-sh-sh ran through the throng, producing comparative silence, Mr. DAYTON spoke in a clear, audible voice, as follows:

HON. W. L. DAYTON WELCOMES MR. LINCOLN.

Respected Sir: In the absence of the Governor of the State, acting by his authority and as his substitute, I give you welcome to the State of New Jersey. [Applause.] Welcome, Sir, to the hearts and the homes of our citizens. We cannot hope to equal in the demonstrations of our attention that magnificent ovation that has accompanied your journey heretofore, but, in the cordiality of our greeting, we are second to none. [Great applause.] We desire to testify to you, Sir, our sincere respect and high appreciation of your personal character, and your public position, to assure you of the loyalty, the unwavering loyalty of this people to the laws and the Constitution, [enthusiastic cheers,] to pledge to you their sympathy, their cordial sympathy and support in all rightful measures tending to the great interests of this country and to the perpetuation of the union in these States. [Applause.] They desire to live in harmony with their brethren as a whole—doing justice to all—asking only a fair return. I am sure, Sir, I do not tread upon forbidden and doubtful ground when I say I prefer one country, one flag, one destiny. [Loud cheers.] Upon you, Sir, on whom so much depends, they feel they can rely for that first great element of success—rectitude of intention. Let me add in conclusion, that burdened as you will be with the cares and responsibilities of government, this united people will follow you to the Capital with their best wishes, their fondest hopes and their earnest prayers. [Applause, and three cheers for LINCOLN.]

MR. LINCOLN'S REPLY TO MR. DAYTON.

MR. DAYTON AND GENTLEMEN OF THE STATE OF NEW-JERSEY: I shall only thank you briefly for this very kind reception given me, not personally, but as the temporary representative of the majesty of the nation. [Applause.] To the kindness of your hearts and of the hearts of your brethren in your State, I should be very proud to respond, but I shall not have strength to address you or other assemblages at length, even if I had the time to do so. I appear before you, therefore, for little else than to greet you and to briefly say farewell. You have done me the very high honor to present your reception courtesies to me through your great man—a man with whom it is an honor to be associated anywhere, and in owning whom no State can be poor. [Applause.] He has said enough, and by the saying of it suggested enough to require a response of an hour well-considered. [Applause.] I could not in an hour make a worthy response to it. I therefore, ladies and gentlemen of New-Jersey, content myself with saying most heartily do I indorse all the sentiments he has expressed. [Applause.] Allow me, most gratefully, to bid you farewell. [Applause.]

58

SHAKING HANDS.

The distinguished gentlemen on the platform were again introduced, but the crowd would not be appeased, and made a rush to get near

Mr. LINCOLN. The unfortunate reporters, who stood by the car, writing on the platform, were suddenly squeezed between the eager multitude and the object of their attention. It was like being in a hydraulic press, or going through a rolling-mill, or being run over by the cars, or pinched between the ferry-boat and the bridge, or suffering *hari kari*. Verily, our reporter's bowels ache when he mentally recalls that excruciating collapse.

In vain did the compressed unfortunates howl with pain—their agonizing cries were regarded as cheers for LINCOLN. In vain did they implore the crowd to stand back; Mr. LINCOLN heightened the excitement and increased the danger by reaching over the heads of the people and shaking hands with a few, which only increased the desire of the many to get nearer, and the torture of those who were near.

The Jersey Police were overwhelmed. Vainly did they brandish their clubs, and push the crowd back. It was like Mrs. Partington trying to sweep back the Atlantic with her broom. Mr. LINCOLN was the focus, and the people the radii; Mr. LINCOLN the hub and the people the spokes, until finally, in obedience to the demand, he became a *spokes*-man himself, and addressed the crowd again.

MR. LINCOLN SPEAKS AGAIN—
HE WILL MAKE NO COMPROMISE.

FELLOW-CITIZENS: I appear before you, as I have on other occasions, simply to see you and to allow you to see me, and so far as the upper tier is concerned (the ladies tier) they have the best of the bargain [laughter,] but as regards the lower tier I intend to make no compromise. [Great laughter and applause.] . . .

A JAM.

The difficult feat now to be performed was to get Mr. LINCOLN through the crowd to the cars. The Police were of no use, rather in the way than otherwise, but by dint of turning his suite into a body-guard, elbowing his way and moving slowly, Mr. LINCOLN reached the car and disappeared within, the multitude peering in at the windows and otherwise behaving with a rudeness that can only be equalled by American multitudes rampantly curious.

THE SPECIAL CAR.

The interior of the car, had been especially fitted up for the occasion by the New-Jersey Railroad Company, cushioned arm chairs were plentiful, and in the centre of the car was a large silver salver, containing a splendid bouquet of flowers.

The train was drawn by the new locomotive *William Pennington,* and was tastefully decorated with flags and streamers. A few minutes after 9 the train started, amid the vociferous cheers of the men and the waving handkerchiefs by the ladies.

Speaking of ladies, it was erroneously stated in the papers yesterday that the lady of AUGUST BELMONT was among those who paid their respects to Mr. LINCOLN on Wednesday. Mrs. BELMONT was not at the Astor House.

TRIP FROM NEW-YORK TO PHILADELPHIA.

Incidents on the Way—Detailed Account up to the Arrival at the City of Brotherly Love.

From Our Special Correspondent.

RAILROAD CAR. ENTERING PHILADELPHIA,
Thursday, Feb 21, 1861

It was with the greatest difficulty that the suite of Mr. LINCOLN were able to obtain foothold upon the platform, from the side of which the special train was to start. The police force, though, doubtless, well meaning, was remarkably inefficient, boisterous and rude. Policeman No. 2, with a baton half as long as himself, pushed, rammed and jammed every member of the party who held and exhibited a ticket, infinitely to the amusement of the enthusiastic crowd, who, not having any occasion for proximity to the cars, were allowed to approach with entire impunity.

At last, all were safely on, and the train, with its distinguished freightage, pushed slowly through the masses of shouting freemen, and handkerchief-waving ladies, until it had left the dépôt, when, with a terrific whoop from the iron horse, it rattled toward Newark at a speed which astonished the cattle on the several hills, unaccustomed as they are to lighting rapidity, or race-horse motion on that eminently safe but rather slow thoroughfare. . . .

Most of the party occupied the forward one of the two cars, while Mr. LINCOLN, the ladies, and a few of the principal members of the suite remained in the hind car. Mr. LINCOLN seemed physically better than at any time since leaving Springfield. The new hat and coat produce an effect that is very perceptible, and at the same time beneficial, though it is very doubtful if the wearer of them knows or cares anything about it. Mrs. LINCOLN, who has sustained the fatigue and the continual pressure of attention with the most wonderful case, has been in the very best of spirits the entire day. She was highly gratified, as, indeed, she should be, at the wonderful reception given to her husband in New-York, and much pleased with the courteous attention paid to herself and family.

We reached Newark at 9½ o'clock, and leaving the cars at the Morris and Essex dépôt, drove through the city in carriages, reentering the cars at the Newark dépôt. Mr. LINCOLN, attended by his suite and the various gentlemen of the party, entered the former dépôt, which was filled with ladies and gentlemen, and was met by Mayor BIGELOW, who, on behalf of the citizens, welcomed the President elect to the thriving City of Newark . . .

Then occurred the jolliest kind of a time. Newark has a population of over seventy thousand, and I think it is entirely safe to say that at least two-thirds of them were out in the streets, thronging, swarming, jostling and hurrying in crowds of wonderful extent. An open barouche drawn by four splendid white horses, had been provided for Mr. LINCOLN, who stood up therein bareheaded during the entire passage from dépôt to dépôt. The streets were filled, the houses were filled, the windows, the doors, the churches, the stoops, the plazas, the roofs, the trees, the ash barrels, the everything you can think of were crowded to repletion with people who swarmed like bees, who seemed touched with electricity, and who must have had throats lined with brass.

Very many private carriages stood along the line, all of which were filled with bright-eyed ladies, who smiled and waved and huzzaed with as much enthusiasm, if not with as much noise, as the ruder specimens of humanity who surged by them on foot. We have never seen a more extensive or prettier display of "women, lovely women," than was made on the main street of Newark during the passage of the procession. Mr. LINCOLN was struck by it, and thought if there are as many brave men as there are fair women in the city, Newark would be a difficult city to take.

Beyond a continual display of enthusiastic demonstration, and of demonstrative enthusiasm, there was nothing particularly new upon this part of the trip. From one lamp post swung the effigy of a Secessionist, dressed in gray coat and pants, and bearing the inscription, "The fate of a Traitor;" but though the sentiment is undoubtedly a correct one, the exhibition of it was in very bad taste, and indicated lack of the finer sensibilities on the part of the amateur executioner.

When the dépôt or station, from which we are to go, was reached, a terrible struggle occurred. An immense crowd followed close upon the Presidential heels, and the hands of the populace rested heavily upon the backs of the gentlemen who surrounded the guest of the city.

The police with mighty effort endeavored to stop the swelling tide, but as well might they have attempted to stem the waves of the ocean. Those far in the rear pushed those in the front and those in turn pushed on, until we who occupied the rank by the cars were in danger of being smashed into parts, jelly or jam. The Committeemen of course made more trouble than any body else; the marshals exhibited more discretion than valor, and the police officers handled with great vigor the gentlemen of the party, while the scally-wags who were doing their best to make a row were treated with the utmost consideration. At last all were in. Mr. LINCOLN made his farewell bow, the crowd cheered lustily, and on we sped. The various members of the company tired, fatigued, mussed, weary and flushed, stretched their shaking limbs across the welcome cushions, and with muttered cursings at the outrageous treatment they had received, endeavored by uneasy nappings to recuperate their almost exhausted strength. . . .

TRENTON,

the capital of the State of New-Jersey. Here Mr. LINCOLN was met by an additional Committee from the citizens, from the Council, and the Legislature. Apparently every precaution had been taken to preserve good order, and to enable the Presidential party to pass quietly and unmolested through the city. We walked between walls of people with great ease, they the meanwhile roaring, tumbling, and seething as one imagines the waves of the Red Sea did when Moses smote and divided them with his little old rod. So far so good, but here it ends. The moment Mr. LINCOLN took his seat in the carriage the mob became ungovernable. With a mighty rush they beat down the line of feeble constables, and without the least regard to decency, or the form of it, swamped the suite, the Committeemen, and the representatives of the Press. It was rather hard on the staid and respectable officers of the army, the venerable Dr. WALLACE, the roystering TODD, the youthful ROBERT, the driving WOOD, the handsome FORBES, and the gallant ELLSWORTH. But it served the Committeemen just right. It did me good to see them pummeled, pushed and squeezed. I felt happy when I heard them yell with impatient rage at some fellow who stepped upon their feet, or ousted them from their place. Committeemen, as a general rule, are nuisances; they are pompous, vain, selfish, and inefficient toadies, all having their little axes to grind, and each bent upon securing for himself the best place, or the most dinner, as the case may chance to be.

62

The reporters having seen that kind of thing before went through the usual motions and were soon free from the crowd in a carriage, and on our way to the State House. For the benefit of laymen I will state that in a crowd as great as the greatest, you can always be sure of getting through it if you follow these instructions: Elevate your elbow high, and bring it down with great force upon the digestive apparatus of your neighbor. He will double up and yell, causing the gentleman in front of you to turn half way round to see what is the matter. Punch him in the same way, step on his foot, pass him, and continue the application until you have reached the desired point. It never fails. With the greatest difficulty, and only after repeated discomfitures, failures and struggles did the entire party find seats in the conveyances. It seemed as if the crowd was the most obstreperous of any I have ever seen.

The route lay through the principal streets of the city, and was very long. Everybody, with his wife and children, was on hand. The day was exceedingly beautiful, the sky was very clear and blue, and the whole affair, even to the depth and quality of the mud, was remarkable for the fact that there was no half-way about it. The extreme verge of everything was touched.

The reception by the Senate and the General Assembly deserves a more complete account than I can at this time conveniently give. Suffice it to say, that on both occasions, Mr. LINCOLN deported himself most admirably, and satisfied one and all of his fitness for the great post to which he has been called. The speech made by him in the Assembly chamber was the longest, the most specific and pronounced of any that he has made on this trip. The declarations that he was, of all men, a lover of peace and of harmony; that he should *enter upon his duties with no prejudices against any section of the country or portion of the people, and that he should, if necessary, put his foot down firmly,* were received with the most enthusiastic applause. His voice was singularly melodious, having all the sympathetic winsomeness of a woman's combined with the serious vigor of a man. All parties were affected. The President elect may congratulate himself upon the undoubted fact, that upon the representatives of the people of New-Jersey he has made an impression, that reflected upon their constituents, will be most beneficial in its result. . . .

But we are entering the precincts of Philadelphia, and I must close. Car joggling is not particularly favorable to accurate composition of elegant chirography, and begging indulgence for errors that on that account may be found herewith, I abruptly close, while the bells chime, the cannon roar, the crowds huzzah and the Committee men secure good places for themselves.

HOWARD. . . .

The Reception at Philadelphia.

PHILADELPHIA, Thursday, Feb. 21.

The Philadelphia train, with Mr. LINCOLN and suite, arrived at Kensington at 4 o'clock this afternoon, and were escorted to the carriages in waiting for them. Mr. LINCOLN's barouche was conspicuous, owing to the gay plumage of the four white horses attached to it. The procession formed in line, headed by a body of mounted police, followed by a cavalcade of citizens representing all party politics, and the Pennsylvania Dragoons. After these came the President elect and his suite, the members of the Common Council, the Committees of the New-Jersey and Pennsylvania Legislatures, and a large number of citizens in carriages.

Mr. LINCOLN along the line of march was hailed everywhere with patriotic emblems and manifestations. About a hundred thousand people gathered along the line of march, notwithstanding that the weather was extremely cold and threatening a snowstorm.

On the arrival at the head-quarters, the Continental Hotel, Mr. LINCOLN was conducted to the balcony and introduced to Mayor HENRY. The noisy multitude below greeted his appearance with wholesome cheering, but both the Mayor's welcome and his reply were unheard, except by those in the immediate vicinity. Mr. LINCOLN displayed great earnestness in the delivery of his speech, which caused the mass to reflect his patriotic views in deafening applause. . . .

MR. LINCOLN'S RESPONSE.

Mr. LINCOLN replied:

MR. MAYOR AND FELLOW-CITIZENS OF PHILADELPHIA: I appear before you to make no lengthy speech, but to thank you for this reception. The reception you have given me to-night is not to me, the man, the individual, but to the man who temporarily represents, or should represent, the majesty of the nation. [Cheers.] It is true, as your worthy Mayor has said, that there is anxiety amongst the citizens of the United States at this time. I deem it a happy circumstance that this dissatisfied position of our fellow-citizens do not point us to anything in which they are being injured, or about to be injured, for which reason I have felt all the while justified in concluding that the crisis, the panic, the anxiety, of the country at this time, is artificial. If there be those who differ with me upon this subject they have not pointed out the substantial [word illegible— eds.] that exists. I do not mean to say that an artificial panic may not do considerable harm; that it has done such I do not deny. The hope that has been expressed by your Mayor, that I may be able to restore peace, harmony and prosperity to the country, is most worthy of him; and happy, indeed, will I be if I shall be able to verify and fulfill that hope. [Tremendous cheering.] I promise you in all sincerity, that I bring to the work a sincere heart. Whether I will bring a head equal to that heart will be for future times to determine. It were useless for me to speak of details of plans now; I shall speak officially next Monday week, if ever. If I should not speak then it were useless for me to do so now. If I do speak then it is useless for me to do so now. When I do speak I shall take such ground as I deem best calculated to restore peace, harmony and prosperity to the country and tend to the perpetuity of the nation and the liberty of these States and these people. Your worthy Mayor has expressed the wish, in which I join with him, that it were convenient for me to remain with your city long enough to consult your merchants and manufacturers; or as it were to listen to the breathings rising within the consecrated walls wherein the Constitution of the United States, and I will add the Declaration of Independence, were originally framed and adopted. [Enthusiastic applause.] I assure you and your Mayor, that I had hoped on this occasion, and upon all occasions during my life, that I shall do nothing inconsistent with the teachings of these holy and most sacred walls. I never asked anything that does not breathe from those walls. All my political warfare has been in favor of the teachings that came forth from these sacred walls. May my right hand forget its cunning, and my tongue cleave to the roof of my mouth, if ever I prove fake to those teachings. Fellow-citizens, I have addressed you longer than I expected to do, and now allow me to bid you good night. . . .

Assassination Fears

Lincoln's inaugural journey took him on to Trenton and Philadelphia— where he gave his most eloquent pre-inaugural speehes—then toward Baltimore where he was scheduled merely to cross town to change trains for the last leg of his long trip to Washington.

But Baltimore was a secessionist hotbed. Armed with reports from detectives that an incredible assassination threat awaited him there, Lincoln was persuaded to take unprecedented precautions. About 4 A.M. on February 23—hours after declaring outside Independence Hall that "I would rather be assassinated on this spot than surrender it"—Lincoln replaced his signature stovepipe hat and frock coat with nondescript outerwear to cross the Baltimore platform covertly. The "fear of ridicule," Lincoln conceded, was not strong enough to argue against these safety measures. Thus disguised, Lincoln later admitted, "I was not the same man." Two hours later, Lincoln arrived in Washington—safe from harm, but about to face an avalanche of criticism.

Even the pro-Republican New York Tribune *was appalled. Though it blamed secessionist "ruffians" for driving Lincoln to secrecy, it lamented the episode as "the only instance recorded in history in which the recognized head of a nation . . . has been compelled, for fear of his life, to enter the capital in disguise." The pro-secessionist* Charleston Mercury *just gloated: "Everybody here is disgusted at this cowardly and undignified entry." Within days, illustrated newspapers began publishing lampoons showing Lincoln wearing disguises ranging from military cloaks to kilts.*

Whether Lincoln came to regret his decision to pass through Baltimore in secrecy is not known. Maryland reluctantly remained in the Union— but the plot that resulted in Lincoln's assassination four years later was born in the same city that Lincoln avoided in 1861.

—H. H.

HIGHLY IMPORTANT NEWS.

Secret Departure of the President Elect from Harrisburgh.

Alleged Plot for His Assassination.

Unexpected Arrival in Washington.

Surprise of the Harrisburgh People, and Indignation of the Baltimoreans.

Good Effect of his Presence in the Federal Capital.

Important Action of the Peace Conference.

Adoption of the Plan of Mr. Franklin, of Pennsylvania.

Mr. Lincoln's Reception of the Peace Delegation.

Facts and Rumors Regarding the New Cabinet.

Interesting Dispatches and Rumors from the South.

Special Dispatch to the New-York Times.

HARRISBURGH, Saturday, Feb. 23 — 8 A.M.

ABRAHAM LINCOLN, the President Elect of the United States, is safe in the capital of the nation. By the admirable arrangement of Gen. SCOTT, the country has been spared the lasting disgrace, which would have been fastened indelibly upon it had Mr. LINCOLN been murdered upon his journey thither, as he would have been had he followed the programme as announced in the papers and gone by the Northern Central Railroad to Baltimore.

On Thursday night after he had retired, Mr. LINCOLN was aroused and informed that a stranger desired to see him on a matter of life and death. He declined to admit him unless he gave his name, which he at once did, and such prestige did the name carry that while Mr. LINCOLN was yet disrobed he granted an interview to the caller.

A prolonged conversation elicited the fact that an organized body of men had determined that Mr. LINCOLN should not be inaugurated, and that he should never leave the City of Baltimore alive, if indeed, he ever entered it.

The list of the names of the conspirators presented a most astonishing array of persons high in Southern confidence, and some whose fame is not confined to this country alone.

Statesmen laid the plan, Bankers indorsed it, and adventurers were to carry it into effect. As they understood, Mr. LINCOLN was to leave Harrisburgh at 9 o'clock this morning by special train, the idea was, if possible, to throw the cars from the road at some point where they would rush down a steep embankment and destroy in a moment the lives of all on board. In case of the failure of this project, their plan was to surround the carriage on the way from dépôt to dépôt in Baltimore, and assassinate him with dagger or pistol shot.

So authentic was the source from which the information was obtained, that Mr. LINCOLN, after counseling with his friends, was compelled to make arrangements which would enable him to subvert the plans of his enemies.

Greatly to the annoyance of the thousands who desired to call on him last night, he declined giving a reception. The final council was held at 8 o'clock.

Mr. LINCOLN did not want to yield, and Col. SUMNER actually cried with indignation; but Mrs. LINCOLN, seconded by Mr. JUDD and Mr. LINCOLN's original informant, insisted upon it, and *at nine o'clock* Mr. LINCOLN *left on a special train.* He wore a Scotch plaid cap and a very long military cloak, so that he was entirely unrecognizable: Accompanied by Superintendent

LEWIS and one friend, he started, while all the town, with the exception of Mrs. LINCOLN, Col. SUMNER, Mr. JUDD, and two reporters, who were sworn to secrecy, supposed him to be asleep.

The telegraph wires were put beyond reach of any one who might desire to use them.

At 1 o'clock the fact was whispered from one to another, and it soon became the theme of most excited conversation. Many thought it was a very injudicious move, while others regarded it as a stroke of great merit.

Dispatches to the Associated Press.

THE DEPARTURE FROM HARRISBURGH.

HARRISBURGH, Saturday, Feb. 23

The people of this city were astounded this morning by an announcement that Mr. LINCOLN had started in a special train for Washington, dispatches having been received requiring his presence in Washington. Reports are busily circulated that there was plot to assassinate him while passing through Baltimore, but such stories are not believed. The Baltimore Committee is here, but did not have an interview with Mr. LINCOLN.

ARRIVAL IN BALTIMORE.

BALTIMORE, Saturday, Feb. 23.

Mr. LINCOLN arrived here at 8 o'clock *incog.,* and went direct to Washington. His family, and the remainder of his party, will arrive at 1 o'clock. Much excitement was occasioned by the *ruse.*

ARRIVAL IN WASHINGTON.

WASHINGTON, Saturday, Feb. 23.

Not a little sensation prevailed throughout the city this morning, as soon as it became known that Mr. LINCOLN had arrived in the early train. It was unsuccessfully sought to conceal the fact, especially from the newspaper press, his presence here being at first communicated to a few political friends in confidence. He was met at the station by several gentlemen of distinction, without any formality, and was immediately driven to Willard's Hotel.

He was yesterday advised to come hither without delay. Preparations had been made to meet him at the station this afternoon, and the Mayor of Washington was to make a welcome address, but Mr. LINCOLN has thus spoiled the programme. About 10 o'clock, Mr. LINCOLN, accompanied by Mr. SEWARD, paid his respects to President BUCHANAN, spending a few minutes in general conversation.

Senator BIGLER and Representative JOHN COCHRANE happened to be at the White House when he entered, and were accordingly introduced to the President elect. Mr. LINCOLN afterwards returned to his hotel.

THE NEWS IN PHILADELPHIA.

PHILADELPHIA, Sunday, Feb. 24.

No community could manifest more anxiety regarding the late movements of Mr. LINCOLN than Philadelphia. Its like has seldom been experienced here, even on the most exciting occasions. The newspaper offices during yesterday were thronged with anxious inquirers.

Extras were in unparalleled demand.

To-day, this subject has been the chief topic of conversation, and statement made by prominent members of the Republican Party, justify the belief that fears on the part of his friends, of an attempt at assassination on the train or procession at Baltimore, was the real sole cause of his flight.

It was discussed among the prominent members of his suite when in this City, and measures were taken to guard against such a calamity. The names of Gen. SCOTT and Gov. HICKS, of Maryland, are prominently mentioned as among those who gave the warning, and Messrs. JUDD and DAVIS as those who acted on it. It is possible that a statement to the public will be published by friends to justify their course, and to remove from Mr. LINCOLN the charge of unwanted apprehension.

THE PRESIDENTIAL PROGRESS.

Various Points—The Flag-Raising—Description of Mrs. Lincoln—Affairs at Harrisburgh.

From Our Special Correspondent.

BUEHLER HOUSE.
HARRISBURGH, Saturday Morning, Feb. 23, 1861.

This is Saturday morning—very early Saturday morning—and but a few hours before the President elect takes the last step in his memorable journey to Washington, the theatre of his unenviable duties. The work performed by those in attendance upon him since they reached the borders of the State of Pennsylvania, has not only been arduous but embarrassing, and attended with circumstances hitherto unencountered and, in some respects, not entirely creditable to the managers of affairs, or to the people of the State. Without exception, probably, the Continental is the finest hotel in the world—its arrangements for the convenience of its guests, its various appointments, the gentlemen in charge, and the entire establishment can be equaled for completeness and suitability nowhere, and yet at the Continental raged such a conflict of rude vulgarity and impertinent curiosity, as I have never seen surpassed in this or any other country. The people were wild. Forgetting that some show of respect was due to the proprietor and the guests of the house, the populace, eager, impulsive, thoughtless and rough, crowded into the hotel, filled the spacious halls, jammed the corridors and prevented ingress or egress for those whose duties, inclination or position required the normal use of doorways and passages. I do not propose now to describe the scenes of ill-breeding that were manifested there, but will simply say that the proceedings were disgraceful to the authorities of the city, insulting to Mr. LINCOLN, and a great injury to the reputation of the citizens of Philadelphia. If we owned the house, and such transactions are the natural result of the entertaining of distinguished guests, we would let every man who was titled beyond a captaincy in the State militia, go to some less known and less elegant quarters, that thereby the quiet and unpretentious persons who travel might enjoy the comforts of the best hotel in the country without meeting blackguards in crowds, and loafers by the score.

Friday's work was a very large "stent." Long before sunrise Mr. LINCOLN and his immediate attendants were up, dressed and breakfasted. They had an important engagement to meet at the dawn of day, and though sleep was the desire of their eye-lids, and rest the burden of their wearied bodies' song, imperative duty called and was obeyed. Gathered around the Independence Hall were, at the least calculation, thirty thousand people. They had come, many of them, from a distance. Hard-fisted farmers, whose votes helped swell the tide which swept, irresistibly, the Republican Party into power; greasy mechanics, sneered at by snobbish South Carolina, but recognized by their fellow freemen as the very foundation of the temple of Liberty; milkmen from their rounds; young clerks, dry goods and otherwise, on their way from lonely bedrooms to dreary stores and shops; students with badge and pipe; Quakers with broad brims and knowing eyes; old men, unshaven, but happy; thousands of intelligent, thinking, understanding, voting, middle-aged men, and other thousands of that peculiar look found only in cities—a knowing, cunning look—had taken the trouble to rise at an unusual hour of the day, on a cold, bleak but bracing morning, that they might witness the performance of a deed, the solemn beauty of which cannot well be overestimated. The data from which one could easily deduce the conclusion that the affair was not one of ordinary occurrence, are these: Mr. LINCOLN, the President elect of the United States, was about to raise and unfurl from the summit of Independence Hall a flag on which were thirty-four stars—and this was to be done as the sun sent forth his first ray from behind the lofty mountains, announcing that the one hundred and twenty-ninth anniversary of WASHINGTON's Birthday was begun. Short and trite as is that sentence, there is food enough for several minutes' study; and as it will be seen, the impression produced upon the immense and motley crowd was great, so we think it might be made to be upon, if properly guaranteed, the entire people of this great Republic. It was a great occasion. The day, the place, the audience, the surroundings, the purpose and meaning of the vast assemblage, all combined to mark it as long to be remembered. The arrival of Mr. LINCOLN was the signal for long-continued and most vociferous applause, after which was performed the ceremony, as previously described in the TIMES, and concerning which, Mr. LINCOLN, when subsequently addressing the Legislative Assemblies of the State, spoke as follows:

"Our friends there had provided a magnificent flag of the country. They had arranged it so that I was given the honor of raising it to the head of its staff; and when it went up, I was pleased that it went to its place by the strength of my own feeble arm. When, according to the arrangement, the cord was pulled, and it flaunted gloriously to the wind without an accident, in the light-glowing sunshine of the morning, I could not help hoping that there was, in the entire success of that beautiful ceremony, at least something of an omen of what is to come. Nor could I help, feeling then as I have often felt, that in the whole of that proceeding I was a very humble instrument. I had not provided the flag; I had not made the arrangement for elevating it to its place; I had applied but a very small portion of even my feeble strength in raising it. In the whole transaction I was in the hands of the people who had arranged it, and if I can have the same generous cooperation of the people of this nation, I think the flag of our country may yet be kept flaunting gloriously."

At no time has so popular an incident occurred during the trip. All things combined to make it not only impressively grand, but emphatically popular. Already the example has been followed in sundry places at Philadelphia, along the road, and here; and doubtless, ere the setting of the sun of the 4th of March, thousands of flags, bearing proudly the thirty-four stars of the united nation, will be displayed from as many domes, exponents of the rising of the people in their majesty, to rebuke the efforts of traitors, who are plotting to destroy our liberties, and to rend asunder that great political fabric which, for seventy years, has borne the brunt of the battle for freedom, and has been the hospitable home for all who were in pursuit of liberty, equality, and fraternal sympathy. Big thing.

From Philadelphia the party was enabled to depart with great comfort. Admirable police regulations kept ample space at the dépôt, and with an entire ease everything passed off as it should. As the train shot off from the station, the assembled crowd gave a farewell salute in the shape of rousing cheers, capital as lung exercise for them, and gratifying to the party for whose especial tympanum they were given. There were two well furnished cars, in addition to the luggage-car, (in which, by the way, were refreshments, emphatically for man and beast,) the former one being kept for the Committees, and the hinder one, which was divided into convenient compartments, for the accommodation of the LINCOLNS, one and all, and the several friends accompanying them. Mr. LINCOLN was fatigued—not so very strange either—and availed himself of the time granted by the printed time-table to take a good hour's sleep. Chancing to pass him while he was enjoying the balmy, I was gratified to be assured on two important points—he does not sleep with his mouth open, nor does he snore; two very important considerations when the party sleeping is a public man, and resting in a railroad car.

Mrs. LINCOLN, who is molded in another fashion, did not sleep—catch her. On the contrary, she was very wide awake. With her was the wife of a Springfield friend, and had they been the centre of attraction at a Saratoga ball-room, they could not have been more entirely complaisant, more brilliant or self-possessed. Ladies are fond of reading about each other. They like to know everything concerning each other, and particularly the weak points—the more the better, and I fear that's not the whole of it. Now it so happens, that an all-wise Providence has seen fit to elevate Mr. LINCOLN to the Presidential chair. Mr. LINCOLN removes his limbs from the desk in his legal office, and goes as per correspondence to the house upon the hill. Of course he takes Mrs. LINCOLN with him, and, as nearly as I can judge, the entire female population are in ecstasies of curiosity to know who she was, what she is, what she looks like, what her manner is, and if she has *presence* of the sort necessary in the exalted station to which she will be soon introduced.

Believing that a large part of this curiosity is laudable, and having it in my power to gratify it, I will at once proceed to do so. Certain metropolitan journals, with hatches to sharpen, have erroneously attributed to Mrs. LINCOLN the features of a Juno, the form of a Venus, and the wisdom of a Minerva. This we cannot indorse, nor can we agree with certain other unscrupulous newspaper men who accuse Mrs. LINCOLN of all that is coarse, ungenial and unrefined. Mrs. LINCOLN does not chew snuff, does not dress in *outré* style, does not walk *à la Zouave,* does not use profane language, nor does she on any occasion, public or private, kick up shindies. These negatives are necessary, because, the affirmative of these propositions has been sent broadcast throughout the land. Mrs. LINCOLN, as she appears to the humble, and somewhat peripatetic individual who represents on this occasion the dignity of the TIMES—is a middle-aged lady, of—well, say forty or perhaps thirty-eight years of age.

On the top of her head, the place where the hair ought to grow—the hair *does* grow, and very luxuriantly, too, of a dark brown color, and elastic fibre. Her head is large and well developed, presenting the organs of firmness and language in a highly developed and well-matured condition. Her forehead is broad; her eye clear and intelligent, and rather blue than gray; her nose is—well, not to put too fine a point on it—is not Grecian; her mouth is large, well shaped, and capable of great expression, while her chin rounds gracefully, balances properly, and goes in a quiet way towards the indorsing of our opinion that she is a *decided*—not obstinate—woman. Her form inclines to stoutness, but is well-fashioned and comely, while her hands and feet are really beautiful, indicating, as does the well-shaped ear, that she has come from a race of people who were well born. Her carriage is good, her manners are pleasant, her greetings are affable, and, without doubt, her intentions are correct. That Mrs. LINCOLN goes to the White House, versed in the goodly knowledge of housewifery and substantial living, rather than skilled in the cunning tricks of politics, and *blesed* with the excitements of Washington life, is a feature for congratulation, rather than for deprecation. She started with Mr. LINCOLN when he was a poor young man, with no more idea of being called to the Presidency than of being a cannibal, she has pursued a quiet home life, rearing and educating a happy family, cheering the man of her choice as he passed through the stormy scenes of life, and content if in all things she made, what few women do make, a good wife and a competent mother. She has been suddenly called to fill an unaccustomed position. To it she goes, taking with her, her sound substratum of common sense, her natural tact, that great aider of us all; the esteem of all who knew her at her old home, and the best wishes of every decent woman in the land.

I shall not weary you with a description of our journey hither. Shorthand would express it thus:—crowds—enthusiasm—little speech—little bow—kissed little girl—God-blessed old man—recognized friend—much affected. The spaces you can fill up at your leisure. . . .

HOWARD.

———

First Inaugural

The tight security on Inauguration Day, March 4, 1861, had never been seen in Washington before. The broad streets between the White House and the Capitol were lined with soldiers, and sharpshooters stood conspicuous guard from rooftops along the route.

Lincoln had prepared his inauguration address with extraordinary care, drafting it in a room above his brother-in-law's general store in Springfield, carrying it in a special satchel during the trip to Washington, and exploding in nervous anger when his son Robert misplaced it at a hotel. The incoming president knew that it would be the most closely read speech of his career so far—and perhaps in the entire history of the shaky Union.

The result was a masterpiece. Lincoln offered an olive branch to the South, a renewed pledge not to interfere with slavery where it existed, but reaffirmed his vow to preserve, protect, and defend the Constitution according to his sacred oath. When incoming Secretary of State Seward, his old New York party rival, suggested a final paragraph that Seward himself would compose, Lincoln demonstrated that he was as gifted a diplomat and editor as he was a writer.

With Lincoln's expert tweaking, the final peroration was memorable: "The mystic chords of memory, stretching from every battlefield, and patriot grave, to every living heart and hearthstone, all over this broad land, will yet swell the chorus of the Union, when again touched, as surely they will be, by the better angels of our nature."

Then Lincoln stepped forward to take the oath of office. Few on the scene missed the irony in the fact that it was administered by a hostile Chief Justice Roger B. Taney, whose pro-slavery Dred Scott decision has helped propel Lincoln back into politics, and, as it turned out, toward the presidency.

—H. H.

THE NEW ADMINISTRATION.

Abraham Lincoln President of the United States.

The Inauguration Ceremonies.

A Tremendous Crowd and No Accidents.

The Inaugural Address.

How it was Delivered and How it was Received.

An Impressive Scene at the Capitol.

Mr. Lincoln's First Audience at the White House.

Visit of the New-York Delegation to Senator Seward.

Mr. Seward Makes a Speech.

What was Done at the Grand Inauguration Ball.

Miscellaneous Incidents of the Occasion.

Our Washington Dispatches.

WASHINGTON, Monday, March 4.

THE DAWNING OF THE DAY.

The day to which all have looked with so much anxiety and interest has come and passed. ABRAHAM LINCOLN has been inaugurated, and "all's well."

At daylight the clouds were dark and heavy with rain, threatening to dampen the enthusiasm of the occasion with unwelcome showers. A few drops fell occasionally before 8 o'clock; but not enough to lay the dust, which, under the impulse of a strong northwest wind, swept down upon the avenue from the cross streets quite unpleasantly. The weather was cool and bracing, and, on the whole favorable to the ceremonies of the day.

MR. LINCOLN.

Mr. LINCOLN rose at 5 o'clock. After an early breakfast the Inaugural was read aloud to him by his son ROBERT, and the completing touches were added, including the beautiful and impassioned closing paragraph. Mr. LINCOLN then retired from his family circle to his closet, where he prepared himself for the solemn and weighty responsibilities which he was about to assume.

Here he remained until it was time for an audience to Mr. SEWARD. Together these statesmen conversed concerning that paragraph of the Inaugural relating to the policy of forcing obnoxious non-resident officers upon disaffected citizens.

When Mr. SEWARD departed, Mr. LINCOLN closed his door upon all visitors, until Mr. BUCHANAN called for him to escort him to the Capitol.

THE THRONG IN THE STREETS.

From early daylight the streets were thronged with people, some still carrying carpet-bags in hand, having found no quarters in which to stop. . . .

THE INAUGURAL PROCESSION.

It was nearly noon when Mr. BUCHANAN started from the White House with the Inaugural procession, which halted before Willard's Hotel to receive the President elect. The order of march you will get from other sources, and I will only observe that the carriage containing Mr. BUCHANAN and Mr. LINCOLN, was a simple open brett, surrounded by the President's mounted guard, in close order, as guard of honor.

The procession, as usual, was behind-hand a little, but its order was excellent. Nothing noteworthy occurred on the route. As it ascended the Capitol hill, towards the north gate, the company of United States Cavalry and the President's mounted guard took their positions each side of the carriage-way by which the President's party entered the north wing of the Capitol to go to the Senate Chamber.

The procession halted until the President and suite entered, and then filed through the troops aforesaid into the grounds.

On the east front, the military took their positions in the grounds in front of the platform, but the United States troops maintained their places outside until the line took up the President and party again after the ceremonies were over, to escort them back to the White House.

ARRANGEMENTS AT THE CAPITOL.

The arrangements at the Capitol were admirably designed, and executed so that everybody who was entitled to admission got in, and everybody who could not go in could see from without. The Senate Chamber was the great point of attraction, but only the favored few were admitted upon the floor, while the galleries were reserved for and occupied by a select number of ladies. The scene which transpired there was most memorable, producing a great and solemn impression upon all present. . . .

A few moments before 12 o'clock, MR. BRECKINRIDGE came in with Mr. HAMLIN upon his arm, and, together, they sat by the side of the President's desk until noon, . . .

The Senate now waited in silence for the President elect. Gradually those entitled to the floor entered. The Diplomatic Corps, in full court dress, came quite early. The Supreme Court followed, headed by the venerable Chief Justice TANEY, who looked as if he had come down from several generations, and finally the House of Representatives filed in. For at least an hour Mr. HAMLIN was acting President of the United States, but at length, a little after 1 o'clock, the doors opened, and the expected dignitaries were announced.

THE OUTGOING AND THE INCOMING.

Mr. BUCHANAN and Mr. LINCOLN entered, arm in arm, the former pale, sad, and nervous; the latter's face slightly flushed, with compressed lips. For a few minutes, while the oath was administered to Senator PEARCE, they sat in front of the President's desk. Mr. BUCHANAN sighed audibly, and frequently, but whether from reflection upon the failure of his Administration, I can't say. Mr. LINCOLN was grave and impassive as an Indian martyr.

APPEARANCE AT THE EAST PORTICO.

When all was ready, the party formed, and proceeded to the platform erected in front of the eastern portico. The appearance of the President elect was greeted, as he entered from the door of the rotunda, with immense cheering by the many thousand citizens assembled in the grounds, filling the square and open space, and perching on every tree, fence or stone affording a convenient point from which to see or hear. In a few minutes the portico was also densely crowded with both sexes.

On the front of the steps was erected a small wooden canopy, under which were seated Mr. BUCHANAN, Chief-Justice TANEY, Senators CHASE and BAKER, and the President elect, while at the left of the small table on which was placed the Inaugural, stood Col. SELDEN, Marshal of the District, an exponent of the security which existed there for the man and the ceremonies of the hour. At the left of the canopy, sat the entire Diplomatic Corps, dressed in gorgeous attire, evidently deeply impressed with the solemnity of the occasion, and the importance of the simple ceremony about to be performed. Beyond them was the Marine band, which played several patriotic airs before and after the reading of the address. To the right of the diplomats sat in solemn dignity, in silk gowns and hats, the members of the Supreme Court. Then came Senators, members of the House, distinguished guests and fair ladies by the score, while the immediate right of the canopy was occupied by the son and Private Secretaries of Mr. LINCOLN. Perched up on one side, hanging on by the railing, surrounding the statue of COLUMBUS and an Indian girl, was Senator WIGFALL, witnessing the pageant.

MR. LINCOLN INTRODUCED.

Everything being in readiness, Senator BAKER came forward and said:

"FELLOW-CITIZENS: I introduce to you ABRAHAM LINCOLN, the President elect of the United States of America."

Whereupon, Mr. LINCOLN arose, walked deliberately and composedly to the table, and bent low in honor of the repeated and enthusiastic cheering of the countless host before him. Having put on his spectacles, he arranged his manuscript on the small table, keeping the paper thereon by the aid of his cane, and commenced in a clear, ringing voice, that was easily heard by those on the outer limits of the crowd, to read his first address to the people, as President of the United States.

RECEPTION OF THE INAUGURAL.

The opening sentence, "Fellow-citizens of the United States," was the signal for prolonged applause, the good Union sentiment thereof striking a tender chord in the popular breast. Again, after defining certain actions to be his duty, he said, "And I shall perform it," there was a spontaneous, and uproarious manifestation of approval which continued for some moments. Every sentence which indicated firmness in the Presidential chair, and every statement of a conciliatory nature, was cheered to the echo; while his appeal to his "dissatisfied fellow-countrymen," desiring them to reflect calmly, and not hurry into false steps, was welcomed by one and all, most heartily and cordially. The closing sentence "upset the watering pot" of many of his hearers, and at this point alone did the melodious voice of the President elect falter.

Judge TANEY did not remove his eyes from Mr. LINCOLN during the entire delivery, while Mr. BUCHANAN, who was probably sleepy and tired, sat looking as straight as he could at the toe of his right boot. Mr. DOUGLAS, who stood by the right of the railing, was apparently satisfied, as he exclaimed, *sotto voce,* "Good," "That's so," "No coercion," and "Good again."

THE OATH OF OFFICE.

After the delivery of the address Judge TANEY stood up, and all removed their hats, while he administered the oath to Mr. LINCOLN. Speaking in a low tone the form of the oath, he signified to Mr. LINCOLN, that he should repeat the words, and in a firm but modest voice, the President took the oath as prescribed by the law, while the people, who waited until they saw the final bow, tossed their hats, wiped their eyes, cheered at the top of their voices, hurrahed themselves hoarse, and had the crowd not been so very dense, they would have demonstrated in more lively ways, their joy, satisfaction and delight.

SHAKING HANDS.

Judge TANEY was the first person who shook hands with Mr. LINCOLN and was followed by Mr. BUCHANAN, CHASE, DOUGLAS, and a host of minor great men. A Southern gentleman, whose name I did not catch, seized him by the hand, and said, "God bless you, my dear Sir; you will save us." To which Mr. LINCOLN replied, "I am very glad that what I have said causes pleasure to Southerners, because I then know they are pleased with what is right." . . .

WHAT MR. BUCHANAN SAID.

In reply to questions, Mr. BUCHANAN said, with a wretched and suspicious leer, "I cannot say what he means until I read his Inaugural; I cannot understand the secret meaning of the document, which has been simply read in my hearing."

WHAT MR. DOUGLAS SAID.

Mr. DOUGLAS said, "He does not mean coercion; he says nothing about retaking the forts, or Federal property—he's all right."

Subsequently, to another querist, DOUGLAS said: "Well, I hardly know what he means. Every point in the address is susceptible of a double construction; but I think he does not mean coercion."

GOING TO THE WHITE HOUSE.

After delaying a little upon the platform, Mr. LINCOLN, and Mr. BUCHANAN, arm in arm, and followed by a few privileged persons, proceeded at a measured pace to the Senate Chamber, and thence to the President's Room, while the Band played "Hail Columbia" "Yankee Doodle" and the "Star Spangled Banner." In a short time the procession was re-formed, and in state, the President and Ex-President were conducted to the White House. . . .

WHAT IS SAID OF THE INAUGURAL.

While conservative people are in raptures over the Inaugural, it cannot be denied that many Southerners look upon it as a precursor of war. They probably will take a calmer view to-morrow. . . . Its conciliatory tone, and frank, outspoken declaration of loyalty to the whole country, captured the hearts of many heretofore opposed to Mr. LINCOLN, and its firm enunciation of purpose to fulfill his oath to maintain the Constitution and laws, challenge universal respect.

THE POLICE AND MILITARY.

The arrangements for the preservation of the peace was admirable. A large special police, with conspicuous badges, were distributed all along the line of procession, and about the Capitol, but their mere presence was generally sufficient to insure order. In a few cases, where individual fights occurred, they interposed so promptly as to prevent a collision becoming general. So, too, they immediately dispersed every gathering of people who manifested the least improper excitement, or attempted to vociferate sentiments intended to be offensive or incendiary.

The several companies of United States Artillery, all under arms, were on the street near their quarters, with horses hitched up, and riders standing by their side, ready to vault into the saddle at an instant's notice. Files of mounted troops were stationed at different points of the City to convey to Head-quarters prompt intelligence of any disturbance.

The turn-out of the District militia was quite imposing. The Washington Light Infantry looked remarkably well. They are a fine-looking set of young men. The National Rifles, the corps whose secession sympathies are well understood here, failed to participate in the parade, but I understand they were on duty at the Armory, ready to turn out if needed to aid in the preserving of the peace.

THE CAPITOL FLAG.

Early in the forenoon, when the flag was unfurled upon the Capitol, one of the halliards gave way, and, splitting in two, the flag flung out like a pennant. For a long while it could not be taken down, though finally an adventurous man climbed to the top of the staff, and, tearing away the ill-omened standard, replaced it with an entire flag of the Union. . . .

THE INAUGURATION CEREMONIES.

Dispatch to the Associated Press.

WASHINGTON, Monday, March 4.

The day was ushered in by a most exciting session of the Senate, that body sitting for twelve hours, from 7 o'clock yesterday evening to 7 o'clock this morning.

As the dial of the clock pointed to 12 o'clock last night, and the Sabbath gave way to Monday, the 4th of March, the Senate Chamber presented a curious and animated appearance. The galleries were crowded to repletion, the ladies' gallery resembling, from the gay dresses of the fair ones there congregated, some gorgeous parterre of flowers, and the gentlemen's gallery seemed one dense black mass of surging, heaving masculines, pushing, strggling and almost clambering over each other's back in order to get a good look at the proceedings. . . .

At ten minutes after 1 o'clock an unusual stir occurred in the Chamber, and the rumor spread like wild-fire that the President elect was in the building.

At fifteen minutes past 1 o'clock, Marshal-in-Chief, Major B. B. FRENCH, entered the Chamber ushering in the President and the President elect. They had entered together from the street through a private covered passage-way on the north side of the Capitol, police officers being in attendance to prevent outsiders from crowding after them.

The line of procession was then formed in the following order

Marshal of the District of Columbia.

Judges of the Supreme Court.

Sergeant at Arms of the Senate.

Committee of Arrangements.

President of the United States, President elect.

Vice-President.

Secretary of the Senate.

Senators.

Diplomatic Corps.

Heads of Departments.

Governors, and others in the Chamber.

When the word was given for the members of the House to fall into the line of the procession, a violent rush was made for the door, accompanied by loud outcries, violent pushing and great disturbance.

After the procession had reached the platform, Senator BAKER, of Oregon, introduced Mr. LINCOLN to the Assembly. On Mr. LINCOLN advancing to the stand, he was cheered, but not very loudly. Unfolding his manuscript, in a loud, clear voice, he read his address, as follows:

THE INAUGURAL ADDRESS.

Fellow-Citizens of the United States:

In compliance with a custom as old as the Government itself, I appear before you to address you briefly, and to take in your presence the oath prescribed by the Constitution of the United States to be taken by the President before he enters on the execution of his office.

I do not consider it necessary for me at present to discuss those matters of Administration, about which there is no special anxiety or excitement.

Apprehension seems to exist among the people of the Southern States that, by the accession of a Republican Administration, their property, and their peace and personal security are to be endangered. There has never been any reasonable cause for such apprehension. Indeed, the most ample evidence to the contrary has all the while existed, and been open to their inspection. It is found in nearly all published speeches of him who now addresses you. I do but quote from one of these speeches, when I declare that "I have no purpose, directly or indirectly, to interfere with the institution of Slavery in the States where it exists. I believe I have no lawful right to do so, and I have no inclination to do so." Those who nominated and elected me did so with a full knowledge that I had made this and many similar declarations, and had never recanted them. And more than this, they placed in the platform for my acceptance, and as a law to themselves and to me, the clear and emphatic resolution which I now read:

Resolved, That the maintenance inviolate of the rights of the States, and especially the right of each State to order and control its own domestic institutions according to its own judgment, exclusively, is essential to that balance of power of which the perfection and endurance of our political fabric depends; and we denounce the lawless invasion, by armed force, of the soil of any State or a Territory, no matter under what pretext, as the gravest of crimes.

I now reiterate these sentiments, and in doing so, I only press upon the public attention the most conclusive evidence of which the case is susceptible, that the property, peace and security of no section are to be in any wise endangered by the new incoming Administration. I add too, that all the protection which, consistently with the Constitution and the laws, can be given, will be cheerfully given to all the States when lawfully demanded, for whatever cause, as cheerfully to one section as to another.

There is much controversy about the delivering up of fugitives from service or labor. The clause I now read is as plainly written in the Constitution as any other of its provisions.

"No person held to service or labor in one State under the laws thereof, escaping into another shall, in consequence of any law or regulation therein, be discharged from such service or labor, but shall be delivered up on claim of the party to whom such service or labor may be due."

It is scarcely questioned that this provision was intended by those who made it for the reclaiming of what we call fugitive slaves, and the intention of the lawgiver is the law. All Members of Congress swear their support to the whole Constitution—to this provision as much as any other. To the proposition, then, that slaves whose cases come within the terms of this clause "shall be delivered up," their oaths are unanimous. Now if they would make the effort in good temper, could they not, with nearly equal unanimity frame and pass a law by means of which to keep good that unanimous oath? There is some difference of opinion whether this clause should be enforced by National or by State authority, but surely that difference is not a very material one. If the slave is to be surrendered, it can be of but little consequence to him or to others by which authority it is done. And should any one, in any case, be content that this oath shall go unkept on a merely unsubstantial controversy, as to how it shall be kept? Again, in any law upon this subject, ought not all the safeguards of liberty known in the civilized and humane jurisprudence to be introduced, so that a free-man be not, in any case, surrendered as a slave? And might it not be well at the same time to provide by law for the enforcement of that clause in the Constitution which guarantees that "the citizens of each State shall be entitled to all the privileges and immunities of citizens in the several States." I take the official oath to-day with no mental reservations, and with no purpose to construe the Constitution or laws by any hyper-critical rules; and while I do not choose now to specify particular acts of Congress as proper to be enforced, I do suggest that it will be much safer for all, both in official and private stations, to conform to, and abide by all, those acts which stand unrepealed, than to violate any of them, trusting to find impunity in having them held to be unconstitutional.

It is seventy-two years since the first inauguration of a President under our National Constitution. During that period, fifteen different and greatly distinguished citizens have in succession administered the Executive branch of the Government. They have conducted it through many perils, and generally with great success. Yet with all this scope for precedent, I now enter upon the same task, for the brief constitutional term of four years, under great and peculiar difficulty. A disruption of the Federal Union, heretofore only menaced, is now formidably attempted. I hold that in contemplation of universal law and of the Constitution, the union of these States is perpetual. Perpetuity is implied, if not expressed, in the fundamental law of all National Governments. It is safe to assert that Government proper never had a provision in its organic law for its own termination. Continue to execute all the express provisions of our national Constitution, and the Union will endure forever, it being impossible to destroy it except by some action not provided for in the instrument itself. Again, if the United States be not a Government proper, but an association of States in the nature of a contract merely, can it, as a contract, be peaceably unmade by less than all the parties who made it. One party to a contract may violate it—break it, so to speak—but does it not require all to lawfully rescind it? Descending from these general principles, we find the proposition that, in legal contemplation, the Union is perpetual, confirmed by the history of the Union itself. The Union is much older than the Constitution. It was formed in fact by the articles of association in 1774. It was matured and continued in the Declaration of Independence, in 1776. It was further matured and the faith of all the then thirteen States, expressly plighted and engaged, that it should be perpetual by the articles of Confederation in 1778 and finally in 1787, one of the declared objects for ordaining and establishing the Constitution was, to form a more perfect Union. But if the destruction of the Union by one, or by a part only of the States, be lawfully possible the Union is less than before, the Constitution having lost the vital element of perpetuity. It follows from these views that no State upon its own mere motion can lawfully get out of the Union; that resolves and ordinances to that effect are legally void, and that acts of violence within any State or States against the authority of the United States are insurrectionary or revolutionary according to circumstances.

I, therefore, consider that, in view of the Constitution and the laws, the Union is unbroken, and, to the extent of my ability, I shall take care, as the Constitution itself expressly enjoins upon me, the laws of the Union be faithfully executed in all the States. Doing this I deem to be only a simple duty on my part. I shall perfectly perform it, so far as practicable, unless my rightful masters, the American people, shall withhold the requisition, or in some authoritative manner direct the contrary. I trust this will not be regarded as a menace, but only as the declared purpose of the Union that it will constitutionally defend and maintain itself.

In doing this, there need be no bloodshed or violence, and there shall be none unless forced upon the national authority. The power confided to me will be used to hold, occupy and possess the property and places belonging to the Government, and collect the duties and imposts, but beyond what may be necessary for these objects there will be no invasion, no using of force against or among the people anywhere.

Where hostility to the United States in any interior section shall be so great and so universal as to prevent competent resident citizens from holding the Federal offices, there will be no attempt to force obnoxious strangers among the people that object. While the strict legal right may exist of the Government to enforce the exercise of these offices, the attempt to do so would be so irritating, and so nearly impracticable withal, that I deem it better to forego for the time the uses of such offices.

The mails, unless repelled, will continue to be furnished in all parts of the Union.

So far as possible, the people everywhere shall have that sense of perfect security which is most favorable to calm thought and reflection. The course here indicated will be followed, unless current events and experience shall show a modification or change to be proper, and in every case and exigency my best discretion will be exercised, according to the circumstances actually existing, and with a view and a hope of a peaceful solution of the national troubles and the restoration of fraternal sympathies and affections. That there are persons in one section or another who seek to destroy the Union at all events, and are glad of any pretext to do it, I will neither affirm or deny. But if there be such I need address no word to them. To those, however, who really love the Union, may I not speak. Before entering upon so grave a matter as the destruction of our national fabric with all its benefits, its memories and its hopes, would it not be well to ascertain why we do it. Will you hazard so desperate a step while there is any [possibility that any] portion of the ills you fly from have no real existence? Will you, while the certain ills you fly to are greater than the real ones you fly from?

Will you risk the commission of so fearful a mistake? All profess to be content in the Union, if all Constitutional rights can be maintained. Is it true, then, that any right plainly written in the Constitution has been denied? I think not. Happily the human mind is so constituted that no party can reach to the audacity of doing this. Think, if you can, of a single instance in which a plainly written provision of the Constitution has ever been denied. If, by the mere force of numbers, a majority should deprive a minority of any clearly written constitutional right, it might, in a moral point of view, justify revolution—certainly would, if such right were a vital one. But such is not our case.

All the vital rights of minorities and individuals are so plainly assured to them by affirmations and negations, guaranties and prohibitions in the Constitution, that controversies never arise concerning them. But no organic law can ever be framed with a provision specifically applicable to every question which may occur in practical administration. No foresight can anticipate nor any document of reasonable length contain express provisions for all possible questions. Shall fugitives from labor be surrendered by National or by State authority? The Constitution does not expressly say. Must Congress protect Slavery in the Territories? The Constitution does not expressly say. From questions of this class spring all our constitutional controversies, and we divide upon them into majorities and minorities.

If the minority will not acquiesce the majority must, or the Government must cease. There is no alternative for continuing the Government but acquiescence on the one side or the other. If a minority in such a case will secede rather than acquiesce, they make a precedent which in turn will ruin and divide them, for a minority of their own will secede from them whenever a majority refuses to be controlled by such a minority.

For instance, may not any portion of a new confederacy, a year or two hence, arbitrarily secede again, precisely as portions of the present Union now claim to secede from it? All who cherish disunion sentiments are now being educated to the exact temper of doing this. Is there such perfect identity of interests among the States to compose a new Union, as to produce harmony only and prevent renewed secession? Plainly, the central idea of secession is the essence of anarchy.

A majority held in restraint by constitutional check and limitations, and always changing easily with deliberate changes of popular opinions and sentiments, is the only true sovereign of a free people. Whoever rejects it, does, of necessity, fly to anarchy or to despotism. Unanimity is impossible. The rule of a minority, as a permanent arrangement, is wholly inadmissible.

So that, rejecting the majority principle, anarchy or despotism in some form is all that is left. I do not forget the position assumed by some that constitutional questions are to be decided by the Supreme Court, nor do I deny that such decisions must be binding in any case upon the parties to a suit, as to the object of that suit, while they are also entitled to very high respect and consideration in all parallel cases by all other Departments of the Government, and while it is obviously possible that such a decision may be erroneous in any given case, still the evil effect following it being limited to that particular case, with the chance that it may be overruled and never become precedent for other cases, can better be borne than could the evils of a different practice. At the same time the candid citizen must confess, that if the policy of the Government upon the vital questions affecting the whole people, is to be irrevocably fixed by the decisions of the Supreme Court, the instant they are made in ordinary litigation between parties in personal actions, the people will have ceased to be their own rulers, having to that extent practically resigned their Government into the hands of that eminent tribunal. Nor is there in this view any assault upon the Court or the Judges.

It is a duty from which they may not shrink to decide cases of property brought before them, and it is no fault of theirs if others seek to turn their decisions to political purposes. One section of the country believes Slavery is right, and ought to be extended, while the other believes it is wrong, and ought not to be extended.

This is the only substantial dispute in the Fugitive Slave clause of the Constitution; and the laws for the suppression of the foreign Slave-trade are each as well enforced, perhaps, as any law can ever be in a community where the moral sense of the people imperfectly supports the law itself.

The great body of the people abide by the dry legal obligation in both cases, and a few break over in each. This, I think, cannot be perfectly cured, and it would be worse in both cases after the separation of the sections than before. The foreign Slave-trade, now imperfectly suppressed, would be ultimately revived, without restriction, in one section, while fugitive slaves now only partially surrendered, would not be surrendered at all by the other.

Physically speaking, we cannot separate—we cannot remove our respective sections from each other, nor build an impassable wall between them. A husband and wife may be divorced, and go out of the presence and beyond the reach of each other—but different parts of our country cannot do this.

They cannot but remain face to face, and intercourse either amicable or hostile must continue between them. Is it possible to make that intercourse more advantageous or more satisfactory after separation than before? Can aliens make treaties easier than friends can make laws? Can treaties be more faithfully enforced between aliens than laws can among friends?

Suppose you go to war, you cannot fight always, and when, after much loss on both sides and no gain on either, you cease fighting, the identical questions as to terms of intercourse are again upon you. This country, with its institutions, belongs to the people who inhabit it. Whenever they shall grow weary of the existing Government, they can exercise their Constitutional right of amending or their revolutionary right to dismember or overthrow it. I cannot be ignorant of the fact that many worthy and patriotic citizens are desirous of having the National Constitution amended. While I make no recommendation of amendment, I fully recognize the full authority of the people over the whole subject to be exercised in either of the modes prescribed in the instrument itself, and I should, under existing circumstances, favor rather than oppose a fair opportunity being afforded the people to act upon it.

I will venture to add that to me the Convention mode seems preferable in that it allows amendment[s] to originate, with the people themselves, instead of only permitting them to take or reject propositions originated by others not especially chosen for the purpose, and which might not be precisely such as they would wish, either to accept or refuse. I understand a proposed amendment to the Constitution, which amendment, however, I have not seen, has passed Congress to the effect that the Federal Government shall never interfere with the domestic institutions of States, including that of persons held for service. To avoid misconstruction of what I have said, I depart from my purpose not to speak of particular amendments, so far as to say that holding such a provision to now be implied constitutional law, I have no objection to its being made express and irrevocable.

The Chief Magistrate derives all his authority from the people, and they have conferred none upon him to fix the terms for a separation of the States. The people themselves, also, can do this if they choose, but the Executive, as such, has nothing to do with it.

His duty is to administer the present Government as it came to his hands, and to transmit it unimpaired by him to his successor. Why should there not be a patient confidence in the ultimate justice of the people? Is there any better for [sic; should be "or"—eds.] equal hope in the world? In our present differences is either party without faith of being in the right?

If the Almighty Ruler of Nations, with His eternal truth and justice, be on your side of the North, or on yours of the South, that truth and that justice will surely prevail by the judgment of this great tribunal, the American people.

By the frame of the Government under which we live, this same people have wisely given their public servants but little power for mischief, and have with equal wisdom provided for the return of that little to their own hands at very short intervals. While the people retain their virtue and vigilance, no Administration, by any extreme wickedness or folly can very seriously injure the Government in the short space of four years.

My countrymen, one and all, think calmly and well upon this whole subject. Nothing valuable can be lost by taking time.

If there be an object to hurry any of you in hot haste to a step which you would never take deliberately, that object will be frustrated by taking time; but no good object can be frustrated by it. Such of you as are now dissatisfied still have the old Constitution unimpaired, and on the sensitive point, the laws of your own framing under it, while the new Administration will have no immediate power, if it would, to change either. If it were admitted that you who are dissatisfied hold the right side in the dispute, there still is no single reason for precipitate action.

Intelligence, patriotism, Christianity and a firm reliance on Him who has never yet forsaken this favored land, are still competent to adjust in the best way all our present difficulty.

In your hands, my dissatisfied fellow-countrymen, and not in mine, is the momentous issue of civil war. The Government will not assail you. You can have no conflict without being yourselves the aggressors.

You have no oath registered in Heaven to destroy the Government, while I shall have the most solemn one to "preserve, protect and defend" it.

I am loth [*sic*] to close. We are not enemies but friends. We must not be enemies.

Though passion may have strained, it must not break our bonds of affection. The mystic chords of memory stretching from every battle-field and patriot's grave to every living heart and hearthstone all over this broad land, will yet swell the chorus of the Union, when again touched, as surely they will be, by the better angels of our nature.

―――――

During the delivery of the Inaugural, which commenced at 1½ o'clock, he was much cheered, especially at any allusion to the Union.

President BUCHANAN and Chief-Justice TANEY listened with the utmost attention to every word of the address, and at its conclusion, the latter administered the usual oath, in making which, Mr. LINCOLN was vociferously cheered.

The Chief-Justice seemed very much agitated, and his hands shook very perceptibly with emotion.

The Inauguration of to-day makes the eighth ceremony of the kind in which Chief-Justice TANEY has officiated, he having administered the oath of office successively to Presidents VAN BUREN, TYLER, POLK, TAYLOR, FILLMORE, PIERCE, BUCHANAN and LINCOLN. The ceremony was exceedingly impressive. . . .

Thus ended for the day-time the Inauguration ceremonies. Though the enthusiasm was not by any means equal to that manifested on former occasions of a similar nature, everything passed off quietly. The amplest civil and military preparations were made by the municipal authorities and Gen. SCOTT to provide for any emergencies that might arise. . . . The officers, it is reported, were continually passing to and fro, and it is said the General was heard to exclaim, "Everything is going on peaceably— thank God Almighty for it!" . . .

―――――

"Wanted—A Policy!"

A month after Lincoln was inaugurated it seemed to many Northerners that his administration was doing nothing to deal with the secession of the Southern states and the formation of a rival government, the Confederate States of America. So far as readers of newspapers could tell, the president spent all his time in making diplomatic and domestic appointments and in holding extended visiting hours, from 10 A.M. to 3 P.M., where all comers were welcome.

They did not realize that, unlike Great Britain and France, the United States had no permanent civil service, which could carry on the normal functions of government during a change in administrations. In the weeks after his inaugural Lincoln had to create a government from scratch, making hundreds of appointments from local postmasters to members of his cabinet. He had almost no staff to assist him—one private secretary, John. G. Nicolay; one assistant secretary, detailed from the Department of Interior, John Hay; and, from time to time, part-time clerks borrowed from other departments to copy routine papers.

Outsiders also did not know that Lincoln met with his cabinet almost every day to discuss the perilous situation at Fort Sumter, which (along with Fort Pickens in Florida) was the last major Union fortress in the seceded states. His civilian and military advisers gave him contradictory opinion. He hesitated before making a decision that might well embroil the nation in war.

Restive over Lincoln's indecisiveness, Secretary of State Seward prepared a memorandum, for the president's eyes only, that, in effect, offered to take over the running of the government. Lincoln quietly pocketed it. It was not so easy to ignore The New York Times, *usually a staunch supporter of the president, when it expressed the same impatience in its editorial headed: "Wanted—A Policy!" Lincoln clipped this and other critical newspaper articles and filed them under the heading "Villainous articles."*

—D. H. D.

WANTED—A POLICY!

The Washington correspondent of one of our morning contemporaries says:

"The point of embarrassment concerning Fort Sumpter, in the President's mind, as announced with entire candor, is, that if it be yielded, and the Federal authority be thus withdrawn under real or supposed necessity, similar reasons may be urged as to Fort Pickens and other points, which are not considered in the same category."

We should be very sorry to think that the President's mind was embarrassed, or his action controlled, in any degree by such considerations at his late day. Undoubtedly in themselves they deserve serious and grave attention. But they should have been weighed and disposed of long ago. It is by no means a new discovery that much may be said on both sides of every question;—and persons who have nothing better to do may amuse themselves by such carefully balanced dialectics. But President LINCOLN has duties and responsibilities on his hands which forbid his indulgence of such tastes. He is required to *act,*—and action requires decision. Certainly it is a momentous question whether Fort Sumpter should be evacuated or not:—there are many reasons to be urged for it and many against it. But Mr. LINCOLN is under the necessity, after full consideration of both sides, to adopt one course or the other;—and when adopted he should act as if no objections had ever been urged against it. If he has decided to evacuate Fort Sumpter, he should do it frankly,—not with apologies or useless "embarrassments." The effect of such a step should have been considered long ago.

It is idle to conceal the fact that the Administration thus far has not met public expectation. The country feels no more assurances as to the future,—knows nothing more of the probable results of the secession movement,—than it did on the day Mr. BUCHANAN left Washington. It sees no indications of an administrative policy adequate to the emergency,—or, indeed, of any policy beyond that of listless waiting to see what may "turn up." There are times when such a policy may be wise;—but not in presence of an active, resolute, and determined enemy. The new Confederacy is moving forward, towards the consummation of its plans, with a degree of vigor, intelligence, and success, of which, we are sorry to say, we see no indications on the part of the Government at Washington. In spite of the immense difficulties with which they have to contend,—the poverty of the country, its utter lack of commerce, of an army and navy, and of credit,—the hostility of its fundamental principles to the sentiments of the Christian world, the utter hollowness of its reasons for revolution, and the universal distrust which it encounters everywhere,—in spite of all these obstacles and discouragements, we cannot conceal the fact that the new Government of which JEFFERSON DAVIS is at the head, has evinced a marvelous degree of energy, and is rapidly assuming the proportions of a solid and formidable Power. Within less than six months they have adopted a Constitution, organized a Government, put all its machinery into working order, established a commercial system and put it in operation, laid the basis of a financial department, organized an army, secured enormous stores and munitions of war, and put themselves in a position to offer a very formidable resistance to any attempted coercion on the part of the United States. And what has been done on our part against them? What single step has been taken by our Government, either to resist their movement from without, or to appeal with vigor and effect to the loyalty which still lives within their borders? JEFFERSON DAVIS will soon have an organized army of 30,000 men at his command:—suppose he decides to march into Mexico, or Virginia, or upon Washington,—what organized means have we to resist and defeat his schemes? They have adopted a revenue system for the express purpose of depleting and damaging our commerce:—what have we done to offset it? With a blindness and a stolidity without a parallel in the history of intelligent statesmanship, we have done everything in our power to aid their efforts, and crown their hostile endeavors with complete success.

The fact is, our Government has done absolutely *nothing,* towards carrying the country through the tremendous crisis which is so rapidly and so steadily settling down upon us. It allows everything to *drift,*—to float along without guidance or impulse of any kind. This might do well enough, if the Southern States were pursuing the same policy. But while we are idle, they are active. While we leave everything at loose ends, they make everything tight and snug for the coming storm. Such a course can have but one result. The President must adopt some clear and distinct policy in regard to secession, or the Union will not only be severed, but the country will be disgraced. No great community can *drift* into ruin, without losing character as well as prosperity. It must, at least, make an effort at self-preservation, if it would avoid the contempt inseparable from imbecility. A nation may be overcome by outward force, or destroyed by internal treachery;—but if it struggles nobly and gallantly against its enemies, whatever else it may lose, it preserves the respect of the world, as well as its own. We are in danger of losing everything—even honor. The public sentiment is already demoralized,—the heart of the people is deadened,—and the patriotism of the country is already paralyzed, to a degree which a year ago we should not have thought possible in any contingency. Rebellion in the popular judgment has ceased to be a crime. Treason has become respectable. Men throughout the North think and talk of the revolution which is crushing the best Constitution the world ever saw,—which is sweeping away a Government which has done more for popular rights and popular interests than any other the earth has ever known, as they would talk of a partisan canvass for control of a village corporation. Deeds of infamy, compared with which ARNOLD's treason shines bright as the sun at noonday, excite scarcely a passing remark, and the fate of the great Republic of the Western world—the great Republic of human history—excites scarcely as much interest as the fluctuations of the Stock market, or the ups and downs of a local canvass.

What is the reason of this sad—this fearful change in the temper and tone of the country? Is patriotism a fiction? Have we suddenly discovered that Governments are but playthings—that loyalty is a delusion—that to stab a nation is to commit no crime? Or does the event vindicate the old faith that Democracy is a delusion—that the people are incapable of self-government, and that bayonets and cannon are the only security for law and order?

Is it not rather that the people have no leaders,—no representatives in the posts of power,—no men filled with the conscious sense of duty, and omnipotent to do what is right through faith in the people whose interests and rights they guard, and whose power they wield? One of the highest and noblest functions of a Government in a free country is to lead the nation,—to go forward as the national honor and welfare may call, and summon the people to rally to the standard set up in their defence. The people look to their Government for guidance in every great emergency. They look to it for courage, for vigor, for indomitable energy, for all the great qualities which give success to nations and glory to success. And when the Government fails them, they are powerless. They have no other leadership—no other means of union—no possibility of making their wishes known or their will felt, but through the action of the Government to which they have intrusted their welfare and delegated their power.

It is the high, imperative duty of President LINCOLN, in this solemn crisis of the nation's fate, to give the American people this guidance and leadership. He was perfectly right in saying at Springfield that upon his shoulders rests a responsibility more weighty than has ever fallen upon any one of his predecessors. That responsibility is not met by supervising the distribution of office. Mr. LINCOLN should reserve his thoughts and his strength for nobler duties than presiding over the wrangling of hungry and selfish hunters for patronage and place. He wastes powers that belong to the nation,—he squanders opportunities which millions upon millions of gold will never bring back, for rescuing the nation from the most fearful perils. We shall not be suspected of any but the most friendly sentiments towards the President of the United States, when we tell him, what the courtiers who hang upon his favor will not dare to whisper,—that he must go up to a higher level than he has yet reached, before he can see and realize the high duties to which he has been called. He has spent time and strength in feeding rapacious and selfish partisans, which should have been bestowed upon saving the Union and maintaining the authority of the Constitution he has solemnly sworn to defend. He has not done what he was expected to do as soon as he should assume the reins of power—summon back, by word and act, the loyalty of the American people to the flag and the Government of their common country. The Union is weaker now than it was a month ago. Its foes have gained courage, and its friends have lost heart. Step by step the new Confederacy marches forward towards solid and secure foundations,—and day by day the bright hopes of the lovers of the Union fade and die away.

The Administration *must have a policy of action,*—clear and definite in the end it aims at, wise and resolute in the means employed, and proclaimed to the people as the standard around which they can rally. What it should be, is not for us to say. That is a matter requiring wise and careful deliberation on the part of those who are responsible; but it should be *decided* upon promptly, and then carried into effect with steady and dauntless resolution.

The President has to decide whether he will *enforce the law* at the hazard of civil war,—or whether he will waive the execution of the law, and *appeal to the people* of the seceded States on behalf of the Union. One or other of these courses he should lose no time in adopting,—simply because every day lost renders less possible the success of either. If he decides to enforce the laws, let him call Congress together and demand the means of doing it. If he decides upon Peace, let him proclaim his purpose,—and seek at once the confidence and favor of the people whom he desires to win. Let him first disarm the fears of War which now unite, by outward pressure, the Southern people,—and then let him proceed to organize a Union party in every Southern State, and to strengthen and encourage it by all the legitimate means at his disposal. Why has SAM HOUSTON, of Texas, been left to fight the battle of the Union alone,—without a word of encouragement, or promise of a man or a dollar from the Government at Washington? Why have the Union men in Louisiana been abandoned without an effort, to the despotism of the minority which has usurped control of their affairs? Why have the noble-hearted champions of the Union and the Constitution in Virginia and Tennessee and Kentucky been ignored utterly in the use of the Executive patronage and in all the public action of the Federal Government? Simply, in our judgment, because the Administration has decided upon no means of meeting the secession movement,—because it has no POLICY. It is going blindly,—living from hand to mouth,—trusting in the chances of the future for deliverance from present and impending perils.

We trust this period of indecision, of inaction, of fatal indifference, will have a speedy end. Unless it does, we may bid farewell to all hope of saving the Union from destruction and the country from anarchy. A mariner might as well face the tempest without compass or helm, as an Administration put to sea amid such storms as now darken our skies, without a clear and definite plan of public conduct. The country looks eagerly to President Lincoln for the dispersion of the dark mystery that hangs over our public affairs. The people want *something* to be decided on—some standard raised—some policy put forward, which shall serve as a rallying point for the abundant but discouraged loyalty of the American heart. In a great crisis like this, there is no policy so fatal as that of having no policy at all.

PART TWO

THE EARLY WAR YEARS
1861–1862

Fort Sumter Falls

*T**he events of Friday, April 12, 1861, put an end to hesitation. The night before, three emissaries from Gen. P. G. T. Beauregard, who commanded the Confederate troops in Charleston, rowed out to Fort Sumter and demanded that the Union commander, Maj. Robert Anderson, surrender. When he refused, Confederate batteries on shore began firing. The 85 officers and men (plus 43 workmen) in the garrison returned fire as best they could, but they were hopelessly outmanned and outgunned by the 4,000 Confederates on shore. After 34 hours of bombardment, the defenders surrendered.*

Initially Washington received the reports with incredulity. President Lincoln was still privately negotiating with commissioners from Virginia in an effort to resolve the crisis. But as the news reports became more detailed he knew he had to act. After an emergency Sunday meeting with his cabinet he drew up a proclamation calling out 75,000 militiamen, to quell an insurrection "too powerful to be suppressed by ordinary Judicial proceedings," and he also summoned a special session of the Congress, to assemble on July 4. The war had begun.

—D. H. D.

FORT SUMPTER FALLEN.

Particulars of the Bombardment.

The Fort on Fire and the Garrison Exhausted.

No Attempt at Reinforcement.

The Cessation of Firing and the Capitulation.

No Lives Lost on Either Side.

Major Anderson and his Men Coming to New-York.

How the News was Received in Washington.

Call for Seventy-Five Thousand Militia.

An Extra Session of Congress.

War Feeling Throughout the Northern and Western States.

Fort Pickens Reinforced.

CHARLESTON, Saturday, April 13—Evening.

Major ANDERSON has surrendered, after hard fighting, commencing at 4½ o'clock yesterday morning, and continuing until five minutes to 1 to-day.

The American flag has given place to the Palmetto of South Carolina.

You have received my previous dispatches concerning the fire and the shooting away of the flagstaff. The latter event is due to Fort Moultrie, as well as the burning of the fort, which resulted from one of the hot shots fired in the morning.

During the conflagration, Gen. BEAUREGARD sent a boat to Major ANDERSON, with offers of assistance, the bearers being Colonels W. P. MILES, and ROGER PRYOR, of Virginia, and LEE. But before it reached him, a flag of truce had been raised. Another boat then put off, containing Ex-Gov. MANNING, Major D. R. JONES and Col. CHARLES ALLSTON, to arrange the terms of surrender, which were the same as those offered on the 11th inst. These were official. They stated that all proper facilities would be afforded for the removal of Major ANDERSON and his command, together with the company arms and property, and all private property, to any post in the United States he might elect. The terms were not, therefore, unconditional.

Major ANDERSON stated that he surrendered his sword to Gen. BEAUREGARD as the representative of the Confederate Government. Gen. BEAUREGARD said he would not receive it from so brave a man. He says Major ANDERSON made a staunch fight, and elevated himself in the estimation of every true Carolinian.

During the fire, when Major ANDERSON's flagstaff was shot away, a boat put off from Morris Island, carrying another American flag for him to fight under—a noteworthy instance of the honor and chivalry of South Carolina Seceders, and their admiration for a brave man.

The scene in the city after the raising of the flag of truce and the surrender is indescribable; the people were perfectly wild. Men on horseback rode through the streets proclaiming the news, amid the greatest enthusiasm.

On the arrival of the officers from the fort they were marched through the streets, followed by an immense crowd, hurrahing, shouting, and yelling with excitement.

Several fire companies were immediately sent down to Fort Sumpter to put out the fire, and any amount of assistance was offered.

A regiment of eight hundred men has just arrived from the interior, and has been ordered to Morris Island, in view of an attack from the fleet which may be expected to-night.

Six vessels are reported off the bar, but the utmost indignation is expressed against them for not coming to the assistance of Major ANDERSON when he made signals of distress.

The soldiers on Morris Island jumped on the guns every shot they received from Fort Sumpter while thus disabled, and gave three cheers for Major ANDERSON and groans for the fleet.

Col. LUCAS, of the Governor's Staff, has just returned from Fort Sumpter, and says Major ANDERSON told him he had pleasanter recollections of Fort Moultrie than Fort Sumpter. Only five men were wounded, one seriously.

The flames have destroyed everything. Both officers and soldiers were obliged to lay on their faces in the casemates, to prevent suffocation.

The explosions heard in the city were from small piles of shell, which ignited from the heat.

The effect of the shot upon the fort was tremendous. The walls were battered in hundreds of places, but no breach was made.

Major ANDERSON expresses himself much pleased that no lives had been sacrificed, and says that to Providence alone is to be attributed the bloodless victory. He compliments the firing of the Carolinians, and the large number of exploded shells lying around attests their effectiveness.

The number of soldiers in the fort was about seventy, besides twenty-five workmen, who assisted at the guns. His stock of provisions was almost exhausted, however. He would have been starved out in two more days.

The entrance to the fort is mined, and the officers were told to be careful, even after the surrender, on account of the heat, lest it should explode.

A boat from the squadron, with a flag of truce, has arrived at Morris Island, bearing a request to be allowed to come and take Major ANDERSON and his forces. An answer will be given to-morrow at 9 o'clock.

The public feeling against the fleet is very strong, it being regarded as cowardly to make not even an attempt to aid a fellow officer.

Had the surrender not taken place, Fort Sumpter would have been stormed to-night. The men are crazy for a fight.

The bells have been chiming all day, gun firing, ladies waving handkerchiefs, people cheering, and citizens making themselves generally demonstrative. It is regarded as the greatest day in the history of South Carolina.

Fort Sumpter Evacuated.

CHARLESTON, *VIA* AUGUSTA, Saturday, April 13.
FORT SUMPTER HAS SURRENDERED.
The Confederate flag floats over its walls.
None of the garrison or Confederate troops are hurt.
Another correspondent says:
The bombarding has closed.
Major Anderson has drawn down the stripes and stars, and displays a white flag, which has been answered from the city, and a boat is on the way to Sumpter.

CHARLESTON, Saturday, April 13—P.M.
The Federal flag was again hoisted over Fort Sumpter, when PORCHER MILES, with a flag of truce, went to the Fort.

In a few minutes the Federal flag was again hauled down by Major ANDERSON, and a white one unfurled.

CHARLESTON, Saturday, April 13.
Gen. BEAUREGARD, with two Aids, have left for Fort Sumpter.

Three fire companies from Charleston are now on their way to Sumpter to quell the fire before it reaches the magazine.

Fort Sumpter has unconditionally surrendered.

Ex-Senator CHESTNUT, Ex-Governor MANNING and W.P. MILES have just landed and marched to Gov. PICKENS' residence, followed by a dense crowd will with joy.

It is reported that the Federal flag was shot away by the Palmetto Guards at Morris Island.

In all two thousand shots have been fired. No Carolinians killed.

Major ANDERSON and his men, under guard, were conveyed to Morris Island.

The bells are ringing out a merry peal, and our people are engaged in every demonstration of joy.

It is estimated that there are nine thousand men under arms on the islands and in the neighborhood.

The Latest Dispatches.

CHARLESTON, Saturday, April 13.

I have seen W. PORCHER MILES, who has just returned from a visit to Fort Sumpter. He assured me that no one was killed at Fort Sumpter. This is reliable, and puts at rest all previous reports about Fort Sumpter.

Maj. ANDERSON has reached the city, and is the guest of Gen. BEAUREGARD.

Our people sympathize with Maj. ANDERSON, but abhor those who were in the steamers off our bar and in sight of our people, and did not even attempt to reinforce him.

The Fairfield regiment, one thousand strong, has just passed the *Courier* office, and their way to Morris Island.

There are now ten thousand men under arms in the harbor and on the coast.

Judge MAGRATH, who has just returned, reports that the wood-work and officers' quarters at Fort Sumpter are all burnt.

None of the officers were wounded.

The Fort will be taken possession of to-night by the Confederate troops.

A boat from one of the vessels outside the harbor communicated with Gen. SIMONS, in command of the forces on Morris Island, and made a request that one of the steamers be allowed to enter the port for the purpose of taking away Major ANDERSON and his command. An arrangement was agreed upon by the parties to stay all proceedings until 9 o'clock to-morrow.

CHARLESTON, Saturday, April 13.

Hostilities have for the present ceased, and the victory belongs to South Carolina. With the display of the flag of truce on the ramparts of Sumpter at 1½ o'clock, the firing ceased, and an unconditional surrender was made.

The Carolinians had no idea that the fight was at an end so soon.

After the flag-staff of ANDERSON was shot away, Col. WIGFALL, Aid to Gen. BEAUREGARD, at his Commander's request, went to Sumpter with a white flag, to offer assistance in extinguishing the flames. He approached the burning fortress from Morris Island, and while the firing was raging on all sides, effected a landing at Sumpter. He approached a port-hole, and was met by Maj. ANDERSON. The Commandant of Fort Sumpter said he had just displayed a white flag, but the firing from the Carolina batteries was kept up nevertheless.

Col. WIGFALL replied that Major ANDERSON must haul down the American flag; that no parley would be granted; surrender or fight was the word. Major ANDERSON then hauled down his flag, and displayed only that of truce.

All firing instantly ceased, and two other of Gen. BEAUREGARD's staff—Ex-Senator CHESTNUT and Ex-Governor MANNING—came over in a boat and stipulated with the Major that his surrender should be unconditional for the present, subject to the terms of Gen. BEAUREGARD.

Major ANDERSON was allowed to remain with his men in actual possession of the fort, while Messrs. CHESTNUT and MANNING came over to the city, accompanied with a member of the Palmetto Guards, bearing the colors of his Company. These were met at the pier by hundreds of citizens, and as they marched up the street to the General's quarters, the crowd was swelled to thousands. Shouts rent the air and wildest joy was manifested on account of the welcome tidings.

After the surrender, a boat with an officer and ten men was sent from one of the four ships in the offing to Gen. SIMONS, commanding on Morris Island, with a request that a merchant ship or one of the vessels of the United States be allowed to enter and take off the commander and garrison of Fort Sumpter.

Gen. SIMONS replied that if no hostilities were attempted during the night, and no effort was made to reinforce or retake Fort Sumpter, he would give an answer at 9 o'clock on Sunday morning.

The officer signified that he was satisfied with this, and returned. This correspondent accompanied the officers of Gen. BEAUREGARD's staff on a visit to Fort Sumpter. None but the officers were allowed to land, however. They went down in a steamer and carried three fire engines for the purpose of putting out the flames. The fire, however, has been previously extinguished by the exertions of Major ANDERSON and his men.

The visitors reported that Major ANDERSON surrendered because his quarters and barracks were destroyed and he had no hope of reinforcements. The fleet lay idly by during the thirty hours of the bombardment, and either could not or would not help him; besides, his me were prostrate from over-exertion.

There were but five of them hurt, four badly and one, it is thought, mortally, but the rest were worn out.

The explosions that were heard and seen from the city in the morning, were caused by the bursting of loaded shells. These were ignited by the fire, and could not be removed quick enough. The fire in the barracks was caused by the quantities of hot shot poured in from Fort Moultrie. Within Fort Sumpter everything but the casemates is in utter ruin. The whole thing looks like a blackened mass of ruins. Many of the guns are dismounted. The side opposite the iron battery of Cummings' Point is the hardest dealt with. The rifled cannon from this place made great havoc with Fort Sumpter. The wall looks like a honey-comb. Near the top is a breach as big as a cart. The side opposite Fort Moultrie is honey-combed extensively, as is that opposite the floating battery.

Fort Moultrie is badly damaged. The officers quarters and barracks are torn to pieces. The frame houses on the islands are riddled with shot in many instances, and whole sides of houses are torn out.

The fire in Fort Sumpter was put out and re-caught three times during the day.

Dr. CRAWFORD, Major ANDERSON's surgeon, is slightly wounded in the face. None of the Carolinians are injured.

Major ANDERSON and all his officers and men are yet in Fort Sumpter. I approached near enough to the wall to see him bid adieu. In addition to this, conversations were had, which have been repeated to me.

A boat was sent from the Fort to-night to officially notify the fleet at the bar that Major ANDERSON had surrendered. It is not known when the Carolinians will occupy Fort Sumpter, or what is to be done with the vanquished.

Everyone is satisfied with the victory, and happy that no blood was shed.

In the city, after the surrender, bells were rung and cannon fired.

CHARLESTON, Sunday, April 14.

Negotiations were completed last night. Major ANDERSON, with his command, will evacuate Fort Sumpter this morning, and will embark on board of the war vessel off our bar.

When Fort Sumpter was in flames, and ANDERSON could only fire his guns at long intervals, the men at our batteries cheered at every fire which the gallant Major made in his last struggles, but looked defiance at the vessels of war, whose men, like cowards, stood outside without firing a gun or attempting to divert the fire of a single battery from Sumpter.

Five of ANDERSON's men are slightly wounded.

CHARLESTON, Sunday, April 14.

The Steamer *Isabel* is now steaming up, and will take Gen. BEAUREGARD to Sumpter, which will be turned over by Major ANDERSON to the

Confederate States. ANDERSON and his command, it is reported, will proceed to New York in the *Isabel.*

CHARLESTON, Sunday, April 14.

Maj. ANDERSON and his men leave to-night in the steamer *Isabel* at 11 o'clock for New-York.

The fleet is still outside.

It was a thrilling scene when Maj. ANDERSON and his men took their formal leave of Fort Sumpter.

THE TIMES CORRESPONDENT IMPRISONED.

WILMINGTON, N.C., Sunday, April 14.

I saw the first gun fired at Fort Sumpter at 4 o'clock, A.M., April 12. I witnessed the battle for six hours. At noon I was arrested by order of Gen. BEAUREGARD as a Federal spy, and I was imprisoned for twenty-four hours, and then sent out of the city by Gov. PICKENS, destitute of funds. In Wilmington I was aided by Mr. PRICE, of the *Daily Journal,* and will be with you in thirty-six hours.

There are conflicting reports as to the number killed. It is generally believed that nobody is hurt.

JASPER.

PROCLAMATION BY THE PRESIDENT.

Seventy-Five Thousand Volunteers and an Extra Session of Congress.
By the President of the United States.
A Proclamation.

Whereas; The laws of the United States have been for some time past, and now are opposed, and the execution thereof obstructed in the States of South Carolina, Georgia, Alabama, Florida, Mississippi, Louisiana and Texas, by combinations too powerful to be suppressed by the ordinary course of Judicial proceedings, or by the powers vested in the Marshals by law,—now, therefore, I, ABRAHAM LINCOLN, President of the United States, in virtue of the power in me vested by the Constitution and the laws, have thought fit to call forth, and hereby do call forth, the militia of the several States of the Union to the aggregate number of seventy-five thousand, in order to suppress said combinations, and to cause the laws to be duly executed.

The details for this object will be immediately communicated to the State authorities through the War Department. I appeal to all loyal citizens to favor, facilitate and aid this effort to maintain the honor, the integrity and the existence of our national Union and the perpetuity of popular government, and to redress wrongs already long enough endured.

I deem it proper to say that the first service assigned to the forces hereby called forth will probably be to repossess the forts, places and property which have been seized from the Union, and in every event the utmost care will be observed, consistently with the objects aforesaid, to avoid any devastation, any destruction of, or interference with property, or any disturbance of peaceful citizens in any part of the country, and I hereby command the persons composing the combinations aforesaid to disperse and retire peaceably to their respective abodes, within twenty days from this date.

Deeming that the present condition of public affairs presents an extraordinary occasion, I do hereby, in virtue of the power in me vested by the Constitution, convene both Houses of Congress. The Senators and Representatives are therefore summoned to assemble at their respective Chambers, at 12 o'clock noon, on Thursday, the fourth day of July next, then and there to consider and determine such measures as in their wisdom the public safety and interest may seem to demand.

In witness whereof, I have hereunto set my hand, and caused the seal of the United States to be affixed.

Done at the City of Washington, this fifteenth day of April, in the year of our Lord one thousand eight hundred and sixty-one, and of the Independence of the United States, the eighty-fifth.

By the President, ABRAHAM LINCOLN
WILLIAM H. SEWARD, Secretary of State. . . .

The News in Washington.

WASHINGTON, Sunday, April 14.

THE EXCITEMENT AT THE CAPITAL.

The excitement here throughout the day has been intense. People gather in groups on the streets, and in hotels, discussing affairs at Charleston and the probabilities of the future.

There is great diversity of opinion relative to the reliability of the news that Major ANDERSON has surrendered. The dispatches to the Associated Press are evidently full of blunders, which cast suspicion on the whole.

DISPATCHES TO THE PRESIDENT.

The President, nevertheless, has intelligence which satisfies him that the news is too true. Private dispatches from Charleston signed by trusty men, also confirm it; but as the telegraph is known to have been constantly tampered with by the secession authorities, it is feared that even private dispatches may have been mutilated for the purpose of cutting the Government off from all possible means of correct information.

THE CREDIBILITY OF THE TELEGRAMS.

The statement that the fleet had asked a cessation of hostilities until morning especially puzzles everybody, for if the Fort had surrendered the fleet could only have asked a cessation for its own sake, and we have thus far no information that it had been engaged. The vessels had only to steam out of range.

Still the opinion of men of high military authority here is that the news of the surrender is too true. They say no battery for the defense of the harbor could long withstand a skillful bombardment by heavy metal, where the garrison assailed is too weak to reply effectively and distract or annoy the assailants.

Besides, it is well-known here, and I have it from an authentic official source. Major ANDERSON's provisions were all exhausted yesterday, leaving him without an ounce to refresh his men after their hard day's work. There is apparently good reason here to believe the report that Major ANDERSON has embarked seaward.

Still many wagers were taken here to-day that the whole story of the surrender is false. The Union men absolutely refuse credence.

STREET FIGHTS IN WASHINGTON.

To-day's excitement has betrayed many secessionists who held public office, and who could not conceal their joy at the reduction of Fort Sumpter. Several fights occurred, and decided knock-downs. Gen. NYE, among others, has knocked down a couple of secessionists within the last day or two. The fact is, Northern men have got tired of having treason crammed offensively down their throats, and are learning to resent it by force, the only argument the chivalry seem to appreciate. . . .

THE COURSE OF VIRGINIA.

Everybody here sees that now war has commenced, the question which the Virginia Convention has to decide is simply whether Virginia will declare war against the United States or stand by the Government; whether she will invite the battle upon her soil, to her utter ruin, or aid in bringing the fratricidal strife to a speedy termination by sustaining the Government and the Union.

THE NORTH A UNIT.

The news from the North of the unanimity of public sentiment in favor of the Government and the strongest policy for the suppression of rebellion gladdens very heart. It is fully believed that all partisan considerations henceforth will be suspended, and that every effort will be directed to saving the country.

THE PRESIDENT'S PROCLAMATION.

You have the President's proclamation, making a requisition for seventy-five thousand volunteers, called from all the adhering States except California and Oregon. That news will thrill like an electric shock throughout the land, and establish the fact that we have a Government at last.

UNANIMITY OF THE CABINET.

The Cabinet is a unit on these measures, and no man among them was more decided and active in their support than Mr. SEWARD, who urged conciliation and forbearance until the Disunionists were put clearly and thoroughly in the wrong.

THE QUOTA OF TROOPS FROM EACH STATE.

The War Department is engaged to-night in calculating the number of troops which each State is entitled to furnish. New York will be entitled probably to ten regiments. Pennsylvania and Massachusetts to a few less. The estimates are based upon the Federal representation of the States.

The proclamation is the fruit of a prolonged Cabinet meeting held last night.

THE BLOCKADE OF SOUTHERN PORTS.

No policy relative to closing the ports of the Seceding States is yet understood to be settled upon in detail. It is probable, however, that arrangements will be speedily made to cut off all communication with them by sea. There need be no doubt about the power of the Government to do this under its authority to prevent smuggling.

But, independent of that, the occasion justifies the Executive in assuming responsibility. He may well emulate Gen. JACKSON, who, when BOB LETCHER asked him under what law he could bring the Nullifier leaders of South Carolina to Washington for trial and execution, replied that if the Attorney-General could not find a law for it, he would get another Attorney-General who could. Self-preservation is the Government's first duty, and its masters, the people, will justify it in every wise measure addressed to that end. . . .

South Blockaded

The firing on Fort Sumter cleared the air. In the North many believed that the Union, with its vast resources, its enormous superiority in manufactures and railroads, and a population of twenty million could easily defeat the Confederacy, with its five million inhabitants. Secretary of State Seward thought the war would be over in ninety days, and the Chicago Tribune *predicted success "within two or three months at the furthest."*

In the South the attack on Fort Sumter precipitated the secession of Virginia, which had teetered between remaining in the Union and joining the Confederacy. By the end of May, North Carolina, Tennessee and Arkansas followed. With its population now increased to nine million, the Confederacy was now a formidable opponent.

To counter these moves, President Lincoln on April 19 issued a proclamation blockading the ports of the seceded states. The purpose was both to prevent the Confederates from importing arms and supplies from Europe and to cut off the export of cotton and tobacco, the main sources of Southern revenue. Congressman Thaddeus Stevens of Pennsylvania condemned the proclamation as "a great blunder," because in terms of international law it "meant we were blockading ourselves." When he confronted the president, Lincoln put on his best countryman air and said, "I don't know anything about the law of nations and I thought it was all right."

—D. H. D.

HIGHLY EXCITING NEWS.

Southern Ports to be Blockaded.

A Day of Riot and Blood in Baltimore.

Pennsylvania and Massachusetts Volunteers Attacked.

Two Massachusetts Men Killed and Several Wounded.

They Return the Fire and Kill Seven of the Rioters.

The Secessionists Nonplussed at Harper's Ferry.

The Arms Destroyed and the Building Burnt.

Departure of the Seventh Regiment of New-York.

The Most Impressive Scene Ever Witnessed in Broadway.

The War Spirit throughout the North.

Proclamation from President Lincoln.

WASHINGTON, Friday, April 19.

The President has issued a proclamation, stating that an insurrection against the Government of the United States has broken out in the States of South Carolina, Georgia, Alabama, Florida, Mississippi, Louisiana and Texas, and the laws of the United States, for the collection of the revenue, cannot be effectually executed therein, conformably to that provision of the Constitution, which requires duties to be uniform throughout the United States, and further a combination of persons engaged in such insurrection have threatened to grant pretended letters-of-marque, to authorize the bearers thereof to commit assaults on the lives, vessels and property of good citizens of the country, carefully engaged in commerce on the high seas, and in the waters of the United States.

And whereas the President says an Executive proclamation has already been issued, requiring the persons engaged in these disorderly proceedings to desist, therefore calling out a militia force for the purpose of repressing the same, and convening Congress in extraordinary session, to deliberate and determine thereon. The President, with a view to the same purposes before mentioned, and to the protection of the public peace, and the lives and property of its orderly citizens, pursuing their lawful occupations, until Congress shall have assembled and deliberated on the said unlawful proceedings, or until the same shall have ceased, has further deemed it advisable to set on foot a BLOCKADE OF THE PORTS within the States aforesaid, in pursuance of the laws of the United States and the laws of the nations, in such cases provided.

For this purpose a competent force will be posted so as to prevent the entrance and exit of vessels from the ports aforesaid.

If, therefore, with a view to violate such blockade, a vessel shall attempt to leave any of the said ports, she will be duly warned by the commander of one of the said blockading vessels, who will indorse on her register the fact and date of such warning; and if the same vessel shall again attempt to enter or leave the blockaded port, she will be captured, and sent to the nearest convenient port for such proceedings against her and her cargo as may be deemed advisable.

ABRAHAM LINCOLN,

President of the United States.

WM. H. SEWARD, Secretary of State. . . .

THE SAFETY OF WASHINGTON.

Many people ask, "Will it be safe for women and children in Washington, in view of the threatened war?" and residents here are receiving numerous appeals from distance friends to leave the city for some more Northern refuge. All such indications of fear are idle. There *has* been danger of an outbreak here and in the neighborhood of the little squad of traitors who are scattered among the great mass of Unionists who comprise the population of the District; but there are not enough of them to get up a respectable riot, and they will not attempt it. As to the seizure of the Capital by a Southern army—that will never be effected if a million men can hold the Stars and Stripes over it,—for above all other points, this is the one which the Government will retain in its possession until it has been proven that the Secessionists can subjugate the rest of the American people,—and that time we apprehend here is not immediately at hand.

THE BENEFITS OF A FIGHT.

If there are still in the North any who hesitate about the propriety of effective measures to support the Government, and who fear and tremble lest a collision of arms is to render a perpetuation of the Union between the North and South impossible, it would do them good to hear the sentiments expressed by Southern gentlemen in this neighborhood—men who know the South, and who have independence enough to express their views freely and without stint. I remember that during the late session of Congress an outspoken and honest Southern member, conversing with a member from New-England with respect to the disturbances between the sections, remarked, "We are going to have a fight with you, and somebody's going to get hurt; but after that we shall like each other better than we ever have since the foundation of the Government."

I confess that at the time it did seem as though the mode suggested was rather a rough sort of introduction to good fellowship; but in conversing today with another Southron, he expressed the same idea, in a form of argument which carried with it great force. "The masses of our people," he said, "don't understand the people of the North. You don't fight duels, nor do various other things which Southern education holds to be indispensable to a reputation for courage. They have consequently settled down into the conviction that 'Yankees' are 'cowards'—and while they despise them for that, they hate them also because they don't give them opportunity for more violent demonstrations upon their persons. They don't *respect* the people of the North—and so they don't believe Northern men when they disclaim any purpose of oppressing the South, and of interfering with Slavery in the States. Cowardice they look upon as the quintessence of meanness—and lying they consider its natural companion. Hence it is that they refuse to give the North credit for an honest motive in its Anti-Slavery sentiments, and hence they believe the demagogues, who profess to see nothing in your hostility to Slavery extension except an offensive purpose to humiliate the South, and force her to inequality in the Union. Now we are about to have a conflict; they will learn that Northern people are not cowards, but as brave and determined as themselves. The knowledge of that fact will inspire them with respect for you, give them confidence in your truth, and make us all better friends than the two sections can ever be until they have each learned, by a stern experience, that the other is worthy of respect and confidence."

There certainly is wisdom and sound logic in the argument,—and if the dread trial by the sword must come, there is some consolation in the anticipation that good will ultimately flow from the evil. . . .

Looking for Leadership

If the attack on Fort Sumter produced an unprecedented outpouring of loyalty in the North, as thousands of volunteers joined the army, vowing to preserve the Union, it also led to vast disorganization as troops began to converge on Washington. On April 19, the Sixth Massachusetts Volunteer Infantry Regiment, which was heading for the capital in response to Lincoln's call, was attacked by secessionist sympathizers as it passed through Baltimore, and at least four soldiers were killed, the first casualties of the Civil War. As rioting continued, several railroad bridges were burned to prevent the passage of Union troops, and for a time Washington was effectively cut off from the rest of the country. Lincoln paced the floor of the White House, looking anxiously for reinforcements. Eventually he broke out in anguish: "Why don't they come! Why don't they come!"

After about a week Washington was relieved by the arrival of troops, but the Union faced crises elsewhere. The commander in charge of Harper's Ferry surrendered without firing a shot. The federal navy yard near Norfolk was evacuated and partly burned because the commandant feared that the Confederates would capture it. The mayor of Baltimore tried to keep any more Union troops from passing through his city, and the governor of Maryland proposed inviting Lord Lyons, the British minister at Washington, to mediate the conflict. Even worse, Robert E. Lee, considered the ablest soldier in the United States army, resigned his commission to join the Confederacy.

This background of disasters makes it easy to understand why The New York Times, a loyal supporter of the Union cause, began to despair and to call for a change in leadership.

—D. H. D.

STARTLING FROM BALTIMORE.

The Northern Troops Mobbed and Fired Upon—The Troops Return The Fire—Four Massachusetts Volunteers Killed and Several Wounded—Several of The Rioters Killed.

BALTIMORE, Friday, April 19.

There was a horrible scene on Pratt-street, to-day. The railroad track was taken up, and the troops attempted to march through. They were attacked by the mob with bricks and stones, and were fired upon. The fire was returned. Two of the Seventh Regiment of Pennsylvania were killed and several wounded.

It is impossible to say what portion of the troops have been attacked. They bore a white flag as they marched up Pratt-street and were greeted with showers of paving-stones. The Mayor of the city went ahead of them with the police. An immense crowd blocked up the streets. The soldiers finally turned and fired on the mob. Several of the wounded have just gone up the street in carts.

At the Washington dépôt, an immense crowd assembled. The rioters attacked the soldiers, who fired into the mob. Several were wounded, and some fatally. It is said that four of the military and four rioters are killed. The city is in great excitement. Martial law has been proclaimed. The military are rushing to the armories.

Civil war has commenced. The railroad track is said to be torn up outside of the city. Parties threaten to destroy the Pratt-street bridge.

As the troops passed along Pratt-street a perfect shower of paving stones rained on their heads.

The cars have left for Washington, and were stoned as they left.

It was the Seventh Regiment of Massachusetts which broke through the mob. Three of the mob are known to be dead and three soldiers. Many were wounded. Stores are closing, and the military rapidly forming. The Minute Men are turning out. . . .

BALTIMORE, Friday, April 19 — 4 P.M.

A town meeting has been called for 4 o'clock.

It is said there have been 12 lives lost.

Several are mortally wounded.

Parties of men half frantic are roaming the streets armed with guns, pistols and muskets.

The stores are closed.

Business is suspended.

A general state of dread prevails.

Parties a short time ago rushed into the telegraph office, armed with hatchets, and cut the wires. Not much damage was done. . . .

OUR BALTIMORE CORRESPONDENCE.
Warlike News from the South—Virginia Seceded—Attack on Harper's Ferry—Gov. Hicks—Excitement in Baltimore—Resignation of Col. Huger, U.S.A., &C.

Correspondence of the New-York Times:

BALTIMORE, Thursday, April 18, 1861.

The news from the South is of the most warlike character. Every effort at preparation is being made for the anticipated conflict; and private dispatches, from unprejudiced sources, represent the feeling of resistance as unanimously extreme.

I have reason to believe, on reliable authority, that the Virginia Convention have, in secret session, by a large majority, repealed the ordinance by which she became a member of the Confederation; that is has not been made public, because of the desire first to mature some plan of prompt and general action; that some fifteen hundred or two thousand troops are now *en route* for Harper's Ferry, and that ere this reaches you that post will be in their possession.

Serious fears are entertained by the Baltimore and Ohio Railroad Company, in consequence of information imparted from different sources, that their bridge over the Potomac will be destroyed. The President, Mr. GARRETT, has this moment, by special engine sent an influential agent there with a view to the protection of the Company's property.

The Norfolk boat of this morning also brings intelligence that the Navy-yard there had been seized, and that vessels had been sunk in the channel, to prevent the men-of-war, lying under the guns of Fortress Monroe, from leaving.

Gov. HICKS has not yet responded, either affirmatively or negatively, to the requirements of the Secretary of War, in regard to the quota of troops from Maryland. The statement in the papers of yesterday that he had done so, are not true.

There is great excitement in this city. A serious disposition is manifested in certain quarters to obstruct the passage of Northern troops through the State. Public opinion is, as yet, too equally divided to permit any open demonstration, and the Mayor and Board of Police are determined on preserving order. The Police force is a well disciplined and efficient one, but has no general authority beyond the Municipal limits.

Col. B. F. HUGER, commandant at the Pikesville Arsenal, near this City, on Monday resigned his commission in the United States service.

The clouds deepen, and all who seriously regard the political atmosphere, are trembling at the impending crash.

CECIL.

THE CITY MILITARY EXCITEMENT.

The Seventh Regiment off for Washington.

The Seventy-first, Twelfth and Sixth Regiments Ordered to Leave To-morrow.

The Metropolis Alive with Military Excitement—The People Bid the Seventh God Speed—The Union and its Flag to be Upheld—The Rhode Island Troops En Route.

Yesterday was a sad, and yet triumphant day for New-York. It was sad that a thousand of our noblest citizens should be so suddenly called away from their homes—perhaps to death—to defend the Constitution and the laws. It was a triumphant vindication of the loyalty of our citizens' thus promptly volunteering to the hardships of a soldier's life. Never before were the people roused to such a pitch of patriotic enthusiasm. There have been gala days, and funeral pageants, and military shows, and complimentary receptions, and triumphal processions that filled the streets with crowds of curious, wondering, sympathetic people, but never has there been developed such a universal, heart-felt, deep-rooted, genuine enthusiasm. The American colors were prominent everywhere—on housetops, on flag-staffs, on horses attached to all kinds of vehicles, on ropes stretched across the streets, on the masts of shipping in the harbor, on breastpins, on the lappets of coats, on the fronts of men's hats—on all sides the glorious old red, white and blue waved in the joyous breeze and dazzled the eye with their bright colors. The awful solemnity of civil war came pressing home to our people who had sons and brothers and fathers just departing, perhaps never to return. The news of the difficulties in Baltimore, the struggle of the troops with the rabble, the reported death of many, the rumors of an attack on the Capital, the tearing up of railroad tracks, and all the attendant horrors of internecine warfare, struck terror into many a stout heart, while the tears of kind-hearted women flowed copiously as a rain-storm. The excitement was heightened to a great degree by the announcement of the fact that the Sixth, Twelfth and Seventy-first Regiments has likewise been ordered to leave for the seat of war this afternoon. Appended are the details of the various movements:

DEPARTURE OF THE SEVENTH REGIMENT.

IMMENSE ENTHUSIASM—EXCITING AND IMPRESSIVE SCENES AND INCIDENTS.

The intelligence that the Seventh Regiment, the "crack" Regiment, the almost adored military body, of this City, would leave for Washington yesterday afternoon, created an excitement scarcely surpassed by anything that has transpired since the first news of the attack on Fort Sumter. Although it was announced that 3 P.M. was the time for the assembling of the regiment at their Armory, over Tompkins Market, Broadway was the scene of gathering for hundreds of people long before noon. The march of the second installment of Massachusetts troops, early in the afternoon, was but an incentive to their patriotism. If they had to wait many hours, as indeed they had, they were prepared to stand on the tip toe of expectation till their favorite Regiment passed, even if nightfall came. The aspect of

Broadway was very gay indeed. Minus the firing of pistols and the explosion of Chinese crackers, it was many Fourth of Julys rolled into one. The Stars and Stripes were everywhere, from the costliest silk, twenty, thirty, forty feet in length, to the homelier bunting, down to the few inches of painted calico that a baby's hand might wave. It would be invidious to say from what buildings the National flag was displayed, because it would be almost impossible to tell from what buildings it did not wave, and never, if flags can be supposed to be animated with any of the feelings of their owners, with a purer devotion to the Union. Evidently, all political partisanship was cast aside. But the gayest, and in this respect, the most remarkable thoroughfare, was Cortlandt-street. Lafayette place, where the Regiment was to form previous to marching, was very attractively dressed—a huge flag being displayed from the Astor Library, among numerous others from private buildings. But Cortlandt-street showed a gathering of flags, a perfect army of them. They were not, in that comparatively brief space from Broadway to the Jersey City Ferry, to be numbered by dozens or by scores, every building seemed like "Captains of Fifties." It was flag, flag, from every window from the first floor to the roof, from every doorway—in short, it was flag, flag,—and of quite large sizes, too, till the wearied eye refused the task of counting them. Such was the display along the route of the "Seventh." Such is and will be the route for all noble troops entering our City from the New-England States. . . .

The excitement in Jersey City, long before they had crossed the ferry, was scarcely less intense, and when they landed there, they found they were by no means in a foreign State. It seemed that all the people of the sister city had turned out. It was a reenaction of what their fellow-townsmen and townswomen had done for them. White handkerchiefs, waved by the ladies' hands, were as numerous as the dog-wood blossoms in Spring, and it was proved that a Jerseyman can raise as hearty a cheer as the best New-Yorker. And so it was till all were fairly disposed of in the cars, and the cars moved off. . . .

One of the members of the Regiment was to have been married on Monday, and the cards of invitation had been issued. But he went yesterday, all the same, to serve his country. The ardent whishes, not only of his friends, but of thousands who never saw his face, will be that he may return at no distant period, unhurt, and with his due share of honor, to fulfill the happy contract. . . .

On the Corn Exchange, as on the Merchants' Exchange, at the Stock Exchange, and in commercial circles generally, the utmost enthusiasm prevailed. As the gallant Seventh Regiment was under marching orders for the National Capital, several young merchants, serving in its rank, bade adieu to their associates at the Corn Exchange. No words of regret were heard, but many an earnest "Good-bye," and "God bless you, my brave fellow." Offers of money to defray expenses were freely made. Assurances to those who were leaving young families behind that these should not be neglected were generously given. The sentiments interchanged were truly inspiring. The Government should be supported, rebellion should be suppressed, the public property defended and the laws enforced. The Corn Exchange is thoroughly satisfied that its representatives—the MALLONS, the HERRICKS, and others—in the ranks of the glorious "Seventh" will do their duty, faithfully and well.

On the railroads between this and Washington, it is intended that the Seventh Regiment shall be preceded by a Pilot Engine, to insure safety. The Engineer Corps have howitzers loaded with grape and canister. Probably the troubles at Baltimore will interfere with the Pilot Engine. . . .

WANTED—A LEADER!

In every great crisis, the human heart demands a leader that incarnates its ideas, its emotions and its aims. Till such a leader appears, everything is disorder, disaster and defeat. The moment he takes the helm, order, promptitude and confidence follow as the necessary result. When we see such results, we know that a hero leads. No such hero at present directs affairs. The experience of our Government for months past has been a series of defeats. It has been one continued retreat. Its path is marked by the wrecks of property destroyed. It has thus far only urged war upon itself. It confidingly enters into compacts with traitors who seek them merely to gain time better to strike a fatal blow. Stung to the quick by the disgraces we have suffered, by the disasters sustained, by the treachery which threatens the annihilation of all order, law, and property, and by the insults heaped upon our National banner, the people have sprung to arms, and demand satisfaction for wounded honor and for violation of laws, which must be vindicated, or we may at once bid farewell to society, to government, and to property, and sink into barbarism.

The spirit evoked within the last fortnight has no parallel since the day of Peter the Hermit. In the last ten days, 100,000 men have sprung to their feet, and, arming and provisioning themselves, are rushing to a contest which can never be quelled till they have triumphed. A holy zeal inspires every loyal heart. To sacrifice comfort, property and life even, is nothing, because if we fail, we must give up these for our children, for humanity, and for ourselves. Where is the leader of this sublime passion? Can the Administration furnish him? We do not question the entire patriotism of every member of it, nor their zeal for the public welfare. The President, in the selection of his Cabinet, very properly regarded the long and efficient services of men in the advocacy of the principles that triumphed in his election. To him the future was seen in the past. But in the few weeks of his official life all past political distinctions have been completely effaced. From a dream of profound peace we awake with our enemy at our throat. Who shall grapple with this foe? Men that can match his activity, quick instincts and physical force. A warrior—not a philosopher; a Cromwell—not a Bacon or a Locke.

Many of the Cabinet, having outlived the hot blood of youth, are vainly attempting to reason with this foe. As well might they oppose a feather to a whirlwind. JEFFERSON DAVIS has surrounded himself with spirits kindred to his own. Think of offering the olive-branch to such men as TOOMBS and WIGFALL. These men are seeking to put a chain about our necks, to secure our humiliation by the destruction of all our national interests, *"Our money, or our life, or both."*

What are we called upon to defend. The welfare of 19,000,000 of freemen, with everything that render life desirable. Were the selection of the Cabinet to be made to-day, would not the past be entirely forgotten in the present? Would not all party ties be completely effaced?

Is not the Cabinet the representative of the past, instead of the present? Is it not exactly in the frame of mind it was in the day of its appointment? From the first its policy has been purely negative, and cooped up in Washington, surrounded on all sides by a hostile population, it still thinks only of self-defense, and yields to the demands of those seeking its destruction in the measured periods of diplomatic intercourse.

Well may the great heart of the North turn away sickened at such a spectacle. Is this a suitable response to the ardor of youth that rushes to the contest regardless of every consequence, and at the risk of severing every tie that can give grace or charm to life? The hope, and the pride, and strength of the country is exposed without plan or forethought for the future, to an able, treacherous and relentless foe. We dread to get the news of the first encounter. We all know how England swayed to and fro under the loss of her best blood in the reckless charge of the light Brigade. How could our more mercurial natures bear up under a similar disaster to the gallant seventh? It is the duty of the members of the Cabinet to look the thing squarely in the face and conscientiously ask themselves this question: "Are we disqualified from age, from inexperience in Executive action, from constitutional timidity, or from inate reluctance to face the horrors of war, to represent this people and country in this hour of travail?" If not, let them earn the gratitude of the people by giving way courteously to the exigencies of the hour, and laying their ambition on the alter of their country. By a timely act of self-sacrifice they may give relief to the anxious heart of this mighty host of earnest, patriotic men who are unselfishly exposing their lives and fortunes without any other object or motive than their country's honor and welfare,—the relief that follows the knowledge that they are directed by bold, strong and competent men, fitted by sterner natures for this revolutionary epoch of their country's history.

Presidential Prerogatives

During the weeks after the fall of Fort Sumter both the Union and the Confederacy prepared for war. Though Lincoln's critics thought he was ineffectual, in fact he moved swiftly to mobilize his country. Because the Congress would not assemble until July, he often had to act on his own, sometimes without clear legal authority. For instance, he directed Gen. Winfield Scott to suspend the privilege of the writ of habeas corpus along the roads used by the military between New York and Washington. This meant that people who attempted to disrupt military convoys could be arrested and imprisoned without charges, and army officers were instructed to ignore all judicial proceedings designed to free them. In May the president made a supplemental call for troops, this time summoning 42,000 volunteers to serve for three years—in contrast to the three months call-up of the militia. Aware that communications between Washington and New York might be disrupted, he authorized payment of $2 million to three prominent New Yorkers to purchase supplies for the army.

When the Congress assembled, in pursuance of his call, on July 4, he submitted a long message, which a clerk read aloud to the legislators. Few paid close attention, and its arguments escaped many of them. Yet the message, which contains some of Lincoln's most eloquent sentences, offered a powerful defense of his policies as president. He intended the message, first, to explain and defend the position he had always held on the illegality of secession. In addition, he offered his only detailed explanation of his actions during the crisis over Fort Sumter, insisting that he acted carefully to avoid hostilities, which the Confederates began without provocation.

Lincoln went on to argue that, because of Southern aggression, he had been obliged to take a number of steps that might not have been strictly legal but were required by necessity. The same necessity, he now urged the Congress, required the raising of an army of at least 400,000 men, at a cost of $400 million.

That recommendation the Congressmen greeted with what newspapers

called "irrepressible applause," and they promptly went beyond the presi-
dent's request to authorize $500 million to field an army of 500,000 men.
—D. H. D.

NATIONAL AFFAIRS.

Special Session of the Thirty Seventh Congress.

Organization of the House of Representatives.

Hon. G.A. Grow Elected Speaker, and Hon. Emerson Etheridge, Clerk.

Message of President Lincoln.

He Recommends an Army of 400,000 Men and the Raising of $400,000,000.

Important Report of the Secretary of the Treasury.

Notice of Important Bills to be Introduced in Congress.

[...]

Special Dispatches from Washington.

WASHINGTON, Friday, July 5.
The President's Message was received and read. It is as follows:

THE MESSAGE.

FELLOW-CITIZENS OF THE SENATE AND HOUSE OF REPRESENTATIVES:
Having been convened on an extraordinary occasion, as authorized by
the Constitution, your attention is not called to any ordinary subject of
legislation. At the beginning of the present Presidential term, four
months ago, the functions of the Federal Government were found to be
generally suspended within the several States of South Carolina, Georgia, Alabama, Mississippi, Louisiana, and Florida, excepting only those
of the Post-office Department. Within these States, all the forts, arsenals,
dock-yards, custom-houses, and the like, including the moveable and
stationary property in and about them, had been seized, and were held in
open hostility to this Government, excepting only Forts Pickens, Baylor

and Jefferson, on and near the Florida coast, and Fort Sumter, in Charleston Harbor, S.C.

The forts thus seized had been put in improved condition, new ones had been built, and armed forces had been organized and were organizing, all avowedly with the same hostile purpose. The forts remaining in the possession of the Federal Government in and near these States were either besieged or menaced by warlike preparations, and especially Fort Sumter was nearly surrounded by well-protected hostile batteries, with guns equal in quality to the best of its own, and outnumbering the latter, as perhaps ten to one—a disproportionate share of the Federal muskets and rifles had somehow found their way into these States, and had been seized to be used against the Government. Accumulations of the public revenue, lying within them, had been seized for the same object—the Navy was scattered in distant seas, leaving but a very small part of it within the immediate reach of the Government.

Officers of the Federal Army had resigned in great numbers, and of those resigning a large proportion had taken up arms against the Government. Simultaneously, and in connection with all this, the purpose to sever the Federal Union was openly avowed. In accordance with this purpose, an ordinance had been adopted in each of these States declaring the States respectively to be separated from the National Union. A formula for instituting a combined Government of those States has been promulgated, and this illegal organization in the character of the "Confederate States," was already invoking recognition, aid and intervention from Foreign Powers.

Finding this condition of things, and believing it to be an imperative duty upon the incoming Executive to prevent, if possible, the consummation of such attempt to destroy the Federal Union, a choice of means to that end became indispensable. This choice was made, and was declared in the Inaugural Address. The policy chosen looked to the exhaustion of all peaceful measures before a resort to any stronger ones. It sought only to hold the public places and property not already wrested from the Government, and to collect the revenue, relying for the rest on time, discussion, and the ballot-box; it promised a continuance of the mails, at Government expense, to the very people who were resisting the Government, and it gave repeated pledges against any disturbances to any of the people or any of their rights, of all that which a President might constitutionally and justifiably do in such a case. Everything was forborne, without which it was believed possible to keep the Government on foot. . . .

It is thus seen that the assault upon and reduction of Fort Sumter was, in no sense, a matter of self-defence on the part of the assailants. They well knew that the garrison in the fort could, by no possibility, commit aggression upon them; they knew—they were expressly notified—that the giving of bread to the few brave and hungry men of the garrison was all which would on that occasion be attempted, unless themselves by resisting so much should provoke more. They knew that this Government desired to keep the garrison in the fort, not to assail them, but merely to maintain visible possession, and thus to preserve the Union from actual and immediate dissolution, trusting, as herein before stated, to time, discussion and the ballot-box for final adjustment, and they assailed and reduced the fort for precisely the reverse object, to drive out the visible authority of the Federal Union and thus force it to immediate dissolution. That this was their object, the Executive well understood; and having said to them in the Inaugural Address "you can have no conflict without being yourselves the aggressors," he took pains, not only to keep this declaration good, but also to keep the case so far from ingenious sophistry, so that the world should not misunderstand it. By the affair at Fort Sumter, with its surrounding circumstances, that point was reached. Then and there, by the assailants of the Government began the conflict of arms, without a gun in sight or in expectancy to return their fire, save only the few in the Fort sent to that harbor years before, for their own protection, and still ready to give that protection in whatever was lawful. In this act, discarding all else, they have forced upon the country the distinct issue—immediate dissolution or blood, and this issue embraces more than the fate of these United States. It presents to the whole family of man the question whether a Constitutional Republic or Democracy, a Government of the people, by the same people, can or cannot maintain its territorial integrity against its own domestic foes. It presents the question whether discontented individuals, too few in numbers to control the Administration according to the organic law in any case, can always upon the pretences made in this case or any other pretences, or arbitrarily without any pretence, break up their Government, and thus practically put an end to free government upon the earth. It forces us to ask "is there in all Republics this inherent and fatal weakness?" Must a Government of necessity be too strong for the liberties of its own people, or too weak to maintain its own existence?

So viewing the issue, no choice was left but to call out the war power of the Government, and so to resist the force employed for its destruction by force for its preservation. The call was made, and the response of the country was most gratifying, surpassing in unanimity and spirit the most sanguine expectations. Yet none of the States, commonly called Slave States, except Delaware, gave a regiment through the regular State organization.

A few regiments have been organized within some others of those States by individual enterprise, and received into the Government service.

Of course the seceded States, so called, and to which Texas had been joined about the time of the inauguration, gave no troops to the cause of the Union. The Border States, so called, were not uniform in their action, some of them being almost for the Union, while others, as in Virginia, North Carolina, Tennessee and Arkansas, the Union sentiment was nearly repressed and silenced. The course taken in Virginia was the most remarkable, perhaps the most important. A Convention, elected by the people of that State, to consider this very question of disrupting the Federal Union, was in session at the Capital of Virginia, when Fort Sumter fell.

To this body the people had chosen a large majority of professed Union men, almost immediately after the fall of Sumter. Many members of that majority went over to the original disunion minority, and, with them, adopted an ordinance for withdrawing the State from the Union. Whether this change was wrought by their great approval of the assault upon Sumter, and their great resentment at the Government's resistance to that assault, is not definitely known.

Although they submitted the ordinance for ratification to a vote of the people, to be taken in a day, then somewhat more than a month distant, the Convention and the Legislature, which was also in session at the same time and place, with leading men of the State, not members of either, immediately commenced acting as if the State was already out of the Union. They pushed military preparations vigorously forward all over the State.

They seized the United States Armory at Harper's Ferry, and the Navy yard at Gosport, near Norfolk. They received, perhaps invited, into their State large bodies of troops, with their warlike appointments, from the so-called seceded States. They formally entered into a treaty of temporary alliance with the so-called Confederate States, and sent members to their Congress at Montgomery, and finally they permitted the insurrectionary Government to be transferred to their capital at Richmond.

The people of Virginia have thus allowed this giant insurrection to make its nest within her borders, and this Government has no choice left but to deal with it where it finds it, and it has the less to regret as the loyal citizens have in due form claimed its protection. These loyal citizens this Government is bound to recognize and protect as being in Virginia. In the Border States, so called, in fact the middle States, there are those who favor a policy which they call armed neutrality. That is, an arming of these States to prevent the Union forces passing one way, or the Disunion the other, over their soil. This would be disunion completed.

Figuratively speaking, it would be the building of an impassable wall along the line of separation, and yet not quite an impassable one, for, under the guise of neutrality, it would tie the hands of the Union-men, and freely pass supplies from among them to the insurrectionists, which it could not do as an open enemy. At a stroke it would take all the trouble off the hands of secession, except only what proceeds from the external blockade.

It would do for the Disunionists that which of all things they most desire—feed them well and give them disunion without a struggle of their own. It recognizes no fidelity to the Constitution, no obligation to maintain the Union; and while very many who have favored it, are doubtless, loyal citizens, it is nevertheless very injurious in effect.

Recurring to the action of the Government, it may be stated that at first a call was made for 75,000 militia, and rapidly following this a proclamation was issued for closing the ports of the insurrectionary districts by proceedings in the nature of blockade. So far all was believed to be strictly legal.

At this point the insurrectionists announced their purpose to enter upon the practice of privateering.

Other calls were made for volunteers to serve three years unless sooner discharged, and also for a large addition to the regular Army and Navy.

These measures, whether strictly legal or not, were ventured upon under what appeared to be a popular demand and a public necessity, trusting then, as now, that Congress would readily ratify them. It is believed that nothing has been done beyond the constitutional competency of Congress.

Soon after the first call for militia it was considered a duty to authorize the commanding General, in proper cases, according to his discretion, to suspend the privilege of the writ of *habeas corpus,* or, in other words, to arrest and detain, without resort to the ordinary processes and forms of law, such individuals as he might deem dangerous to the public safety. This authority has purposely been exercised but very sparingly. Nevertheless the legality and propriety of what has been done under it are questioned, and the attention of the country has been called to the proposition that one who is sworn to take care that the laws be faithfully executed should not himself violate them.

Of course some consideration was given to the question of power and propriety before this matter was acted upon. The whole of the laws which were required to be faithfully executed were being resisted and failing of execution in nearly one-third of the States. Must they be allowed to finally fail of execution, even had it been perfectly clear that by the use of the means necessary to their execution, some single law, made in such extreme tenderness of the citizen's liberty, that practically it relieves more of the guilty than the innocent, should to a very limited extent be violated? To state the question more directly, are all the laws but one to go unexecuted and the Government itself to go to pieces lest that one be violated? Even in such a case, would not the official oath be broken if the Government should be overthrown, when it was believed that disregarding the single law would tend to preserve it? But it was not believed that this question was presented. It was not believed that any law was violated. The provision of the Constitution that the privilege of the writ of *habeas corpus* shall not be suspended unless when in cases of rebellion or invasion the public safety may require it, is equivalent to a provision that such privilege may be suspended when in cases of rebellion or invasion the public safety does require it. It was decided that we have a case of rebellion and that the public safety does require the qualified suspension of the privilege of the writ which was authorized to be made. Now it is insisted that Congress, and not the Executive, is vested with this power.

But the Constitution is silent as to which, or who, is to exercise the power, and as the provision was plainly made for a dangerous emergency, it cannot be believed that the framers of the instrument intended that in every case the danger should run its course until Congress could be called together, the very assembling of which might be prevented, as was intended in this case by the rebellion. No more extended argument is now afforded, as an opinion at some length will probably be presented by the Attorney-General. Whether there shall be any legislation upon the subject; and if so, what, is submitted entirely to the better judgment of Congress. The forbearance of this Government had been so extraordinarily and so long continued, as to lead some foreign nations to shape their action, as if they supposed the early destruction of our National Union was probable.

While this, on discovery, gave the Executive some concern, he is now happy to say that the sovereignty and rights of the United States are now everywhere practically respected by foreign Powers, and a general sympathy with the country is manifested throughout the world. . . .

It is now recommended that you give the legal means for making this contest a short and decisive one; that you place at the control of the Government for the war at least 400,000 men and $400,000.000; that number of men is about one-tenth of those of proper ages within the regions where apparently all are willing to engage, and the sum is less than a twenty-third part of the money value owned by the men who seem ready to devote the whole. A debt of six hundred millions of dollars now is a less sum per head than was the debt of our Revolution when we came out of that struggle, and the money value in the country bears even a greater proportion to what it was then than does the population. Surely each man has as strong a motive now to preserve our liberties as each had then to establish them.

A right result at this time will be worth more to the world than ten times the men and ten times the money. The evidence reaching us from the country leaves no doubt that the material for the work is abundant, and that it needs only the hand of legislation to give it legal sanction, and the hand of the Executive to give it practical shape and efficiency.

One of the greatest perplexities of the Government is to avoid receiving troops faster than it can provide for them; in a word, the people will save their Government, if the Government itself will do its part only indifferently well.

It might seem at first thought to be of little difference whether the present movement at the South be called secession or rebellion. The movers, however, well understand the difference. At the beginning they knew that they could never raise their treason to any respectable magnitude by any name which implies violation of law; they knew their people possessed as much of moral sense, as much of devotion to law and order, and as much pride in its reverence for the history and government of their common country, as any other civilized and patriotic people.

They knew they could make no advancement directly in the teeth of these strong and noble sentiments. Accordingly they commenced by an insidious debauching of the public mind. They invented an ingenious sophism, which, if conceded, was followed by perfectly logical steps through all the incidents of the complete destruction of the Union. The sophism itself is that any State of the Union may, consistently with the nation's Constitution, and therefore lawfully and peacefully, withdraw from the Union, without the consent of the Union, or of any other State.

The little disguise, that the supposed right is to be exercised only for just cause, themselves to be the sole judges of its justice, is too thin to merit any notice. With rebellion thus sugar-coated they have been drugging the public mind of their section for more than thirty years, until at length they have brought many good men to a willingness to take up arms against the Government the day after some assemblage of men have enacted the farcical pretense of taking their State out of the Union, who could have been brought to no such thing the day before.

This sophism derives much, perhaps the whole of its currency, from the assumption that there is some omnipotent and sacred supremacy pertaining to a State, to each State of our Federal Union. Our States have neither more nor less power than that reserved to them in the Union by the Constitution, no one of them ever having been a State out of the Union. The original ones passed into the Union even before they cast off their British colonial dependence, and the new ones came into the Union directly from a condition of dependence, excepting Texas, and even Texas, in its temporary independence, was never designated a State.

The new ones only took the designation of States on coming into the Union, while that name was first adopted for the old ones in and by the Declaration of Independence. Therein the united Colonies were declared to be *free* and *independent* States. But even then the object plainly was not to declare their independence of one another or of the Union, but directly the contrary, as their mutual pledge and their mutual action before, at the time and afterwards, abundantly show.

The express plighting of faith by each and all of the original thirteen States in the articles of Confederation two years later, that the Union shall be perpetual, is most conclusive, having never been States, either in substance or in name, outside of the Union. Whence this magical omnipotence of State rights, asserting a claim of power to lawfully destroy the Union itself? Much is said about the sovereignty of the States, but the word even is not in the National Constitution, nor, as is believed, in any of the State Constitutions.

What is a sovereignty, in the political sense of the term? Would it be far wrong to define it a political community without a political superior? Tested by this, no one of our States, except Texas, was a sovereignty, and even Texas gave up the character on coming into the Union, by which act she acknowledged the Constitution of the United States, and the laws and treaties of the United States made in pursuance thereof. The States have their *status* in the Union, and they have no other legal *status*. If they break from this, they can only do so against law and by revolution.

The Union, and not themselves separately, procured their independence and their liberty. By conquest or purchase the Union gave each of them whatever of independence and liberty it has. The Union is older than any of the States, and, in fact it created them as States. Originally some dependent colonies made the Union, and in turn the Union threw off their old dependence for them, and made them States, such as they are. Not one of them ever had a State Constitution independent of the Union.

Of course it is not forgotten that all the new States formed their Constitutions before they entered the Union, nevertheless dependent upon and preparatory to coming into the Union. Unquestionably, the States have the power and rights reserved to them in and by the national Constitution, but among these surely are not included all conceivable powers, however mischievous or destructive, but, at most, such only as were known in the world at one time as governmental powers, and certainly a power to destroy the Government itself, had never been known as a governmental, as a mere administrative power. This relative matter of National power and State rights as a principle, is no other than the principle of generality and locality. Whatever concerns the whole should be confined to the General Government, while whatever concerns only the State should be left exclusively to the State. This is all there is of original principle about it. Whether the National Constitution in defining boundaries between the two has applied the principle with exact accuracy is not to be questioned. We are all bound by that defining, without question. What is now combated is the position that Secession is consistent with the Constitution, is lawful and peaceful.

It is not contended that there is any express law for it, and nothing should ever be implied as law which leads to unjust or absurd consequences. The nation purchased with money the countries out of which several of these States were formed. Is it just that they shall go off without leave and without refunding? The nation paid very large sums, in the aggregate, I believe, nearly a hundred millions, to relieve Florida of the aboriginal tribes. Is it just that she shall now be off without consent, or without any return? The nation is now in debt for money applied to the benefit of these so-called Seceding States in common with the rest.

Is it just either that creditors shall go unpaid, or the remaining States pay the whole? A part of the present National Debt was contracted to pay the old debts of Texas.

Is it just, that she shall leave and pay no part of this herself? Again, if one State may secede, so may another; and when all shall have seceded none is left to pay the debts. Is this quite just to creditors? Did we notify them of this sage view of ours when we borrowed their money? If we now recognize this doctrine by allowing the seceders to go in peace, it is difficult to see what we can do if others choose to go, or to extort terms upon which they will promise to remain. The Seceders insist that our Constitution admits of secession.

They have assumed to make a National Constitution of their own, in which, of necessity, they have either discarded or retained the right of secession, as they insist it exists in ours.

If they have discarded it, they thereby admit that on principle it ought not to exist in ours; if they have retained it, by their own construction of ours, that [*sic*; should be "they"—eds.] show that to be consistent they must secede from one another whenever they shall find it the easiest way of settling their debts, or effecting any other selfish or unjust object. The principle itself is one of disintegration, and upon which no Government can possibly endure.

If all the States save one should assert the power to drive that one out of the Union, it is presumed the whole class of seceder politicians would at once deny the power, and denounce the act as the greatest outrage upon State rights. But suppose that precisely the same act, instead of being called driving the one out, should be called the seceding of the others from that one, it would be exactly what the seceders claim to do, unless, indeed, they make the point that the one, because it is a minority, may rightfully do what the others, because they are a majority, may not rightfully do. These politicians are subtle and profound in the rights of minorities. They are not partial to that power which made the Constitution, and speaks from the preamble, calling itself, "We, the people."

It may well be questioned whether there is to-day a majority of the legally qualified voters of any State—except, perhaps, South Carolina—in favor of disunion. There is much reason to believe that the Union men are the majority in many, if not in every other one of the co-called seceded States. The contrary has not been demonstrated in any one of them.

It is ventured to affirm this even of Virginia and Tennessee, for the result of an election held in military camps, where the bayonets are all on one side of the question voted upon, can scarcely be considered as demonstrating popular sentiment. At such an election, all that large class who are at once for the Union, and against coercion, would be coerced to vote against the Union.

It may be affirmed without extravagance, that the free institutions we enjoy have developed the powers and improved the condition of our whole people beyond any example in the world. Of this we now have a striking and impressive illustration. So large an army as the Government has now on foot was never before known, without a soldier in it but who has taken his place there of his own free choice. . . .

Our adversaries have adopted some declaration of independence, in which, unlike the good, old one penned by JEFFERSON, they omit the words, "all men are created equal." Why? They have adopted a temporary Constitution in the preamble of which, unlike our good old one signed by WASHINGTON, they omit, "We, the people," and substitute "we, the Deputies of the sovereign and independent States."

Why? why this deliberate pressing out of view the rights of men and the authority of the people? This is essentially a people's contest. On the side of the Union, it is a struggle for maintaining in the world that form and substance of government whose leading object is to elevate the condition of men; to lift artificial weights from all shoulders; to clear the paths of laudable pursuit for all; to afford all an unfettered start and a fair chance in the race of life, yielding to partial and temporary departures from necessity.

This is the leading object of the Government for whose existence we contend. I am most happy to believe that the plain people understand and appreciate this. It is worthy of note that while in this, the Government's hour of trial, large numbers of those in the Army and Navy who have been favored with the offices, have resigned, and proved false to the hand which pampered them, not one common soldier or common sailor is known to have deserted his flag. Great honor is due to those officers who remained true despite the example of their treacherous associates, but the greatest honor and the most important fact of all, is the unanimous firmness of the common soldiers and common sailors. To the last man, so far as known, they have successfully resisted the traitorous efforts of those whose commands but an hour *before,* they obeyed as absolute law.

This is the patriotic instinct of plain people. They understand without an argument that the destroying of the Government, which was made by WASHINGTON, means no good to them. Our popular Government has often been called an experiment. Two points in it our people have settled: the successful establishing and the successful administering of it. One still remains—its successful maintenance against a formidable internal attempt to overthrow it.

It is now for them to demonstrate to the world that those who can fairly carry an election can also suppress a rebellion; that ballots are the rightful and peaceful successor of bullets, and that when ballots have fairly and constitutionally decided, there can be no successful appeal back to bullets; that there can be no successful appeal except to ballots themselves. At succeeding elections such will be a great lesson of peace, teaching men that what they cannot take by an election neither can they take it by a war; teaching all the folly of being the beginners of a war.

Lest there be some uneasiness in the minds of candid men as to what is to be the course of the Government towards the Southern States, after the rebellion shall have been suppressed, the Executive deems it proper to say it will be his purpose then as ever, to be guided by the Constitution and the laws, and that he probably will have no different understanding of the powers and duties of the Federal Government, relatively to the rights of the States and the people under the Constitution than that expressed in the Inaugural Address.

He desires to preserve the Government, that it may be administered for all as it was administered by the men who made it. Loyal citizens everywhere have the right to claim this of their Government, and the Government has no right to withhold or neglect it. It is not perceived that in giving it there is any coercion, any conquest, or any subjugation in any just sense of these terms.

The Constitution provided, and all the States have accepted the provision, "That the United States shall guarantee to every State in this Union a republican form of government," but if a State may lawfully go out of the Union, having done so, it may also discard the republican form of government; so that to prevent its going out is an indispensable means to the end of maintaining the guarantee mentioned, and when an end is lawful and obligatory, the indispensable means to it are also lawful and obligatory.

It was with the deepest regret that the Executive found the duty of employing the war power in defense of the Government. Forced upon him, he could but perform this duty or surrender the existence of the Government. No compromise, by public servants, could, in this case, be a cure; no: that compromises are not often proper, but that no popular Government can long survive a marked precedent that those who carry an election can only save the Government from immediate destruction by giving up the main point upon which the people gave the election. The people themselves, and not their servants, can safely reverse their own deliberate decisions.

As a private citizen, the Executive could not have consented that these institutions shall perish, much less would he, in betrayal of so vast and so sacred a trust as these free people had confided to him. He felt that he had no moral right to shrink nor even to count the chances of his own life in what might follow.

In full view of his great responsibility, he has so far done what he has deemed his duty. You will now, according to your own judgment, perform yours. He sincerely hopes that your views and your actions may so accord with his, as to assure all faithful citizens who have been disturbed in their rights, of a certain and speedy restoration to them, under the Constitution and the laws, and having thus chosen our cause without guile and with pure purpose, let us renew our trust in God and go forward without fear and with manly hearts.

ABRAHAM LINCOLN.

JULY 4, 1861.

First Income Tax

After readily authorizing President Lincoln's request for appropriations to carry on the war, the Congress faced the harder task of determining where the money should come from. Before 1861 the federal government had been financed almost entirely by revenue from customs duties and by the sales of public lands. Both these sources dried up with the outbreak of war. No excise taxes had been levied for more than a generation, and there was no internal revenue service.

In the search for new sources of funds, the legislators received little guidance from the president. Concentrating on the military effort, Lincoln gave almost total control of economic planning to his Secretary of the

Treasury, Salmon P. Chase. When Chase came to him with drafts of pro-posed financial legislation, the president approved, saying: "You under-stand these things. I do not." After the Secretary and Republican leaders in Congress agreed on legislation he gave it his hearty support.

The first financial legislation of Lincoln's administration was the com-plicated act passed on August 5, 1861. In addition to raising tariff rates, the Congress imposed a "direct tax" allocating to each state a quota based on population, not wealth. This was the only form of taxation believed to be authorized under the Constitution. Since it obviously favored the rich states at the expense of the poor, a counterweight was introduced in the form of an income tax, which was initially 3 percent of incomes in excess of eight hundred dollars a year. Lincoln approved this measure, even though many of his advisers doubted its constitutionality. The income tax was abandoned in 1872, and later the Supreme Court declared this form of taxation unconstitutional. Not until the ratification of the 16th Amend-ment in 1913 was Congress authorized to impose income taxes.

The income tax and the tariff together brought in only modest sums, and even after Congress enacted a sweeping internal revenue act in 1862, revenue from all taxes combined did not pay for the cost of the war. So the Secretary of the Treasury had to resort to borrowing heavily and, begin-ning in 1862, to the issuance of paper money ("greenbacks") to meet the needs of the army.

—D. H. D.

THE NEW TARIFF—THE DIRECT TAX—THE INCOME TAX—VIRTUAL REPEAL OF SUB-TREASURY LAW.

The first of August, 1861, will be a memorable day in the fiscal history of the United States. It records the passage through both Houses of Congress, within a few hours, of four measures of fundamental importance, each of them well entitled to the most careful and deliberate examination. Such is the hot-haste under which they have been passed through Congress, and so imperfect the telegraphic communications, that it is next to impossible to state their provisions with any reasonable approach to accuracy. We learn enough, however, to know that each of them is of vital concern to the coun-try. It has not been thought necessary to afford our moneyed classes, or property-holders, or the public Press of this City, any opportunity whatever of examining any of these measures before their passage. And even now it is difficult to ascertain precisely the contents of the laws actually passed. From the best lights we can obtain, we suppose the general results to be as follows:

The Secretary of the Treasury at the opening of Congress informed them that the public service would require $320,000,000 in addition to existing appropriations;—that of this sum $240,000,000 should be raised on loan, and $80,000,000 by increased customs or by taxation. He stated as a fundamental necessity for sustaining the public credit that a sufficient portion of this $80,000,000 should be pledged to the payment of the interest and gradual redemption of the principal of the public debt, including the proposed loans of $240,000,000. Members of Congress responded at once, in very patriotic speeches, to this call of the Secretary, announcing in swelling phrase, that not only two hundred and forty millions, but four hundred or even five hundred millions should be raised if necessary. Loan bills were accordingly pushed through both Houses, providing for two hundred and fifty millions to be borrowed, one hundred millions at twenty years, another hundred at three years, and the remaining fifty millions on Treasury notes.

The House of Representatives, sustaining the conservative policy of the Secretary, and anxious to secure the highest market price for these large amounts of stock, introduced a specific clause into the proposed loan law by which they pledged certain revenues to the payment of the debt. The Senate, for reasons which we will not now discuss, struck out the clause, so that the bill was passed without it, and on discovering this important omission, very earnest appeals were made to Congress by experienced bankers and others in this City, to restore the clause if possible; and it was proposed to do so, by inserting it in a supplemental bill, which had become necessary to modify certain provisions of the law. The two Houses having disagreed on certain provisions of this supplemental bill, it was left to a Committee of Conference. Mr. STEVENS, from that Committee, yesterday reported to the House, in answer to Mr. F. A. CONKLING, of this City, who had advocated the pledge of revenues, as recommended by Secretary CHASE, "that the Senate *would not consent to that,* and that, rather than lose the bill, the Committee of Conference had agreed to abandon that clause."

His report was then adopted by the House, and the bill was passed without the pledge, by 83 to 34. The character of the loan, as standing on the naked, unsupported credit of the Government, and any consequent depreciation in market price, whatever it may be, is, therefore, wholly due to the Senate.

At this stage of the matter it was, that a fundamental change was made, without beat or drum or notice to the country, by which the Sub-Treasury policy, established with so much care by Mr. VAN BUREN, and sustained by all his successors, was virtually thrown to the winds. This skillful *coup d'état,* totally revolutionizing the long-settled policy of the country, was effected by simply providing:

"That the proceeds of the loan," (being this mere trifle of two hundred and fifty millions of dollars,) "instead of being immediately paid into the Treasury in gold and silver, as now required, the money derived from the loan may remain in *solvent Banks* until it shall be drawn out in pursuance of law."

It is just possible that these avails may be drawn from these solvent Banks *in* gold and silver, but we will hazard the conjecture that the Banks will prefer to pay them in their own notes, and that the greater part of the immense disbursements of the Government will not be paid in gold and silver at all. The Secretary will, doubtless, exert his best powers to select only solvent Banks to discharge this immense office of safely keeping these enormous amounts. If the Banks selected should chance to be very numerous or widely scattered, or if any considerable number of them should find it inconvenient to pay over these avails in gold and silver, we shall not be greatly surprised if some of the States in which they are situated should permit them to suspend a duty so difficult of performance.

We will only add, that if the war is to be carried on with paper money not redeemable in gold and silver, it will certainly cost vastly more than if paid in coin. Whether the Government itself, in such a state of things, will deem it necessary to pay its own obligations in gold and silver, the future will disclose. We only say, that this fundamental change in the public depository will be regarded as a feature of some importance, especially if the stock is to be offered in any large masses in foreign countries.

And next, as to the revenues themselves, with which the interest is to be paid.

The House at first proposed a Direct Tax of thirty millions, but in view of its operating unequally on the interior States, in its necessary distribution under the Constitution by population only, the amount was reduced to twenty millions, and an income tax was laid on the proceeds of all kinds of property, professions, trades or occupations, exceeding $600 yearly. The House also made some increase on the existing Tariff—and had taxed tea, coffee, and sugar.

The Senate, before receiving this bill, had discussed a measure of their own, mainly advocated by Mr. SIMMONS, of Rhode Island, and had come to the conclusion to add *ten per cent.* (with some unimportant exceptions) to the present Morrill Tariff—with a provision that except on certain articles no impost should exceed *fifty per cent. ad valorem.*

Mr. SUMNER, as Chairman of the Committee on Foreign Relations, deemed it his duty to expostulate against this addition to the Morrill tariff, as being already so objectionable to England and France; for which suggestion he was stoutly rebuked in debate by Mr. FESSENDEN, and the tariff portion of the bill thus increased accordingly passed the Senate. They also adopted 5 per cent. as the rate to be levied on all incomes above $1,000, excepting income derived from the public debt, which was fixed at 2½ per cent. The measure thus strangely compounded of the original

Senate bill and of amendments to the House bill, was sent yesterday to the House. A Committee of Conference was immediately raised, and resulted in the compromise stated more particularly in our telegraphic report, so that the final result now seems to be a bill embracing the new Tariff—the Direct Tax and the Income Tax—in which the Tariff stands increased as above stated. The Direct Tax is fixed at twenty millions, and the Income Tax at *three* per cent. on the excess of all incomes over $800, but raising it to *five* per cent. on incomes received from property held in this country by citizens of the United States residing abroad.

Mr. WICKLIFFE, of Kentucky, asked for a single day's delay, to enable the bill to be printed and more carefully examined by the members, but Mr. STEVENS could not agree to the delay, and the bill was accordingly passed yesterday, by 89 to 39.

It will not be surprising if the bill, at some future time, should require some amendment. It has, however, but few details, as the whole power of regulating all the details of the collection of the Income Tax is committed by the law to the Secretary of the Treasury. It could hardly be left to better hands.

We complete this historical statement of these measures, which we believe to be accurate in the main, by adding that the large amount thus extracted from incomes permitted a reduction on coffee from five to *four* cents a pound, and on sugar from two-and-a half to *two* cents,—a modification which will doubtless be acceptable to many of our countrymen, and particularly to consumers in the Western States.

Lincoln Curbs Frémont

In late August 1861, Gen. John C. Frémont, who commanded the Union forces in Missouri, faced a Confederate invasion from the southwest and widespread guerrilla warfare elsewhere in the state. Convinced that he had to take drastic action, Frémont, without consulting his superiors in Washington, issued a proclamation freeing the slaves of all Confederate sympathizers.

Lincoln considered Frémont's proclamation an act of insubordination. He intended to keep control of all actions relating to slavery and emancipation in his own hands. He realized that the proclamation gave a heavy blow to Unionist sentiment, especially in the border states. Gen. Robert Anderson, the hero of the Fort Sumter fight who was now in command of the Department of Kentucky, wrote that if he did not immediately repudiate Frémont's action "Kentucky will be lost to the Union."

But the president also knew that Frémont, who had been the first presidential candidate of the Republican Party in 1856, had a large following among abolitionists and had to be handled with care. Sorely beset, he wrote the general, "in a spirit of caution and not of censure," requesting him to modify his proclamation, because it would "alarm our Southern friends, and turn them against us—perhaps even ruin our rather fair prospects for Kentucky." When Frémont proved unwilling to modify his proclamation without a direct order, the president "very cheerfully" gave that command.

Lincoln's action saved Kentucky and the other border states for the Union, but it aroused intense hostility in parts of the North. Senator Benjamin F. Wade of Ohio sneered at Lincoln's pusillanimous course and said that it was all that could be expected "of one, born of poor white trash and educated in a slave State."

—D. H. D.

THE GREAT REBELLION.

Movements of the Rebel Forces Near Washington.

Reconnoissances in Force.

Wholesale Destruction of the Property of Union Men.

Important Letter from the President to Gen. Fremont.

[...]

Letter from the President to Gen. Fremont.

WASHINGTON, Saturday, Sept. 14.

The following letter, from President LINCOLN to Major-Gen. FREMONT, was transmitted to the latter the 12th inst.:

WASHINGTON, D.C., Sept. 11, 1861,

Major-Gen. John C. Fremont:

SIR: Yours of the 8th, in answer to mine of 2d inst., was just received. Assuming that you upon the ground could better judge of the necessities of your position, than I could at this distance, on seeing your proclamation of Aug. 30, I perceived no general objection to it; the particular objectionable clause, however, in relation to the confiscation of property, and the liberation of slaves, appeared to me to be objectionable in its nonconformity to the act of Congress, passed the 6th of last August upon the same subjects, and hence I wrote you expressing my wish that that clause should be modified accordingly. Your answer just received, expresses the preference on your part that I should make an open order for the modification, which I very cheerfully do. It is therefore ordered that the said clause of said proclamation be so modified, held and construed as to conform with and not to transcend the provisions on the same subject contained in the act of Congress, entitled "An act to confiscate property used for insurrectionary purposes, approved Aug. 6, 1861," and that said act be published at length with this order. Your obedient servant,

(Signed)

A. LINCOLN. . . .

Cabinet Shakeup

Lincoln never wanted to appoint Simon Cameron to his cabinet in the first place, but the wily Pennsylvanian claimed that a post was promised him in return for his support of Lincoln at the Chicago nominating convention. Reluctantly naming Cameron Secretary of War, Lincoln was hardly surprised that he ran his department so inefficiently. The Joint Congressional Committee on the Conduct of War, which probed into war contracts, exposed countless scandals and waste. Thousands of pistols were sold to the government at $25 each, when the fair price on a proper competitive basis would not have exceeded $14.50, horses that could have been bought for $60 or less were sold to the War Department for $117, and so on and so on. Lobbying agents received huge commissions on all these deals.

Nobody charged that Cameron was personally corrupt, but he was responsible for his department and its contracts. Lincoln's mail bag was full of complaints against the secretary, filled with injunctions that he must go.

In December, when the president, as was customary, asked the heads of departments to prepare accounts of their activities, to be blended into his annual message to Congress, Cameron gratuitously included in his report an announcement that "clearly a right of the Government to arm slaves" and "employ them in the service against the rebels." Then he published his report, without informing the president.

Lincoln was furious. He did not fire Cameron outright, because the Pennsylvanian still had considerable political support and the president remembered how abolitionists had rallied around General Frémont when he made a similar proclamation. So quietly he arranged for the resignation of Cassius M. Clay, the United States minister to Russia, and named Cameron to take Clay's place. According to Democratic newspapers, the president was sending Cameron to Siberia.

As his replacement Lincoln selected Edwin M. Stanton, who was prickly and independent but also incorruptible. Stanton served as Secretary of War for the rest of the struggle.

—D. H. D.

IMPORTANT FROM WASHINGTON.

Resignation of Secretary Cameron.

Nomination of Edwin P. Stanton, of Pennsylvania, as his Successor.

Mr. Cameron to be Minister to Russia.

Information Concerning Our Consular System.

An Interesting Communication to Congress from Secretary Seward.

Operations of the Blockading Fleet

Recent Important Captures on the South Carolina Coast.

An Exposition of Frauds in the House

Our Special Washington Dispatches

WASHINGTON, Monday, Jan. 13.

THE RETIREMENT OF SECRETARY CAMERON FROM THE WAR DEPARTMENT.

Washington was never more astounded than it was to-day, by the announcement that Secretary CAMERON had retired from the war Department. The thing was wholly unexpected, and no man was more surprised than Mr. CAMERON himself. It seems that the change made is wholly the work of the President. The first agitation of the subject in the President's mind occurred last Thursday. Yesterday he had formed his conclusion, and addressed a note to Mr. CAMERON informing him of it. This note was received by Mr. CAMERON last night, and was the first intimation he had that a change in the Cabinet was determined on. It is needless to deny that the War

Minister was surprised and agitated, but the President assured him of his personal good-will by the tender of the very honorable position of Minister to Russia, in place of Mr. CLAY, who has desired to be recalled.

We are not allowed to know the reasons of the President for this change, but we can safely venture the opinion that it results from his conviction that the country desires, and has long desired, a change. It would be useless to deny, also, that the President and his friends felt that Mr. CAMERON has not been recently sympathizing with the Administration, but, on the contrary, has been in active sympathy with politicians in Washington who are zealously and bitterly opposing the President and his measures.

It is not known whether Col. SCOTT, Assistant Secretary of War, will retire with his chief. The Assistant Secretary is an appointment of the President's who holds him in high esteem, and he can retain him; but of course he will not, nor would Col. SCOTT remain, unless on the invitation of Mr. STANTON.

There is much doubt expressed to-night whether Mr. CAMERON will be confirmed by the Senate as Minister to Russia, but he will be, I think, without doubt.

BEN. Wade was the chief competitor urged upon the President as Secretary of War, in place of CAMERON. . . .

Death of Willie

The Lincolns were fond and indulgent parents, especially toward their younger sons. Willie was only ten when they came to Washington, and Thomas (always called Tad) was eight. Ignorant of the dangers of war, the boys found the White House a wonderful place to play, and they enjoyed firing at invisible Confederates with make-believe guns from the roof of the White House and drilling the other neighborhood children.

Willie was especially precocious. When Col. Edward D. Baker, an old friend of the family, was killed at Balls' Bluff, Willie was moved to write a poem, which was published in the Washington National Republican. *Both parents doted on him, and Mary Lincoln often said that he "would be the hope and stay of her old age."*

But in February 1862, the boys fell ill, with what was called "bilious fever" (probably typhoid). Despite devoted care from both parents, Willie died on February 20. His parents were devastated with grief. When Lincoln looked at his dead boy's face he could only say brokenly, "He was too good for this earth . . . but then we loved him so." Mary Lincoln never recovered from their loss.

—D. H. D.

NEWS FROM WASHINGTON.

Sympathy of Congress for the President and his Family.

Agreement Between the Railroad Men and the Government.

Our Special Washington Dispatches.

WASHINGTON, Friday, Feb. 21.

THE FUNERAL OF THE PRESIDENT'S SON.

The funeral of the President's son will take place next Monday.

NO ILLUMINATION.

The following was addressed to the Senate and House of Representatives, but Congress adjourned before it was transmitted to them:

The President of the United States was last evening plunged into affliction by the death of a beloved child. The Heads of Departments, in consideration of this distressing event, have thought it would be agreeable to Congress, and to the American people, that the official and private buildings occupied by them, should not be illuminated in the evening of the 22d inst.   (Signed)

WM. H. SEWARD,	S. P. CHASE,
E. M. STANTON,	GIDEON WELLES,
EDWARD BATES,	M. BLAIR. . . .

Gradual Emancipation

Lincoln's policy for the liberation of the slaves grew by stages. At the outbreak of the war he kept reminding himself that his presidential oath forbade him to indulge his "abstract judgment on the moral question of slavery." In his inaugural address he disclaimed any intent to overthrow the "established institutions"—meaning slavery—of the Southern states. But that pledge did not prevent him from devoting a great deal of his time and thought to plans for a conservative, voluntary, gradual emancipation.

Part of his plan was to encourage the slaveholding border states still in the Union—Delaware, Maryland, Kentucky, and Tennessee—to provide for the gradual emancipation of their slaves, with compensation provided by the federal government. His message of March 6, 1862, urged the Congress to adopt a resolution supporting this plan. This was the first time an American president had ever proposed any form of emancipation of the slaves. Lincoln cherished this plan. No fewer than three times during this spring he met with congressmen from the border states, earnestly entreating them to accept his plan, but in the end none of them agreed.

In Lincoln's mind a corollary to emancipation was the colonization of freed blacks outside of the United States. For years he had supported the work of the American Colonization Society, which by transporting freedmen to Africa, would simultaneously free "our land from the dangerous presence of slavery" and restore "a captive people to their long-lost father-land." He did not favor the forcible deportation of blacks, but, doubting that the two races could ever live together on terms of equality, he urged African-American leaders to form colonies of their people, whether in Central America or in the Caribbean.

In time Lincoln came to see the futility of both colonization and gradual emancipation and he came slowly to realize that the only solution was the abolition of slavery.

—D. H. D

THE PRESIDENT ON EMANCIPATION.

If proof were wanting of the patriotic ardor of the President for the peace and well-being of the country, it would be found abundantly in the message sent yesterday to Congress. Mr. LINCOLN appreciates the infinite difficulty of the Slavery question. He evidently despairs of prostrating the institution by force of the war-power; he looks to its existence in full vigor, throughout the Gulf States at least, when the war shall have ended. The utmost reach of his practical dealing with the subject is to strip it of political influence in National affairs. To effect this capital object, there is certainly no way so sure as to destroy the identity of interest between Border Slave States and those at the southward; and this object the President's suggestion proposes to attain. It takes the form of a joint resolution submitted to the consideration of Congress. The possibility of one or more States discovering the impolicy of retaining slave-labor is assumed. To such the joint resolution offers pecuniary aid in the task of emancipation, by engaging to pay a sum prefixed for each enslaved negro set at liberty. This bounty the President evidently believes will turn the scale in favor of freedom. Satisfied of the good faith of the National Government in its professions of non-intervention in the legislation of the States, the States will be ready to look favorably upon a plan which, while it makes the merit of the act of emancipation their own, throws the cost elsewhere. And as the plan is adopted, one after another of the northerly Slave States will array themselves on the side of the free communities of the North.

In considering the Presidential project, a number of difficulties will no doubt suggest themselves to Congress. Any State disposed to part with its negroes will naturally offer them in the best market. The extreme South, in the supposition raised by Mr. LINCOLN that Slavery will there retain all its vitality, will compete with the North in the purchase of the discarded labor; and must of necessity offer prices which the North will be unable to pay. When peace shall be restored—always assuming the President to be right in regard to Slavery in the Gulf States—Kentucky will be able to get $130,000,000 for her negroes at the South, while the North, presupposing the round price of $200—the highest rate heretofore named, and considered practicable—would be able to offer only one-third of that amount. If by an act of gradual emancipation Kentucky is thus able at any moment to get the larger sum for her slaves, what temptation to the passage of such an act will be the offer of the smaller? Congress will also have to weigh well that incessantly recurring question, what shall be done with the negroes when freed? Their freedom in any border State will no doubt be followed by their expulsion. Even from Illinois, Mr. LINCOLN's immediate State, the blacks are about to be expelled. Will it not be necessary for the National Government to provide also for their removal from the country, and their colonization and christianization in a new and distant home? And will not this cost, added to the other, constitute a total from which the country, already startled at the coming terror of war-taxation, will draw back appalled?

We fear that the Presidential plan will not achieve the good for which it is so patriotically designed. It will not induce any Slave State to discard Slavery; it will not, therefore, weaken any of the ties between the collective Slave States. It will offer no sufficient reason for departing, even in appearance, from the doctrine that, with Slavery in the States, the National Government has no concern whatever. It will be attended with an expense too overwhelming to be regarded favorably by a people who have already upon their shoulders the burden present and prospective of a debt several thousands of millions—a burden placed there by Slavery. But let the plan have full discussion; let it also have full credit, as evidence that the Government contemplates no forcible interference with the institutions of any State, rebellious or loyal, and desirable good may grow out of it.

Lincoln vs. McClellan

After the Union defeat at the first battle of Bull Run (July 21, 1861), Lincoln brought in Gen. George Brinton McClellan, who had achieved minor victories in western Virginia, to command the forces around Washington. McClellan's brilliance in reorganizing the troops led the president to entrust to him command of all the forces in the Federal armies. When Lincoln warned that the new responsibilities would require vast labor, McClellan responded: "I can do it all."

But during the winter Lincoln began to have increasing doubts. Coordinating military operations in Virginia, in the Ohio Valley and in Missouri was an enormous task, especially when McClellan needed to devote most of his attention to the Army of the Potomac in preparation for an advance into Virginia. Then McClellan fell ill with typhoid fever and, always secretive, he had entrusted his plans to no one—not even the president. Frustrated by McClellan's inaction, Lincoln on January 27, 1862, issued his remarkable General War Order No. 1, commanding all the Union armies to make a simultaneous advance on February 22, Washington's birthday.

He probably did not intend his order to be obeyed literally; it was designed to stir McClellan into action. The general resented Lincoln's "interference," referring to the president in his private letters as "the original gorilla," but he finally produced a plan for an advance, one that Lincoln basically disapproved. McClellan wanted to take the Army of the Potomac down the Potomac to attack Richmond from the east. Eventually the president agreed, but before allowing McClellan to begin, he relieved him from his position as general in chief, so that he could devote himself solely to the Army of the Potomac. McClellan grudgingly acquiesced and began the disastrous Peninsula Campaign.

—D. H. D.

IMPORTANT FROM WASHINGTON.

War Bulletin Issued by the President.

The Order for a Forward Movement.

Gen. McClellan Relieved of the Command-in-Chief.

He Takes the Field at the Head of the Army of the Potomac.

A New Division of Departments.

Gen. Fremont Assigned to a Command in Western Virginia and Eastern Tennessee.

Gen. Halleck in Command of the Department of the Mississippi.

Enthusiastic Reception of Gen. McClellan by the Army.

Important Proceedings of Congress.

[OFFICIAL]
War Bulletins.

EXECUTIVE MANSION,
WASHINGTON, Jan. 27, 1862.

THE PRESIDENT'S GENERAL WAR ORDER, NO. 1.

Ordered, That the 22d day of February, 1862, be the day for a general movement of the land and naval forces of the United States against the insurgent forces.

That especially,

The army at and about Fortress Monroe,

The army of the Potomac,

The army of Western Virginia,

The army near Munfordsville, Ky.,

The army and flotilla at Cairo,

And a naval force in the Gulf of Mexico,

be ready for a movement on that day.

That all other forces, of both land and naval, with their respective commanders, obey existing orders for the time, and be ready to obey additional orders when duly given.

That the Heads of Departments, and especially the Secretaries of War and of the Navy, with all their subordinates, and the General-in-Chief, with all other commanders and subordinates of the land and naval forces, will severally be held to their strict and full responsibilities for the prompt execution of this order.

ABRAHAM LINCOLN.

THE PRESIDENT'S GENERAL WAR ORDER, NO. 2.

Ordered, First, that the Major-General commanding the army of the Potomac proceed forthwith to organize that part of said army destined to enter upon active operations, including the reserve, but excluding the troops to be left in the fortification about Washington, into four army corps, to be commanded according to seniority of rank, as follows:

First corps to consist of four divisions, and to be commanded by Maj.-Gen. I. McDowell.

Second corps to consist of three divisions, and to be commanded by Brig.-Gen. E.V. Sumner.

Third corps to consist of three divisions, and to be commanded by Brig.-Gen. S.P. Heintzelman.

Fourth corps to consist of three divisions, and to be commanded by Brig.-Gen. E.L. Ketes.

2. That the divisions now commanded by the officers above assigned to the commands of corps shall be embraced in, and form part of their respective corps.

3. The forces left for the defence of Washington will be placed in command of Brig.-Gen. James Wadsworth, who shall also be military Governor of the District of Columbia.

4. That this order be executed with such promptness and dispatch as not to delay the commencement of the operations, already directed to be undertaken by the army of the Potomac.

5. A fifth army corps to be commanded by Maj.-Gen. N. P. Banks, will be formed from his own and Gen. Shields' (late Gen. Lander's) Division.

ABRAHAM LINCOLN.

THE PRESIDENT'S GENERAL WAR ORDER, NO. 3.

Major-Gen. McCLELLAN having personally taken the field at the head of the army of the Potomac, until otherwise ordered, he is relieved from the command of the other Military Departments, he retaining command of the Department of the Potomac.

Ordered, further, That the two Departments now under the respective commands of Generals HALLECK and HUNTER, together with so much of that under Gen. BUELL as lies west of a north and south line, indefinitely drawn through Knoxville, Tenn., be consolidated and designated the Department of the Mississippi, and that until otherwise ordered Maj.-Gen. HALLECK have command of said Department.

Ordered, also, That the country west of the Department of the Potomac and east of the Department of the Mississippi be a Military Department, to be called the Mountain Department, and that the same be commanded by Major-General FREMONT; that all the Commanders of Departments, after the receipt of this order by them respectively, report severally and directly to the Secretary of War, and that prompt, full and frequent reports will be expected of all and each of them.

ABRAHAM LINCOLN.

Our Special Washington Dispatches.

WASHINGTON, Wednesday, March 12.

GEN. M'CLELLAN AND THE ARMY OF THE POTOMAC.

The Department having formally announced that Gen. McClellan has taken the field in person, it is not improper to say that he left Washington last Monday, and is leading his great Potomac army upon the flying rebels of Virginia. His reception among the troops, as he passed to their head, was one of the grandest ever witnessed in the country. The largest body of men ever put in motion at once since the battle of Solferino moved from the banks of the Potomac on that day. For many miles, on divers roads, the embattled ranks pressed forward, and the cheers that hailed the General at one point of the lines was taken up by regiment after regiment, and division after division, until the whole vast army rent the heavens with shouts of welcome.

Gen. McClellan rode through the ranks in motion his cap ever in his hand, returning the salutes of the enthusiastic soldiers. It is only hoped by his friends that the country will patiently give him half the time that was accorded to the Western General who pursued his foe from Lexington, Missouri, to Arkansas.

GEN. M'CLELLAN'S POSITION.

The relief of Gen. McClellan from the command of the Western Department, is only just to him. It would be wrong to keep him responsible for campaigns which, while he is in the field, he cannot personally supervise. While his enemies see in this change his humiliation, his friends see his justification and safety.

Planning the Proclamation

On September 4, Robert E. Lee's Army of Northern Virginia, flush with a series of victories over Union forces, began its invasion of Maryland, intent on carrying the war to the North. In a hasty reshuffling of commanders, President Lincoln again put General McClellan in command of the Army of the Potomac. For the next two weeks Union forces trailed the Confederates until the two armies met head-on at Antietam (or Sharpsburg) in Maryland on September 17.

Five days later, on September 22, Lincoln issued his Preliminary Proclamation of Emancipation. He arrived at his decision after months of painful deliberation. He was, and always had been, antislavery, but he did not believe that the Constitution gave him, as president, the power to abolish slavery. Moreover, he realized that many, perhaps most, Northerners who were willing to fight a war to preserve the union were unwilling to fight to free the slaves.

This was emphatically true of the majority in the border states of Maryland, Kentucky and Missouri. On the other hand, sentiment for emancipation was growing in the North and religious denominations barraged the president with demands that he strike down the evil institution. Still he hesitated, telling one group of petitioners that he feared an emancipation proclamation would be as ineffective as the pope's bull against the comet.

By early summer of 1862 Lincoln felt that the time had come to act, and carefully, without consulting anyone, he began drafting his proclamation. In July he read it to the cabinet. The members approved, but Secretary Seward urged him not to issue it in the wake of the recent series of Federal defeats, lest it sound like "our last shriek, on the retreat," but to wait for a Union victory. McClellan's success at Antietam gave him the opportunity he had longed for.

145

Just one month before announcing the historic Emancipation Proclamation, Abraham Lincoln dropped a strong hint that he would do nothing of the kind.

Under pressure for months from abolitionists and so-called Radicals within his own Republican Party, Lincoln found himself, on August 19, the victim of a harsh attack by antislavery editor Horace Greeley, who called the president's reluctance to "confiscate" human property held by Rebels "strangely and disastrously remiss." Three days later, Lincoln replied with a famous letter reiterating: "My paramount object in this struggle is to save the Union, and is not either to save or destroy slavery. If I could save the Union without freeing any slave I would do it. . . ."

What Greeley and other critics did not know is that Lincoln had already drafted a proclamation of emancipation, had read it to his cabinet, and was waiting only for a Union battlefield victory to add teeth to a formal announcement. Lincoln's maneuvering was intended to assure the public that preservation of the Union, not freedom for blacks, remained the chief goal of his administration. Lincoln hoped to put the lid on the inevitable anger from border slave states still loyal to the Union. Just months from mid-term Congressional elections, Lincoln also hoped to prevent a Republican debacle at the hands of angry, pro-slavery Northern voters.

In the end, Lincoln's tactically cautious remarks on the eve of his epochal announcement served principally to arm future generations of historians who questioned his sincerity as an emancipator. In that sense Lincoln's plan may be said to have backfired. But when, three days after the Union victory at the Battle of Antietam, Lincoln stunned the nation with his announcement, The Times *promptly declared it "the great event of the day." The paper reprinted the entire proclamation, highlighting in italics its momentous promise that 100 days hence all slaves held in rebellious states "shall be then, thenceforward, and forever free." The death of the national sin of slavery seemed finally in sight when Ralph Waldo Emerson concluded of Lincoln: "He has been permitted to do more for America than any other American man."*

—H. H.

HIGHLY IMPORTANT.

A Proclamation by the President of the United States.

The War Still to be Prosecuted for the Restoration of the Union.

A Decree of Emancipation.

All Slaves in States in Rebellion on the First of January Next to be Free.

The Gradual Abolition and Colonization Schemes Adhered to.

Loyal Citizens to be Remunerated for Losses' Including Slaves.

WASHINGTON, Monday, Sept. 22.

By the President of the United States of America:

A PROCLAMATION.

I, ABRAHAM LINCOLN, President of the United States of America, and Commander-in-Chief of the Army and Navy thereof, do hereby proclaim and declare, that hereafter, as heretofore, the war will be prosecuted for the object of practically restoring the constitutional relation between the United States and the people thereof in which States that relation is, or may be suspended or disturbed; that it is my purpose, upon the next meeting of Congress, to again recommend the adoption of a practical measure tendering pecuniary aid to the free acceptance or rejection of all the Slave States so called, the people whereof may not then be in rebellion against the United States, and which States may then have voluntarily adopted, or thereafter may voluntarily adopt, the immediate or gradual abolishment of Slavery within their respective limits; and that the efforts to colonize persons of African descent with their consent, upon the Continent or elsewhere, with the previously obtained consent of the governments existing there, will be continued.

That on the first day of January, in the year of our Lord one thousand eight hundred and sixty-three, all persons held as slaves within any State, or any designated part of a State, the people whereof shall then be in rebellion against the United States shall be then, thenceforward, and forever, free; and the Executive Government of the United States, including the military and naval authority thereof, will recognize and maintain the freedom of such persons, and will do no act or acts to repress such persons, or any of them, in any efforts they may make for their actual freedom.

That the Executive will, on the first day of January aforesaid, by proclamation, designate the States and parts of States, if any, in which the people thereof, respectively, shall then be in rebellion against the United States;

and the fact that any State, or the people thereof, shall on that day be in good faith represented in the Congress of the United States by members chosen thereto at elections wherein a majority of the qualified voters of such State shall have participated, shall, in the absence of a strong countervailing testimony, be deemed conclusive evidence that such State and the people thereof have not been in rebellion against the United States.

That attention is hereby called to an act of Congress entitled "An act to make an additional article of war," approved March 13, 1862, and which act is in the words and figure following:

"Be it enacted by the Senate and House of Representatives of the United States of America in Congress assembled, That hereafter the following shall be promulgated as an additional article of war for the government of the army of the United States, and shall be obeyed and observed as such.

ARTICLE—All officers or persons in the military or naval service of the United States are prohibited from employing any of the forces under their respective commands for the purpose of returning fugitives from service or labor who may have escaped from any person to whom such service or labor is claimed to be due, and any officer who shall be found guilty by a Court-martial of violating this article shall be dismissed from the service.

SECTION 2. And be it further enacted, that this act shall take effect from and after its passage."

Also the ninth and tenth sections of an act entitled "An act to suppress insurrection, to punish treason and rebellion, to seize and confiscate property of rebels, and for other purposes," approved July 17, 1862, and which sections are in the words and figures following:

SEC. 9. And be it further enacted, that all slaves of persons who shall hereafter be engaged in rebellion against the Government of the United States, or who shall, in any way give aid or comfort thereto, escaping from such [text illegible] and taking refuge within the lines of the army; and all slaves captured from such persons or [text illegible] them and coming under the control of the government of the United States, and all slaves [text illegible].

Sec. 10. [text illegible] slave escaping into any State, Territory or the District of Columbia, from any of the States, shall be delivered up, or in any way impeded or hindered of his liberty, except for crime or some offence against the laws, unless the person claiming said fugitive shall first make oath that the person to whom the labor or service of such fugitive is alleged to be due, is his lawful owner, and has not been in arms against the United States in the present rebellion, nor in any way given aid and comfort thereto, and no person engaged in the military or naval service of the United States shall, under any pretence whatever, assume to decide on the validity of the claim of any person to the service or labor of any other person, or surrender up any such person to the claimant, on pain of being dismissed from the service.

And I do hereby enjoin upon and order all persons engaged in the military and naval service of the United States, to observe, obey and enforce, within their respective spheres of service, the act and sections above recited.

And the Executive will in due time recommend that all citizens of the United States who shall have remained loyal thereto throughout the rebellion, shall (upon the restoration of the constitutional relation between the United States and their respective States and people, if the relation shall have been suspended or disturbed,) be compensated for all losses by acts of the United States, *including the loss of slaves.*

In witness whereof, I have hereunto set my hand, and caused the seal of the United States to be affixed.

Done at the City of Washington, this Twenty-second day of September, in the year of our Lord one thousand eight hundred and sixty-two, and of the Independence of the United States the eighty-seventh.

ABRAHAM LINCOLN.

By the President.

WILLIAM H. SEWARD, Secretary of State.

GENERAL NEWS FROM WASHINGTON.

Our Special Washington Dispatches.

WASHINGTON, Monday, Sept. 22.

THE PRESIDENT'S PROCLAMATION.

The great event of the day here is the proclamation of the President ordering the execution of the war measures of the last Congress, and promising freedom to the slaves in all States that persist in the rebellion against the Government. This act, so long expected, so long delayed, bids fair to simplify at once the issues of the war, and immediately to array against each other the unconditionally loyal and the rebellious of all shades and grades. If the cause of the Union and free institutions is strongest, this test will show it, and the only question of its triumph will then be the power in the Government to execute its policy with courage and vigor. . . .

PART THREE

COMMANDER-IN-CHIEF
1862–1864

Lincoln at the Front

*N*ortherners praised the quasi victory that Gen. George B. McClellan won over the invading Confederate army at Antietam, Maryland, as a triumph. McClellan himself was exultant, writing his wife: "I fought the battle splendidly . . . it was a masterpiece of art." Others were not so sure. September 17, 1862, was the bloodiest day of the war, when 12,410 Union soldiers were killed or wounded. Afterward Lee's army was allowed to retreat, without harassment, back across the Potomac River.

Desiring to see for himself the condition of the army after the great battle, Lincoln, with almost no notice, slipped out of the capital on October 1 to visit the troops and to talk with their general. Contrary to this report in The Times, the soldiers received him with little enthusiasm, and McClellan seemed more interested in preening himself on his recent success than in planning a new advance.

Lincoln went ahead with the grand review of the troops that McClellan had hastily arranged, but his heart was not in it. As one officer reported, Lincoln offered the soldiers "not a word of approval nor even a smile of approbation." To an Illinois friend who accompanied him the president confided that the vast Army at the Potomac was not a fighting force but only "General McClellan's bodyguard."

—*D. H. D.*

FROM SHARPSBURGH.

The Visit of the President.

Correspondence of the New-York Times.

SHARPSBURGH, Md., Friday, OCT. 8, 1862.
The prevailing monotony of the camp was agreeably relieved to-day by the presence upon the ground of President LINCOLN, accompanied by Gen. McCLELLAN, Gen. MARCY, Col. SWEITZER, Col. SACKETT, Col. HUNT, J. J. C. KENNEDY, Chief Censor, Marshal W. B. LAWSON and others, followed by a cavalcade.

Gen. McCLELLAN entertained the President at his headquarters last night. This morning the party started out for the purpose of reviewing the troops in the vicinity of Sharpsburgh and Williamsport, the portion of the army at Harper's Ferry having been visited by the President yesterday. The party entered the village of Sharpsburgh at 11½ A.M., to the great delight of the citizens, many of whom had never before seen either the President or Gen. McCLELLAN. The population of the place is not large, but what few inhabitants it contains did their utmost, by cheering, waving flags and handkerchiefs, to express their unbound gratification at being honored by such distinguished visitors. Numerous vehicles, containing citizens from adjoining towns, were drawn up on the sides of the roads, thereby affording the occupants a fine opportunity for observing the President as he passed. They mingled their expressions of delight with those of the residents, and we have reason to suppose that the President was favorably impressed both with their candor and loyalty.

The party moved slowly through the village and proceeded to Gen. FITZ-JOHN PORTER's headquarters, where they remained half an hour, in the meantime receiving the lavish hospitality of a gentleman and soldier. The officers on Gen. PORTER's Staff successfully united their efforts in attentions to the President. The troops first reviewed were Gen. SYKES Division, of PORTER's Corps, among whom were conspicuous the red uniforms of the gallant Fifth New York Regiment. It is needless to add that all the troops reviewed presented a fine and imposing appearance. The lines were well formed and admirably preserved throughout the entire ceremony. An objection may be urged in keeping the troops exposed to a hot sun for two hours awaiting the arrival of the President. Some delay is usually experienced on such occasions, but it seems as though two hours was too much an allowance of time. The President approached SYKES' Division, supported on his right by Gen. McCLELLAN and on his left by Gen. PORTER.

The customary salute of twenty-one guns was fired from the artillery attached to the division. The President then advanced and trotted his horse leisurely before the different regiments and batteries, amid the hearty cheers of the troops, the music of bands and the beating of drums. In passing a color it was gracefully dipped, which compliment was acknowledged by the President with uncovered head. In a similar manner all the regiments in the corps were reviewed, after which the party again repaired to Gen. PORTER's headquarters. While there, the President, surrounded by officers of note, including Gen. McCLELLAN, Gen. MARCY and others who accompanied him from Washington, also Gens. PORTER and MORRELL, with the senior officers of their staffs, were taken in photograph by an artist connected with the establishment of BRADY.

The President next proceeded to review Gen. REYNOLDS', formerly HOOKER's corps, when he again met with a most welcome reception. Having reviewed that corps, he passed on to Gen. FRANKLIN's, encamped near Williamsport, being received all along the route with repeated cheers. Toward dark the President and his escort returned to Gen. McCLELLAN's headquarters.

The review consumed nearly six hours' time. The President expressed himself eminently satisfied with the discipline and appearance of the troops, and is, doubtless, convinced of their bravery and patriotism.

The familiar face of Gen. McCLELLAN was not unrecognized as he passed along the ranks, and more than one acclamation was intended for his special benefit. The President will probably leave for Washington to-morrow.

To-day, while passing over a field on the right of the main road, just above Sharpsburgh, an officer espied what he first considered to be an unexploded shell, but upon further examination it proved to be a 12-pounder field-piece buried in the earth. The piece was probably dismounted during the battle of Antietam, and the rebels not having the means to transport it across the river at the time of their hasty retreat, conceived the idea of giving it an underground berth. One of the trunions, however, appeared above the surface sufficiently far to lead to the discovery of the gun. It was not spiked, and was apparently in good order.

WHIT.

General Walks the Plank

No Union commander of the Civil War ever promised so much, and delivered so little, as McClellan. Popular with his men, whom he ably transformed from a ragtag collection of regiments into a polished, well-drilled army, *"Little Mac"* often tested Lincoln's patience with his chronic reluctance to take the army on the offensive against the rebels.

Moreover, McClellan was a Democrat who did little to disguise his antipathy for Lincoln's policy on emancipation. Had he been more aggressive on the field, the general's politics might have been overlooked. But McClellan botched the great invasion of the Virginia Peninsula earlier in 1862, and missed several chances to turn the near-draw at Antietam into a decisive victory.

Worried, Lincoln set off in October to visit McClellan's Maryland headquarters and prod him into action. There, The Times *reported,* the president was cheered warmly when reviewing the troops. The mood changed when the two men met alone. The president lectured the general harshly about his "over-cautiousness," while McClellan, as usual, complained that his men and horses were too exhausted to fight. The two did pose for the first photograph ever taken of a commander-in-chief on a battlefield. But the stately pictures barely disguised their true feelings. McClellan, for example, had complained bitterly to his wife about critics who were "greatly my inferiors socially, intellectually & morally." About Lincoln in particular he wrote: "There never was a truer epithet applied to a certain individual than that of the 'Gorilla.' "

Less than a month later, Lincoln stunned the nation by relieving McClellan as commander of the Army of the Potomac—"entirely unexpected to all," reported The Times. *"I said I would remove him if he let Lee's army get away from him,"* Lincoln told a supporter, *"and I must do so. He has got 'the slows.' "*

—*H. H.*

HIGHLY IMPORTANT.

Gen. McClellan Relieved of His Command.

Gen. Burnside in Command of the Army of the Potomac.

Probable Escape of Main Rebel Army.

Longstreet's Corps Recently at Culpepper Court-House.

The Forces Under Hill and Stuart the Rebel Rear Guard.

The Army Headquarters at Salem.

Jackson only Ten Miles Off with Seventy Thousand Men.

Bragg Said to be at Gordonsville with a Heavy Force.

A Battle Expected at Waterloo.

HEADQUARTERS OF THE ARMY OF THE POTOMAC,
SALEM, Va., Saturday, Nov. 8 — 12 o'clock, noon.

The order relieving Major-Gen. MCCLELLAN from the command of the army of the Potomac was received at headquarters at 11 o'clock last night. It was entirely unexpected to all, and therefore every one was taken by surprise.

On its receipt, the command was immediately turned over to Gen. BURNSIDE.

Gen. MCCLELLAN and his Staff will leave to-morrow for Trenton, where he is ordered to report.

The order was delivered to him by Gen. BUCKINGHAM, in person.

His last official act was the issuing of an address to his soldiers, informing them in a few words that the command had devolved on Gen. BURNSIDE, and taking an affectionate leave of them.

There is no other news worthy of mention, excepting that the army is on motion.

Gen. McClellan At Warrenton.

WASHINGTON, Saturday, Nov. 8 — 10:40 P.M.

Dispatches received here to-day from the Army of the Potomac show Gen. MCCLELLAN's headquarters to be at Warrenton, and that he is following the rebels south, their force being on the west side of the Blue Ridge, while his is on the east. It is admitted by his friends that the enemy is beyond his reach till it suits them to turn and make a stand.

Signing the Proclamation

Abraham Lincoln began his 1863 New Year's Day by presiding over a White House reception, patiently shaking hundreds of hands before retreating to his office at noon for the quiet ceremony that would change America forever.

No one had thought to summon a photographer, an artist, or even a reporter to record the scene. Lincoln simply sat down at his cabinet table, the document spread out before him, and picked up a pen to affix the presidential signature. Then, to the surprise of the handful of eyewitnesses, he set the pen down—and began massaging one massive hand with the other.

"I have been shaking hands since nine o'clock this morning," he explained, "and my right arm is almost paralyzed. If my name ever goes into history it will be for this act, and my whole soul is in it. If my hand trembles when I sign the proclamation, all who examine the document hereafter will say, 'He hesitated.'" Then, pausing only until circulation returned to his hand, he took the pen and firmly wrote "Abraham Lincoln" on the final Emancipation Proclamation.

"The South had fair warning, that if they did not return to their duty, I should strike at this pillar of their strength," he said to Indiana Congressman Schuyler Colfax that evening. "The promise must now be kept, and I shall never recall one word."

Technically, the proclamation freed only those slaves in areas over which the federal government had no control. Like the Declaration of Independence, to which it was immediately compared, Lincoln's edict required the force of arms to turn its promise into reality. But for the first time it called for black recruits to fight for their freedom in Union ranks. "We shout for joy," wrote Frederick Douglass, "that we live to record this righteous decree."

—H. H.

EMANCIPATION.

President Lincoln's Proclamation.

The Slaves in Arkansas, Texas, Mississippi, Alabama, Florida, Georgia, South Carolina and North Carolina Declared to be Free.

Parts of Louisiana and Virginia Excepted.

The Negroes to be Received into the Armed Service of the United States.

WASHINGTON, Thursday, Jan. 1, 1863.

By the President of the United States of America—a Proclamation:

Whereas, on the twenty-second day of September, in the year of our Lord one thousand eight hundred and sixty-two, a Proclamation was issued by the President of the United States containing among other things the following, to wit:

That on the first day of January, in the year of our Lord one thousand eight hundred and sixty-three, all persons held as slaves within any State or designated part of a State, the people whereof shall there be in rebellion against the United States, shall be then, thenceforth, and *forever free;* and the Executive Government of the United States, including the Military and Naval authority thereof will recognize and maintain the freedom of such persons, and will do no act or acts to repress such persons or any of them in any effort they may make for their actual freedom. That the Executive will, on the first day of January aforesaid, by Proclamation, designate the States and parts of States, if any, in which the people therein, respectively, shall then be in rebellion against the United States, and the fact that any State or the people thereof, shall on that day be in good faith represented in the Congress of the United States by Members chosen thereto at elections wherein a majority of the qualified voters of such States shall have participated, shall in the absence of strong countervailing testimony, be deemed conclusive evidence that such State and the people thereof, are not then in rebellion against the United States."

Now, therefore, I, ABRAHAM LINCOLN, President of the United States, by virtue of the power in me vested, as Commander-in-Chief of the Army and Navy of the United States, in time of actual armed rebellion against the authority and Government of the United States, and as a fit and necessary war measure for suppressing said rebellion, do, on this first day of January, in the year of our Lord one thousand eight hundred sixty-three, and in accordance with my purpose so to do, publicly proclaimed for the full period of one hundred days from the day of the first above-mentioned order, and designate as the States and parts of the States wherein the people thereof respectively are this day in rebellion against the United States, the following, to wit:

ARKANSAS, TEXAS, LOUISIANA—except the parishes of St. Bernard, Plequemines, Jefferson, St. John, St. Charles, St. James, Ascension Assumption, Terre Bonne, Lafourche, St. Mary, St. Martin, and Orleans, including the City of New-Orleans—MISSISSIPPI, ALABAMA, FLORIDA, GEORGIA, SOUTH CAROLINA, NORTH CAROLINA and VIRGINIA—except the forty-eight counties designated as West Virginia, and also the counties of Berkley, Accomac, Northampton, Elizabeth City, York, Princess Ann and Norfolk, including the cities of Norfolk and Portsmouth, and which excepted parts, are for the present, left precisely as if this proclamation were not issued.

And, by the virtue of the power, and for the purpose aforesaid, I do aver and declare that all persons held as slaves within said designated States and parts of States are, and henceforward, shall be FREE, and that the Executive Government of the United States, including the military and naval authorities thereof, will recognize and maintain the freedom of said persons.

And I hereby enjoin upon the people so declared to be free, to abstain from all violence unless in necessary self-defence, and I recommend to them that in all cases, when allowed, they labor faithfully for reasonable wages.

And I further declare and make known that such persons of suitable condition, will be received into the armed service of the United States, to garrison forts, positions, stations, and other places, and to man vessels of all sorts in said service.

And, upon this—sincerely believed to be an act of justice, warranted by the Constitution—upon military necessity—I invoke the considerate judgment of mankind and the gracious favor of Almighty God.

In witness whereof I have hereunto set my hand and caused the seal of the United States to be affixed.

Done at the City of Washington, this first
[SEAL.]   day of January, in the year of Our Lord
one thousand eight hundred and sixty-three,
and of the Independence of the United States
of America the eighty-seven,
(Signed)   ABRAHAM LINCOLN.
By the President, WM. H. SEWARD, Secretary of State.

Revolutionizing Banking

Early in his political career, Lincoln had been a strong supporter of a national banking system. The once-hot issue cooled with the demise of his original political party, the Whigs, and the bloody struggle over slavery. But the Civil War drained national resources so quickly that the need for major reform became obvious to ensure the government's solvency and finance the war; and to fund a postwar era that might require millions more to compensate loyal slave-owners for their freed chattel.

"In view of the actual financial embarrassments of the government, and of the greater embarrassments sure to come," the president asked his Secretary of the Treasury, Salmon P. Chase, to devise a plan for "a uniform currency, in which taxes, subscriptions to loans and all other ordinary public dues" would be paid. In a detailed news article that assumed the tone of an editorial, The Times *argued strongly for the new policy:*

"No State or private securities, of any kind . . . can be so secure, in the end, as those of the Nation," the paper wrote.

The following year, Lincoln could convincingly call the new national banking system "acceptable" to both "capitalists and the people." The new system, he accurately predicted, "will create a reliable and permanent influence in support of the national credit, and protect the people against losses in the use of paper money."

Day-to-day management of the war left Lincoln little time to direct national economic policy. Relying almost entirely on Secretary Chase, a political irritant but a brilliant administrator, Lincoln's administration all but revolutionized America's tax, banking, and currency policy.

—H. H.

THE NATIONAL BANKING PROJECT.

The Certainty With Which it Will Give us a Sound National Currency.

Necessity For a Sound National Currency.

WASHINGTON, D.C., Thursday, Jan. 29, 1863.

It is the undoubted duty of Congress to see to it that the country has a sound national currency. Such a currency, based on national law, either of gold or silver, or in some other form, is indispensable to national prosperity. Gold and silver, for the purposes of a circulating medium, have entirely disappeared, and, in the language of President MADISON, in 1815, until the precious metals shall again become available for all the uses of currency, "it devolves on the wisdom of Congress to provide a substitute which shall equally engage the confidence and accommodate the wants of the citizens throughout the Union." War has again brought upon us the financial condition, under pressure of which, Mr. MADISON wrote,—and that has become an imminent necessity which he laid down as a solemn duty. In fulfilling this duty at the present crisis, we are compelled to resort to paper representatives of value, and the question is simply between a purely national currency, a currency issued by State Corporations, or a mixture of both. In other words, Congress has to determine whether the National currency shall take the field exclusively, or whether it will subject the country to the manifold evils growing out of competition between the latter and local currency, about the constitutionality or legality of which there is a decided and radical difference of opinion. It may be maintained, with great confidence, that the two classes of circulation are incompatible, and that the system of local bank paper, while suffered to exist, destroys all hope of a National paper currency, and thus defeats a plain provision of the Constitution. In ordinary times, when the currency was gold and silver, and all the operations of the Government were carried on in these mediums, the banks were, in effect, mere agencies of the people to carry on private transactions. Then it might have been unwise to interfere with local bank circulations. Then Congress could afford to forego, for the time, resort to the power conferred upon it; but in the existing condition of affairs, it has no right to neglect a single resource, and especially one in use of which it only discharged a hitherto suspended obligation.

MR. CHASE'S FREE BANKING SYSTEM.

The well-guarded Free Banking system proposed by Mr. CHASE, commends itself in that it promises the needed currency. The central idea of that measure is the establishment of one sound, uniform circulation, of equal value throughout the country, upon the foundation of National credit, combined with private capital. The proposed circulating notes will bear a common impression, be authenticated by a common authority, be redeemable by the private associations issuing them, and secured by the pledge of United States stocks. Receivable everywhere for public dues, except customs, they will have an equal value in every part of the Union. They are effectively guarded against depreciation— at least more effectually than any local paper currency. If notes, based entirely upon United States bonds are not safe, what others can be? We cannot now have private circulating notes based on specie; and as the *power* of the Government (for its preservation and maintenance) over the resources of the whole country is superior to any other, so its pecuniary responsibility is greater. If the Government falls, all *values* are destroyed. While the Government stands its resources of taxation are equal to every emergency, illimitable and unquestionable. No State or private securities, of any kind, therefore, can be so secure, in the end, as those of the Nation.

The proposed free banking system then, will give us a needed national currency, unequaled to-day in the elements of convenience and security. Its circulating notes, too, will save the loss by broken bank bills, computed at present to be equal to about five per cent. of the entire issue. They will save also the losses now sustained on local currency in the way of exchange, amounting to from one-eighth of one to one and a quarter per cent. on every transaction—equal probably to an average of one per cent. on the entire circulation, which is extracted from the people for the sole benefit of the bankers. Add to these considerations the fact that the demand for United States Bonds as a basis for banking business under the proposed bill, will create a steady market for them, and enable the Government to negotiate loans at favorable terms, and we see that the burdens of war have in a measure been alleviated through a diminution of the rates of interest, or a participation in the profits of circulation, without the least risk of a great money monopoly. The system provides a National Bank, in effect, whose management is directly in the hands of the people themselves.

THE GOVERNMENT AND THE PEOPLE CONSOLIDATED.

In addition to all these public advantages thus set forth, is another of no light import—the interest of labor and capital of the banks, and the Government, and the people, as so forcibly stated by Hon. R. J. WALKER, would for the first time become inseparably united and consolidated. The people would have acquired a new and direct interest in the support of the Government, because their currency would depend for safety on the maintenance of that Government. Each bank would become a powerful auxiliary for the overthrow of rebellion, and would feel constrained to lend its every exertion to that end. Then, just as the banks are strengthened and their capital and profits are increased, would be funded more and more Treasury notes, and the country would be saved from a redundant and depreciated currency. While Congress abdicates its authority to regulate the currency, leaving to the States the power to provide the circulating medium, it places in the hands of the latter the sinews of war, and clothes them with a power to overthrow the Government. If there were no other reason, this of itself should be ample argument for the prompt substitution of some *National* currency in place of that driven out of circulation by the war.

S.

————

The Draft and the Dodgers

Jefferson Davis signed a Confederate conscription act on April 16, 1862. But when Abraham Lincoln signed the national conscription act about a year later he broke new ground for the federal government. It was another huge jolt for a society already roiled by civil war and emancipation.

Under the new draft law, all able-bodied male citizens, along with immigrants who intended to become citizens, between the ages of twenty and *forty-five, became eligible for conscription for up to three years' military service. A draftee could provide a substitute, or pay $300 to secure an exemption.*

Not surprisingly, the new policy proved wildly unpopular. Critics, together with fearful men of draft age, argued that the exemption and substitution clauses unfairly favored the wealthy. Within months, the draft fueled vocal resistance and violent civic unrest in a number of Northern cities. Frustrated, Lincoln railed: "Are we degenerate? Has the manhood of our race run out?"

Recognizing the draft legislation's one glaring flaw, Lincoln eventually urged Congress to rescind the $300 exemption clause and signed the revised law. Substitutions, long traditional in the American military, remained permissible.

The nation's first draft had the unexpected effect of stimulating volunteers to re-enlist. All told, the draft lasted for two years, but fewer than 47,000 draftees ever entered the service; around 118,000 substitutes were ushered into the military. Together, these inductees accounted for only 6 percent of the total men in arms. Although he was well past conscription age himself, Abraham Lincoln paid for a substitute of his own; one John S. Staples, a Pennsylvanian.

—H. H.

THE CONSCRIPTION BILL.

The New Bill for Raising Armies—What It is, and What It Promises.

Correspondence of the New-York Times.

WASHINGTON, Sunday, March 1, 1863.

The Senate, last night, after a protracted debate, concurred in the amendments made by the House to the bill to organize the militia of the United States. . . . It goes now to the President, and will, doubtless, become a law before the final adjournment.

There is an undreamed of power in this bill—undreamed of less than a year ago. It is not to the numbers that it adds to the available forces of the Government. It is not in the extraordinary powers which it confers. It is not in its comprehensive details, nor in all these combined that will be found the great good which will come of the most gigantic innovation upon established usage that has ever been recorded. The life-spring principle of the bill is in its very title—in the declaration by which the distinctions of imaginary lines are swept away, and the repudiation of a *heresy* which bred the necessity for such a law. Fighting against rebellion, which is sought to be justified by the declaration of State Rights, and organizing, equipping, governing its armies upon a principle which was nothing but a recognition of the doctrine which gave birth to its armed assailants. This is what the Administration has been doing from the beginning. Bending to *State* demands—standing motionless on the air-drawn borders of small and great States, and begging of the Executives of a few arbitrary divisions of territory the privilege of drawing upon the resources of the country for the support of the parent that raised them. The friends of the Republic will have cause for exceeding great joy that at last this fatal barrier has been broken, and the fact proclaimed that the country is a nation—divided into sections only for the convenience of local interests, and always with the understanding that these divisions are to melt away whenever rebellion or invasion shall render it essential for the common good that such boundaries be forgotten. This is the fundamental, underlying principle of the bill for the enrollment of the militia of the United States. It is, I confess, a startling reversal of the almost settled theories of the country—but if it kills, it kills only that upon the heretofore barren soil, where dwarfed shrubs of decentralization struggled for existence, there may grow up a giant nation, vigorous to repel and mighty to protect.

The details of the bill, though so greatly overshadowed by the principle it initiates, are, however, equal to the necessities of the hour. Its provisions are broad and comprehensive, and, if rightly administered, it will do away with all necessity for the interposition of any others than those charged with the prosecution of war.

It is not new organizations, new regiments and new officers that are wanted. The evil of fresh regiments with inexperienced officers, has well nigh been the destruction of the army. It has cost millions of dollars, thousand of lives, months of fatal delays and the loss of fruitful opportunities. Here again, came over the army and the nation, the blast of that upas tree—State authority. To the estimated necessities of localities, to the ambition of men, and all the littleness of partisanship—to the making of all things political, from the Supervisor of a town up to the return of a Senator of the United States—for the benefit of all the intermediate legislators, judges, representatives in Congress, mayors of cities and governors of States—to the packing of Conventions and to the greasing of the machinery of party organizations—to all these, as well as to the pecuniary profit of an almost endless number of go-betweens, has the Army of the Nation been made subordinate. Commissions, from Colonels down, have been held up to the purchase of those who could best pay, either in money or in kind. "Give me something for this," has been the culture cry, and those who could give have bought. Look down the registers of the men who command, and trace, as you can easily do, the price so many have paid. It may not be palpable figures, but, nevertheless, the figures are there. Said a Governor of a State, early last Fall, to a man who had served, faithfully and well, up from the ranks to the Captaincy of a Company almost decimated in the field, "Come to me, and you shall have the command of one of the new cavalry regiments I am to organize." After waiting a reasonable time, and hearing nothing more, the Captain went home to his State, to see the Governor. The Governor was, to say the least, frank. "Oh," said he, "I cannot possibly fulfill my promise. The fact is, I was run so hard last Fall that I had to promise all the positions I had to gentlemen of influence." This is one of a thousand cases that I could recite—but even one is one too many. I could name you instances where boys of nineteen have been sent with field commissions to regiments whose officers had been killed on the desperate fields of Fair Oaks and Antietam. Governors in executive chambers make such selections, but Generals and Colonels, lighted by the blaze of the enemy's cannon, will find different material out of which to make their subordinate officers. That Governors, who know nothing of the merits of aspirants, have been set aside, and men whose interests make them careful, have been substituted, as the appointing power, though it may lessen the Executive stature, will give strength and vigor alike to the soldier and the commander.

A kindred evil is also squelched by that provision of the bill which prevents the army from being at times an aggregation of town meetings. "Election of officers." Do you know what a curse that has been? To be sure, it has been practically ignored at all times, when it has suited the convenience of Governors to be oblivious of that right which is nominally given to the enlisted men. But, nevertheless, the principle has remained, and in many instances has been practiced. Electioneering at home is bad enough—pot-house politicians in pot-houses are pitiable sights. I need not ask you a second time to say "yes" to those two propositions. But electioneering at home is commendable compared with electioneering in camp. A pot-house is a paradise, and pot-house politicians are lords of the manor, compared with a tent for the arena and soldiers for the canvassers. Discipline! You may as well talk to the northeast wind as to talk discipline to men whose votes are to be sought by the disciplinarian, whose commission may depend upon the "sweet voices" of those to be restrained. Under the old order of things—it was human nature that it should be so— he who favored most was most favored. Under the new order of things, those who enforce obedience will be best rewarded, and the men will be relieved from the excitement, the bickering, the demoralization of camp canvassing. And for that reason they will be better led, better cared for, better organized and more efficient. While a few bad selections will be made by the Generals, the many will be of best. You may say that it is hard to so decide against the right of the men to select—against the right of Governors to appoint. But readers, soldiers and Governors must recollect that the right to choose is the normal right of peace—a right that, like a thousand other rights, is engulphed by the relentless wages of war. Somebody has truly said, that "war is a terrible necessity." He might have added, "a necessity that knows no law." The voices of the governed are lost in the roar of the cannon—let them be silent until the governed have conquered peace, and they will come again to be heard. They are not dead, but sleeping.

It there is a necessity for a further increase of men—there can be but little occasion for more officers—the ranks of the old regiments will be filled up. The new recruits will be interwoven with the veterans of the Peninsula, of Shiloh, of Roanoke, of Pea Ridge, of Lexington, and Boston Mountain and Murfreesboro; having, by ready example, the drill, the discipline, the cool courage and efficiency of those who have survived battle-fields that have been made memorable by their valor and their endurance. So the officers who have won their spurs will have full ranks gathered under the old riddled banners. Shreds and patches they are; but, tattered and torn as they may be, they are worth all the flaunting standards of new regiments that could be sent to the front by all our Governors within the next year. So by the new law are preserved the historic recollections of the regiments that went out strong both in spirit and in numbers, but that now have only the daring will—the numbers, alas, sleeping where they foremost fell.

Another essential feature of the bill is that which provides for the arrest and return of the deserters of the past two years. This will prove a preventive in the future and a cure for the past. Do you know what an army of deserters could be gathered together in the States? Absenteeism has been as much the curse of the country and the army as it was of Ireland. It is not the poorest that have gone. It would be little if, here and there, only the lower grades left the field and the service. Unfortunately, however, in too many cases it is the well-to-do—those who have some position at home, and some little influence—that take leave of the camp. It is those who have the strength to get furloughs (and those who need them and do not get them) who overstay them, that constitute the bulk of the absentees. These, once returned to the army, would raise the aggregate available force *more than one hundred thousand men,* not counting those who are unfit for the labor and fatigue of the camp and the field. Think of such an increase of the army, without a draft, and then think if it will not go a long way toward rendering a draft unnecessary? The new law designates the machinery by which deserters may be sought out and returned. Returning deserters will deter from desertion. How much of crime is prevented by innate aversion to crime? Is it not the fear of detection, quite as much as conscience, that protects communities from depredations? At any rate, it is the dread of certain recapture, and the disgrace of being returned in durance that will put a stop to absenteeism.

Congress has done well, in declaring principles and in training provisions. Will the President, and those charged with the Executive powers conferred by the bill, prove equal to the enactment? I believe they will. Differ as men may about the policy which Mr. STANTON has pursued, there are none that will not concede to him patience, energy, perseverance and a grasp of details that few possess. I have seen something of public men, and in these essentials he exceeds any I have known. I am familiar with the working of the War Department, and I know that he masters all its intricacies, and by the aid of Mr. WATSON, controls all its ramifications. He has the industry to devise details for the fulfillment of the requirements of the statute and nerve enough to compel obedience to its provisions.

Is not the day dawning? Legal and certain provisions made for supplying the wastage of war, and those to execute who recognize their duty, and are willing to assume the responsibility of acting. What shall, with these in our hands, prevent us from rescuing the nation from disintegration, and mankind from the despair of seeing the last cornerstone of republicanism crumbling beneath the blows of traitors to God, to their country, and humanity? In the concentration of the strength of the nation shines bright and clear the North Star of Hope. Let us follow where it leads, accepting its guidance that we may realize its promise.

LEO.

Education for All

The idea for a federally supported public college system predated Lincoln's presidency by a full decade. But the proposal gained new momentum during the Civil War under the leadership of Senator Justin S. Morrill of Vermont.

Under the Land-Grant College Act, as it was formally known, each state received 30,000 acres of federal land for each member of its Congressional delegation. The states were to sell the lands and use the funds to establish agricultural and industrial colleges. The bill had actually passed the House and Senate before Lincoln took office, only to be vetoed by his predecessor, James Buchanan, who questioned the constitutionality of distributing federal lands to the states.

Revived and strengthened, the legislation sailed through Congress again in late 1861, and was signed by Lincoln the following July. Over the next thirty years, the federal government would distribute thirteen million acres of land to the states, with profits from their sale helping to establish sixty-nine land-grant colleges, including institutions that eventually became Iowa State, Michigan State, the University of Wisconsin and Pennsylvania State University.

When The Times *assessed the early impact of the bill in March 1863, it found that New York, Pennsylvania, Illinois, Rhode Island and several other states had already signed up for the program to create schools specializing in agricultural and mechanical training.*

By opening access to vocational training on a national scale, the legislation created yet another major change in American society. Until the Civil War, institutions of higher education generally specialized in philosophy, foreign languages and literature; the emphasis was on intellectual pursuits, not practical skills. The state schools created under the Morrill Act offered affordable paths to job-related scientific and industrial training for the first time.

Speaking in Wisconsin, one of the states that would create a new college under the Morrill Act, Lincoln had declared the year before he ran for the White House: "Free labor insists on universal education." As president, Lincoln, with Senator Morrill, made the promise a reality.

—H. H.

NEWS FROM WASHINGTON.

WASHINGTON, Saturday, April 25.

Agricultural Colleges.

The act of July 2, 1862, donating public lands to the several States and Territories which may provide colleges for the benefit of agriculture and the mechanic arts, requires that they shall accept the grants within two years. The act requires that, within five years after its passage, the States so accepting shall have built, or in course of erection, one or more of these colleges. The following States have already accepted: New-York, Pennsylvania, Illinois, Rhode Island, Minnesota, Vermont, Kansas, Kentucky, Missouri and Iowa. The General Land Office has in course of preparation a series of instructions to guide the State officers charged with carrying the law into effect. These, before being issued, will be submitted to the Secretary of the Interior for approval.

War Tests Civil Liberties

The controversy over Lincoln's unprecedented exercise of presidential power—including emancipation, suspension of the writ of habeas corpus, arbitrary arrests, military trials and the occasional shutdown of opposition newspapers—percolated for two years when it boiled over with the 1863 military arrest of an antiwar congressman, Clement L. Vallandigham of Ohio, a Democrat. Seized after making a provocative anti-administration speech in his home state, Vallandigham was imprisoned and later banished to the Confederacy.

In May, a group of angry New York Democrats staged a mass protest rally in Albany, led by the prominent local leader Erastus Corning (ancestor of a later, long-term Democratic mayor). Urged on by Governor Horatio Seymour, who warned that "our liberties are overthrown," they rebuked the president, declaring their "determination to stand by the Constitution."

Always sensitive to charges of tyranny, even as he was testing the limits of presidential constitutional authority in wartime, Lincoln saw the attack by the Democrats as an opportunity to offer a comprehensive public defense of his emergency powers. In an age in which presidents did not speak out publicly on controversial issues, Lincoln became his own spin doctor and a master at releasing important correspondence to the press for mass publications.

Lincoln issued his reply to the Albany Democrats on June 12, and within days it became front-page news in papers throughout the North. The message made a strong case for his actions, arguing that "the public safety requires them" in times of "rebellion or invasion." In the best known passage, he asked: "Must I shoot a simple-minded soldier boy who deserts, while I must not touch the hair of a wily agitator who induces him to desert? . . . I think that, in such a case, to silence the agitator and save the boy is not only constitutional, but withal, a great mercy."

—*H. H.*

THE PRESIDENT ON ARBITRARY ARRESTS

President Lincoln in Reply to the Albany Democratic Resolutions.

Able and Interesting Discussion of the Case of Vallandigham.

Mr. Lincoln's Reply.

EXECUTIVE MANSION, WASHINGTON, June 12, 1863.
Hon. Erastus Corning and others:

GENTLEMEN: Your letter of May 19, inclosing the resolutions of a public meeting held at Albany, N.Y., on the 16th of the same month, was received several days ago.

The resolutions, as I understand them, are resolvable into two propositions—first, the expression of a purpose to sustain the cause of the Union, to secure peace through victory, and to support the Administration in every constitutional and lawful measure to suppress the rebellion; and secondly, a declaration of censure upon the Administration for supposed unconstitutional action, such as the making of military arrests. And, from the two propositions, a third is deduced, which is that the gentlemen composing the meeting are resolved on doing their part to maintain our common Government and country, despite the folly or wickedness, as they may conceive, of any Administration. This position is eminently patriotic, and as such, I thank the meeting, and congratulate the nation for it. My own purpose is the same; so that the meeting and myself have a common object, and can have no difference, except in the choice of means or measures for effecting that object.

And here I ought to close this paper, and would close it, if there were no apprehension that more injurious consequences than any merely personal to myself might follow the censures systematically cast upon me for doing what, in my view of duty, I could not forbear. The resolutions promise to support me in every constitutional and lawful measure to suppress the rebellion; and I have not knowingly employed, nor shall knowingly employ, any other. But the meeting, by their resolutions, assert and argue that certain military arrests, and proceedings following them, for which I am ultimately responsible, are unconstitutional. I think they are not. The resolutions quote from the Constitution the definition of treason, and also the limiting safeguards and guarantees therein provided for the citizen on trials for treason, and on his being held to answer for capital or otherwise infamous crimes, and, in criminal prosecutions, his right to a speedy and public trial by an impartial jury. They proceed to resolve "that these safeguards of the rights of the citizen against the pretensions of arbitrary power were intended more *especially* for his protection in times of civil commotion." And apparently to demonstrate the proposition, the resolutions proceed: "They were secured substantially to the English people *after* years of protracted civil war, and were adopted into our Constitution at the *close* of the revolution." Would not the demonstration have been better, if it could have been truly said that these safeguards had been adopted and applied *during* civil wars and *during* our revolution, instead of *after* one and at the *close* of the other? I, too, am devotedly for them *after* civil war, and *before* civil war, and at all times, "except when, in cases of rebellion or invasion, the public safety may require" their suspension. The resolutions proceed to tell us that the safeguards "have stood the test of seventy-six years of trial, under our republican system, under circumstances which show that while they constitute the foundation of all free government, they are the elements of the enduring stability of the republic." No one denies that they have so stood the test up to the beginning of the present rebellion, if we except a certain occurrence at New-Orleans; nor does any one question that they will stand the same test much longer after the rebellion closes. But these provisions of the Constitution have no application to the case we have in hand, because the arrests complained of were not made for treason—that is, not for *the* treason defined in the Constitution, and upon the conviction of which the punishment is death—nor yet were they made to hold persons to answer for any capital or otherwise infamous crimes; nor were the proceedings following, in any constitutional or legal sense, "criminal prosecutions." The arrests were made on totally different grounds, and the proceedings following accorded with the grounds of the arrests. Let us consider the real case with which we are dealing, and apply to it the parts of the Constitution plainly made for such cases.

Prior to my installation here, it had been inculcated that any State had a lawful right to secede from the National Union, and that it would be expedient to exercise the right whenever the devotees of the doctrine should fail to elect a President to their own liking. I was elected contrary to their liking; and, accordingly, so far as it was legally possible, they had taken seven States out of the Union, had seized many of the United States forts, and had fired upon the United States flag, all before I was inaugurated, and, of course, before I had done any official act whatever. The rebellion thus began soon ran into the present civil war; and, in certain respects, it began on very unequal terms between the parties. The insurgents had been preparing for it more than thirty years, while the Government had taken no steps to resist them. The former had carefully considered all the means which could be turned to their account. It undoubtedly was a well-pondered reliance with them that in their own unrestricted efforts to destroy Union, Constitution and law all together, the Government would, in great degree, be restrained by the same Constitution and law from arresting their progress. Their sympathizers pervaded all departments of the Government, and nearly all communities of the people. From this material, under cover of "liberty of speech," "liberty of the Press," and *"habeas corpus,"* they hoped to keep on foot among us a most efficient corps of spies, informers, suppliers, and aiders and abettors of their course in a thousand ways. They knew that in times such as they were inaugurating, by the Constitution itself, the *"habeas corpus,"* might be suspended; but they also knew they had friends who would make a question as to *who* was to suspend it; meanwhile their spies and others might remain at large to help on their cause. Or if, as has happened, the Executive should suspend the writ, without ruinous waste of time, instances of arresting innocent persons might occur, as are always likely to occur in such cases; and then a clamor could be raised in regard to this, which might be, at least, of some service to the insurgent cause. It needed no very keen perception to discover this part of the enemy's programme, so soon as by open hostilities their machinery was fairly put in motion. Yet, thoroughly imbued with a reverence for the guaranteed rights of individuals, I was slow to adopt the strong measures which by degrees I have been forced to regard as being within the exceptions of the Constitution and as indispensable to the public safety. Nothing is better known to history than that courts of justice are utterly incompetent to such cases. Civil courts are organized chiefly for trials of individuals, or, at most, a few individuals acting in concert; and this in quiet times, and on charges of crimes well defined in the law. Even in times of peace bands of horse-thieves and robbers frequently grown too numerous and powerful for the ordinary courts of justice. But what comparison, in numbers, have such bands ever borne to the insurgent sympathizers in many of the loyal States? Again, a jury too frequently has at least one member more ready to hang the panel than to hang the traitor. And yet, again, he who dissuades one man from volunteering, or induces one soldier to desert, weakens the Union cause as much as he who kills a Union soldier in battle. Yet this dissuasion or inducement may be so conducted as to be no defined crime of which any civil court would take cognizance.

Ours is a case of rebellion—so called by the resolutions before me—in fact, a clear, flagrant, and gigantic case of rebellion; and the provision of the Constitution that "the privilege of the writ of *habeas corpus* shall not be suspended, unless when, in cases of rebellion or invasion, the public safety may require it," is *the* provision which specially applies to our present case. This provision plainly attests the understanding of those who made the Constitution, that ordinary courts of justice are inadequate to "cases of rebellion,"—attests their purpose that, in such cases, men may be held in custody whom the courts, acting on ordinary rules, would discharge. *Habeas corpus* does not discharge men who are proved to be guilty of defined crime; and its suspension is allowed by the Constitution on purpose that men may be arrested and held who cannot be proved to be guilty of defined crime, "when, in cases of rebellion or invasion, the public safety may require it." This is precisely our present case—a case of rebellion, wherein the public safety does require the suspension. Indeed, arrests by process of courts, and arrests in cases of rebellion, do not proceed altogether upon the same basis. The former is directed at the small percentage of ordinary and continuous perpetration of crime, while the latter is directed at sudden and extensive uprisings against the Government, which, at most, will succeed or fail in no great length of time. In the latter case, arrests are made, not so much for what has been done, as for what probably would be done. The latter is more for the preventive and less for the vindictive than the former. In such cases the purposes of men are much more easily understood than in cases of ordinary crime. The man who stands by and says nothing when the peril of his Government is discussed, cannot be misunderstood. If not hindered, he is sure to help the enemy; much more, if he talks ambiguously—talks for his country with "buts" and "ifs" and "ands." Of how little value the constitutional provisions I have quoted will be rendered, if arrests shall never be made until defined crimes shall have been committed, may be illustrated by a few notable examples. Gen. JOHN C. BRECKINRIDGE, Gen. ROBERT E. LEE, Gen. JOSEPH E. JOHNSTON, Gen. JOHN B. MAGRUDER, Gen. WILLIAM B. PRESTON, Gen. SIMON B. BUCKNER, and Commodore FRANKLIN BUCHANAN, now occupying the very highest places in the rebel war service, were all within the power of the Government since the rebellion began, and were nearly as well known to be traitors then as now. Unquestionably if we had seized and held them, the insurgent cause would be much weaker. But no one of them had then committed any crime defined in the law. Every one of them, if arrested, would have been discharged on *habeas corpus* were the writ allowed to operate. In view of these and similar cases, I think the time not unlikely to come when I shall be blamed for having made too few arrests rather than too many.

By the third resolution the meeting indicate their opinion that military arrests may be constitutional in localities where rebellion actually exists, but that such arrests are unconstitutional in localities where rebellion or insurrection does not actually exist. They insist that such arrests shall not be made "outside of the lines of necessary military occupation and the scenes of insurrection." Inasmuch, however, as the Constitution itself makes no such distinction, I am unable to believe that there is any such constitutional distinction. I concede that the class of arrests complained of can be constitutional only when, in cases of rebellion or invasion, the public safety may require them; and I insist that in such cases they are constitutional *wherever* the public safety does require them; as well in places to which they may prevent the rebellion extending as in those where it may be already prevailing; as well where they may restrain mischievous interference with the raising and supplying of armies to suppress the rebellion as where the rebellion may actually be; as well where they may restrain the enticing men out of the army as where they would prevent mutiny in the army; equally constitutional at all places where they will conduce to the public safety, as against the dangers of rebellion or invasion. Take the particular case mentioned by the meeting. It is asserted, in substance, that Mr. VALLANDIGHAM was, by a military commander, seized and tried, "for no other reason than words addressed to a public meeting, in criticism of the course of the Administration, and in condemnation of the military orders of the General." Now if there be no mistake about this; if this assertion is true and the whole truth; if there was no other reason for the arrest, then I concede that the arrest was wrong. But the arrest, as I understand, was made for a very different reason. Mr. VALLANDIGHAM avows his hostility to the war on the part of the Union; and his arrest was made because he was laboring, with some effect, to prevent the raising of troops; to encourage desertions from the army; and to leave the rebellion without an adequate military force to suppress it. He was not arrested because he was damaging the political prospects of the Administration, or the personal interests of the Commanding-General, but because he was damaging the army, upon the existence and vigor of which the life of the nation depends. He was warring upon the military, and this gave the military constitutional jurisdiction to lay hands upon him. If Mr. VALLANDIGHAM was not damaging the military power of the country, then his arrest was made on mistake of fact, which I would be glad to correct on reasonably satisfactory evidence.

I understand the meeting, whose resolutions I am considering, to be in favor of suppressing the rebellion by military force—by armies. Long experience has shown that armies cannot be maintained unless desertion shall be punished by the severe penalty of death. The case requires, and the law and the Constitution sanction, this punishment. Must I shoot a simple-minded soldier boy who deserts, while I must not touch a hair of a wily agitator who induces him to desert? This is none the less injurious when effected by getting a father, or brother, or friend, into a public meeting, and there working upon his feelings till he is persuaded to write the soldier boy that he is fighting in a bad cause, for a wicked Administration of a contemptible Government, too weak to arrest and punish him if he shall desert. I think that in such a case, to silence the agitator and save the boy is not only constitutional, but withal a great mercy.

If I be wrong on this question of constitutional power, my error lies in believing that certain proceedings are constitutional when, in cases of rebellion and invasion, the public safety does not require them: in other words, that the Constitution is not, in its application, in all respects the same, in cases of rebellion or invasion involving the public safety, as it is in times of profound peace and public security. The Constitution itself makes the distinction; and I can no more be persuaded that the Government can constitutionally take no strong measures in time of rebellion, because it can be shown that the same could not be lawfully taken in time of peace, than I can be persuaded that a particular drug is not good medicine for a sick man, because it can be shown not to be good food for a well one. Nor am I able to appreciate the danger apprehended by the meting that the American people will, by means of military arrests during the rebellion, lose the right of public discussion, the liberty of speech and the Press, the law of evidence, trial by jury, and *habeas corpus,* throughout the indefinite peaceful future, which I trust lies before them, any more than I am able to believe that a man could contract so strong an appetite for emetics during temporary illness as to persist in feeding upon them during the remainder of his healthful life.

In giving the resolutions that earnest consideration which you request of me, I cannot overlook the fact that the meeting speak as, "democrats." Nor can I, with full respect for their known intelligence, and the fairly presumed deliberation with which they represented their resolutions, be permitted to suppose that this occurred by accident, or in any way other than that they preferred to designate themselves "Democrats" rather than "American citizens." In this time of national peril I would have preferred to meet you upon a level one step higher than any party platform; because I am sure that, from such more elevated position, we could do better battle for the country we all love than we possibly can from those lower ones where, from the force of habit, the prejudices of the past, and selfish hopes of the future, we are sure to expend much of our ingenuity and strength in finding fault with, and aiming blows at each other. But, since you have denied me this, I will yet be thankful, for the country's sake, that not all Democrats have done so. He on whose discretionary judgment Mr. VALLANDIGHAM was arrested and tried is a Democrat, having no old party affinity with me; and the judge who rejected the constitutional view expressed in these resolutions, by refusing to discharge Mr. VALLANDIGHAM on *habeas corpus* is a Democrat of better days than these, having received his judicial mantle at the hands of President JACKSON. And still more, of all those Democrats who are nobly exposing their lives and shedding their blood on the battle-field, I have learned that many approve the course taken with Mr. VALLANDIGHAM, while I have not heard of a single one condemning it. I cannot assert that there are none such. And the name of President JACKSON recalls an instance of pertinent history.

After the battle of New-Orleans, and while the fact of the treaty of peace had been concluded was well known in the city, but before official knowledge of it had arrived, Gen. JACKSON still maintained martial or military law. Now, that it could be said the war was over, the clamor against martial law, which had existed from the first, grew more furious. Among other things a Mr. LOUAILLIER published a denunciatory newspaper article, Gen. JACKSON arrested him. A lawyer by the name of MOREL procured the United States Judge HALL to order a writ of *habeas corpus* to relieve Mr. LOUAILLIER. Gen. JACKSON arrested both the lawyer and the judge. A Mr. HOLLANDER ventured to say of some part of the matter that "it was a dirty trick." Gen. JACKSON arrested him. When the officer undertook to serve the writ of *habeas corpus* Gen. JACKSON took it from him, and sent him away with a copy. Holding the judge in custody a few days, the General sent him beyond the limits of his encampment, and set him at liberty, with an order to remain till the ratification of peace should be regularly announced, or until the British should have left the southern coast. A day or two more elapsed, the ratification of the treaty of peace was regularly announced, and the judge and others were fully liberated. A few days more, and the judge called Gen. JACKSON into court and fined him a thousand dollars for having arrested him and the others named. The general paid the fine, and there the matter rested for nearly thirty years, when Congress refunded principal and interest. The late Senator Douglas, then in the House of Representatives, took a leading part in the debates, in which the constitutional question was much discussed. I am not prepared to say whom the journals would show to have voted for the measure.

It may be remarked: First, that we had the same Constitution then as now; secondly, that we then had a case of invasion, and now we have a case of rebellion; and, thirdly, that the permanent right of the people to public discussion, the liberty of speech and of the Press, the trial by jury, the law of evidence, and the *habeas corpus,* suffered no detriment whatever by that conduct of Gen. JACKSON, or its subsequent approval by the American Congress.

And yet, let me say, that in my own discretion, I do not know whether I would have ordered the arrest of Mr. VALLANDIGHAM. While I cannot shift the responsibility from myself, I hold that, as a general rule, the commander in the field is the better judge of the necessity in any particular case. Of course, I must practice a general directory and revisory power in the matter.

One of the resolutions expresses the opinion of the meeting that arbitrary arrests will have the effect to divide and distract those who should be united in suppressing the rebellion, and I am specifically called on to discharge Mr. VALLANDIGHAM. I regard this as, at least, a fair appeal to me on the expediency of exercising a constitutional power which I think exists. In response to such appeal I have to say, it gave me pain when I learned that Mr. VALLANDIGHAM had been arrested—that is, I was pained that there should have seemed to be a necessity for arresting him—and that it will afford me great pleasure to discharge him so soon as I can, by any means, believe the public safety will not suffer by it. I further say, that as the war progresses, it appears to me, opinion and action, which were in great confusion at first, take shape and fall into more regular channels, so that the necessity for strong dealing with them gradually decreases. I have every reason to desire that it should cease altogether, and far from the least is my regard for the opinions and wishes of those who, like the meeting at Albany, declare their purpose to sustain the Government in every constitutional and lawful measure to suppress the rebellion. Still, I must continue to do so much as may seem to be required by the public safety.

A. LINCOLN.

New York Draft Riots

The worst civil disturbance in the history of America, except for the Civil War itself, was the three days of violent rioting that erupted in New York City in July 1863. The draft riots cost at least 100 lives, along with millions in property damage. Pro-administration officials were dragged into the streets and beaten, and demonstrators threatened the homes and businesses of prominent local Republicans.

Rioters, mostly new Irish-Americans who were unwilling draftees in a war to abolish slavery, destroyed a conscription office in Lower Manhattan, set fire to the Colored Orphans' Asylum uptown, lynched and sexually mutilated African-Americans and beat up policemen. Eventually, President Lincoln was compelled to order exhausted veterans of the recent Battle of Gettysburg to travel north to New York and help put down the ugly protest.

New York's Democratic governor, Horatio Seymour, who admitted that the riots were a "disgrace," nonetheless argued that the administration should suspend the military draft until the Supreme Court could decide its constitutionality. The president was willing to make a few concessions to restore public order, including the creation of a commission to investigate New York's draft quota, which critics believed was unfairly high.

But his reply to Seymour Lincoln was blunt: "I can not consent to suspend the draft in New-York, as you request, because, among other reasons, time is too important. . . . We are facing an enemy who, as I understand, drives every able bodied man he can reach, into his ranks, very much as a butcher drives bullocks into a slaughter-pen."

—H. H.

THE DRAFT IN NEW-YORK.

Important Correspondence Between Gov. Seymour and the President.

The Draft to be Proceeded With.

WASHINGTON, Saturday, Aug. 9.

The Following is Gov. SEYMOUR'S Letter to the President on the Question of the Draft in New-York:

"STATE OF NEW YORK, EXECUTIVE DEPARTMENT,
ALBANY, Aug. 3, 1863.

To the President of the United States:

SIR: At my request a number of persons have called upon you with respect to the draft in this State, more particularly as it affected the Cities of New-York and Brooklyn. To avoid misapprehensions I deem it proper to state my views and wishes in writing. As the draft was one of the causes of the late riot in the City of New-York, and as that outbreak has been urged by some as a reason for its immediate execution in that City, it is proper that I should speak of that event.

At the moment when the militia of the City were absent in pursuance of your request, and when the forces of the General Government were withdrawn from its fortifications, leaving it defenceless against any attack from abroad or the riot within its limits, the Provost-Marshal commenced the draft without consultation with the authorities of the State or of the City. The harsh measure of raising troops by compulsion has heretofore been avoided by this Government, and is now resorted to from the belief on its part that it is necessary for the support of our arms. I know you will agree with me that justice and prudence alike demand that this lottery for life shall be conducted with the utmost fairness and openness, so that all may know that it is impartial and equal in its operations. It is the right of every citizen to be assured that in all public transactions there is strict impartiality in a matter so deeply affecting the persons and happiness of our people. This is called for by every consideration.

I am happy to say that in many of the districts in this State the enrolled lists were publicly exhibited, the names were placed in the wheels, from which they were to be drawn in the presence of men of different parties, and of known integrity, and the drawings were conducted in a manner to avoid suspicion of wrong. . . . Unfortunately this was not done in the

District of New-York when the draft was commenced. The excitement caused by this unexpected draft led to an unjustifiable attack upon the enrolling officers, which ultimately grew into the most destructive riot known in the history of our country. Disregard for law, and the disrespect for judicious tribunals, provided their natural results of robbery and arson, accompanied by murderous outrages upon a helpless race, and for a time the very existence of the commercial metropolis of our country was threatened.

In the sad and humiliating history of this riot, it is gratifying that the citizens of New-York, without material aid from the State or nation, were able of themselves to put down this dangerous insurrection. I do not underrate the value of the services rendered by the military or naval officers of the General Government who were stationed in that City, for the public are under great and lasting obligations to them for their courage and skill, and their wise and prudent counsels. But they had at their command only a handful of good troops, who alone were entirely unequal to the duty of defending the vast amount of national property which was endangered. The rioters were subdued by the exertions of the City officials, civil and military, the people, the Police, and a small body of only twelve hundred men, composed equally of the State and National forces, who availed themselves of the able advice and direction of the distinguished military men to whom I have alluded. It gives a gratifying assurance of the ability of the greatest City of our continent to maintain order in its midst, under circumstances so disadvantageous, against an uprising so unexpected, and having its origin in questions deeply exciting to the minds of the great masses of its population. . . .

While this deplorable riot has brought disgrace upon the great City in which it occurred, it is due to the character of its population to say that they were able to put it down without aid from any other quarter, to save their City and to rescue their own and the Government property from the violence of a mob at a critical moment, when they had sent their armed men to save the national capital from falling into the hands of hostile arms. For this patriotic service they have already received your thanks and the gratitude of the nation. However much we may denounce and deplore the violence of bad or misguided men, it would be alike unjust and ungrateful to urge the execution of the draft in any spirit of resentment, or to show any unwillingness to see that the most exact justice is observed in the execution of the measure, and in fixing the amount of the quotas. I am sure that you will unite with me in repelling any counsels suggested by excited passions or partisan prejudices; for you have on more than one occasion acknowledged the generous and patriotic promptitude with

Lincoln, the railsplitter, in a large painting probably made for the 1860 campaign.

Lincoln speaks before 1,200 people at Cooper Union in New York on February 27, 1860. Four daily newspapers printed the entire 7,715-word speech the next day. It was Lincoln's first front-page article, and it brought him national prominence.

The home where Lincoln was born on February 12, 1809, at Rock Spring Farm, on Nolin Creek in Hardin (now LaRue) County, Kentucky.

Street scene of the Springfield the Lincolns knew. In the first year of their marriage, they lived in the Globe Tavern (first building on left), where their son, Robert, was born.

Lawyers Abraham Lincoln and Anthony Thornton plead for their clients, May 16, 1856, in the old courthouse, Shelbyville, Illinois. *(by B. G. Funk)*

Lincoln speaks on slavery as Stephen Douglas waits behind him, in this artist's rendition of one of the 1858 Lincoln-Douglas debates for the U.S. Senate.

Willie Lincoln, son of
Abraham Lincoln, around
1855. He died in the
White House in 1862.

Lincoln and Tad
in 1865. His
youngest son was
the only member
of his family ever
photographed
with him.

A fanciful scene of Lincoln at home with Mrs. Lincoln and their
two sons, Robert Todd Lincoln (in uniform) and Thomas,
who was called Tad.

Mary Todd Lincoln in
her inaugural gown.
*(Photograph by
Mathew Brady, 1861)*

Lincoln in 1862,
around the time of the
Preliminary Emancipation
Proclamation.
*(Photograph by
Mathew Brady, 1862)*

Lincoln in June 1860,
a month after he was
nominated for President.

The photograph that Lincoln believed helped make him President: the Cooper Union portrait.
(Photograph by Mathew Brady, February 27, 1860)

Lincoln as he appeared days before delivering the Gettysburg Address in November 1863.
(Photograph by Alexander Gardner)

Abraham Lincoln, flanked by detective Allan Pinkerton (left) and Gen. John A. McClernand, pose for photographer Alexander Gardner near Sharpsburg, Maryland, on October 3, 1862, during the president's visit to the Army of the Potomac two weeks after its victory at the Battle of Antietam.

(Photograph by Alexander Gardner)

Antietam, 1862. President Lincoln visits Gen. George B. McClellan and his staff near Sharpsburg, Maryland, on October 3, 1862, a few weeks after the Battle of Antietam. Lincoln was there to try to persuade McClellan to move his troops and attack Gen. Robert E. Lee's army. But McClellan declined to attack and was dismissed as commander of the Army of the Potomac a few days later. Pictured (left to right) are: Col. Delos B. Sacket, Capt. G. Monteith, Lt. Col. N. B. Sweitzer, Gen. G. W. Morell, Gen. Andrew A. Humphreys, Gen. McClellan, Scout Adams, Col. Alexander S. Webb, Capt. George Armstrong Custer, President Lincoln, Col. Lewis C. Hunt, Gen. Fitz-John Porter, Allan Pinkerton, Col. Fred T. Locke, Surgeon Letterman, and Col. R. N. Batchelder. *(Photograph by Alexander Gardner)*

Lincoln with private
secretaries Nicolay
and Hay in 1863.
*(Photograph by
Alexander Gardner)*

Period lithograph of Lincoln and his wife receiving guests
at the White House.

The town of Gettysburg as it looked in 1863, with crowds gathered on the day Lincoln made his famous address.

The first page of Lincoln's best-known address.

An artist's view of Lincoln giving the Gettysburg Address on November 19, 1863.

(Painting by Fletcher G. Ransom)

Artist Francis B. Carpenter's painting of President Lincoln
and cabinet members at the reading of the Emancipation
Proclamation, July 22, 1862.

Lincoln delivers his "with malice toward none" speech at his
Second Inauguration on March 4, 1865.

John Wilkes Booth,
the President's assassin.

David Herold was sentenced to death for
conspiring in Lincoln's assassination.

Lewis Powell, one of the four conspirators.

George Atzerodt, the conspirator assigned to assassinate Vice President Andrew Johnson.

Mary Surratt, another conspirator, was the first woman to be executed by the federal government.

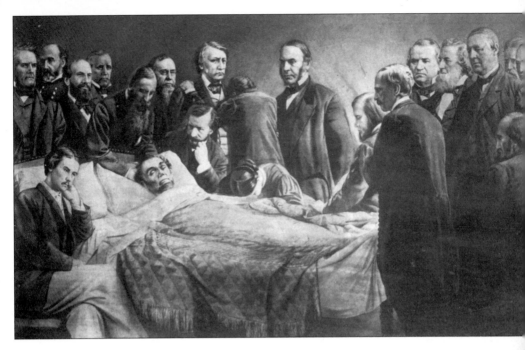

The President on his deathbed with members of his cabinet standing
near him and son Robert seated by his side.

(Photo montage by Alexander Gardner)

Lincoln's hearse and funeral procession passing down
Twelfth Street in Chicago.

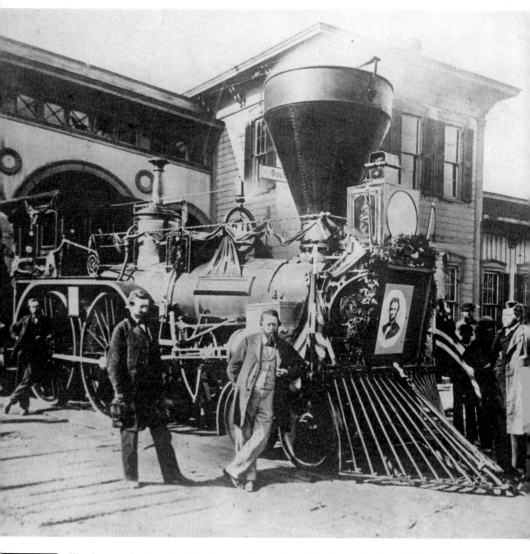

The locomotive bearing the nine-car funeral train is shown before it left Washington on April 21, 1865. The train stopped at Baltimore, Harrisburg, Philadelphia, New York, Albany, Buffalo, Cleveland, Indianapolis, Chicago, and finally Springfield.

The assassination of President Lincoln at Ford's Theatre,
April 14, 1865. *(Print by Currier & Ives)*

Placing the hoods on the conspirators at their execution,
July 7, 1865. *(Photograph by Alexander Gardner)*

which the City of New-York has responded to calls made upon it by you in moment of sudden peril. . . . After a careful examination I am satisfied that the quotas now demanded from Congressional Districts in New-York and Kings County are glaringly unjust. Either the names enrolled in these Districts greatly exceed the true numbers or the enrollments in other parts of the State are grossly deficient. The practical injustice will be the same in either case. . . . I ask that the draft may be suspended in this State, as has been done elsewhere, until we shall learn the results of recruiting, which is now actively going on throughout the State, and particularly in the City of New-York. I am advised that large numbers are now volunteering. Whatever credit shall hereafter be allowed to this State, it is certain there is a balance in its favor. It is but just that the delinquent States should make up for their deficiency before New-York, which has so freely and generously responded to the calls of the Government, shall be refused the opportunity to continue its voluntary support of the armies of the Union; there is another point which profoundly excites the public mind which has been brought to your attention by persons from this and other States; our people have been taught that laws must be upheld and respected at every cost and every sacrifice; that the conscription act, which demands their persons and perhaps their lives, must be promptly obeyed, because it is a statute of our Government; to support the majesty of law, a million of men had gone forth from Northern homes to the battle-fields of the South, more than 200,000 have been laid in bloody graves, or have perished in lingering disease. . . . It is believed by at least one half of the people of the loyal States that the Conscription act, which they are called upon to obey, because it stands upon the statute book, is in itself a violation of the supreme constitutional law, there is a fear and suspicion that, while they are threatened with the severest penalties of the law, they are deprived of its protection. In the minds of the American people the duty of obedience and the right to protection are inseparable. If it is, therefore, proposed on the one hand to exact obedience at the point of the bayonet, and upon the other hand to shut off by military power all approach to our judicial tribunals, and to deny redress for wrongs, we have reason to fear the most ruinous results. These disasters may be produced as well by bringing laws into contempt, and by a destruction of respect for the decisions of Courts, as by open resistance. This Government and our people have more to fear from an acquiescence in the disorganizing teachings that war suspends their legal rights, or destroy their legal remedy, than they have to fear from resistance to the doctrine that measures can be enforced without regard to the decisions of judicial tribunals. . . . I earnestly urge that the Government interpose no obstructions to the earliest practicable judicial decision upon this point. Our accustomed procedures give to our citizens the right to bring all questions affecting personal liberty or compulsory service in a direct and summary manner to the judges and courts of the State or nation. The decisions which would thus naturally be rendered within a brief period, and after full and ample discussion, would make such a current of judicial opinion as would satisfy the public mind that the act is either valid or void. The right of this Government to enforce military service in any other mode than that pointed out by the Constitution cannot be established by a violent enforcement of the statute. It must be determined ultimately by the judiciary. . . . I do not dwell upon what I believe would be the consequence of a violent harsh policy before the constitutionality of the act is tested. You can scan the immediate future as well as I. The temper of the people today you can readily learn by consulting as I have done with men of all political parties and of every profession and occupation, the nation's strength is in the hearts of the people. Estrange them, divide them, and the foundations fall, the structure must perish. I am confident you will feel that acquiescence in my request will be but a small concession for our Government to make to our people, and particularly that it should assure itself and them of the accordance of its subordinate laws with the supreme law of the land. It will be but a little price to pay for the peace of the public mind, It will abate nothing from the dignity, nothing from the sovereignty of the nation to show a just regard for the majesty of the law, and a paternal interest in the wishes and welfare of our citizens.

Truly yours, &c.,   HORATIO SEYMOUR.

REPLY OF THE PRESIDENT.

EXECUTIVE MANSION, WASHINGTON, Aug. 7.
His Excellency, Horatio Seymour, Governor of New-York, Albany, N.Y.:

Your communication of the 3d instant has been received and attentively considered. I cannot consent to suspend the draft in New-York, as you request, because, among other reasons, TIME is too important. . . .

I do not object to abide a decision of the United States Supreme Court, or of the judges thereof, on the constitutionality of the draft law. In fact, I should be willing to facilitate the obtaining of it. But I cannot consent to lose the time while it is being obtained. We are contending with an enemy who, as I understand, drives every able-bodied man he can reach into his ranks, very much as a butcher drives bullocks into a slaughter pen. No time is wasted, no argument is used. This produces an army which will soon turn upon our now victorious soldiers already in the field, if they shall not be sustained by recruits as they should be. It produces an army with a rapidity not to be matched on our side, if we first waste time to reexperiment with the volunteer system, already deemed by Congress, and palpably, in fact, so far exhausted as to be inadequate, and then more time to obtain a Court decision as to whether a law is constitutional which requires a part of those not now in the service to go to the aid of those who are already in it; and still more time to determine with absolute certainty that we get those who are to go, in the precise legal proportion to those who are not to go. My purpose is to be in my action just and constitutional, and yet practical, in performing the important duty with which I am charged, of maintaining the unity and the free principles of our common country.

Your obedient servant,

A. LINCOLN.

Blacks in the Military

Though Union forces had triumphed at Gettysburg, hope for a quick end to the war evaporated when Confederates under Robert E. Lee retreated into Virginia unmolested. And that wasn't all the bad news.

Under siege from critics on all sides—antiwar Democrats impatient for peace, antidraft civilians fearful of conscription, antiblack Unionists resentful about black recruitment, as well as black soldiers angered over unequal pay—Lincoln found himself on the political defensive as the bloody summer of 1863 drew to a close.

An opportunity to capture the high ground came in August, when citizens in Springfield, Illinois, invited him to address a Grand Mass Meeting of "unconditional Union men." Wrote the event's chairman, "A visit to your old home town would not be inappropriate if you can break away from the pressure of public duties."

Lincoln was tempted. "I think I will go, or send a letter—probably the latter," he replied. He was still not free of the nineteenth-century tradition against presidential speech-making. Writing another of his brilliant state papers designed to be published in the press, Lincoln sent it to Springfield with this advice to the speaker: "Read it very slowly."

A result was one of Lincoln's most impassioned public statements—an eloquent justification for emancipation, capped by a rebuke to those who opposed blacks in the military: "There will be some black men who can remember that, with silent tongue, and clenched teeth, and steady eye, and well-poised bayonet, they have helped mankind on to this great consummation, while, I fear, there will be some white ones, unable to forget that, with malignant heart, and deceitful speech, they have strove to hinder it."

Lincoln's message announced no new initiative, but it did make clear that he would not retreat from old policies firmly in place. "It ought to be pretty well understood by this time," The Times editorial acknowledged, "that the President is not a man who takes steps backwards."

—H. H.

The President's Letter.

President LINCOLN's letter to the Springfield Convention has all his characteristic solidity of sense and aptness of expression. It hits, as his written efforts always do, the very heart of his subject. Its contrast in downright directness of sentiment and style with many of the missives that used to be sent from the White House, in the days when glittering generalities were thought the only courtly language, is odd enough: but "plain people," who make up, in fact, the real people, like ABRAHAM LINCOLN none the less for this ingenuous freedom. . . .

Upon the question of the Emancipation Proclamation, and the employment of blacks as soldiers, the President is no less explicit. The Proclamation, he says, was designed for a military end exclusively. He has the testimony of commanders in the field that it has contributed to that end; among which commanders are some who have no affinity with the Republican party, and who judge solely by military considerations. . . . The President's argument for the employment of colored troops is unanswerable. He declares that it has practicably operated to the advantage of our arms—that "at least one of our successes could not have been achieved, when it was, but for the aid of black soldiers"—and he contends that the military considerations in this matter ought to prevail. Those who oppose the war outright may consistently oppose the employment of black soldiers which contribute to its success. But those who favor the war are bound to consent to all available means for its effective prosecution, and to form their judgment by the military standard solely.

But the great charm of this free-and easy, familiar letter, is its utter freedom from everything like a partisan spirit. Doubtless there are some minor views in it with which many good War Democrats would not exactly coincide; but the dominant sentiment of the production cannot but find an echo in every truly loyal heart, without distinction of party. Every line shows the one supreme desire and determination to subordinate everything to the maintenance of the Union. Every opinion is shaped, every principle applied, with exclusive reference to that end. It is a noble example. It ought to carry a moral power of far greater account than any mere argumentation. If all loyal men would faithfully keep to this criterion, rigidly excluding all thought of party interests and party associations, the Union cause would quickly gather a new strength that would amaze everybody. The differences about the methods and policies best calculated to speed on the national triumph would dwindle and sink out of sight. Confidence would be reposed in the superior information and opportunities for correct judgment possessed by the Government; and there would be a generous emulation everywhere to support the Government in its chosen modes of action. It is party spirit, infinitely more than the true national spirit, that keeps up the bickerings about the means employed. Party spirit has no business in this conflict. It should be put under the ban. It should be driven relentlessly from the sight and hearing of men. It is a happy thing that President LINCOLN sets his face so firmly against it. The very best proof of his fitness for his present weighty responsibilities is to be found in the fact that he has a soul possessed of this magnanimity, and a mind capable of these conceptions of patriotic duty.

THE PRESIDENT'S LETTER.

An Argument Addressed to the Opponents of the War Policy of the Administration.

Letter to the Union Convention at Springfield, Ill.

EXECUTIVE MANSION, WASHINGTON, Aug. 16, 1863.
Hon. James C. Conkling:

MY DEAR SIR: Your letter inviting me to attend a mass meeting of unconditional Union men, to be held at the Capital of Illinois on the 3d of September, has been received. It would be very agreeable to me thus to meet my old friends at my own home, but I cannot just now be absent from this city so long as a visit there would require.

The meeting is to be of all those who maintain unconditional devotion to the Union; and I am sure that my old political friends will thank me for tendering, as I do, the nation's gratitude to those other noble men whom no partisan malice or partisan hope can make false to the nation's life.

There are those who are dissatisfied with me. To such I would say, you desire peace, and you blame me that we don't have it. But how can we attain it? There are but three conceivable ways. First, to suppress the rebellion by force of arms. This I am trying to do. Are you for it? If you are, so we are agreed. If you are not for it, a second way is to give up the Union. I am against this. If you are, you should say so plainly. If you are not for force, not yet for dissolution, there only remains some imaginary compromise. . . .

A compromise, to be effective, must be made either with those who control the rebel army, or with the people first liberated from the domination of that army by the success of our army. Now, allow me to assure you that no word or intimation from the rebel army, or from any of the men controlling it, in relation to any peace compromise, has ever come to my knowledge or belief. All charges and intimations to the contrary are deceptive and groundless. And I promise you that if any such proposition shall hereafter come, it shall not be rejected and kept secret from you. I freely acknowledge myself to be the servant of the people, according to the bond of service, the United States Constitution; and that, as such, I am responsible to them.

But, to be plain. You are dissatisfied with me about the negro. Quite likely there is a difference of opinion between you and myself upon that subject. I certainly wish that all men could be free, while you I suppose, do not. Yet, I have neither adopted nor proposed any measure which is not consistent with even your view, provided that you are for the Union.

I suggested compensated emancipation, to which you replied that you wished not to be taxed to buy negroes. But I had not asked you to be taxed to buy negroes, except in such a way as to save you from greater taxation to save the Union exclusively by other means.

You dislike the Emancipation Proclamation, and perhaps would have it retracted. You say it is unconstitutional. I think differently. I think that the Constitution invests its Commander-in-Chief with the law of war in time of war. The most that can be said, if so much, is that slaves are property. Is there, has there ever been, any question that by the law of water, property, both of enemies and friends, may be taken when needed?

And is it not needed whenever taking it helps us or hurts the enemy? Armies the world over destroy enemy's property when they cannot use it; and even destroy their own to keep it from the enemy. Civilized belligerents do all in their power to help themselves or hurt the enemy, except a few things regarded as barbarous or cruel. Among the exceptions are the massacre of vanquished foes and non-combatants, male and female.

But the Proclamation, as law, is valid or is not valid. If it is not valid, it needs no retraction. If it is valid, it cannot be retracted, any more than the dead can be brought to life. Some of you profess to think that its retraction would operate favorably for the Union. Why better after the retraction than before the issue?

There was more than a year and a half of trial to suppress the rebellion before the Proclamation was issued, the last one hundred days of which passed under an explicit notice that it was coming unless averted by those in revolt returning to their allegiance. The war has certainly progressed as favorably for us since the issue of the Proclamation as before.

I know as fully as one can know the opinions of others, that some of the commanders of our armies in the field who have given us our most important victories, believe the emancipation policy and the aid of colored troops constitute the heaviest blows yet dealt to the rebellion; and that at least one of those important successes could not have been achieved when it was but for the aid of black soldiers.

Among the commanders holding these views are some who have never had any affinity with what is called Abolitionists, or with "Republican party politics," but who hold them purely as military opinions. I submit their opinions as being entitled to some weight against the objections often urged that emancipation and arming the blacks are unwise as military measures, and were not adopted as such in good faith.

You say that you will not fight to free negroes. Some of them seem to be willing to fight, for you—but no matter. Fight you then, exclusively, to serve the Union. I issued the Proclamation on purpose to aid you in saving the Union.

Whenever you shall have conquered all resistance to the Union, if I shall urge you to continue fighting, it will be an apt time then for you to declare that you will not fight to free negroes.

I thought that in your struggle for the Union, to whatever extent the negroes should cease helping the enemy, to that extent it weakened the enemy in his resistance to you. Do you think differently? I thought that whatever negroes can be got to do as soldiers, leaves just so much less for white soldiers to do in saving the Union. Does it appear otherwise to you? But negroes, like other people, act upon motives. Why should they do anything for us if we will do nothing for them? If they stake their lives for us they must be prompted by the strongest motive, even the promise of their freedom. And the promise being made, must be kept. . . .

Peace does not appear so distant as did. I hope it will come soon, and come to stay; and so come as to be worth the keeping in all future time.

I will then have been proved that, among freemen, there can be no successful appeal from the ballot to the bullet, and that they who take such appeal are sure to lose their case, and pay the cost.

And then there will be some black men who can remember that, with silent tongue, and clenched teeth, and steady eye, and well poised bayonet, they have helped mankind on this great consummation, while I fear there will be some white men unable to forget that, with malignant heart and deceitful speech, they have striven to hinder it.

Still, let us not be over sanguine of a speedy final triumph. Let us be quite sober. Let us diligently apply the means, never doubting that a just God, in his own good time, will give us the rightful result.

Yours, very truly,   A. LINCOLN.

Gettysburg Address

Abraham Lincoln was not the principal orator at the solemn ceremonies consecrating the new national soldiers' cemetery for casualties of the Battle of Gettysburg. That honor was assigned to Edward Everett of Massachusetts, who had run for vice president on one of the tickets opposing Lincoln in the 1860 election. Lincoln was asked to deliver only "a few appropriate remarks."

But, as Everett generously conceded to the president the next day, "I should be glad if I could flatter myself that I came as near to the central idea of the occasion, in two hours, as you did in two minutes." Most contemporaries eventually reached the same conclusion. But while The Times *published the full text of Lincoln's 272 words on its front page, few immediately appreciated its astonishing craftsmanship or its transfiguring defense of equality and democracy.*

On the other hand, legends that insist that the speech was indifferently received at the cemetery, and condemned or ignored by journalists, are gross exaggerations. At the time, the Gettysburg Address elicited a wholly partisan response: Republican adherents praised it ("It will live among the annals of the war"), and Democratic opponents condemned it ("silly, flat and dishwatery").

Another legend that has stubbornly clung to Lincoln's greatest speech is that the president dashed it off haphazardly—even, as one myth maintained, on the back of an envelope on the train to Gettysburg.

In fact, Lincoln worked diligently on the address, drafting it at the White House, reading versions to a few friends, and rewriting it repeatedly until he was fully satisfied that it was equal to the occasion. He even edited it after delivering it. Asked to write a fresh copy by hand for a war relief auction, he changed the phrase, "this nation shall have a new birth of freedom," altering it to read, for the first time: "this nation, under God. . . ."

—H. H.

THE HEROES OF JULY.

A Solemn and Imposing Event.

Dedication of the National Cemetery at Gettysburgh.

Immense Numbers of Visitors.

Oration by Hon. Edward Everett—Speeches of President Lincoln, Mr. Seward and Governor Seymour.

The Programme Successfully Carried Out.

The ceremonies attending the dedication of the National Cemetery commenced this morning by a grand military and civic display, under command of Maj.-Gen. COUCH. The line of march was taken up at 10 o'clock, and the procession marched through the principal streets to the Cemetery, where the military formed in line and saluted the President. At 11½ the head of the procession arrived at the main stand. The President and members of the Cabinet, together with the chief military and civic dignitaries, took position on the stand. The President seated himself between Mr. SEWARD and Mr. EVERETT after a reception marked with the respect and perfect silence due to the solemnity of the occasion, every man in the immense gathering uncovering on his appearance.

The military were formed in line extending around the stand, the area between the stand and military being occupied by civilians, comprising about 15,000 people and including men, women and children. The attendance of ladies was quite large. The military escort comprised one squadron of cavalry, two batteries of artillery and a regiment of infantry, which constitutes the regular funeral escort of honor for the highest officer in the service.

After the performance of a funeral dirge, by BIRGFIELD, by the band, an eloquent prayer was delivered by Rev. Mr. STOCKTON . . .

MR. EVERETT then commenced the delivery of his oration, which was listened to with marked attention throughout. . . .

PRESIDENT LINCOLN'S ADDRESS.

The President then delivered the following dedicatory speech:

Fourscore and seven years ago our Fathers brought forth upon this Continent a new nation, conceived in liberty and dedicated to the proposition that all men are created equal. [Applause.] Now we are engaged in a great civil war, testing whether that nation, or any nation so conceived and so dedicated, can long endure. We are met on a great battle-field of that war. We are met to dedicate a portion of it as the final resting place of those who here gave their lives that that nation might live. It is altogether fitting and proper that we should do this. But in a larger sense we cannot dedicate. We cannot consecrate, we cannot hallow this ground. The brave men, living and dead, who struggled here have consecrated it far above our power to add or detract. [Applause.] The world will little note nor long remember, what we say here, but it can never forget what they did here. [Applause.] It is for us, the living, rather to be dedicated here to the refinished [*sic*; should be "unfinished"—eds.] work that they have thus far nobly carried on. [Applause.] It is rather for us to be here dedicated to the great task remaining before us, that from these honored dead we take increased devotion to that cause for which they here gave the last full measure of devotion; that we here highly resolve that the dead shall not have died in vain; [applause] that the Nation shall under God have a new birth of freedom, and that Government of the people, by the people and for the people, shall not perish from the earth. [Long continued applause.]

Three cheers were then given for the President and the Governors of the States.

After the delivery of the addresses, the dirge and the benediction closed the exercises, and the immense assemblage separated at about 4 o'clock. . . .

THE GETTYSBURGH CELEBRATION.

From our Special Correspondent.

GETTYSBURGH, Penn.
THURSDAY Evening, Nov. 19, 1863.

All the noteworthy incidents of the celebration here to-day have already been sent off to you by telegraph, and it would have gratified your correspondent exceedingly if he could also have got off, but fate, combined with the miserable railroad arrangements, has ordained that he should spend another night in this over-crowded village. The only train that has been permitted to leave here, to-day, was the special train bearing the President and his party, which left at 6 o'clock this evening. Even the mail train, which should have left at 8 o'clock this morning, was detained for fear it would come in collision with some of the numerous trains that have been following each other in rapid succession from Hanover Junction, bringing visitors to the Dedication. How they are all to sleep here to-night it is difficult to imagine. All the hotels as well as the private houses were filled to overflowing last night. Every housekeeper in Gettysburgh has opened a temporary hotel, and extends unbounded hospitality to strangers—for a consideration. People from all parts of the country seem to have taken this opportunity to pay a visit to the battle-fields which are hereafter to make the name of Gettysburgh immortal. The Dedication ceremonies were apparently a minor consideration, for even while Mr. EVERETT was delivering his splendid oration, there were as many people wandering about the fields, made memorable by the fierce struggles of July, as stood around the stand listening to his eloquent periods. They seem to have considered, with President LINCOLN, that it was not what was *said* here, but what was *done* here, that deserved their attention. During the last three days, the scenes of the late battles have been visited by thousands of persons from every loyal State in the Union, and there is probably not a foot of the grounds that have not been trodden over and over again by reverential feet. But little over four months have passed away since the champions of Slavery and Freedom met here in deadly strife, and already the name of Gettysburgh has become historical, and its soil is classic ground. This, too, while the contest is yet undecided, and the camp-fires of the contending armies still illumine the Southern sky. If the people of the North can thus forestall history, it is because the manifest justice of their cause enables them to see the future in the present, and to behold in the fresh made graves of their fallen sons the shining monuments of their glory in ages to come.

The National Cemetery which has been consecrated to-day by such imposing ceremonies is located in the very midst of the fierce strife of those terrible July days, and many of the Union heroes fell on the ground comprised within its inclosure. It is little over half a mile to the south of the Gettysburgh Court-house, in the outskirts of the town, on what is called Prospect Hill, which is but a continuation of the elevated ridge known as Cemetery Hill. This hill, it will be recollected, formed the northernmost line of the Union armies during the last two days of the battle, and was several times stormed by the rebel infantry without success. The new cemetery is contiguous to the town cemetery of Gettysburgh and comprise 17¼ acres. It was purchased by the State of Pennsylvania at something like $25,000, and is to be devoted exclusively to the loyal dead who fell in the three days' battles. The present appearance of the cemetery is not very inviting, but the plan on which it is laid out is excellent, and when it is finished and covered with green sward, it will be one of the most beautiful burial-grounds in the country. . . .

The position of the new cemetery is very fine, and commands a view of the whole country for miles around, including the entire ground covered by the Union and rebel lines. It is less than a quarter of a mile from the house occupied by Gen. MEADE as his headquarters, about half a mile from Culp's Hill, where the hardest fighting occurred on the 3d of July, and about two miles from Round Top, which was occupied by the extreme left of the Union lines, and was the scene of the hand-to-hand fight of the 2d.

In wandering around these battle-fields, one is astonished and indignant to find at almost every step of his progress the carcasses of dead horses, which the negligence, or laziness or stupidity of the people of Gettysburgh have permitted to remain above ground since the battle, and which still breed pestilence in the atmosphere of this whole region. I am told that more than a score of deaths have resulted from this neglect in the village of Gettysburgh, during the past summer; and in the house in which I was compelled to seek lodgings there are now two boys sick with typhoid fever, attributed to this cause. Within a stone's throw of the whitewashed hut occupied as the headquarters of Gen. MEADE I counted yesterday no less than ten carcasses of dead hoses, lying on the ground where they were struck by the shells of the enemy.

The ceremonies of the Dedication to-day, of which you have already read a full account, passed off without accident, and nearly in accordance with the programme previously published. There was not, however, so large a military display as was anticipated, and the procession was unexpectedly slim, for the reason that most of the guests who were expected to join it were either off viewing the battle-fields, or hurried up to the cemetery before the procession started. The opening prayer, by Rev. Mr. STOCKTON, was touching and beautiful, and produced quite as much effect upon the audience as the classic sentences of the orator of the day. President LINCOLN's brief address was delivered in a clear, loud tone of voice, which could be distinctly heard at the extreme limits of the large assemblage. It was delivered (or rather read from a sheet of paper which the speaker held in his hand) in a very deliberate manner, with strong emphasis, and with a most business-like air. . . .

Soon after the arrival of the President at Gettysburgh last evening, he was serenaded by a Baltimore band, and after numerous calls for "the President," "Old ABE," "Uncle ABE," "Father ABRAHAM," "the next President," &c., &c., was induced to make his appearance at the door. He said he was tired, and did not feel like speaking, and as a man who did not feel like talking was apt to say foolish things, he begged to be excused from making a speech. The audience cheered the sentiment, and the President, taking it for granted he was excused, retired to his room. . . .

When War Ends

Lincoln devoted much of his third annual message to Congress to a careful accounting of the administration record on ending slavery. The president seemed particularly proud that in slaveholding Union states like Maryland, long opposed even to restraining "the extension of slavery," debate now focused on "the best mode of removing slavery" altogether.

The president pledged once again that he would never renege on the Emancipation Proclamation; proposed that an oath to obey the Proclamation be part of any plan to re-admit a rebel state into the Union; defended the recruitment of African-Americans for the Union military; and argued passionately that armed force was still necessary to restore the Union and democracy. He ended the message with fervent thanks to the fighting men of the army and navy, "from commander to sentinel . . . to whom, more than to others, the world must stand indebted for the home of freedom disenthralled, regenerated, enlarged and perpetuated."

While one Southern newspaper reacted to the message by branding Lincoln a "Yankee monster of inhumanity and falsehood," the president's private secretary rejoiced that the message was ecstatically received by Congress, where "men acted as if the millennium had come."

Lincoln took advantage of the good will in Washington by issuing a proclamation of amnesty and reconstruction that same day. Overriding members of his own party who advocated harsher terms, the president proposed that only 10 percent of a rebel state's 1860 voters swear allegiance to federal authority to gain readmission to the Union. Exempting only high-ranking Confederates, Lincoln added a generous amnesty provision that did, however, require rebel states to recognize the Emancipation Proclamation and outlaw slavery.

The war still raged, but Lincoln was looking to the future—and a Union at peace.

—H. H.

PRESIDENT'S MESSAGE.

Fellow-citizens of the Senate and House of Representatives:

Another year of health and of sufficiently abundant harvests has passed. For these, and especially for the improved condition of our national affairs, our renewed and profoundest gratitude is due. We remain in peace and friendship with foreign Powers. The efforts of disloyal citizens of the United States to involve us in foreign wars to aid an inexcusable insurrection have been unavailing. . . .

When Congress assembled a year ago, the war had already lasted nearly twenty months, and there had been many conflicts on both land and sea, with varying results; the rebellion had been pressed back into reduced limits; yet the tone of public feeling and opinion, at home and abroad, was not satisfactory. With other signs, the popular elections then just past indicated uneasiness among ourselves while, amid much that was cold and menacing, the kindest words coming from Europe were uttered in accents of pity that we were too blind to surrender a hopeless cause. Our commerce was suffering greatly by a few armed vessels built upon and furnished from foreign shores, and we were threatened with such additions from the same quarters as would sweep our trade from the seas and raise our blockade. We had failed to elicit from European Governments anything hopeful upon this subject.

The preliminary Emancipation Proclamation, issued in September, was running its assigned period to the beginning of the new year. A month later, the final proclamation came, including the announcement that colored men of suitable condition would be received in the war service. The policy of emancipation and of employing black soldiers gave to the future a new aspect, about which hope and fear and doubt contended in uncertain conflict. According to our political system, as a matter of civil administration the Government has no lawful power to effect emancipation in any State, and for a long time it had been hoped that the rebellion could be suppressed without resorting to it as a military measure. It was all the while deemed possible that the necessity for it might come, and that if it should, the crisis of the contest would then be presented. It came, and, as was anticipated, was followed by dark and doubtful days.

Eleven months having now passed, we are permitted to take another review. The rebel borders are pressed still further back, and by the complete opening of the Mississippi, the country dominated by the rebellion is divided into distinct parts with no practical communication between them. Tennessee and Arkansas have been substantially cleared of insurgent control, and influential citizens in each—owners of slaves and advocates of Slavery at the beginning of the rebellion—now declare openly for emancipation in their respective States. Of these States not included in the Emancipation Proclamation, Maryland and Missouri, neither of which three years ago would tolerate any restraint upon the extension of Slavery into new Territories, only dispute now as to the best mode of removing it within their own limits.

Of those who were slaves at the beginning of the rebellion, full one hundred thousand are now in the military service, about one-half of which number actually bear arms in the ranks—thus giving the double advantage of taking so much labor from the insurgent cause and supplying the places which otherwise must be filled with so many white men. So far as tested, it is difficult to say they are not as good soldiers as any. No servile insurrection or tendency to violence or cruelty has marked the measures of emancipation and arming the blacks. These measures have been much discussed in foreign countries, and, contemporary with such discussion, the tone of public sentiment there is much improved. At home the same measures have been fully discussed, supported, criticised and denounced, and the annual elections following are highly encouraging to those whose official duty it is to bear the country through this great trial. Thus we have the new reckoning. The crisis which threatened to divide the friends of the Union is past.

Looking now to the present and future, and with a reference to a resumption of the National authority, in the States wherein that authority has been suspended, I have thought fit to issue a proclamation—a copy of which is herewith transmitted—on examination of this proclamation it will appear (as is believed) that nothing is attempted beyond what is amply justified by the Constitution. True, the form of an oath is given, but no man is coerced to take it. The man is only promised a pardon in case he voluntarily takes the oath. The Constitution authorizes the Executive to grant or withhold the pardon at his own absolute discretion, and this includes the power to grant on terms, as is fully established by judicial and other authorities. It is also preferred that is in any of the States named a State Government shall be recognized and guaranteed by the United States, and that under it the State shall, on the constitutional conditions be protected against invasion and domestic violence.

The constitutional obligation of the United States to guarantee every State in the Union a Republican form of Government, and to protects the State in the cases stated, is explicit and full. But why tender the benefits of this provision only to a State Government set up in this particular way? This section of the Constitution contemplates a case wherein the element within a State favorable to Republican government in the Union may be too feeble for an opposite and hostile element external to or even within the State, and such are precisely the cases with which we are now dealing.

An attempt to guarantee and protect a revived State Government, constructed in the whole or in preponderating part from the very element against whose hostility and violence it is to be protected, is simply absurd. There must be a test by which to separate the opposing elements, so as to build only from the sound, and that test is a sufficiently liberal one which accepts as sound whoever will make a sworn recantation of his former movements.

But if it be proper to require, as a test of admission to the political body, an oath of allegiance to the United States and to the Union under it, why not also to the laws and proclamations in regard to Slavery?

Those laws and proclamations were enacted and put forth for the purpose of aiding in the suppressing of the rebellion. To give them their fullest effect there had to be a pledge for their maintenance. In my judgment they have aided and will further aid the cause for which they were intended.

To now abandon them would be not only to relinquish a lever of power, but would also be a cruel and astounding breach of faith.

I may add, at this point, while I remain in my present position, I shall not attempt to retract or modify the Emancipation Proclamation, nor shall I return to Slavery any person who is free by the terms of that proclamation, or by any of the acts of Congress.

For these and other reasons it is thought best that support of these measures shall be included in the oath, and it is believed that the Executive may lawfully claim it in return for pardon and restoration of forfeited rights, which he has a clear constitutional power to withhold altogether or grant upon terms he shall deem wisest for the public interest. It should be observed, also, that this part of the oath is subject to the modifying and abrogating power of legislation and supreme judicial decision.

The proposed acquiescence of the National Executive in any reasonable temporary State arrangement for the freed people, is made with the view of possibly modifying the confusion and destitution which must at best attend all classes by a total revolution of labor throughout the whole States. It is hoped that the already deeply afflicted people in those States may be somewhat more ready to give up the cause of their affliction, if, to this extent, this vital matter be left to themselves, while no power of the National Executive to prevent an abuse is abridged by the proposition.

The suggestion in the proclamation as to maintaining the political framework of the States on what is called reconstruction, is made in the hope that it may do good, without danger of harm. It will save labor, and avoid great confusion. But why any proclamation now upon this subject? This subject is beset with the conflicting views that the step might be delayed too long, or be taken too soon. In some States the elements for resumption seem ready for action but remain inactive, apparently for want of a rallying point—a plan of action. Why shall A adopt the plan of B, rather than B that of A? And if A and B should agree, how can they know but that the General Government here will reject their plan? By the proclamation a plan is presented which may be accepted by them as a rallying point—and which they are assured in advance will not be rejected here. This may bring them to act sooner than they otherwise would.

The objections to a premature presentation of a plan by the National Executive consists in the danger of committals on points which could be more safely left to further documents. Care has been taken to so shape the demurement as to avoid embarrassment from this source, saying that on certain terms certain classes will be pardoned with rights restored. It is not said that other classes or other terms will never be included, saying that reconstruction will be accepted if presented in a specific way. It is not said it will never be accepted in any other way. The movements by State action for emancipation in several of the States not included in the Emancipation Proclamation are matters of profound gratulation.

And while I do not repeat in detail what I have heretofore so earnestly urged upon this subject, my general views and feelings remain unchanged; and I trust that Congress will omit no fair opportunity of aiding these important steps to the great consummation. In the midst of other cares, however important, we must not lose sight of the fact that the war power is still our main reliance. To that power alone can we look for a time, to give confidence to the people in the contested regions, that the insurgent power will not again overrun them. Until that confidence shall be established, little can be done anywhere for what is called reconstruction. Hence our chiefest care must still be directed to the army and navy, which have thus far borne their harder part so nobly and well. And it may be esteemed fortunate that in giving the greatest efficiency to these indispensable arms, we do honorably recognize the gallant men, from commander to sentinel, who compose them, and to whom, more than to others, the world must stand indebted for the home of freedom, disenthralled, regenerated, enlarged and perpetuated.

(Signed)   ABRAHAM LINCOLN.

DECEMBER 8, 1863.

The following proclamation is appended to the message:

PROCLAMATION.

Whereas, In and by the Constitution of the United States, it is provided that the President shall have power to grant reprieves and pardons for offences against the United States, except in cases of impeachment—and, whereas, a rebellion now exists whereby the loyal State Governments of several States have for a long time been subverted, and many persons have committed and are now guilty of treason against the United States,

And whereas, With reference to said rebellion and treason laws have been enacted by Congress declaring forfeitures and confiscation of property and liberation of slaves, all upon terms and conditions therein stated, and also declaring that the President was thereby authorized at any time thereafter, by proclamation, to extend to persons who may have participated in the existing rebellion in any State or part thereof, pardon and amnesty, with such exceptions and at such times and on such conditions as he may deem expedient for the public welfare.

Whereas, The Congressional declaration for limited and conditional pardon accords with the well-established judicial exposition of the pardoning power, and

Whereas, With reference to the said rebellion the President of the United States has issued several proclamations with provisions in regard to the liberation of slaves, and

Whereas, It is now desired by some persons heretofore engaged in the said rebellion to resume their allegiance to the United States, and to reinaugurate loyal State Governments within and for their respective States; therefore I, ABRAHAM LINCOLN, President of the United States, do proclaim, declare and make known to all persons who have directly or by implication participated in the existing rebellion, except as herein excepted, that a full pardon is hereby granted to them and each of them, with restoration of all rights of property, except as to slaves, and in property cases where the rights of third parties shall have intervened, and upon the condition that every such person shall take and subscribe an oath and thenceforward keep and maintain said oath inviolate, and which oath shall be registered for permanent preservation, and shall be of the tenor and effect, following, to wit:

I,———, do solemnly swear, in presence of Almighty God, that I will henceforth faithfully support, protect and defend the Constitution of the United States and the Union of the States thereunder, and that I will in like manner abide by and faithfully support all acts of Congress passed during the existing rebellion with reference to slaves, so long and so far as not repealed, modified or held void by Congress or by decision of the Supreme Court, and that I will in like manner abide by and faithfully support all proclamations of the President made during the existing rebellion having reference to slaves, so long and so far as not modified or declared void by decision of the Supreme Court. So help me God.

The persons accepted from the benefits of the foregoing provisions are: All who are, or shall have been civil or diplomatic officers or agents of the so-called Confederate Government; all who have left judicial stations under the United States to aid the rebellion; all who are, or shall have been military or naval officers of said so-called Confederate Government above the rank of Colonel in the army, of Lieutenant in the navy; all who left seats in the United States Congress to aid the rebellion; all the resigned commissions in the army or navy of the United

States and afterward aided the rebellion, and all who have engaged in any way in treating colored persons, or white persons in charge of such, otherwise than lawfully as prisoners of war, and which persons may have been found in the United States service as soldiers, seamen, or in any other capacity; and I do further proclaim, declare and make known that, whenever, in any of the States of Arkansas, Texas, Louisiana, Mississippi, Tennessee, Alabama, Georgia, Florida, South Carolina and North Carolina, a number of persons not less than one-tenth in number of the votes cast in such States at the Presidential election of the year of our Lord 1860, each having taken the oath aforesaid and not having since violated it, and being a qualified voter by the election law of the State existing immediately before the so-called act of Secession, and excluding all others, shall reestablish a State Government which shall be Republican, and in no wise contravening said oath, such shall be recognized as the true government of the State, and the State shall receive thereunder the benefit of the constitutional provision, which declares that

"The United States shall guarantee to every State in this Union a Republican form of government, and shall protect each of them against invasion on application of the Legislature, or of the Executive, when the Legislature cannot be convened, against domestic violence."

And I do further proclaim, declare and make known, that any provision which may be adopted by such State Government in relation to the freed people of such State, which shall recognize and declare their permanent freedom, provide for their education, and which may yet be consistent as a temporary arrangement, with their present condition as a laboring, landless and houseless class, will not be objected to by the National Executive.

And it is engaged as not improper that, in construction a loyal State Government in any State, the name of the State, the boundary, the subdivisions, the Constitution, and the general code of laws, as before the rebellion, be maintained, subject only to the modifications made necessary by the conditions herein before stated and such others if any not contravening said conditions and which may be deemed expedient by those framing the new State Government. To avoid misunderstanding, it may be proper to say that this proclamation, so far as it relates to State Governments, has no reference to States wherein loyal State Governments have all the while been maintained, and for the same reason it may be proper to further say, that whether members sent to Congress from any State shall be admitted to seats constitutionally, rests exclusively with the respective Houses, and not to any extent with the Executive. And still further, that this proclamation is intended to present the people of the States wherein the national authority has been suspended, and loyal State Governments have been subverted, a mode in and by which the national authority and loyal State Governments may be reestablished within said States, or in any of them. And, while the mode presented is the best, the Executive can suggest with his present impressions, it must not be understood that no other possible mode would be acceptable.

Given under my hand at the City of Washington, the eighth day of December, A.D. one thousand eight hundred and sixty-three, and of the independence of the United States of America the eighty-eighth.

ABRAHAM LINCOLN.

By the President—

Wm. H. Seward, Secretary of State.

Grant Takes Command

For some time, Lincoln had been a frustrated commander-in-chief in search of a successful general. Pope, McClellan, McDowell, Burnside, Halleck and Meade had all disappointed him, but looking west Lincoln finally found his man. Troops under Ulysses S. Grant typically took high casualties, but always prevailed. After triumphs at Fort Donelson and Shiloh in 1862, Grant had laid relentless siege to Vicksburg. The South's citadel city quietly surrendered on July 4, 1863, while most Americans breathlessly followed the news from Gettysburg.

Grant's triumph did not elude Lincoln. Although some advisers, including his own wife, urged him to bypass a man they derided as a battlefield butcher and a drunk, Lincoln stubbornly defended Grant's potential. When a congressional delegation urged Lincoln to dismiss Grant because of his alleged insobriety, the president asked the visitors (according to legend) to find out what brand of whiskey the general favored because, "If it made fighting generals like Grant, I should like to get some of it for distribution." Privately, Lincoln confided: "I can not spare this man. He fights."

Finally, in March 1864, the president summoned Grant to Washington, handed him command of all Union forces, and declared his support for whatever plan he designed to win the war.

Grant was the guest of honor that week at a huge White House reception, at which the general had to stand on a sofa so he could be seen alongside the towering Lincoln amidst the throng of admirers. Just a few weeks later, Lincoln expressed pleasure at Grant's most recent victories. "It is the dogged pertinacity of Grant that wins," he said. It took another full year, and tens of thousands more dead and wounded, but Grant eventually repaid Lincoln's confidence.

—H. H.

GEN. GRANT IN COMMAND.

His Official Order Announcing the Fact.

Present Headquarters to be with the Army of the Potomac.

Departure of the General from Nashville for the East.

General Sherman Assumes Command at Nashville.

NASHVILLE, Thursday, March 17.

Gen. GRANT formally assumed the command of the armies of the United States to-day. The following is his order on the subject:

HEADQUARTERS OF THE ARMIES OF THE UNITED STATES,
NASHVILLE, Tenn., March 17, 1864.

GENERAL ORDERS, No. 12.—In pursuance of the following order of the President:

EXECUTIVE MANSION, WASHINGTON, D.C., March 10, 1864.—Under the authority of the Act of Congress to appoint the grade of Lieutenant-General in the army, of February 29, 1864, Lieutenant-General ULYSSES S. GRANT, U.S.A., is appointed to the command of the armies of the United States.

(Signed)   ABRAHAM LINCOLN.

—I assume command of the armies of the United States. Headquarters will be in the field, and, until further orders, will be with the Army of the Potomac. There will be an officer headquarters in Washington, D.C., to which all official communications will be sent, except those from the army where the headquarters are at the date of their address.

(Signed,)   U.S. GRANT,

Lieutenant-General,
NASHVILLE, Thursday, March 17. . . .

The Great Forgery Uproar

In *May 1864, two pro-Democratic newspapers,* The New York World *and* New York Journal of Commerce, *published a sensational exclusive: a new proclamation by President Lincoln, calling for 400,000 new troops to put down the rebellion. No one was more surprised by the story than Lincoln himself. Though he was privately considering such a move he had written no such proclamation. The report was an audacious forgery, intended, some later said, to inflate the price of gold and benefit currency speculators.*

Lincoln's response was quick and decisive. Employing unusually harsh language, the president commanded local military authorities "to arrest and imprison" "the editors, proprietors and publishers" of the offending newspapers. Their "false and spurious proclamation," he charged, had been "wickedly and traitorously printed and published" to "give aid and comfort to the enemies of the United States, and to the rebels now at war against the Government, and their aides and abettors."

The following day, editors from four other New York papers wrote Lincoln to offer their view that the fraud had been perpetrated by a man masquerading as an Associated Press messenger, hinting that it was only because of the late hour that more journals had not succumbed to the counterfeit scheme. In a May 20 editorial, The Times *also blamed the A.P. imposter for distributing the "false as hell" proclamation. At the editors' urging, Lincoln quickly released the prisoners, except for the editor of* The New York World, *Joseph Howard. The anti-Lincoln newspapers resumed operations by May 21; Howard was paroled in August.*

Historians have made much of the episode, some arguing that it demonstrated Lincoln's willingness to violate the Constitution to quash dissent. But the World *remained a relentless critic of the president, opposing his re-election with racist editorials and slanted news coverage. It was never interfered with again.*

—H. H.

THE FORGED PROCLAMATION.

Public Excitement and Indignation.

Suppression of the World and Journal of Commerce.

Military Seizure of their Offices.

Three Thousand Five Hundred Dollars Reward for the Forger.

By the publication of the following atrocious forgery in the *World* and *Journal of Commerce,* yesterday morning, great excitement was created among our citizens until the fact that it was utterly false, concocted by enemies of the Union and of the Administration, became patent. Their indignation was aroused, and was neither reserved nor unstinted in its expression. But meantime it had operated in Wall-street, had found its way on the steamer to Europe, and had secured against the Administration an unusual amount of declamation and condemnation.

EXECUTIVE MANSION, May 17, 1864.

Fellow-Citizens of the United States:

In all seasons of exigencies it becomes a nation carefully to scrutinize its line of conduct, humbly to approach the Throne of Grace, and meekly to implore forgiveness, wisdom and guidance.

For reasons known only to Him, it has been decreed that this country should be the scenes of unparalleled outrage, and this nation the monumental sufferer of the nineteenth century. With a heavy heart, but an undiminished confidence in our cause, I approach the performance of a duty rendered imperative by my sense of weakness before the Almighty, and of justice to the people.

It is not necessary that I tell you that the first Virginia campaign under Lieut.-Gen. GRANT, in whom I have every confidence, and whose courage and fidelity the people do well to honor, is virtually closed. He has conducted his great enterprise with discreet ability. He has inflicted great loss upon the enemy. He has crippled their strength and defeated their plans.

In view, however, of the situation in Virginia, the disaster at Red River, the delay at Charleston, and the general state of the country, I, ABRAHAM LINCOLN, do hereby recommend that Thursday, the 26th day of May, A.D., 1864, be solemnly set apart throughout these United States as a day of fasting, humiliation and prayer.

Deeming, furthermore, that the present condition of public affairs presents an extraordinary occasion, and in view of the pending expiration of the service of (100,000) one hundred thousand of our troops, I, ABRAHAM LINCOLN, President of the United States, by virtue of the power vested in me by the Constitution and laws, have thought fit to call forth, and hereby do call forth, the citizens of the United States, between the ages of (18) eighteen and (45) forty-five years, to the aggregate number of (400,000) four hundred thousand, in order to suppress the existing rebellious combinations, and to cause the due execution of the laws.

And furthermore, in case any State or number of States shall fail to furnish by June 15 next their assigned quotas, it is hereby ordered that the same be raised by an immediate and peremptory draft.

The details for this object will be communicated to the State authorities through the War Department.

I appeal to all loyal citizens to favor, facilitate and aid this effort to maintain the honor, the integrity and the existence of our national Union, and the perpetuity of popular government. . . .

(Signed)   ABRAHAM LINCOLN.

By the President:

WILLIAM H. SEWARD.

Secretary of State.

The above was received by the TIMES publication office about 3:30 A.M. The night clerk sent it up to the night editor, who suspected it at once, for several reasons, viz: it came without the usual Associated Press envelope; the handwriting was strange, not being that of anyone known to be connected with the office of the Association; in addition, the usual nightly indication that everything was in had been received from that office fifteen minutes before. These facts were sufficient to cause the suppression of the document, but to render the matter positively sure, a messenger was sent to the Associated Press office, who soon returned with the statement that the "Proclamation" was bogus, and was not promulgated through that office. In the meantime, the night editor of the *Daily News,* suspecting the affair, had sent to the TIMES' Editorial Rooms to ascertain how the matter was regarded there, and upon receiving the assurance that it was undoubtedly a forgery, and would not be printed in the TIMES, the *News* also concluded to suppress it. As soon as the copy was received in the TIMES' Editorial Rooms information was sought as to the party who delivered it, but the only thing that could be ascertained was, that a boy had rushed in, thrown it on the counter and rushed out.

Early yesterday morning the *World* discovered its serious error, and bulletined a reward of $500 for the discovery of the forger of the proclamation. It also published, in an extra, a disclaimer and explanation.

The following official denial of the proclamation was received from the Secretary of State; and to it is appended the disclaimer of the Agent of the Associated Press.

DEPARTMENT OF STATE, WASHINGTON, May 18, 1864.

To the Public:

A paper purporting to be a proclamation of the President, countersigned by the Secretary of State, and bearing date of the 17th day of May, is reported to this Department as having appeared in the New-York *World* of this date. *This paper is an absolute forgery.*

No proclamation of this kind or any other has been made or proposed to be made by the President, or issued or proposed to be issued by the State Department or any other Department of the Government.

WILLIAM H. SEWARD,
Secretary of State.

AGENCY ASSOCIATED PRESS,
No. 145 BROADWAY, May 18 — 11 A.M.

The alleged proclamation of the President calling for four hundred thousand men was not received at this agency, and we have no knowledge or belief in its authenticity.

D.H. CRAIG, Agent.

At the Produce Exchange, immediately after the close of the regular business hours, an indignation meeting was organized. Mr. R. P. GETTY called the meeting to order, and in a few pertinent remarks introduced a series of resolutions, expressive of the views of all patriotic produce merchants. Mr. JAMES P. WALLACE, in seconding the resolutions, spoke in the strongest manner, condemnatory of the infamous hoax, its authors, and all concerned in giving it publicity. The resolutions, as unanimously adopted, read as follows:

Whereas, There was published in the *Journal of Commerce* and *World* newspapers of this morning what purported to be a proclamation by the President of the United States, calling for four hundred thousand additional men, and also appointing a day of fasting and prayer; and

Whereas, Said proclamation proves to have been a forgery of the most nefarious and villainous kind; therefore,

Resolved, That in view of the present condition of our country, the authors of such forgery, and the publishers of it, (if such knowingly,) are unworthy of our support and confidence, and deserve the reprobation and denunciation of every loyal man in this community, and merit the severest punishment which either civil or military law can justly inflict.

MILITARY OCCUPATION OF THE WORLD AND JOURNAL OF COMMERCE OFFICES.

Pursuant, as was understood, to orders received last evening from Washington for the seizure of the offices of the *World* and *Journal of Commerce,* the arrest of the publishers and proprietors and the suppression of the papers, Gen. DIX detailed a force of the Reserve Guard for the purpose.

At a few minutes before 9 o'clock, Lieut. G. TUTHILL, in command of twelve men, appeared at the *World* office; possession was taken of the publication office, a guard placed therein, and the Lieutenant visited the editorial and composing rooms. He made no arrests, but directed a cessation of business, and took possession of the premises.

The office of the *Journal of Commerce* was seized by a detachment of twelve men of the Reserve Corps, under command of Capt. CANDY, about nine o'clock last evening. Our reporter was informed that Mr. HALLOCK, one of the proprietors, was arrested at the office, and that officers were dispatched to effect the arrest of Messrs. PRIME and STONE, the other members of the firm. The office of the *Journal* was closed, and work was stopped in the composing-room, but the printing of the weekly was allowed to go on, as it does not contain the forged proclamation.

It is stated by the assistant foreman of the *Journal* that the copy of the bogus proclamation was handed into the office about 3¼ o'clock yesterday morning, when only four men were in the composing-room. The copy was cut into slips without being read, and set up by the different by the different hands, who thought they were doing a great thing in getting out so important a document. The editors of the *Journal,* it is alleged, were all away, and knew nothing of the proclamation until they read it in the paper. It was also stated that the editors had prepared an article, which was set up, for publication this morning, disavowing all complicity in the matter, and offering a reward of $1,000 for the discovery of the perpetrator of the forgery.

THE REWARDS OFFERED.

The *World* offers $500 for the discovery of the party or parties perpetrating the forgery.

The *Journal of Commerce* offers a reward of $1,000 for the same.

The Associated Press publishes the following:

ONE THOUSAND DOLLARS REWARD.

At an early hour on Wednesday morning, a fraudulent Proclamation, signed by the President, was delivered in manuscript to each of the editors of the morning papers in this City. By direction of the Executive Committee of the Associated Press, and with the approval of the publishers of the *Journal of Commerce, Tribune, Express, World,* TIMES, *Herald* and *Sun,* the Association will pay a reward of one thousand dollars for such evidence as may lead to the conviction of the author of the above-named fraudulent document.

D.H. CRAIG.

General Agent N.Y. Associated Press.

No. 145 Broadway, May 18, 1864.

Here are three thousand five hundred dollars ($3,500) offered. The messenger who delivered the copies at the different offices was doubtless unaware that he was the tool of traitors. Let him come out at once and give the names of his employers. He will gain honor and money. Other rewards will doubtless be offered, and all the skill and ingenuity that detective patriotism possesses will be used to discover the villainous perpetrator of this scandalous fraud.

Letter from the Editors of the Suppressed Journals.

To the Editor of the New-York Times:

Will you oblige us by publishing in your columns the following statement of the proceedings of the Government this evening toward the *World* and the *Journal of Commerce,* regarding the publication in our morning's issues of the forged proclamation, purporting to be signed by President LINCOLN, appointing a day of fasting and prayer, and calling into the military service 400,000 men.

The document in question was written on their manifold paper, such as is used for all the dispatches sent to the several newspapers of our Association, and had every external appearance and mark to identify it as a genuine dispatch arriving in the regular course of business.

It was delivered at our office late at night, at the time of the receipt of our latest news, too late, of course, for editorial supervision, but, as it happened, not before our printing offices were closed.

It was delivered at all, or nearly all of the newspaper offices, and was published in part of the morning editions of the *Journal of Commerce* and *World,* and as we are informed in a part of the editions of one or more of our cotemporaries.

Early this morning the fact that the dispatch had not been sent by the agent of the Associated Press became known to us, and its fraudulent character was at once announced upon our bulletin boards, and a reward of $500 offered by us for the discovery of the forger. The Executive Committee of the Associated Press also offered a similar reward of $1,000, as the fraud had attempted to be perpetrated upon all the journals composing our association.

We took pains in the afternoon to apprise Gen. DIX of the facts in the case, and gave him such information in regard to the circumstances of the forgery as might assist him in the discovery of its author. The Government was at once put in possession of the facts in the case.

Nevertheless, this evening Gen. Dix, acting under preemptory orders from the Government, placed our offices under a strong military guard, and issued warrants for the arrest of the editors and proprietors of the *World* and *Journal of Commerce,* and their imprisonment in Fort Lafayette. A vessel was lying under steam at one of the wharves, to convey us thither.

Chancing to meet one of the officers of Gen. DIX's Staff, charged with the execution of this order, we proceeded in his company to the headquarters of the Department of the East, and were informed by Gen. DIX that the order for our arrest had been suspended, but that the order for the suppression of the publication of the *World* and *Journal of Commerce* had not been rescinded, and that we could not be permitted to enter our offices, which continue under the charge of the military guards.

We protest against this proceeding. We protest against the assumption of our complicity with this shameless forgery implied in the order for our arrest. We protest against the suppression of our journals for the misfortune of being deceived by a forgery not less ingenious nor plausible than the forged report of the Confederate Secretary of War, which Secretary SEWARD made the basis of diplomatic action.

PRIME, STONE, HALE & HALLOCK, (*Journal of Commerce.*)
MANTON MARBLE, (*World.*) New York, May 18, 1864.

PART FOUR

THE MARTYRED PRESIDENT
1864–1865

The Business of Politics

In the early months of 1864, Lincoln's renomination was seriously in doubt. For one thing, tradition argued against it. No president since Andrew Jackson had sought, much less won, re-election. Worse, the Republican Party seemed for a time hopelessly split. The radical wing hoped to cajole its unsuccessful 1856 contender, former general John C. Frémont, into the race, while another potential challenger loomed inside Lincoln's cabinet: the ambitious Secretary of the Treasury, Salmon P. Chase.

Lincoln eventually outflanked them both, winning renomination by acclamation when the Republicans, briefly renamed the National Union party, convened at Baltimore in early June. One of the great unsolved mysteries surrounding the convention remains the replacement of Vice President Hannibal Hamlin with a longtime Democrat, the military Governor of Tennessee, Andrew Johnson. No one has ever proven whether Lincoln knew, accepted, or even engineered the change in the ticket. If he participated in the dump Hamlin effort, however, it certainly ranks as a tragic mistake. Johnson later succeeded Lincoln, and proved to be a disastrous chief executive.

The convention also adopted a platform plank calling for a constitutional amendment to outlaw slavery everywhere. Lincoln called it "a fitting, and necessary conclusion to the final success of the Union cause."

Lincoln's own labors were only beginning. He entered the campaign a decided underdog, having taken the political risk of redefining the war in midrebellion as a battle to destroy slavery, not a fight to preserve the Union. The Democrats, meeting in Chicago, drafted a platform advocating peace, and nominated an old adversary to challenge Lincoln for the

White House, none other than former Gen. George B. McClellan. The most important campaign in American history was under way.

—H. H.

PRESIDENTIAL.

Lincoln & Johnson.

Proceedings of the National Union Convention Yesterday.

Unanimous Renomination of President Lincoln.

Gov. Andy Johnson, of Tennessee, for Vice-President.

The Loyal Platform.

Slavery Must Perish by the Constitution.

Emancipation, the Monroe Doctrine, Economy and the Pacific Railroad.

Enthusiastic Scenes at the Nomination.

The Final Adjournment.

BALTIMORE, WEDNESDAY, JUNE 8.

The Convention reassembled at 10 o'clock this morning, President Denison in the Chair. . . .

The hall was, if possible, more crowded than on yesterday, every nook and corner being occupied.

REPORTS OF COMMITTEES. . . . THE PLATFORM.

Mr. RAYMOND, of New-York, from the Committee on Resolutions, reported the following resolutions:

Resolved, That it is the highest duty of every American citizen to maintain against all their enemies the integrity of the Union, and the paramount authority of the Constitution and the laws of the United States, and that laying aside all differences and political opinions, we pledge ourselves as Union men, animated by a common sentiment, and aiming at a common object, to do everything in our power to aid the Government in quelling by force of arms the rebellion now raging against its authority, and in bringing to the punishment due to their crimes the rebels and traitors arrayed against it. [Prolonged applause.]

Resolved, That we approve the determination of the Government of the United States not to compromise with rebels or to offer any terms of peace except such as may be based upon an "unconditional surrender" of their hostility and a return to their just allegiance to the Constitution and the laws of the United States; and that we call upon the Government to maintain this position and to prosecute the war with the utmost possible vigor to the complete suppression of the rebellion, in full reliance upon the self-sacrifices, the patriotism, the heroic valor and the undying devotion of the American people to their country and its free institutions. [Applause.]

Resolved, That as Slavery was the cause, and now constitutes the strength, of this rebellion, and as it must be always and everywhere hostile to the principles of Republican Government, justice and the national safety demand its utter and complete extirpation from the soil of the Republic; [applause,] and that we uphold and maintain the acts and proclamations by which the Government, in its own defence, has aimed a death-blow at this gigantic evil. We are in favor, furthermore, of such an amendment to the Constitution, to be made by the people in conformity with its provisions, as shall terminate and forever prohibit the existence of Slavery within the limits or the jurisdiction of the United States. [Applause.] . . .

. . . *Resolved,* That we approve and applaud the practical wisdom, the unselfish patriotism and unswerving fidelity of the Constitution and the principles of American liberty with which ABRAHAM LINCOLN has discharged, under circumstances of unparalleled difficulties, the great duties and responsibilities of the Presidential office; that we approve and indorse, as demanded by the emergency and essential to the preservation of the nation, and as within the Constitution, the measures and acts which he has adopted to defend the nation against its open and secret foes; that we approve especially the proclamation of emancipation and the employment as Union soldiers of men heretofore held in slavery [applause]; and that we have full confidence in his determination to carry these and all other constitutional measures essential to the salvation of the country into full and complete effect. . . .

Resolved, That we are in favor of the speedy construction of the railroad to the Pacific.

209

Resolved, That the national faith pledged for the redemption of the public debt must be kept inviolate, and that for this purpose we recommend economy and rigid responsibility in the public expenditures, and a vigorous and just system of taxation: that it is the duty of every loyal State to sustain the credit and promote the use of the national currency. [Applause.]

Resolved, That we approve the position taken by the Government that the people of the United States can never regard with indifference the attempt of any European Power to overthrow by force or to supplant by fraud, the institutions of any Republican Government on the Western Continent; [prolonged applause,] and that they will view with extreme jealousy, as menacing to the peace and independence of this our country, the efforts of any such Power to obtain new footholds for Monarchical Governments, sustained by a foreign military force in near proximity to the United States. [Long-continued applause.]

The reading of the resolution elicited the wildest outbursts of enthusiasm, especially the emancipation and Anti-Slavery sentiments enunciated.

The mention of the name of ABRAHAM LINCOLN was received with tremendous cheering, the whole house rising and waving hats and handkerchiefs.

The resolution indorsing the Monroe doctrine was also received with great applause.

On motion of Mr. BUSHNELL, of Connecticut, the resolutions were adopted by acclamations. . . .

THE DRAFT

Report of Provost-Marshal-General Fry—Recommendation that the $300 Clause be Repealed.

[. . .]

To the President:

SIR: I beg leave to submit to you a report made to me by the Provost-Marshal-General, showing the result of the draft now going on to fill the deficiency in the quotas of certain States, and recommending a repeal of the clause in the Enrollment Act, commonly known as "the three hundred dollar clause." The recommendation of the Provost-Malshal-General is approved by this Department; and I trust that it will be recommended by you to Congress.

The recent successes that have attended our arms leads to the hope that by maintaining our military strength and giving it such increase as the extended field of operations may require, an early termination of the war may be attained. But to accomplish this it is absolutely necessary that efficient means be taken with vigor and promptness to keep the army up to its strength and supply deficiencies occasioned by the losses in the field.

To that end resort must be had to a draft. But ample experience has now shown that the pecuniary exemption from service frustrates the object of the Enrollment Law by furnishing money instead of men.

An additional reason for repealing the exemption clause is, that it is contemplated to make the draft for comparatively a short term. The burden of military service will therefore be lightened. But its certainty of furnishing troops is an absolute essential to success.

I have the honor to be your obedient servant,

(Signed)   EDWIN M. STANTON
                                  Secretary of War,

———

Beating the Odds, Again

True to tradition, Lincoln did no personal campaigning in 1864. "I believe it is not customary for one holding the office, and being a candidate for re-election, to do so," he explained. In a September draft memo that he never issued, he provided a hint of how he might have debated pro-peace Democrats. "Much is being said about peace," Lincoln wrote, "and no man desires peace more ardently than I. Still I am yet unprepared to give up the Union for peace which, so achieved, could not be of much duration."

For much of the campaign, Lincoln believed he would lose the election. Concerned that as president McClellan might overturn the Emancipation Proclamation, Lincoln called Frederick Douglass to the White House and plotted an elaborate scheme to alert as many slaves to their legal freedom as possible before November. However impractical, the plan demonstrated Lincoln's sincerity as a liberator.

Growing less confident of his chances week by week, Lincoln went so far as to ask his cabinet to sign, sight unseen, a memorandum in August that pledged cooperation with the new administration.

The momentum changed decisively when Gen. William T. Sherman captured Atlanta on September 1. Suddenly, after more than three weary, bloody, frustrating years of war, victory seemed within reach. Later that month, Lincoln placated the radical dissents within his own party by dismissing the conservative postmaster general, Montgomery Blair, ensuring the elimination of Frémont's third-party challenge.

On November 8, Lincoln polled 55 percent of the popular vote— 2,213,665 to McClellan's 1,802,237. The electoral avalanche was even bigger. Lincoln won 22 of 25 states, amassing 212 electoral votes to Mc-Clellan's 21. Especially heartening to Lincoln was the fact that soldiers, counted separately, voted an overwhelming 78 percent for the president.

—H. H.

VICTORY!

Glorious Result Yesterday.

Election of Lincoln and Johnson.

Terrible Defeat of McClellan.

The Union Triumphant.

New-England a Solid Phalanx.

New-York for Lincoln and Fenton

Defeat of Governor Seymour and His Friends.

Gain of Five Union Congressmen in the State.

Election of Raymond, Dodge, Darling, Conklin and Humphrey.

Pennsylvania Union on the Home Vote.

Heavy Union Gains.

Maryland and Delaware all Right.

Heavy Union Gains in New-Jersey.

The Great Northwest Solid for Lincoln.

Details of the Returns.

The Vote of the City.

President and Governor.

Peace Nears, Slavery Ends

Peace, reunion and freedom never seemed closer than they did on February 1, 1865. The Confederate vice president, Alexander H. Stephens, left Richmond that day en route to Gen. Ulysses S. Grant's Virginia headquarters to propose terms for a cessation of hostilities. The story was judged by The Times *to be more important than even the big news from Washington, where Congress made history by ratifying the Thirteenth Amendment to the Constitution abolishing slavery.*

Proclaiming it "a king's cure for all the evils," the president was so jubilant that he signed the official Congressional resolution—"Approved, February 1, 1865. Abraham Lincoln"—even though he was not legally required to do so. (Six days later, the Senate grumpily passed another resolution declaring that the president's "approval was unnecessary.") Lincoln, it seemed, wanted his name on the document that, once and for all, promised the complete destruction of the institution against which he had fought for nearly thirty years. The Abolitionist *editor William Lloyd Garrison told Lincoln, "You have done mighty work for the freedom of all mankind."*

A crowd gathered outside the White House to serenade the president; greeting them, Lincoln expressed pride that his home state of Illinois had become the first to ratify the amendment. "It winds the whole thing up," he said of the amendment. It was "the fitting if not indispensable adjunct to the consummation of the great game we are playing." According to a reporter's account of his impromptu remarks, Lincoln ended by congratulating "all present, himself, the country and the whole world upon this great moral victory."

Lincoln did not live to see the ratification of the Thirteenth Amendment. He was killed eight months before it became law.

—H. H.

THE PEACE QUESTION.

Its Latest Aspect.

Three Commissioners Coming from Richmond.

They Apply for Admission to General Grant's Lines.

A. H. Stephens of Georgia, R. M. T. Hunter of Virginia, and A. J. Campbell of Alabama.

A Flag of Truce and a Parley.

General Grant in Communication with the Government.

Expected Arrival of the Commissioners at Annapolis.

Special Dispatch to the New-York Times.

WASHINGTON, TUESDAY, JAN. 31.

In regard to the rebel Peace Commissioners, the following facts are known:

ALEXANDER H. STEPHENS of Georgia, R. M. T. HUNTER of Virginia, and A. J. CAMPBELL of Alabama, the latter formerly of the United States Supreme Court, arrived at Gen. GRANT's lines last Sunday afternoon and desired permission to come to Gen. GRANT's headquarters.

After considerable delay and parley they were allowed to come to Gen. GRANT's headquarters at City Point. It appears that Gen. GRANT immediately notified the Government of the fact, but up to this time we are not aware of the decision arrived at, though they are expected to reach Washington presently, via Annapolis.

FROM GEN. GRANT'S LINES.

The Commissioners Appear in Front of Petersburgh—Application for a Permit to Come Through—Scenes under the Flag-of-Truce—Excitement among the Soldiers.

From Our Special Correspondent.

HEADQUARTERS, FIFTH ARMY CORPS.
SUNDAY, JAN. 29, 1864—10 A.M.

For many days the weather has been intensely cold, and many cases of frost-bitten feet, ears, cheeks, &c., on our picket lines are reported. To-day the intense cold had moderated, and though the sun shone brightly and the air was calm, the road were solid and travelers many.

214

In front of Col. HARRIMAN's brigade, of WILCOX's division, Ninth Corps, about noon today, a flag of truce was displayed on the parapet of the enemy's works, a few rods to the right of the crater. The bearer of the flag states, that "Hon. ALEXANDER H. STEPHENS, Vice-President of the Southern Confederacy, and Hon. R. M. T. HUNTER, of Virginia, were desirous of proceeding to Gen. GRANT's headquarters; that they were expected, and would have approached our lines via the James River, but were unable to do so, owing to the ice in the stream."

The message sent by the bearer of the Confederate flag of truce was sent at once to the headquarters of the Ninth Corps.

The news that Messrs. STEPHENS and HUNTER were awaiting permission to enter our lines flew like wildfire through the camp. They were distinguished men; they had made names for themselves before the war began, before acquiescing in the severance of the Republic, and the Union soldiers, who are reading men, knew it. Curiosity is one of the failings of the Union soldier, and, as the news of the flag passed from camp to camp, tents were evacuated, from bomb-proofs temporarily-buried soldiers emerged, pickets brought their rifled-muskets to an "order," and all, not otherwise engaged, covered the parapets of the works of the main and picket lines. As you know, for many days there has been a tacit understanding along this part of the line that there should be no firing; but, until to-day, the members of the corps did not think it conducive to their health to exhibit themselves prominently.

The white flag, however, brought both Unionists and Confederates within plain, point-blank shooting range of each other, and waiting for a reply to the rebel request, they showed themselves in clouds on the works of the contending armies. "How are you Fort Fisher!" says the Yanks; "Good-bye, European importations;" "Have you heard from HOOD?" "Did you know that your Virginian, THOMAS, had presented to OLD ABE a 'worsted Hood'!" and many other remarks of a like nature.

The "Confeds" seemed to take it all in good part, and made, in some instances, quite happy replies, such as, "Fort Fisher may be gone up, but why don't you take Fort Crater?" "GWIN's a fool, and we don't care a d—n for anything more from Europe;" and "HOOD's hoodwinked old THOMAS, and you'll hear from him directly, I recon."

So they passed the time intervening before the reply came. Men who, a few moments later, might be engaged in mortal combat, whiled away the closing hours of the beautiful Sabbath in seemingly friendly intercourse. But does any one dream that, if on the midst of this sort of national gathering, the order had been given, "Prepare for action," any of the soldiers, so jocose and free from care, would have disobeyed the command? No! But, shoulder to shoulder, they would have repeated the lesson they have been endeavoring to teach the foes of their country for these long years. In the soldier's life there is sunshine and shadow, but, alas! the shadow predominates. The Union soldier lives on in the hope that through the shadow will finally break the sun of peace, reflecting around the bank of adversity's clouds a rainbow of victory, telling in unmistakable colors of a "Union" conquered and thereafter indivisible.

As the bright orb of day neared the western horizon, and glanced upon the lofty spires of the yet unconquered "Cockade City," an officer from the headquarters of the Ninth Corps neared our foremost line. All were on the tiptoe of excitement; but, soldierlike, the gallant Colonel kept his own counsel; and, improvising a flag of truce from a white handkerchief, proceeded to scale the works; and, with one companion, advanced to the neutral ground.

After some minutes' waiting, he was met by four officers of the Confederacy, and a conference was held within a stone's throw of the scene of the terrible tragedy of the 30th of July last. What the result of this interview was, was not made public; but, it is believed that no word had been received from Gen. GRANT, and as a consequence, the "distinguished gentlemen" from Georgia and Virginia would have to bide their time, perhaps until to-morrow.

As the flags receded from each other, the thousands who covered the works suddenly disappeared, walking into their tents, crawling into their holes and descending into their boombproofs, to speculate upon the meaning of such a seemingly urgent desire on the part of the Vice-President and Ex United States Senator to enter the Union lines. Speculation upon this subject is not only rife among the soldiers, but among other thinking men, and the most extravagant propositions are put forth. Of course it is useless to speculate. It may be that the visit of these noted Southern gentlemen will be productive of good; but time alone will tell.

—G. F. WILLIAMS

FROM WASHINGTON.

Abolition of Slavery.

Passage of the Constitutional Amendment.

One Hundred and Nineteen Yeas Against Fifty-six Nays.

Exciting Scene in the House.

Enthusiasm over the Result.

The Peace Mission in the Senate.

A Resolution Calling for Information.

Passage of Retaliation Resolutions in the Senate.

Special Dispatches to the New-York Times.

THE PASSAGE OF THE CONSTITUTIONAL AMENDMENT.

The great feature of the existing rebellion was the passage to-day by the House of Representatives of the resolutions submitting to the Legislatures of the several States an amendment to the Constitution abolishing slavery. It was an epoch in the history of the country, and will be remembered by the members of the House and spectators present as an event in their lives. At 3 o'clock, by general consent, all discussion having ceased, the preliminary votes to reconsider and second the demand for the previous question were agreed to by a vote of 113 yeas, to 58 nays; and amid profound silence the Speaker announced that the yeas and nays would be taken directly upon the pending proposition. During the call, when prominent Democrats voted aye, there was suppressed evidence of applause and gratification exhibited in the galleries, but it was evidence that the great interest centered entirely upon the final result, and when the presiding officer announced that the resolution was agreed to by yeas 119, nays 56, the enthusiasm of all present, save a few disappointed politicians, knew no bounds, and for several moments the scene was grand and impressive beyond description. No attempt was made to suppress the applause which came from all sides, every one feeling that the occasion justified the fullest expression of approbation and joy.

Rebels Rejected

Did Lincoln really believe that a meeting with Rebel commissioners could abruptly end four years of Civil War? The president left no hints about his true thoughts, but he apparently felt obliged to travel to Union headquarters in February 1865 to entertain the enemy peace proposals.

There, he endured what must have been an awkward reunion with the Confederate vice president, Stephens, the tiny Georgia Whig with whom he had served in Congress during the Mexican War. Seeing him wrapped in his huge overcoat, Lincoln later recalled with a laugh: "Didn't you think it was the biggest shuck and the littlest ear that ever you did see?"

As a Times *headline reported a week before Lincoln's fifty-sixth birthday, on February 5, 1865, "The Rebel Propositions Said to have been*

Inadmissible." Indeed, the Rebel and his fellow commissioners proposed a truce accompanied by abrogation of the Emancipation Proclamation. Lincoln might have briefly considered sacrificing his executive order in the expectation that the Thirteenth Amendment would soon render it superfluous. But in the end, no doubt recalling his innumerable pledges never to recall "a word of it," he rejected the offer.

Lincoln probably knew that history was on his side. A few days after returning from the failed Hampton Roads conference, he sat for a life mask that sculptor Clark Mills hoped to use for a heroic statue to celebrate Lincoln's accomplishments. Seeing it later, the president's private secretary thought it "sad and peaceful in its infinite repose . . . a look as of one on whom sorrow and care had done their worst without victory." The overall impression was "of unspeakable sadness and all-suffering strength."

In truth, Lincoln's astonishing vitality was fading. Thin and haggard after four years of war, he complained privately about circulatory problems and relentless exhaustion. And now he turned his attention to his second inaugural.

—H. H.

THE PEACE CONFERENCE

Return of President Lincoln and Mr. Seward to Washington.

The Rebel Commissioners Gone Back to Richmond.

Various Rumors in Regard to the Conference and Its Results.

The Rebel Propositions Said to have been Inadmissible.

Reported Appointment of Thirteen Commissioners on Either Side.

Rumors of a Truce of Thirty Days.

FROM WASHINGTON.

WASHINGTON, D.C., SATURDAY, FEB. 4.
President LINCOLN and Secretary SEWARD arrived here from Fortress Monroe, at 10 o'clock this morning.

They had an informal conference with Mr. STEPHENS and his associates, Messrs. HUNTER and CAMPBELL, on board the *River Queen,* in Hampton Roads.

The conference occupied four hours, and is positively known to have resulted in no change of attitude, either of the Government or of the rebels. In other words it was a failure.

The *Star* has the following particulars of the return of President LINCOLN, and Secretary SEWARD.

"President LINCOLN and Secretary SEWARD arrived in Washington at 9:15 this morning, by special train from Annapolis, on their return of Fortress Monroe."

The President, who left here on Thursday at 11:30 A.M., accompanied by Mr. GEORGE KOONTZ, of the Baltimore and Ohio Railroad Company, arrived at Annapolis at 1:15 P.M., and, in company with Mr. KOONTZ, proceeded to the Naval Academy, where the steamer *Colyer* had steamed up, and, going on board, left immediately, and arrived at Fortress Monroe at an early hour yesterday morning.

The two boats, *Mary Martin,* bearing the rebel deputation to Fortress Monroe, and the *River Queen,* on which Mr. SEWARD went down, were lashed side by side, during which time the President and Secretary of State, and the rebel deputation, had a protracted interview.

The boats separated about dusk, and the *River Queen* started immediately for Annapolis, where she arrived early this morning.

The special train which was in waiting for the party left that place at 7:30 this morning, and arrived here, as stated above, at 9:25.

Gens. WILLIAMS and INGALL'S, who came up on the *Colyer* last night were on board the same train, as were also Mr. R. S. CREW, of the State Department, who went down with Mr. SEWARD, and Major ECKERT, Superintendent of the United States Military Telegraph, and Charles Forbes, attaché of the White House, who accompanied the President."

REPORTS FROM BALTIMORE.

FIRST DISPATCH.

BALTIMORE, SATURDAY, FEB. 4.

President LINCOLN and Secretary SEWARD, accompanied by Gen. INGALLS, arrived at Annapolis this morning, and left at 6 o'clock for Washington.

Nothing is yet known as to the result of their conference with the Confederate Commissioners.

SECOND DISPATCH.

BALTIMORE, SATURDAY, FEB. 4.

A special dispatch to the Baltimore *American,* from Annapolis, this morning, after announcing the arrival there of President LINCOLN and Secretary SEWARD on board of Gen. GRANT's flag-of-truce boat, says:

The prospects of an early settlement of our National difficulties are brighter.

It was rumored on board of the steamer that an armistice of thirty days would take place, but this, of course, is only mere rumor. . . .

THE LATEST.

WASHINGTON, SATURDAY, FEB. 4.

Much surprise was occasioned this morning by the early return of President LINCOLN and Secretary SEWARD, and it was not long before many conflicting reports were circulated regarding the result of their mission.

The antagonistic positions of the two Governments were known on the return of Mr. Blair from Richmond—no one desiring peace on the basis of unconditional submission to the Union, and the other on the basis of separate independence and recognition.

It was clear that the rebels themselves did not anticipate a ready compliance with their demands, while there was an earnest desire on the part of the President to do all that was compatible with honor and public expediency in the premises, and who evinced not a little anxiety to induce an accommodation.

It was briefly announced by telegraph, this morning, that President LINCOLN and Secretary SEWARD had returned to Washington, after a conference with the rebel commissioners, which resulted in no change of the attitude of the Government or of the rebels.

Private telegrams have since been received, making inquiry as to the truth of this statement, because the whole truth had not been stated with regard to the prospective and immediate results from Richmond.

Now, that brief telegram sent over the wires this morning is reliable, and it was obtained from the best authority.

No details have yet been made known, nor is it probable that they will transpire, the President and Secretary SEWARD being the only parties present on our side, and the conference being entirely informal, more in the character of a general conversation to elicit the views of all who composed it, than a grave diplomatic discussion.

Beyond this, whatever may be said, must be mere speculation.

The conversation did not result in any agreement. The main feature involving the questions of separation of, and submission to the Union having been left undecided, of course those of a minor character could have no existence, and so the parties separated.

As far as can be ascertained nothing was said as to future meetings, and the issue seems to be left precisely where it was before the conference.

There is no verification of the report circulating to-day, that they had agreed upon a general exchange of prisoners.

Various Statements About the Peace Conference.

Special Dispatch to the Commercial Advertiser.

WASHINGTON, SATURDAY, FEB. 4.

In pursuance of a notification by telegraph from the President, the Cabinet assembled at 11 o'clock this morning. The President has, doubtless, laid before the members the result of his mission.

The general opinion here is that the rebel emissaries presented four propositions, all of which were positively inadmissible.

Some pretend that thirteen commissioners are to be appointed on either side.

The President and Mr. SEWARD are very reticent about the result of their negotiations with the rebel "commissioners," and no particulars are yet known of the details of the interview. There is, however, a general feeling of satisfaction among those in the President's confidence, and the result of the negotiations is regarded as highly favorable to peace. Senators, who have Secretary SEWARD seen this morning, express the utmost assurance that peace is only a question of days.

From what a member of the Cabinet intimated at the Capitol this afternoon, Mr. LINCOLN went down firmly believing that the rebel envoys are prepared to make Union and emancipation a base of operations.

Even the Sun Came Out

One of the greatest speeches of his career, Abraham Lincoln's second inaugural address was delivered beneath gray skies outside the United States Capitol on March 4, 1865. But as the president spoke, the sun burst through the clouds. The symbolism was not lost on the new chief justice of the Supreme Court—Salmon P. Chase, his onetime rival—who called it "an auspicious omen of the dispersion of the clouds of war." Lincoln himself admitted, "it made my heart jump."

Best remembered for its reconciliatory conclusion, this briefest of presidential inaugurals actually devoted more words to a fire-and-brimstone defense of the war as heaven-sent punishment for the national sin of slavery. Insisting that emancipation had sanctified the Union cause, Lincoln defended wartime sacrifices, even if God willed that the fighting continue "until every drop of blood drawn with the lash, shall be paid by another drawn with the sword."

Changing to a benevolent note, Lincoln ended the speech with the sublime call for a mutually blameless peace:

"With malice toward none; with charity for all; with firmness in the right, as God gives us to see the right, let us strive on to finish the work we are in; to bind up the nation's wounds; to care for him who shall have borne the battle, and for his widow, and his orphan—to do all which may achieve and cherish a just, and a lasting peace, among ourselves, and with all nations."

One newspaper of the day thought the concluding sentiments deserved to be "printed in gold." Lincoln believed that the speech would "wear as well as—perhaps better than—any thing I have ever produced." But he was also aware that it was "not immediately popular," explaining, "Men are not flattered by being shown that there has been a difference of purpose between the Almighty and them."

—H. H.

THE INAUGURATION.

A Stormy Morning but a Clear Afternoon.

The Procession to the Capitol.

Imposing Display—Enthusiasm Among the People.

The Inauguration Ceremonies.

Vice-President Johnson Sworn in by Mr. Hamlin.

President Lincoln takes the Oath for the Second Term.

His Inaugural Address.

The Changes of Four Years—Both Sides Disappointed at the Length of the War.

The Situation Very Hopeful.

Our Object—a Just and Lasting Peace Among Ourselves and with Others.

The Inauguration of President Lincoln.

Dispatches to the Associated Press.

WASHINGTON, SATURDAY, MARCH 4.

The procession is now forming, though a heavy rain is falling, and the streets are almost impassable with mud.

The avenue is filled with a dense mass of people.

The ceremonies will take place in the Senate Chamber.

SECOND DISPATCH.

The procession reached the Capitol at about quarter to twelve o'clock, escorting the President elect.

At a subsequent period, the President and Vice-President, together with the Justices of the Supreme Court, Members and Ex-Members of Congress, Foreign Ministers, and other persons of distinction, assembled in the Senate Chamber.

There the Vice-President elect took the oath of office, preceding it by an address.

Chief Justice Chase administered the oath of office on the eastern portico, when the President delivered his Inaugural Address.

There was a very large attendance, and the scene was one of marked interest.

THIRD DISPATCH.

The rain has ceased, and the procession is now passing down the avenue. This display is exceedingly grand. The sidewalks are jammed with people, and every window and house-top was filled with ladies and gentlemen, who are waving handkerchiefs and hats with great enthusiasm.

The visiting Philadelphia Fire Department and ours, attract great attention by their beautifully adorned apparatus.

Many bands of music are interspersed throughout the whole procession, and the line is one continual ring of music.

The *Chronicle* is represented in the procession by a large truck with a press upon it printing a *Chronicle Junior,* and scattering them to the dense mass of humanity.

The procession was one hour passing a given point, and the length of it is probably over a mile.

The Navy-yard delegation has a monitor in line, with the turret turning.

The streets are almost in an impassable condition, which makes the display not as magnificent as it would have been, though it is exceedingly beautiful.

One feature in the procession is the colored troops and the Odd-Fellows, with their band of music.

FOURTH DISPATCH.

The weather has cleared off bright and beautiful.

The President and others reached the platform. The band played "Hail to the Chief." Salutes were fired, and the President was cheered by an immense throng, composed of civilians and the military.

After delivering the Inaugural Address he was again cheered, salutes were fired, and the band played.

THE INAUGURAL ADDRESS.

Fellow-Countrymen:

At this second appearing to take the oath of the Presidential office, there is less occasion for an extended address than there was at the first. Then a statement somewhat in detail of a course to be pursued seemed very fitting and proper. Now, at the expiration of four years, during which public declarations have been constantly called forth on every point and phase of the great contest which still absorbs the attention and engrosses the energies of the nation, little that is new could be presented.

The progress of our arms, upon which all else chiefly depends, is as well known to the public as to myself, and it is, I trust, reasonably satisfactory and encouraging to all. With high hope for the future, no prediction in regard to it is ventured.

On the occasion corresponding to this four years ago, all thoughts were anxiously directed to an impending civil war. All dreaded it; all sought to avoid it. While the inaugural address was being delivered from this place, devoted altogether to saving the Union without war, insurgent agents were in the city seeking to destroy it without war—seeking to dissolve the Union and divide the effects by negotiation. Both parties deprecated war, but one of them would make war rather than let the nation survive, and the other would accept war rather than let it perish, and the war came.

One-eighth of the whole population were colored slaves, not distributed generally over the Union, but localized in the Southern part of it. These slaves constituted a peculiar and powerful interest. All knew that this interest was somehow the cause of the war. To strengthen, perpetuate and extend this interest, was the object for which the insurgents would rend the Union by war, while the Government claimed no right to do more than to restrict the territorial enlargement of it.

Neither party expected for the war the magnitude and the duration which it has already attained. Neither anticipated that the cause of the conflict might cease, or even before the conflict itself should cease. Each looked for an easier triumph, and a result less fundamental and astounding.

Both read the same Bible and pray to the same God, and each invokes His aid against the other. It may seem strange that any men should dare to ask a just God's assistance in wringing their bread from the sweat of other men's faces, but let us judge not, that we be not judged. The prayers of both should [*sic*; Lincoln said "could"—eds.] not be answered. That of neither has been answered fully. The Almighty has his own purposes. Woe unto the world because of offences, for it must needs be that offences come, but woe to that man by whom the offence cometh. If we shall suppose that American slavery is one of these offences, which in the Providence of God must needs come, but which having continued through His appointed time, He now wills to remove, and that He gives to both North and South this terrible war as the woe due to those by whom the offence came. Shall we discern there is any departure from those Divine attributes which the believers in a living God always ascribe to him? Fondly do we hope, fervently do we pray, that this mighty scourge of war may speedily pass away. Yet, if God wills that it continue until all the wealth piled by the bondsman's two hundred and fifty years of unrequited toil shall be sunk, and until every drop of blood drawn with the lash shall be paid by another drawn with the sword, as was said three thousand years ago; so, still it must be said, that the judgments of the Lord are true and righteous altogether.

With malice toward none, with charity for all, with firmness in the right, as God gives us to see right, let us [strive on to] finish the work we are in, to bind up the nation's wounds, to care for him who shall have borne the battle and for his widow and his orphans, to do all which may achieve and cherish a just and a lasting peace among ourselves and with all nations.

Lincoln Inspects Richmond

Richmond, the Confederate capital, fell on April 3, 1865. The very next day, ignoring the personal danger such a visit posed, Lincoln set off by boat from Union headquarters at City Point in Virginia to inspect the city's smoldering ruins. Accompanied only by his young son Tad, a small unit of sailors, Adm. David Dixon Porter, and one White House guard, Lincoln stepped off a rowboat on the Richmond shoreline, and walked unannounced into the city.

No conqueror entered a captured city with less pomp and circumstance.

Within minutes, an elderly newly freed slave stepped forward to squint at the tall stranger in the black stovepipe hat. "Bless the Lord! There is the great Messiah!" he shouted. "Glory, Hallelujah." While white citizens peered at the scene from behind drawn curtain, a crowd of African-Americans quickly surrounded the president, weeping, shouting and cheering. When some dropped to their knees, Lincoln, now in tears himself, insisted: "Don't kneel to me. You must kneel to God only."

Lincoln eventually made his way to the Confederate "White House," abandoned only a few days earlier by Jefferson Davis and the remnants of the rebel government. There, he sat in Davis's old chair and asked only for a glass of water. Later, he toured the city and visited the state house designed by Thomas Jefferson. He found the floors littered with Confederate currency, and evidently picked up a worthless note or two as souvenirs. When doctors recovered his wallet after his murder ten days later, they found some of the notes still there.

—H. H.

GRANT—LEE

Progress of the Rout of Lee's Army.

Another Brilliant Victory.

Desperate and Sanguinary Battle Near Burkesville.

Sheridan Attacks the Enemy and Routs Them.

Capture of Six Rebel Generals.

Generals Ewell, Custis Lee, Corse, Kershaw, Button, and De Barre Taken Prisoners.

Large Captures of Prisoners, Guns, Wagons and Munitions.

Lee's Army Broken Up.

Sheridan Still Pressing on with Cavalry and Infantry.

Full Details of the Victory.

Official Reports from President Lincoln, Secretary Stanton, Gens. Grant, Sheridan, Wright and Humphreys.

[...]

Hon. Secretary of War:

At 11:15 P.M. yesterday, at Burkesville Station, Gen. GRANT sends me the following from Gen. SHERIDAN.

A. LINCOLN.

DISPATCH FROM GEN. SHERIDAN.

THURSDAY, APRIL 6. — 11:15 P.M.

Lieut.-Gen Grant:

I have the honor to report that the enemy made a stand at the intersection of the Burkes Station Road with the road upon which they were retreating.

I attacked them with two divisions of the Sixth Army Corps, and routed them handsomely, making a connection with the cavalry. I am still pressing on with the cavalry and infantry. Up to the present time we have captured Gens. EWELL, KERSHAW, BUTTON, CORSE, DEBARE and CURTIS LEE, several thousand prisoners fourteen pieces of artillery, with caissons, and a large number of wagons. If the thing is pressed I think Lee will surrender.

P.H. SHERIDAN, Major-Gen. Comd'ing.

FROM RICHMOND.

Visit of President Lincoln to Richmond—His Interview with Prominent Citizens—Immense Enthusiasm of the Colored Population—The City Perfectly Tranquil—Navigation on the James Again Resumed.

From Our Own Correspondent.

HEADQUARTERS, ARMY OF THE JAMES.
RICHMOND, TUESDAY, APRIL 4, 1865.

The most interesting fact to be recorded to-day is the visit of the President to Richmond.

Mr. LINCOLN, accompanied by his young son and Admiral PORTER, arrived at the Rockette at 2 P.M., in the *Malvern,* and proceeded at once to the mansion of Ex-President DAVIS, now the headquarters of Maj.-Gen. WEITZEL.

The arrival of the President soon got noised abroad, and the colored population turned out in great force, and for a time blockaded the quarters of the President, cheering vociferously.

It was to be expected, that a population that three days since were in slavery, should evince a strong desire to look upon the man whose edict had struck forever the manacles from their limbs. A considerable number of the white population cheered the President heartily, and but for the order of the Provost-marshal, issued yesterday, ordering them to remain within their homes quietly for a few days, without doubt there would have been a large addition to the number present. After a short interval the President held a levee—Gen. DEVINS introducing all the officers present. The President shook hands with each, and received the hearty congratulations of all.

The Presidential, party attended by Gens. WEITZEL, DEVINS, SHEPLEY, and a brilliant staff of officers, then made a tour round the city—drove rapidly round the capitol—stopping for a few moments to admire CRAWFORD's magnificent statue of Washington, in the grounds of the capitol, and returned to Gen. WEITZEL's headquarters at 5:30.

The President and party left Richmond at 6:30 P.M.

Admiral FARRAGUT arrived here this morning on a flying visit, and returned to City Point this evening down the "James."

It is very satisfactory to be able to state that the torpedoes have been removed, and that six of our gunboats are at the present time lying off the "Rocketts."

The destruction of property by the fire, yesterday, is enormous, and must amount to tens of millions of dollars. The dense volumes of smoke, and the intense heat, rendered it impossible to form an adequate idea of the extent of the property destroyed yesterday. The entire business portion of the city is a heap of smouldering ruins, and nothing but the absence of wind saved the entire city from destruction. There is but one feeling of unmitigated disgust expressed by the residents at this barbarous outrage.

It is positively asserted that Gen. BRECKINRIDGE gave the order that the tobacco and the government workshops should be set fire to, and the close proximity of other valuable property rendered its escape from destruction almost impossible.

The greater portion of the tobacco destroyed is said to have belonged to France and England.

A regular mail communication between this and City Point will be established to-morrow, under the superintendence of Lieut. PARKER, who has been stationed at City Point for some time in the same capacity. Lieut. PARKER has taken possession of the old post-office, which is well adapted for the purpose. . . .

The publication of the *Whig* newspaper is resumed, under the management of one of its proprietors, who has always been opposed to secession. I inclose the first copy issued of the reformed journal, which states the circumstances under which its publication is permitted to be resumed.

It is asserted that two or three of the most prominent citizens sought and obtained an interview with Mr. LINCOLN during his short stay here. I have been requested not to mention their names.

Many startling rumors are afloat respecting the rebel army, but they cannot be traced to a reliable source. It is reported that JEFF. DAVIS and Gen. R. E. LEE were both captured this morning, but as the President had received no confirmation of the fact of its being so, it is scarcely probable that it is true.

It is believed that Gen. LEE's army is divided—one part on either side of the Appomattox, and that Gen. GRANT will be able to prevent their again uniting.

It is gratifying to state that the city is perfectly tranquil, and that the general behavior of our troops is all that could be desired, and has elicited the admiration of the citizens generally.

R. D. FRANCIS.

Surrender at Appomattox

"If the thing is pressed I think Lee will surrender," Lincoln wired General Grant on April 7. "Let the thing be pressed." Though victory seemed inevitable, Lincoln was anxious. The commander-in-chief hoped to be on the scene himself when the fighting stopped. But after spending much of April at the front in Virginia as Grant's forces squeezed the last vestiges of strength from the Confederate army, Lincoln and his family reluctantly headed back to Washington by steamer on the eighth. By the time they arrived the following evening, General Lee had already surrendered to General Grant.

The "thing" had been pressed, but Lincoln had missed the historic climax.

The president found the capital thronged with celebrants. Church bells rang and bonfires illuminated the streets. That night, he briefly greeted exuberant crowds who called for him at the White House.

The following morning, despite rain and chill, well-wishers paraded to the presidential mansion, standing in the mud as bands played, cannons fired and supporters shouted themselves hoarse until Lincoln appeared at an upstairs window. "I am very greatly rejoiced to find that an occasion has occurred so pleasurable that the people cannot restrain themselves," the haggard but smiling Lincoln declared to more cheers. He was contemplating a major speech for the following night—on Reconstruction—at which he would raise the delicate issue of voting rights for blacks and he begged the crowd to excuse him until then. But the onlookers were in no mood to disperse.

As always, Lincoln found a way. "I have always thought 'Dixie' one of the best tunes I have ever heard," he said. "Our adversaries over the way attempted to appropriate it, but I insisted yesterday that we fairly captured it" as "our lawful prize." To waves of laughter and applause, he concluded: "I now request the band to favor me with its performance."

Right on cue, one of the marching bands on the lawn struck up the Confederate anthem, and then quickly followed it with a performance of "Yankee Doodle Dandy." They were the last songs Abraham Lincoln heard until the orchestra at Ford's Theatre played "Hail to the Chief" in his honor on the night he was killed, four days later.

—H. H.

UNION

Victory!

Peace!

Surrender of General Lee and His Whole Army.

The Work of Palm Sunday.

Final Triumph of the Army of the Potomac.

The Strategy and Diplomacy of Lieut.-Gen. Grant.

Terms and Conditions of the Surrender.

The Rebel Arms, Artillery, and Public Property Surrendered.

Rebel Officers Retain Their Side Arms, and Private Property.

**Officers and Men Paroled and Allowed to
Return to Their Homes.**

The Correspondence Between Grant and Lee.

OFFICIAL.

WAR DEPARTMENT, WASHINGTON,
APRIL 9, 1865 — 9 O'CLOCK P.M.

To Maj.-Gen. Dix:

This department has received the official report of the SURRENDER, THIS DAY OF GEN. LEE AND HIS ARMY TO LIEUT.-GEN. GRANT, on terms proposed by Gen. GRANT.

Details will be given as speedily as possible.

EDWIN M. STANTON,
Secretary of War.

HEADQUARTERS ARMIES OF THE UNITED STATES,
4:30 P.M., APRIL 9.

Hon. Edwin M. Stanton, Secretary of War:

GEN. LEE SURRENDERED THE ARMY OF NORTHERN VIRGINIA THIS AFTERNOON, upon terms proposed by myself. The accompanying additional correspondence will show the conditions fully.

(Signed)
U. S. GRANT, Lieut.-Gen'l.

SUNDAY, APRIL 9, 1865.

GENERAL—I received your note of this morning, on the picket line, wither I had come to meet you and ascertain definitely what terms were embraced in your proposition of yesterday with reference to the surrender of this army.

I now request an interview in accordance with the offer contained in your letter of yesterday for that purpose.

Very respectfully, your obedient servant,
R. E. LEE, General.

To Lieut.-Gen. GRANT, Commanding United States Armies.

Gen. R. E. Lee, Commanding Confederate States Armies.

Your note of this date is but this moment, 11:50 A.M., received.

In consequence of my having passed from the Richmond and Lynchburgh road to the Farmville and Lynchburgh road, I am at this writing about four miles West of Walter's church, and will push forward to the front for the purpose of meeting you.

Notices sent to me, on this road, where you wish the interview to take place, will meet me.

Very respectfully, your ob'd't servant,

U. S. GRANT

Lieutenant-General.

APPOMATTOX COURT-HOUSE, APRIL 9, 1865.

General R. E. Lee, Commanding C. S. A.:

In accordance with the substance of my letters to you on the 8th inst., I propose to receive the surrender of the Army of Northern Virginia on the following terms, to wit:

Rolls of all the officers and men to be made in duplicate, one copy to be given to an officer designated by me, the other to be retained by such officers as you may designate.

The officers to give their individual paroles not to take arms against the Government of the United States until properly exchanged, and each company or regimental commander sign a like parole for the men of their commands.

The arms, artillery and public property to be packed and stacked and turned over to the officers appointed by me to receive them.

This will not embrace the side-arms of the officers, nor their private horses or baggage. This done, EACH OFFICER AND MAN WILL BE ALLOWED TO RETURN TO THEIR HOMES, not to be disturbed by United States authority so long as they observe their parole and the laws in force where they reside.

Very respectfully,

U. S. GRANT, Lieutenant-General.

HEADQUARTERS ARMY OF NORTHERN VIRGINIA,

APRIL 9, 1865.

Lieut.-Gen. U. S. Grant, Commanding U. S. A.:

GENERAL—I have received your letter of this date, CONTAINING THE TERMS OF SURRENDER OF THE ARMY OF NORTHERN VIRGINIA, as proposed by you; As they are substantially the same as those expressed in your letter of the 8th inst., THEY ARE ACCEPTED. I will proceed to designate the proper officers to carry the stipulations into effect.

Very respectfully,

Your obedient servant,

R. E. LEE, General.

THE PRELIMINARY CORRESPONDENCE.

The following is the previous correspondence between Lieut.-Gen. GRANT and Gen. LEE, referred to in the foregoing telegram to the Secretary of War.

CLIFTON HOUSE, VA., APRIL 9, 1865.

Hon. Edwin M. Stanton, Secretary of War:

The following correspondence has taken place between Gen. LEE and myself. *There has been no relaxation in the pursuit during its pendency.*

U. S. GRANT, Lieutenant-General.

APRIL 7, 1865.

General R. E. Lee, Commanding C. S. A.:

GENERAL: The result of the last week must convince you of the hopelessness of further resistance on the part of the Army of Northern Virginia in this struggle. I feel that it is so and regard it as my duty to shift from myself the responsibility of any further effusion of blood, by asking of you the surrender of that portion of the Confederate State Army, known as the Army of Northern Virginia.

Very Respectfully,

Your obedient servant,

U. S. GRANT,

Lieutenant-General,

Commanding Armies of the United States.

APRIL 7, 1865.

General: I have received your note of this date.

Though not entirely of the opinion you express of the hopelessness of further resistance on the part of the army of Northern Virginia, I reciprocate your desire to avoid useless effusion of blood, and therefore, before considering your proposition, *ask the terms you will offer, on condition of its surrender.*

R. E. LEE, General.

To Lieut.-Gen. U. S. GRANT, Commanding Armies of the United States.

APRIL 8, 1865.

To Gen. R. E. Lee, Commanding C. S. A.:

GENERAL—Your note of last evening in reply to mine of same date, asking the conditions on which I will accept the surrender of the Army of Northern Virginia, is just received.

In reply, I would say that *peace being my first desire, there is but one condition that I insist upon,* viz.:

That the men surrendered shall be disqualified for taking up arms again against the Government of the United States until properly exchanged.

I will meet you, or designate officers to meet any officers you may name, for the same purpose, at any point agreeable to you, for the purpose of arranging definitely the terms upon which the surrender of the Army of Northern Virginia will be received.

Very respectfully, your obedient servant,

U. S. GRANT, Lieut.-General,

Commanding armies of the United States.

APRIL 8, 1865.

GENERAL: I received, at a late hour, your note of to-day, in answer to mine of yesterday.

I did not intend to propose the surrender of the Army of Northern Virginia, but *to ask the terms* of your proposition. To be frank, I do not think the emergency has arisen to call for the surrender.

But as *the restoration of peace should be the sole object of all,* I desire to know whether your proposals would tend to that end.

I cannot, therefore, meet you with a view to surrender the Army of Northern Virginia, but *as far as your proposition may affect the Confederate States forces under my command, and tend to the restoration of peace,* I should be pleased to meet you at 10 A.M., to-morrow, on the old stage road to Richmond, between the picket lines of the two armies.

Very respectfully, your obedient servant,

R. E. LEE,

General, C. S. A.

To Lieut.-Gen. GRANT, Commanding Armies of the United States.

APRIL 9, 1865.

General R. E. Lee, Commanding C. S. A.:

GENERAL: Your note of yesterday is received. As I have no authority to treat on the subject of peace, the meeting proposed for 10 A.M. to-day could lead to no good. I will state, however, General, that *I am equally anxious for peace with yourself;* and the whole North entertain the same feeling. *The terms upon which peace can be had are well understood. By the South laying down their arms, they will hasten that most desirable event, save thousands of human lives, and hundreds of millions of property not yet destroyed.*

Sincerely hoping that all our difficulties may be settled *without the loss of another life,* I subscribe myself,

Very respectfully,

Your obedient servant,

U. S. GRANT,

Lieutenant-General United States Army.

Assassin Marks His Man

Abraham Lincoln had spoken from the upstairs windows of the White House many times with impromptu, often innocuous remarks. The day after the band played "Dixie" he returned to the window but with a serious, lengthy, carefully written policy statement on Reconstruction. "We meet this evening, not in sorrow," Lincoln began, "but in gladness of heart." A "righteous and speedy peace" seemed imminent, for which the president praised Grant and his army. Then he turned his attention to the restoration of the Union.

The historian Don E. Fehrenbacher wrote that the address reflected Lincoln's intention to go "to work again after having finished one heavy task." It was, Fehrenbacher argued, "a voice interrupted in the middle of a sentence," which is perhaps why the anti-Republican New York World *thought Lincoln groped in his address "like a traveler in an unknown country without a map."*

That night, however, Lincoln became the first president to publicly discuss giving the right to vote to African Americans—if only, in the beginning, to war veterans and the "very intelligent." One person in the crowd who heard the momentous proposal was a Maryland-born former matinee idol named John Wilkes Booth. "That means nigger citizenship," he whispered to his fellow conspirator in the assassination plot, Lewis Powell. "Now, by God, I will put him through it. That will be the last speech he will ever make."

—H. H.

235

THE NEW ERA.

Important Speech by the President

His Views on Peace and Reconstruction.

The Policy of the Administration.

The Proper Relations Between the Several States to be Restored.

The New State Government of Louisiana.

Why it Should Not be Interfered With.

The Question of the Status of the Seceded States Not to be Raised.

A New Proclamation to the South Foreshadowed.

WASHINGTON, TUESDAY, APRIL 11.

The executive departments, including the President's mansion, are again illuminated to-night and adorned with transparencies and national flags, as were also many places of business and private dwellings. Bonfires blazed in many parts of the city and rockets were fired. Thousands of persons of both sexes repaired to the Executive mansion, and after several airs had been played by the band, the President, in response to the numerous calls, appeared at an upper window. The cheering with which he was greeted having ceased, he spoke as follows:

THE PRESIDENT'S SPEECH

We meet this evening not in sorrow, but in gladness of heart. The evacuation of Petersburgh and Richmond, and the surrender of the principal insurgent army, give hopes of a righteous and speedy peace, whose joyous expression cannot be restrained. In the midst of this, however, He from whom all blessings flow must not be forgotten. A call for a national thanksgiving is being prepared, and will be duly promulgated. Nor must those whose harder part gives us the cause of rejoicing be overlooked. Their honors must not be parceled out with others. I myself was near the front, and had the high pleasure of transmitting much of the good news to you. But no part of the honor for plan and execution is mine. To Gen. GRANT, his skillful officers and brave men, all belongs. The gallant navy stood ready, but was not in reach to take active part. By these recent successes the reinauguration of the national authority—reconstruction, which has had a large share of thought from the first—is pressed much more closely upon our attention. It is fraught with great difficulty. Unlike a war between independent nations, there is no authorized organ for us to treat with. No one man has the authority to give up the rebellion for any other man. We must simply begin with and mould from disorganized and discordant elements. Nor is it a small additional embarrassment that we, the loyal people, differ among ourselves as to the mode, manner and measure of reconstruction. As a general rule, I abstain from reading to reports of attacks upon myself, wishing not to be provoked by that to which I cannot properly offer an answer. In spite of this precaution, however, it comes to my knowledge that I am much censured for some supposed agency in setting up and seeking to sustain the new State Government of Louisiana. In this I have done just so much and no more than the public knows. In the annual message of December, 1863, and the accompanying proclamation, I presented a plan of reconstruction, as the phrase goes, which I promised, if adopted by any State, would be acceptable to and sustained by the Executive Government of the nation. I distinctly stated that this was not the only plan which might, possibly, be acceptable; and I also distinctly protested that the Executive claimed no right to say when or whether members should be admitted to seats in Congress from such States. This plan was in advance submitted to the then cabinet, and approved by every member of it. One of them suggested that I should then and in that connection apply the Emancipation Proclamation to the theretofore excepted parts of Virginia and Louisiana, that I should drop the suggestion about apprenticeship for freed people, and that I should omit the protest against my own power in regard to the admission of members of Congress. But even he approved every part and parcel of the plan which has since been employed or touched by the action of Louisiana. The new constitution of Louisiana, declaring emancipation for the whole State, practically applies the proclamation to the part previously excepted. It does not adopt apprenticeship for freed people, and is silent, as it could not well be otherwise, about the admission of members to Congress. So that as it applied to Louisiana every member of the Cabinet fully approved the plan. The message went to Congress, and I received many commendations of this plan, written and verbal, and not a single objection to it, from any professed emancipationist came to my knowledge until after the news reached Washington that the people of Louisiana had begun to move in accordance with it. From about July, 1862, I had corresponded with different persons supposed to be interested in seeking a reconstruction of a State government for Louisiana. When the message of 1863, with the plan before mentioned, reached New-Orleans, Gen. BANKS wrote me that he was confident that the people, with his military cooperation, would reconstruct substantially on that plan. I wrote to him and some of them to try it. They tried it, and the result is known. Such has been my only agency in getting up the Louisiana government. As to sustain it, my promise is out, as before stated. But as bad promises are better broken than kept, I shall treat this as a bad promise and break it whenever I shall be convinced that keeping it is adverse to the public interest, but I have not yet been so convinced.

I have been shown a letter on this subject, supposed to be an able one, in which the writer expresses regret that my mind has not seemed to be definitely fixed on the question, whether the seceded States, so called, are in the Union or out of it. It would, perhaps, add astonishment to his regret were he to learn that since I have found professed Union men endeavoring to answer that question I have purposely forborne any public expression upon it. As appears to me, that question has not been, nor yet is a practically material one, and that any discussion of it while it thus remains practically immaterial, could have no effect other than the mischievous one of dividing our friends. As yet, whatever it may become, that question is bad as the basis of a controversy, and good for nothing at all—a merely pernicious abstraction. We all agree that the seceded States, so called, are out of their proper practical relation with the Union, and that the sole object of the government, civil and military, in regard to those States, is to again get them into their proper practical relation. I believe that it is not only possible, but, in fact, easier, to do this without deciding, or even considering, whether those States have ever been out of the Union, than with it. Finding themselves safely at home, it would be utterly immaterial whether they had been abroad. Let us all join in doing the acts necessary to restore the proper practical relations between those States and the nation, and each forever after innocently indulge his own opinion whether in doing the acts he brought the States from without into the Union, or only gave them proper assistance, they never having been out of it. The amount of constituency, so to speak, on which the Louisiana Government rests, would be more satisfactory to all if it contained 50,000, or 30,000, or even 20,000, instead of 12,000, as it does. It is also unsatisfactory to some that the elective franchise is not given to the colored man. I would myself prefer that it were now conferred on the very intelligent, and on those who serve our cause as soldiers. Still the question is not whether the Louisiana government, as it stands, is quite all that is desirable. The question is, will it be wiser to take it as it is, and help to improve it, or to reject and disperse? Can Louisiana be brought into proper practical relation with the Union sooner by sustaining or by discarding her new State government? Some twelve thousand voters in the heretofore slave State of Louisiana have sworn allegiance to the Union, assumed to be the rightful political power of the State, held elections, organized a State government, adopted a Free State constitution, giving the benefit of public schools equally to black and white, and empowering the Legislature to confer the elective franchise upon the colored man. This Legislature has already voted to ratify the constitutional amendment recently passed by Congress, abolishing slavery throughout the nation. These twelve thousand persons are thus fully committed to the Union and to perpetuate freedom in the State; committed to the very things, and nearly all things, the nation wants, and they ask the nation's recognition and its assistance to make good this committal. Now if we reject and spurn them we do our utmost to disorganize and disperse them. We in fact say to the white man, you are worthless or worse; we will neither help you, nor be helped by you. To the blacks, we say: This cup of liberty which these, your old masters, held to your lips, we will dash from you, and leave you to the chances of gathering the spilled and scattered contents in some vague and undefined when, where and how. If this course, discouraging and paralizing both white and black, have any tendency to bring Louisiana into proper practical relations with the Union, I have so far been unable to perceive it. If, on the contrary, we recognize and sustain the new government of Louisiana, the converse of all this is made true. We encourage the hearts and nerve of the arms of 12,000 to adhere to their work, and argue for it, and proselyte for it, and fight for it, and feed it, and grow it and ripen it to a complete success. The colored man, too, in seeing all united for him, is inspired with vigilance, and energy, and daring to the same end. Grant that he desires the elective franchise, will he not attain it sooner by saving the already advanced steps toward it, than by running backward over them? Concede that the new government of Louisiana is to what it should be as the egg is to the fowl, we shall sooner have the fowl by hatching the egg, than by smashing it. [Laughter.] Again, if we reject Louisiana we also reject one vote in favor of the proposed amendment to the national constitution. To meet this proposition it has been argued that no more than three-fourths of those States which have not attempted secession are necessary to validly ratify the amendment. I do not commit myself against this further than to say that such a ratification would be questionable, and sure to be persistently questioned, while a ratification by three-fourths of all the States would be unquestioned and unquestionable. I repeat the question. Can Louisiana be brought into proper practical relation with the Union sooner by sustaining, or by discarding her new State Government? What has been said of Louisiana will apply to other States. And yet so great peculiarities pertain to each State, and such important and sudden changes occur in the same State, and withal so new and unprecedented is the whole case, that no exclusive and inflexible plan can safely be prescribed as to details and collaterals. Such exclusive and inflexible plan would surely be come a *new* entanglement. Important principles may and must be inflexible. In the present situation, as the phrase goes, *it may be my duty to make some new announcement to the people of the South.* I am considering and shall not fail to act when satisfied that action will be proper.

The President, during the delivery of the above speech, was frequently interrupted by applause, and on its conclusion, in the midst of the cheering, the band struck up a patriotic air, when he bowed and retired.

Ford's Theatre, April 14, 1865

The extent of the conspiracy is still the subject of vigorous debate among historians. Did it reach all the way to Jefferson Davis and the Confederate secret service? Or was it the vengeful act of a racist Southern sympathizer, frustrated that the war ended before he could execute an elaborate plot to kidnap and ransom Lincoln for Confederate prisoners of war?

All that is known for sure is that John Wilkes Booth pulled the trigger that ended Abraham Lincoln's life at approximately 10:13 P.M. on Good Friday, April 14, 1865, as Lincoln, his wife and their young guests, Henry Rathbone and Clara Harris, sat in the presidential box at Ford's Theatre on Tenth Street watching the British stage comedy "Our American Cousin."

Lincoln was carried gingerly across the street to a boarding house, where he died at 7:22 the following morning. He never regained consciousness. No American president had ever been assassinated before and newspapers raced to print accounts of the great tragedy with breathtaking speed. By morning, before the president even took his last breath, special editions appeared on the streets throughout the country announcing the "awful event."

In the days that followed, The New York Times *and other major dailies marked the event with pages and pages of articles that carried heavy black column rules, signaling unprecedented national mourning. The comprehensive coverage examined every detail of Lincoln's death struggle, the attack on Secretary of State William H. Seward and the escape and pursuit of Booth and his fellow conspirators. The all-consuming national tragedy not only elevated Abraham Lincoln to the status of exalted martyr, it also tested the nation's press.*

"I cannot bring myself to believe that any human being lives who would do me any harm," Lincoln had insisted only nine days before his murder. But on the way to his country house near Washington a bullet had once knocked the hat off his head. It was never determined who pulled the trigger or why.

—H. H.

AWFUL EVENT.

President Lincoln Shot by an Assassin.

The Deed Done at Ford's Theatre Last Night.

The Act of a Desperate Rebel.

The President Still Alive at Last Accounts.

No Hopes Entertained of His Recovery.

Attempted Assassination of Secretary Seward.

Details of the Dreadful Tragedy.

[OFFICIAL.]

WAR DEPARTMENT,
WASHINGTON, APRIL 15 — 1:30 A.M.

Maj.-Gen. Dix:

This evening at about 9:30 P.M., at Ford's Theatre, the President, while sitting in his private box with Mrs. LINCOLN, Mrs. HARRIS, and Major RATHBURN, was shot by an assassin, who suddenly entered the box and approached behind the President.

The assassin then leaped upon the stage, brandishing a large dagger or knife, and made his escape in the rear of the theatre.

The pistol ball entered the back of the President's head and penetrated nearly through the head. The wound is mortal. The President has been insensible ever since it was inflicted, and is now dying.

About the same hour an assassin, whether the same or not, entered Mr.

SEWARD'S apartments, and under the pretence of having a prescription, was shown to the Secretary's sick chamber. The assassin immediately rushed to the bed, and inflicted two or three stabs on the throat and two on the face. It is hoped the wounds may not be mortal. My apprehension is that they will prove fatal.

The nurse alarmed Mr. FREDERICK SEWARD, who was in an adjoining room, and hastened to the door of his father's room, when he met the assassin, who inflicted upon him one or more dangerous wounds. The recovery of Frederick SEWARD is doubtful.

It is not probable that the President will live throughout the night.

Gen. GRANT and wife were advertised to be at the theatre this evening, but he started to Burlington at 6 o'clock this evening.

At a Cabinet meeting at which Gen. GRANT was present, the subject of the state of the country and the prospect of a speedy peace was discussed. The President was very cheerful and hopeful, and spoke very kindly of Gen. LEE and others of the Confederacy, and of the establishment of government in Virginia.

All the members of the Cabinet except Mr. SEWARD, are now in attendance upon the President.

I have seen Mr. SEWARD, but he and FREDERICK were both unconscious.

EDWIN M. STANTON,
SECRETARY OF WAR.

Detail of the Occurence.

WASHINGTON, FRIDAY, APRIL 14 — 12:30 A.M.

The President was shot in a theatre to-night, and is, perhaps, mortally wounded. Secretary SEWARD was also assassinated.

SECOND DISPATCH.

WASHINGTON, FRIDAY, APRIL 14.

President LINCOLN and wife, with other friends, this evening visited Ford's Theatre for the purpose of witnessing the performance of "American Cousin."

It was announced in the papers that Gen. GRANT would also be present, but he took the late train of cars for New-Jersey.

The theatre was densely crowded, and everybody seemed delighted with the scene before them. During the third act, and while there was a temporary pause for one of the actors to enter, a sharp report of a pistol was heard, which merely attracted attention, but suggesting nothing serious, until a man rushed to the front of the President's box, waving a long dagger in his right hand, and exclaiming *"Sic semper tyrannis,"* and immediately leaped from the box, which was in the second tier, to the stage beneath, and ran across to the opposite side, making his escape amid the bewilderment of the audience from the rear of the theatre, and, mounting a horse, fled.

The screams of Mrs. LINCOLN first disclosed the fact to the audience that the President had been shot, when all present rose to their feet, rushing toward the stage, many exclaiming "Hang him! Hang him!"

The excitement was of the wildest possible description, and of course there was an abrupt termination of the theatrical performance.

There was a rush toward the President's box, when cries were heard: "Stand back and give him air." "Has any one stimulants." On a hasty examination, it was found that the President had been shot through the head, above and back of the temporal bone, and that some of the brain was oozing out. He was removed to a private house opposite to the theatre, and the Surgeon-General of the army, and other surgeons sent for to attend to his condition.

On an examination of the private box blood was discovered on the back of the cushioned rocking chair on which the President had been sitting, also on the partition and on the floor. A common single-barreled pocket pistol was found on the carpet.

A military guard was placed in front of the private residence to which the President had been conveyed. An immense crowd was in front of it, all deeply anxious to learn the condition of the President. It had been previously announced that the wound was mortal; but all hoped otherwise. The shock to the community was terrible.

The President was in a state of syncope, totally insensible, and breathing slowly. The blood oozed from the wound at the back of his head. The surgeons exhausted every effort of medical skill, but all hope was gone. The parting of his family with the dying President is too sad for description.

At midnight, the Cabinet, with Messrs. SUMNER, COLFAX and FARNSWORTH, Judge CURTIS, Gov. OGLESBY, Gen. MEIGS, Col. HAY, and a few personal friends, with Surgeon-General BARNES and his immediate assistants, were around his bedside.

The President and Mrs. LINCOLN did not start for the theatre until fifteen minutes after eight o'clock. Speaker COLFAX was at the White House at the time, and the President stated to him that he was going, although Mrs. LINCOLN had not been well, because the papers had announced that Gen. GRANT and they were to be present, and, as Gen. GRANT had gone North, he did not wish the audience to be disappointed.

He went with apparent reluctance and urged Mr. COLFAX to go with him; but that gentleman had made other engagements, and with Mr. ASH-MAN, of Massachusetts, bid him good bye.

When the excitement at the theatre was at its wildest height, reports were circulated that Secretary SEWARD had also been assassinated.

On reaching this gentleman's residence a crowd and a military guard were found at the door, and on entering it was ascertained that the reports were based on truth.

Everybody there was so excited that scarcely an intelligible word could be gathered, but the facts are substantially as follows:

About 10 o'clock a man rang the bell, and the call having been answered by a colored servant, he said he had come from Dr. VERDI, Secretary SEWARD's family physician, with a prescription, at the same time holding in his hand a small piece of folded paper, and saying in answer to a refusal that he must see the Secretary, as he was entrusted with particular directions concerning the medicine.

He still insisted on going up, although repeatedly informed that no one could enter the chamber. The man pushed the servant aside, and walked heavily toward the Secretary's room, and was then met by Mr. FREDERICK SEWARD, of whom he demanded to see the Secretary, making the same representation which he did to the servant. What further passed in the way of colloquy is not known, but the man struck him on the head with a "billy," severely injuring the skull and felling him almost senseless. The assassin then rushed into the chamber and attacked Major SEWARD, Paymaster of the United States army and Mr. HANSELL, a messenger of the State Department and two male nurses, disabling them all, he then rushed upon the Secretary, who was lying in bed in the same room, and inflicted three stabs in the neck, but severing, it is thought and hoped, no arteries, though he bled profusely.

The assassin then rushed down stairs, mounted his horse at the door, and rode off before an alarm could be sounded, and in the same manner as the assassin of the President.

It is believed that the injuries of the Secretary are not fatal, nor those of either of the others, although both the Secretary and the Assistant Secretary are very seriously injured.

Secretaries STANTON and WELLES, and other prominent officers of the government, called at Secretary SEWARD's house to inquire into his condition, and there heard of the assassination of the President.

They then proceeded to the house where he was lying, exhibiting of course intense anxiety and solicitude. An immense crowd was gathered in front of the President's house, and a strong guard was also stationed there, many persons evidently supposing he would be brought to his home.

The entire city to-night presents a scene of wild excitement, accompanied by violent expressions of indignation, and the profoundest sorrow—many shed tears. The military authorities have dispatched mounted patrols in every direction, in order, if possible, to arrest the assassins. The whole metropolitan police are likewise vigilant for the same purpose.

The attacks both at the theatre and at Secretary SEWARD's house, took place at about the same hour—10 o'clock—thus showing a preconcerted plan to assassinate those gentlemen. Some evidence of the guilt of the party who attacked the President are in the possession of the police.

Vice-President JOHNSON is in the city, and his headquarters are guarded by troops.

Another Account.

Special Dispatch to the New-York Times.

WASHINGTON, FRIDAY, APRIL 14.
11:15 P.M.

A stroke from Heaven laying the whole of the city in instant ruins could not have startled us as did the word that broke from Ford's Theatre a half hour ago that the President had been shot. It flew everywhere in five minutes, and set five thousand people in swift and excited motion on the instant.

It is impossible to get at the full facts of the case, but it appears that a young man entered the President's box from the theatre, during the last act of the play of "Our American Cousin," with pistol in hand. He shot the President in the head and instantly jumped from the box upon the stage, and immediately disappeared through the side scenes and rear of the theatre, brandishing a dirk knife and dropping a kid glove on the stage.

The audience heard the shot, but supposing it fired in the regular course of the play, did not heed it till Mrs. LINCOLN's screams drew their attention. The whole affair occupied scarcely half a minute, and then the assassin was gone. As yet he has not been found.

The President's wound is reported mortal. He was at once taken into the house opposite the theatre.

As if this horror was not enough, almost the same moment the story ran through the city that Mr. SEWARD had been murdered in his bed.

Inquiry showed this to be so far true also. It appears a man wearing a light coat, dark pants, slouch hat, called and asked to see Mr. SEWARD, and was shown to his room. He delivered to Major SEWARD, who sat near his father, what purported to be a physician's prescription, turned, and with one stroke cut Mr. SEWARD's throat as he lay on his bed, inflicting a horrible wound, but not severing the jugular vein, and not producing a mortal wound.

In the struggle that followed, Major SEWARD was also badly, but not seriously, wounded in several places. The assassin rushed down stairs, mounted the fleet horse on which he came, drove his spurs into him, and dashed away before any one could stop him.

Reports have prevailed that an attempt was also made on the life of Mr. STANTON.

MIDNIGHT.

The President is reported dead. Cavalry and infantry are scouring the city in every direction for the murderous assassins, and the city is over-whelmed with excitement. Who the assassins were no one knows, though every body supposes them to have been rebels.

SATURDAY MORNING — 1 O'CLOCK.

The person who shot the President is represented as about 30 years of age, five feet nine inches in height, sparely built, of light complexion, dressed in dark clothing, and having a genteel appearance. He entered the box, which is known as the State box, being the upper box on the right hand side from the dress-circle in the regular manner, and shot the President from behind, the ball entering the skull about in the middle, behind, and going in the direction of the left eye; it did not pass through, but apparently broken the frontal bone and forced out the brain to some extent. The President is not yet dead, but is wholly insensible, and the Surgeon-General says he cannot live till day-break. The assassin was followed across the stage by a gentleman, who sprang out from an orchestra chair. He rushed through the side door into an alley, thence to the avenue and mounted a dark bay horse, which he apparently received from the hand of an accomplice, dashed up F, toward the back part of the city. The escape was so sudden that he effectually eluded pursuit. The assassin cried *"sic sempre"* in a sharp, clear voice, as he jumped to the stage, and dropped his hat and a glove.

Two or three officers were in the box with the President and Mrs. LINCOLN, who made efforts to stop the assassin, but were unsuccess-ful, and received some bruises. The whole affair, from his entrance into the box to his escape from the theatre, occupied scarcely a minute, and the strongest of the action found everybody wholly unprepared. The assault upon Mr. SEWARD appears to have been made almost at the same moment as that upon the President. Mr. SEWARD's wound is not dangerous in itself, but may prove so in connection with his recent in-juries. The two assassins have both endeavored to leave the city to the northwest, apparently not expecting to strike the river. Even so low down as Chain Bridge, cavalry have been sent in every direction to in-tercept them.

The President still lies insensible. Messrs. STANTON, WELLS, MCCUL-LOCH, SPEED and USHER are with him, as also the Vice-President, the Surgeon-General, and other Surgeons.

There is a great throng about the house, even at this hour.

2 O'CLOCK A.M.

The President still lives, but lies insensible, as he has since the first moment, and no hopes are entertained that he can survive.

The most extravagant stories prevail, among which one is to effect, that Gen. GRANT was shot while on his way to Philadelphia, of course this is not true.

Another is, that every member of Mr. SEWARD's family was wounded in the struggle with the assassin there. This also is untrue. Mr. FRED. SEWARD, the Assistant Secretary, and Major CLARENCE SEWARD, of the army, were wounded, neither of them dangerously.

The Condition of the President.

WASHINGTON, APRIL 15—2:12 A.M.

The President is still alive; but he is growing weaker. The ball is lodged in his brain, three inches from where it entered the skull. He remains insensible, and his condition is utterly hopeless.

The Vice-President has been to see him; but all company, except the members of the Cabinet and of the family, is rigidly excluded.

Large crowds still continue in the street, as near to the house as the line of guards allows.

"Our Great Loss"

Easter Sunday, 1865—"Black Easter," as it became known—found public buildings and private homes throughout the North draped in bunting and crape, the official "habiliments of woe." Engravings and lithographs of the murdered president appeared in shop windows from Broadway in New York to Pennsylvania Avenue in Washington, and in loyal cities across the country. At churches and synagogues—April 16 also was the Jewish holiday of Passover—ministers and rabbis alike preached sermons comparing Lincoln to Jesus or Moses, sacrificing his life for his people, dying before he could reach the "promised land."

247

"Our Great Loss," as The New York Times *described it in thick black headlines the following morning, cloaked an entire nation in unprecedented grief, even as readers breathlessly followed the frantic search for the missing assassin, John Wilkes Booth, and the "brief" but "impressive" inauguration of Lincoln's successor, Andrew Johnson.*

Reporting the fast-breaking events as well as the deep need for analysis and reflection, the newspaper devoted three full black-ruled pages to the calamity; a gripping report on Lincoln's last moments alive, details on multicity funeral plans, reactions from Albany and local pulpits, and both a reprinted text and generous appraisal of what The Times *called "the last address of the president to the country"—his stirring inaugural—in fact his penultimate speech.*

For those who noticed, the paper also carried reminders that Lee's surrender and Lincoln's death notwithstanding, the war was not yet fully over; the rumor that the Confederate Gen. Joseph E. Johnston's stubborn army had surrendered in North Carolina had been proven false. And in Richmond, the occupied former rebel capital, 3,000 captured Union soldiers languished in the notorious Libby Prison.

Lincoln had called for "forgiveness and good will," The Times *reminded its readers. That spirit would be severely tested in the days to come.*

—H. H.

OUR GREAT LOSS.

Death of President Lincoln.

The Songs of Victory Drowned in Sorrow.

Closing Scenes of a Noble Life.

The Great Sorrow of an Afflicted Nation.

Party Differences Forgotten in Public Grief.

Vice-President Johnson Inaugurated as Chief Executive.

Mr. Seward will Recover.

John Wilkes Booth Believed to be the Assassin.

Manifestations of the People Throughout the Country.

OFFICIAL DISPATCHES.

WAR DEPARTMENT, WASHINGTON,
APRIL 15—4:10 A.M.

To Maj.-Gen. Dix:

The President continues insensible and is sinking.

Secretary SEWARD remains without change

FREDERICK SEWARD'S skull is fractured in two places, besides a severe cut upon his head.

The attendant is still alive, but hopeless. Maj. SEWARD'S wound is not dangerous.

It is now ascertained with reasonable certainty that two assassins were engaged in the horrible crime, WILKES BOOTH being the one that shot the President, and the other companion of his whose name is not known, but whose description is so clear that he can hardly escape. It appears from a letter found in BOOTH'S trunk that the murder was planned before the 4th of March, but fell through then because the accomplice backed out until "Richmond could be heard from." BOOTH and his accomplice were at the livery stable at six o'clock last evening, and left there with their horses about ten o'clock, or shortly before that hour.

It would seem that they had for several days been seeking their chance, but for some unknown reason it was not carried into effect until last night.

One of them has evidently made his way to Baltimore—the other has not yet been traced.

EDWIN M. STANTON,
Secretary of War.

WAR DEPARTMENT, WASHINGTON, APRIL 15.

Major-Gen. Dix:

ABRAHAM LINCOLN died this morning at twenty-two minutes after seven o'clock.

EDWIN M. STANTON,
Secretary of War.

WAR DEPARTMENT,
WASHINGTON, APRIL 15—3 P.M.

Maj.-Gen. Dix, New-York:

Official notice of the death of the late President, ABRAHAM LINCOLN, was given by the heads of departments this morning to ANDREW JOHNSON, Vice-President, upon whom the constitution devolved the office of

President. Mr. JOHNSON, upon receiving this notice, appeared before the Hon. SALMON P. CHASE, Chief Justice of the United States, and took the oath of office, as President of the United States, assumed its duties and functions. At 12 o'clock the President met the heads of departments in cabinet meeting, at the Treasury Building, and among other business the following was transacted:

First—The arrangements for the funeral of the late President were referred to the several Secretaries, as far as relates to their respective departments.

Second—WILLIAM HUNTER, Esq., was appointed Acting Secretary of State during the disability of Mr. SEWARD, and his son, FREDERICK SEWARD, the Assistant Secretary.

Third—The President formally announced that he desired to retain the present Secretaries of departments of his Cabinet, and they would go on and discharge their respective duties in the same manner as before the deplorable event that had changed the head of the government.

All business in the departments was suspended during the day.

The surgeons report that the condition of Mr. SEWARD remains unchanged. He is doing well.

No improvement in Mr. FREDERICK SEWARD.

The murderers have not yet been apprehended.

—EDWIN M. STANTON,
Secretary of War.

THE ASSASSINATION.

Additional Details of the Lamentable Event.

WASHINGTON, SATURDAY, APRIL 15.

The assassin of President LINCOLN left behind him his hat and a spur.

The hat was picked up in the President's box and has been identified by parties to whom it has been shown as the one belonging to the suspected man, and accurately described as the one belonging to the suspected man by other parties, not allowed to see it before describing it.

The spur was dropped upon the stage, and that also has been identified as the one procured at a stable where the same man hired a horse in the evening.

Two gentlemen who went to the Secretary of War to apprize him of the attack on Mr. LINCOLN met at the residence of the former a man muffled in a cloak, who, when accosted by them, hastened away.

It had been Mr. STANTON's intention to accompany Mr. LINCOLN to the theatre, and occupy the same box, but the press of business prevented.

It therefore seems evident that the aim of the plotters was to paralyze the country by at once striking down the head, the heart and the arm of the country.

As soon as the dreadful events were announced in the streets, Superintendent RICHARDS, and his assistants, were at work to discover the assassin.

In a few moments the telegraph had aroused the whole police force of the city.

Maj. WALLACH and several members of the City Government were soon on the spot and every precaution was taken to preserve order and quiet in the city.

Every street in Washington was patrolled at the request of Mr. RICHARDS.

Gen. AUGUR sent horses to mount the police.

Every road leading out of Washington was strongly picketed, and every possible avenue of escape was thoroughly guarded.

Steamboats about to depart down the Potomac were stopped.

The Daily *Chronicle* says:

"As it is suspected that this conspiracy originated in Maryland, the telegraph flashed the mournful news to Baltimore and all the cavalry was immediately put on active duty. Every road was picketed and every precaution taken to prevent the escape of the assassin. A preliminary examination was made by Messrs. RICHARDS and his assistants. Several persons were called to testify and the evidence as elicited before an informal tribunal, and not under oath, was conclusive to this point. The murderer of President LINCOLN was JOHN WILKES BOOTH. His hat was found in the private box, and identified by several persons who had seen him within the last two days, and the spur which he dropped by accident, after he jumped to the stage, was identified as one of those which he had obtained from the stable where he hired his horse.

This man BOOTH has played more than once at Ford's Theatre, and is, of course, acquainted with its exits and entrances, and the facility with which he escaped behind the scenes is well understood.

The person who assassinated Secretary SEWARD left behind him a slouched hat and an old rusty navy revolver. The chambers were broken loose from the barrel, as if done by striking. The loads were drawn from the chambers, one being but a rough piece of lead, and the other balls smaller than the chambers, wrapped in paper, as if to keep them from falling out.

CLOSING SCENES.

Particulars of His Last Moments—Record of His Condition Before Death—His Death.

WASHINGTON, SATURDAY, APRIL 15 — 11 O'CLOCK A.M.

The *Star* extra says:

"At 7:20 o'clock the President breathed his last, closing his eyes as if falling to sleep, and his countenance assuming an expression of perfect serenity. There were no indications of pain, and it was not known that he was dead until the gradually decreasing respiration ceased altogether.

Rev. Dr. GURLEY, of the New-York-avenue Presbyterian Church, immediately on its being ascertained that life was extinct, knelt at the bedside and offered an impressive prayer, which was responded to by all present.

Dr. GURLEY then proceeded to the front parlor, where Mrs. LINCOLN, Capt. ROBERT LINCOLN, Mrs. JOHN HAY, the Private Secretary, and others, were waiting, where he again offered a prayer for the consolation of the family.

The following minutes, taken by Dr. ABBOTT, show the condition of the late President throughout the night:

11 o'clock—Pulse 44.

11:05 o'clock—Pulse 45, and growing weaker.

11:10 o'clock—Pulse 45.

11:15 o'clock—Pulse 42.

11:20 o'clock—Pulse 45; respiration 27 to 29.

11:25 o'clock—Pulse 42.

11:32 o'clock—Pulse 48, and full.

11:40 o'clock—Pulse 45.

11:45 o'clock—Pulse 45; respiration 22.

12 o'clock—Pulse 48; respiration 22.

12:15 o'clock—Pulse 48; respiration 21—echmos both eyes

12:30 o'clock—Pulse 45.

12:32 o'clock—Pulse 60.

12:35 o'clock—Pulse 66.

12:40 o'clock—Pulse 69; right eye much swollen, and echmos.

12:45 o'clock—Pulse 70.

12:55 o'clock—Pulse 80; struggling motion of arms.

1 o'clock—Pulse 86; respiration 30.

1:30 o'clock—Pulse 95; appearing easier.

1:45 o'clock—Pulse 86—very quiet, respiration irregular.

Mrs. LINCOLN present.

2:10 o'clock—Mrs. LINCOLN retired with ROBERT LINCOLN to an adjoining room.

2:30 o'clock—President very quiet—pulse 54—respiration 28.

2:52 o'clock—Pulse 48—respiration 30.

3 o'clock—Visited again by Mrs. LINCOLN.

3:25 o'clock—Respiration 24 and regular.

3:35 o'clock—Prayer by Rev. Dr. GURLEY.

4 o'clock—Respiration 26 and regular.

4:15 o'clock—Pulse 60—respiration 25.

5:50 o'clock—Respiration 28—regular—sleeping.

6 o'clock—Pulse falling—respiration 28.

6:30 o'clock—Still falling and labored breathing.

7 o'clock—Symptoms of immediate dissolution.

7:22 o'clock—Death.

Surrounding the death-bed of the President were Secretaries Stanton, Welles, Usher, Attorney-General Speed, Postmaster-General Dennison, M. B. Field, Assistant Secretary of the Treasury; Judge Otto, Assistant Secretary of the Interior; Gen. Halleck, Gen. Meigs, Senator Sumner, R. F. Andrews, of New-York; Gen. Todd, of Dacotah; John Hay, Private Secretary; Gov. Oglesby, of Illinois; Gen. Farnsworth, Mrs. and Miss Kenney, Miss Harris, Capt. Robert Lincoln, son of the President, and Doctors E. W. Abbott, B. K. Stone, C. D. Gatch, Neal Hall, and Mr. Lieberman. Secretary McCulloch remained with the President until about 5 o'clock, and Chief-Justice Chase, after several hours' attendance during the night, returned early this morning.

Immediately after the President's death a Cabinet meeting was called by Secretary STANTON, and held in the room in which the corpse lay. Secretaries STANTON, WELLES and USHER, Postmaster-General DENNISON, and Attorney-General SPEED, were present. The results of the conference are as yet unknown.

Removal of the Remains to the Executive Mansion— Feeling in the City.

WASHINGTON, SATURDAY, APRIL 15.

The President's body was removed from the private residence opposite Ford's Theatre to the executive mansion this morning at 9:30

o'clock, in a hearse, and wrapped in the American flag. It was escorted by a small guard of cavalry, Gen. AUGUR and other military officers following on foot.

A dense crowd accompanied the remains to the White House, where a military guard excluded the crowd, allowing none but persons of the household and personal friends of the deceased to enter the premises, Senator YATES and Representative FARNSWORTH being among the number admitted.

The body is being embalmed, with a view to its removal to Illinois.

Flags over the department and throughout the city are at half-mast. Scarcely any business is being transacted anywhere either on private or public account.

Our citizens, without any preconcert whatever, are draping their premises with festoons of mourning.

The bells are tolling mournfully. All is the deepest gloom and sadness. Strong men weep in the streets. The grief is wide-spread and deep and in strange contrast to the joy so lately manifested over our recent military victories.

This is indeed a day of gloom.

Reports prevail that Mr. FREDERICK W. SEWARD, who was kindly assisting the nursing of Secretary SEWARD, received a stab in the back. His shoulder blade prevented the knife or dagger from penetrating into his body. The prospects are that he will recover.

A report is circulated, repeated by almost everybody, that BOOTH was captured fifteen miles this side of Baltimore. If it be true, as asserted, that the War Department has received such information, it will doubtless be officially promulgated.

The government departments are closed by order, and will be draped with the usual emblems of mourning.

The roads leading to and from the city are guarded by the military, and the utmost circumspection is observed as to all attempting to enter or leave the city.

AUTOPSY UPON THE BODY OF ABRAHAM LINCOLN.

WASHINGTON, SATURDAY, APRIL 15.

As autopsy was held this afternoon over the body of President LINCOLN by Surgeon-General BARNES and Dr. STONE, assisted by other eminent medical men.

The coffin is of mahogany, is covered with black cloth, and lined with lead, the latter also being covered white satin.

A silver plate upon the coffin over the breast bears the following inscription:

ABRAHAM LINCOLN.
SIXTEENTH PRESIDENT OF THE UNITED STATES.
Born July 12, 1809.*
Died April 15, 1865.

The remains have been embalmed.

A few locks of hair were removed from the Presiden's head for the family previous to the remains being placed in the coffin.

THE ASSASSINS.

Circumstances Tending to Inculpate G. H. Booth—Description of his Confederate in the Crime.

WASHINGTON, SATURDAY, APRIL 15.

There is no confirmation of the report that the murderer of the President has been arrested.

Among the circumstances tending to fix a participation in the crime on BOOTH, were letters found in his trunk, one of which, apparently from a lady, supplicated him to desist from the perilous undertaking in which he was about to embark, as the time was inauspicious, the mine not yet being ready to be sprung.

The *Extra Intelligencer* says: "From the evidence obtained it is rendered highly probable that the man who stabbed Mr. SEWARD and his sons, is JOHN SURRATT, of Prince George County, Maryland. The horse he rode was hired at NAYLOR's stable, on Fourteenth-street. SURRATT is a young man, with light hair and goatee. His father is said to have been postmaster of Prince George County."

About 11 o'clock last night two men crossed the Anacostia Bridge, one of whom gave his name as BOOTH, and the other as SMITH. The latter is believed to be JOHN SURRATT.

Last night a riderless horse was found, which has been identified by the proprietor of one of the stables previously mentioned as having been hired from his establishment.

255

*This date was given in error. Lincoln's actual birth date was February 12.—eds.

Accounts are conflicting as to whether BOOTH crossed the bridge on horseback or on foot; but as it is believed that he rode across it, it is presumed that he had exchanged his horse.

From information in the possession of the authorities it is evident that the scope of the plot was intended to be much more comprehensive.

The Vice-President and other prominent members of the Administration were particularly inquired for by suspected parties, and their precise localities accurately obtained; but providentially, in their cases, the scheme miscarried.

A boat was at once sent down the Potomac to notify the gunboats on the river of the awful crime, in order that all possible means should be taken for the arrest of the perpetrators.

The most ample precautions have been taken, and it is not believed the culprits will long succeed in evading the overtaking arm of justice.

The second extra of the *Evening Star* says:

"Col. INGRAHAM, Provost-Marshal of the defences north of the Potomac, is engaged, in taking testimony to-day, all of which fixes the assassination upon J. WILKES BOOTH.

Judge OLIN, of the Supreme Court of the District of Columbia, and Justice MILLER, are also engaged to-day, at the Police Headquarters, on Tenth-street, in taking the testimony of a large number of witnesses.

Lieut. TYRELL, of Col. INGRAHAM's staff, last night proceeded to the National Hotel, where BOOTH had been stopping, and took possession of his trunk, in which was found a Colonel's military dress-coat, two pairs of handcuffs, two boxes of cartridges and a package of letters, all of which are now in the possession of the military authorities.

One of these letters, bearing the date of Hookstown, Md., seems to implicate BOOTH. The writer speaks of "the mysterious affair in which you are engaged," and urges BOOTH to proceed to Richmond, and ascertain the views of the authorities there upon the subject. The writer of the letter endeavors to persuade BOOTH from carrying his designs into execution at that time, for the reason, as the writer alleges, that the government had its suspicions aroused. The writer of the letter seems to have been implicated with Booth in "the mysterious affair" referred to, as he informs BOOTH in the letter that he would prefer to express his views verbally; and then goes on to say that he was out of money, had no clothes, and would be compelled to leave home, as his family were desirous that he should dissolve his connection with BOOTH. This letter is written on note paper, in a small neat hand, and simply bears the signature of "Sam."

At the Cabinet meeting yesterday, which lasted over two hours, the future policy of the government toward Virginia was discussed, the best feeling prevailed. It is stated that it was, determined to adopt a very liberal policy, as was recommended by the President. It is said that this meeting was the most harmonious held for over two years, the President exhibiting throughout that magnanimity and kindness of heart which has ever characterized his treatment of the rebellious States, and which has been so [word illegible] requited on their part.

One of the members of the Cabinet remarked to a friend he met at the door, that "The government was to-day stronger than it had been for three years past."

WASHINGTON, SATURDAY, APRIL 15—3:30 P.M.

To-day no one is allowed to leave the city by rail conveyance, or on foot, and the issuing of passes from the Headquarters of the Department of Washington has been suspended by Gen. AUGER.

Probable Attempt of the Assassins to Escape into Canada— Order from the War Department.

[Circular.]

WAR DEPARTMENT,
PROVOST MARSHAL GENERAL'S BUREAU,
WASHINGTON, D. C.—9:40 A.M., APRIL 15.

It is believed that the assassins of the President and Secretary SEWARD are attempting to escape to Canada. You will make a careful and thorough examination of all persons attempting to cross from the United States into Canada, and will arrest all suspicious persons. The most vigilant scrutiny on your part, and the force at your disposal, is demanded. A description of the parties supposed to be implicated in the murder will be telegraphed you to-day. But in the meantime be active in preventing the crossing of any suspicious persons.

By order of the Secretary of War,

N. L. JEFFERS, Brevet Brig.-Gen.,
Acting Provost-Marshal General.

THE SUCCESSION.

Mr. Johnson Inaugurated as President.

The Oath Administered by Secretary Chase.

He Will Perform His Duties Trusting in God.

WASHINGTON, SATURDAY, APRIL 15 — 12 A.M.

ANDREW JOHNSON was sworn into office as President of the United States by Chief-Justice Chase, to-day, at eleven o'clock.

Secretary MC CULLOUGH and Attorney-General SPEED, and others were present.

He remarked:

"The duties are mine. I will perform them, trusting in God.

SECOND DISPATCH.

WASHINGTON, SATURDAY, APRIL 15.

At an early hour this morning, Hon. EDWIN M. STANTON, Secretary of War, sent an official communication to Hon. ANDREW JOHNSON, Vice-President of the United States, that in consequence of the sudden and unexpected death of the Chief Magistrate, his inauguration should take place as soon as possible, and requesting him to state the place and hour at which the ceremony should be performed.

Mr. JOHNSON immediately replied that it would be agreeable to him to have the proceedings take place at his rooms in the Kirkwood House as soon as the arrangements could be perfected.

Chief Justice CHASE was informed of the fact and repaired to the appointed place in company with Secretary MCCULLOUGH, of the Treasury Department, Attorney-General SPEED, J. P. BLAIR, Sr., Hon. MONTGOMERY BLAIR, Senators FOOT, of Vermont, RAMSAY, of Minnesota, YATES, of Illinois, STEWART, of Nevada, HALE, of New Hampshire, and Gen. FARNSWORTH, of Illinois.

At eleven o'clock the oath of office was administered by the Chief Justice of the United States, in his usual solemn and impressive manner.

Mr. JOHNSON received the kind expressions of the gentlemen by whom he was surrounded in a manner which showed his earnest sense of the great responsibilities so suddenly devolved upon him, and made a brief speech, in which he said:

"The duties of the office are mine. I will perform them. The consequences are with God. Gentlemen, I shall lean upon you. I feel that I shall need your support. I am deeply impressed with the solemnity of the occasion and the responsibility of the duties of the office I am assuming.

Mr. JOHNSON appeared to be in remarkably good health, and has a high and realizing sense of the hopes that are centred upon him. His manner was solemn and dignified, and his whole bearing produced a

most gratifying impression upon those who participated in the ceremonies.

It is probable that during the day President JOHNSON will issue his first
proclamation to the American people.

It is expected, though nothing has been definitely determined upon,
that the funeral of the late President LINCOLN will take place on or about
Thursday next. It is supposed that his remains will be temporarily deposited in the Congressional Cemetery.

OUR GREAT LOSS

The Assassination of President Lincoln.

Details of the Fearful Crime.

Closing Moments and Death of the President.

Probable Recovery of Secretary Seward.

Rumors of the Arrest of the Assassins.

The Funeral of President Lincoln to Take Place Next Wednesday.

Expressions of Deep Sorrow Throughout the Land.

[...]

Last Moments of the President.

Interesting Letter from Maunsell B. Field, Esq.

On Friday evening, April 14, 1865, I was reading the evening paper in
the reading-room of Willard's Hotel, at about 10½ o'clock, when I was
startled by the report that an attempt had been made a few minutes before
to assassinate the President at Ford's Theatre. At first I could scarcely
credit it, but in a few minutes the statement was confirmed by a number of
people who came in separately, all telling the same story. About fifteen
minutes previously I had parted with Mr. MELLER, of the Treasury Department, and he had retired to his room. Immediately on receiving this
intelligence I notified him of it, and we together proceeded to the scene of
the alleged assassination. We found not only considerable crowds on the

streets leading to the theatre, but a very large one in front of the theatre, and of the house directly opposite, where the President had been carried after the attempt upon his life. With some difficulty I obtained ingress to the house. I was at once informed by Miss HARRIS, daughter of Senator HARRIS, that the President was dying, which statement was confirmed by three or four other persons whom I met in the hall; but I was desired not to communicate his condition to Mrs. LINCOLN, who was in the front parlor. I went into this parlor, where I found Mrs. LINCOLN, no other lady being present, except Miss HARRIS, as already mentioned. She at once recognized me, and begged me to run for Dr. STONE, or some other medical man. She was not weeping, but appeared hysterical, and exclaimed in rapid succession, over and over again: "Oh! why didn't he kill me? why didn't he kill me?" I was starting from the house to go for Dr. STONE, when I met at the door, Major ECKERT, of the War Department, who informed me he was going directly to STONE's house, STONE having already been sent for, but not having yet arrived. I then determined to go for Dr. HALL, whose precise residence I did not know. Upon inquiring of the crowd, I was told it was over FRANK TAYLOR's bookstore, on the avenue. This proved to be a mistake, and I was compelled to return to his actual residence on the avenue, above Ninth-street. I found the doctor at home and dressed, and he at once consented to accompany me. Arrived in the neighborhood of the house, I had great difficulty in passing the guard, and only succeeded at last in having the doctor introduced, admission being refused to myself. I returned to Willard's, it now being about 2 o'clock in the morning, and remained there until between 3 and 4 o'clock, when I again went to the house where the President was lying, in company with Mr. ANDREWS, late Surveyor of the port of New-York. I obtained ingress this time without any difficulty, and was enabled to take Mr. ANDREWS in with me. I proceeded at once to the room in which the President was lying, which was a bedroom in an extension, on the first or parlor floor of the house. The room is small, and is ornamented with prints—a very familiar one of LANDSEER's, a white horse, being prominent directly over the bed. The bed was a double one, and I found the President lying diagonally across it, with his head at the outside. The pillows were saturated with blood, and there was considerable blood upon the floor immediately under him. There was a patchwork coverlet thrown over the President, which was only so far removed, from time to time, as to enable the physicians in attendance to feel the arteries of the neck or the heart, and he appeared to have been divested of all clothing. His eyes were closed and injected with blood, both the lids and the portion surrounding the eyes being as black as if they had been bruised by violence. He was breathing regularly, but with effort, and did not seem to be struggling or suffering.

The persons present in the room were the Secretary of War, the Secretary of the Navy, the Postmaster-General, the Attorney-General, the Secretary of the Treasury, (who, however, remained only till about 5 o'clock,) the Secretary of the Interior, the Assistant-Secretary of the Interior, myself, Gen. AUGUR, Gen. HALLECK, Gen. MEIGS, and, during the last moments, Capt. ROBERT LINCOLN and Maj. JOHN HAY. On the foot of the bed sat Dr. STONE; above him, and directly opposite the President's face, an army surgeon, to me a stranger; another army surgeon was standing, frequently holding the pulse, and another gentleman, not in uniform, but whom I understood to be also an army surgeon, stood a good deal of the time leaning over the head-board of the bed.

For several hours the breathing above described continued regularly, and apparently without pain or consciousness. But about 7 o'clock a change occurred, and the breathing, which had been continuous, was interrupted at intervals. These intervals became more frequent and of longer duration, and the breathing more feeble. Several times the interval was so long that we thought him dead, and the surgeon applied his finger to the pulse, evidently to ascertain if such was the fact. But it was not till 22 minutes past 7 o'clock in the morning that the flame flickered out. There was no apparent suffering, no convulsive action, no rattling of the throat, none of the ordinary premonitory symptoms of death. Death in this case was a mere cessation of breathing.

The fact had not been ascertained one minute when Dr. GURLEY offered up a prayer. The few persons in the room were all profoundly affected. The President's eyes after death were not, particularly the right one, entirely closed. I closed them myself with my fingers, and one the surgeons brought pennies and placed them on the eyes, and subsequently substituted for them silver half-dollars. In a very short time the jaw commenced slightly falling, although the body was still warm. I called attention to this, and had it immediately tied up with a pocket handkerchief. The expression immediately after death was purely negative, but in fifteen minutes here came over the mouth, the nostrils, and the chin, a smile that seemed almost an effort of life. I had never seen upon the President's face an expression more genial and pleasing. The body grew cold very gradually, and I left the room before it had entirely stiffened. Curtains had been previously drawn down by the Secretary of War.

Immediately after the decease, a meeting was held of the members of the Cabinet present, in the back parlor, adjacent to the room in which the President died, to which meeting I, of course, was not admitted. About fifteen minutes before the decease, Mrs. LINCOLN came into the room, and threw herself upon her dying husband's body. She was allowed to remain there only a few minutes, when she was removed in a sobbing condition, in which, indeed, she had been during all the time she was present.

After completing his prayer in the chamber of death, Dr. GURLEY went into the front parlor, where Mrs. LINCOLN was, with Mrs. and Miss KINNEY and her son ROBERT, Gen. TODD, of Dacotah, (a cousin of hers,) and Gen. FARNSWORTH, of Illinois. Here another prayer was offered up, during which I remained in the hall. The prayer was continually interrupted by Mrs. LINCOLN's sobs. Soon after its conclusion, I went into the parlor, and found her in a chair, supported by her son ROBERT. Presently her carriage came up, and she was removed to it. She was in a state of tolerable composure at that time, until she reached the door, when, glancing at the theatre opposite, she repeated three or four times: "That dreadful house!—that dreadful house!"

Before I myself left, a guard had been stationed at the door of the room in which the remains of the late President were lying. Mrs. LINCOLN had been communicated with, to ascertain whether she desired the body to be embalmed or not, and the Secretary of War had issued various orders, necessary in consequence of what had occurred.

I left the house about 8:30 o'clock in the morning, and shortly after met Mr. Chief-Justice CHASE, on his way there. He was extremely agitated, as, indeed, I myself had been all through the night. I afterward learned that, at the Cabinet meeting referred to, the Secretary of the Treasury and the Attorney-General were appointed a committee to wait on the Vice-President, which they did, and he was sworn into office early in the morning by the Chief-Justice.

MAUNSELL B. FIELD.

THE GREAT CALAMITY.

WASHINGTON, APRIL 16.

THE CORPSE.

The corpse of the late President has been laid out in the room known as the "guests' room," northwest wing of the White House. It is dressed in the suit of black clothes worn by him at his late Inauguration. A placid smile rests upon his features, and the deceased seems to be in a calm sleep. White flowers have been placed upon the pillow and over the breast.

The corpse of the President will be laid out in state in the east room on Tuesday, in order to give the public an opportunity to see once more the features of him they loved so well. The preparations are being made, to that end, under the supervision of the upholsterer. The catafalque upon which the body will rest is to be placed in the south part of the east room, and is somewhat similar in style to that used on the occasion of the death of President HARRISON. Steps will be placed at the side to enable the public to mount to a position to get a perfect view of the face. The catafalque will be lined with fluted white satin, and on the outside it will be covered with black cloth and black velvet.

THE FUNERAL.

The funeral of President LINCOLN will take place on Wednesday next. Rev. Dr. GURLEY, of the New-York-avenue Presbyterian Church, where the President and his family have been accustomed to worship, will doubtless be the officiating clergyman.

The remains will be temporarily deposited in the vault of the Congressional Cemetery, and hereafter taken to Mr. LINCOLN's home at Springfield, Illinois.

THE FUNERAL CAR.

The funeral car, which is being prepared for the occasion, is to be a magnificent affair. It is to be built on a hearse body. Its extreme length will be fourteen feet. The body of the car will be covered, with black cloth, from which will hang large festoons of clothes on the sides and ends, gathered and fastened by large rosettes of white and black satin over bows of white and black velvet. The bed of the car, on which the coffin will rest, will be eight feet from the ground, in order to give a full view of the coffin; and over this will rise a canopy, the support of which will be draped with black cloth and velvet. The top of the car will be decorated with plumes. The ear will be drawn by six or eight horses, each led by a groom.

BOOTH NOT ARRESTED.

Up to this time it has not been ascertained that the assassin of the President has been captured.

THE PRESIDENT'S PLACE OF WORSHIP.

This morning, at the New-York-avenue Presbyterian Church, which Mr. LINCOLN formerly attended, a large crowd of persons assembled in anticipation that the pastor, Rev. P. D. GURLEY, D. D., would make some allusion to the nation's great calamity. The pulpit and the choir, and the President's pew were draped in mourning.

THE ASSASSINATION A CONSPIRACY.

The Extra *Star* has the following:

"Developments have been made within the past twenty-four hours, showing conclusively the existence of a deep laid plot of a gang of conspirators, including members of the order of the Knights of the Golden Circle, to murder President LINCOLN and his Cabinet. We have reason to believe that Secretary SEWARD received, several months since, an intimation from Europe that something of a very desperate character was to transpire at Washington; and it is more than probable that the intimation had reference to the plot of the assassination.

THE CONSPIRACY.

The pickets encircling this city on Friday night, to prevent the escape of the parties who murdered President LINCOLN and attempted the assassination of Secretary SEWARD and his sons, were fired upon at several points by concealed foes. Arrests of the parties charged with the offence will be promptly made.

It was ascertained some weeks ago, from personal friends of the late President, that he had received several private letters warning him that an attempt would probably be made upon his life. But to this he did not seem to attach much, if any, importance. It has always been thought that he was not sufficiently careful of his individual safety on his last visit to Virginia.

It is known that on frequent occasions he would start from the Executive mansion for his Summer country residence at the Soldier's Home without the cavalry escort, which often hurried and overtook him before he had proceeded far. It has always been understood that this escort was accepted by him only on the importunity of his friends as a matter of precaution.

The President before retiring to bed, would, when important military events were progressing, visit the War Department, generally alone, passing over the dark intervening ground, even at late hours, on repeated occasions; and after the warning letters had been received, several close and intimate friends armed for any emergency were careful that he should not continue his visits without their company. For himself, the President seemed to have no fears.

The above facts have heretofore been known to the writer of this telegram, but for prudential reasons, he has not stated them until now.

THE LAST HOURS OF THE PRESIDENT.

As everything pertaining to the last hours of the late President must be interesting to the public, the following incidents of the last day of his life have been obtained from several sources.

His son, Capt. LINCOLN, breakfasted with him on Friday morning, having just returned from the capitulation of LEE, and the President passed a happy hour listening to all the details. While at breakfast he heard that Speaker COLFAX was in the house, and sent word that he wished to see him immediately in the reception room. He conversed with him nearly an hour about his future policy as to the rebellion, which he was about to submit to the Cabinet. Afterwards he had an interview with Mr. HALE, Minister to Spain, and several Senators and Representatives.

At 11 o'clock the Cabinet and Gen. GRANT met with him, and in one of the most satisfactory and important Cabinet meetings held since his first inauguration, the future policy of the Administration was harmoniously and unanimously agreed on. When he adjourned Secretary STANTON said he felt that the government was stronger than at any previous period since the rebellion commenced.

In the afternoon the President had a long and pleasant interview with Gen. OGLESBY, Senator YATES, and other leading citizens of his State.

In the evening Mr. COLFAX called again, at his request, and Mr. ASHMUN, of Massachusetts, who presided over the Chicago Convention of 1860, was present. To them he spoke of his visit to Richmond; and when they stated that there was much uneasiness at the North while he was at the rebel capital, for fear that some traitor might shoot him, he replied jocularly that he would have been alarmed himself if any other person had been President and gone there, but that he did not feel any danger whatever. Conversing on a matter of business with Mr. ASHMUN, he made a remark that he saw Mr. ASHMUN was surprised at; and immediately with his well-known kindness of heart said, "You did not understand me, ASHMUN, I did not mean what you inferred, and I will take it all back and apologize for it." He afterward gave Mr. ASHMUN a card to admit himself and friend early the next morning, to converse further about it.

Turning to Mr. COLFAX he said: "You are going with Mrs. Lincoln and me to the theatre, I hope." But Mr. COLFAX had other engagements, expecting to leave the city the next morning.

He then said to Mr. COLFAX, "Mr. SUMNER has the gavel of the Confederate Congress, which he got at Richmond, to hand to the Secretary of War. But I insisted then that he must give it to you; and you tell him for me to hand it over." Mr. ASHMUN alluded to the gavel which he still had, and which he had used at the Chicago Convention, and the President and Mrs. LINCOLN, who was also in the parlor, rose to go to the theatre. It was half an hour after the time they had intended to start, and they spoke about waiting half an hour longer, for the President went with reluctance, as Gen. GRANT had gone North, and he did not wish the people to be disappointed, as they had both been advertised to be there. At the door he stopped, and said: "COLFAX, do not forget to tell the people in the mining region as you pass through them, what I told you this morning about the development, when peace comes, and I will telegraph you at San Francisco." He shook hands with both gentlemen with a pleasant good-bye, and left the Executive Mansion, never to return to it alive.

The President and Cabinet, at the meeting, today, intrusted to Assistant Secretary of the Treasury, HARRINGTON, the general arrangement of the programme for the funeral of the late President. Maj. FRENCH, the Commissioner of Public Buildings, will attend to the carrying out of so much of it as directly appertains to the corpse, and Maj.-Gen. AUGUR, in charge of the defences of Washington, will be in charge of the military part of the procession. Assistant Secretary HARRINGTON has been in consultation, to-night, relative to the arrangements, with Gov. OGLESBY, Senator YATES and Ex-Representative ARNOLD, of Illinois, and Gens. GRANT, HALLECK and AUGUR and Admirals FARRAGUT and SHUBRICK.

The funeral ceremonies of the late President will take place on Wednesday. The time for the remains to leave the city, as well as the route by which they will be taken to Springfield, is as yet undetermined. The procession will form at 11 o'clock, and the religious services will commence at noon, at which hour throughout the whole land, the various religious societies have been requested to assemble in their respective places of worship for prayer. The procession will move at 2 P.M. Details will be made known as soon as perfected.

The acting Secretary of State has issued the following address: *To the People of the United States:*

The undersigned is directed to announce that the funeral ceremonies of the lamented Chief Magistrate will take place at the Executive Mansion, in this city, at 12 o'clock noon on Wednesday, the 19th instant.

The various religious denominations throughout the country are invited to meet in their respective places of worship at that hour for the purpose of solemnizing the occasion with appropriate ceremonies.

(Signed)   W. HUNTER,
Acting Secretary of State.

DEPARTMENT OF STATE, WASHINGTON, APRIL 17, 1865.
WASHINGTON, SATURDAY, APRIL 15.

To-day, Surgeon General BARNES, Dr. STONE, the late President's family physician; Drs. CRANE, CURTIS, WOODWARD, TOFT and other eminent medical men, performed an autopsy on the body of the President.

The external appearance of the face was that of a deep black stain about both eyes. Otherwise the face was very natural.

The wound was on the left side of the head behind, on a line with and three inches from the left ear.

The course of the ball was obliquely forward, toward the right eye, crossing the brain obliquely a few inches behind the eye, where the ball lodged.

In the track of the wound were found fragments of bone which had been driven forward by the ball.

The ball was found imbedded in the anterior lobe of the west hemisphere of the brain.

The orbit plates of both eyes were the seat of comminuted fracture, and the orbits of the eyes were filled with extravasated blood.

The serious injury to the orbit plates was due to the centre coup, the result of the intense shock of so large a projectile fired so closely to the head.

The ball was evidently a derringer, hand cast, and from which the neck had been clipped.

A shaving of lead had been removed from the ball in its passage of the bones of the skull, and was found in the orifice of the wound. The first fragment of bone was found two and a half inches within the brain: the second and a larger fragment about four inches from the orifice. The ball lay still further in advance. The wound was half an inch in diameter.

A silver plate upon the coffin over the breast bears the following inscription:

ABRAHAM LINCOLN.   267
SIXTEENTH PRESIDENT OF THE UNITED STATES,
Born July 12, 1809.*
Died April 15, 1865.

*See note on page 255.— eds.

The remains have been embalmed.

A few locks of hair were removed from the Presiden's head for the family previous to the remains being placed in the coffin.

The New President.

Inauguration of Andrew Johnson.

Brief and Impresive Ceremonies.

The Oath of Office Administered on Saturday by Chief-Justice Chase.

President Johnson's Inaugural address.

WASHINGTON, SUNDAY, APRIL 16.

Yesterday morning Attorney-General SPEED waited upon Hon. ANDREW JOHNSON, Vice-President of the United States, and officially informed him of the sudden and unexpected decease of President LINCOLN, and stated that an early hour might be appointed for the inauguration of his successor. The following is a copy of the communication referred to:

WASHINGTON CITY, APRIL 15, 1865

SIR: ABRAHAM LINCOLN, President of the United States, was shot by assassin last evening at Ford's Theatre, in this city, and died at the hour of twenty-two minutes after seven o'clock. About the same time at which the President was shot, an assassin entered the sick chamber of Hon. W. H. SEWARD, Secretary of State, and stabbed him in several places in the throat, neck and face, severely, if not mortally, wounding him. Other members of the Secretary's family were dangerously wounded by the assassin while making his escape.

By the death of President LINCOLN, the office of President has devolved, under the Constitution, upon you. The emergency of the government demands that you should immediately qualify, according to the requirements of the Constitution, and enter upon the duties of the President of the United States. If you will please make known you pleasure, such arrangements as you deem proper will be made.

Your obedient servants,

HUGH McCULLOCH,
Secretary of the Treasury.

EDWIN M. STANTON,
Secretary of War.
GIDEON WELLES,
Secretary of the Navy.
WILIAM DENNISON,
Postmaster-General.
J. P. USHER,
Secretary of the Interior.
JAMES SPEED,
Attorney-General.
To ANDREW JOHNSON, Vice-President of the United States.

Mr. JOHNSON requested that the ceremony take place at his rooms at the Kirkwood House, in this city, at 10 o'clock in the morning.

Hon. SALMON P. CHASE, Chief-Justice of the Supreme Court of the United States, was notified of the fact, and desired to be in attendance to administer the oath of office. . . .

After the presentation of the above letter, the Chief Justice administered the following oath to Mr. JOHNSON:

"I do solemnly swear that I will faithfully execute the office of President of the United States, and will, to the best of my ability, preserve, protect and defend the Constitution of the United States."

After receiving the oath, and, being declared President of the United States, Mr. JOHNSON remarked:

ADDRESS OF PRESIDENT JOHNSON.

"Gentlemen, I must be permitted to say that I have been almost overwhelmed by the announcement of the sad event which has so recently occurred. I feel incompetent to perform duties so important and responsible as those which have been so unexpectedly thrown upon me. As to an indication of any policy which may be presented by me in the administration of the government, I have to say that that must be left for the development as the Administration progresses. The message or declaration must be made by the acts as they transpire. The only assurance that I can now give of the future is by reference to the past. The course which I have taken in the past in connection with this rebellion, must be regarded as a guarantee of the future. My past public life, which has been long and laborious, has been founded as I, in good conscience believe, upon a great principle of right, which lies at the basis of all things. The best energies of my life have been spent in endeavoring to establish and perpetuate the principles of free government, and I believe that the government, in passing through its present trials, will settle down upon principles consonant with popular rights, more permanent and enduring than heretofore. I must be permitted to say, if I understand the feelings of my own heart, I have long labored to ameliorate and alleviate the condition of the great mass of the American people. Toil and an honest advocacy of the great principles of free government have been my lot. The duties have been mine—the consequences are God's. This has been the foundation of my political creed, I feel that in the end the government will triumph, and that these great principles will be permanently established. In conclusion, gentlemen, let me say that I want your encouragement and countenance. I shall ask and rely upon you and others in carrying the government through its present perils. I feel in making this request that it will be heartily responded to by you and all other patriots and lovers of the rights and interests of a free people."

At the conclusion of the above remarks, the President received the kind wishes of the friends by whom he was surrounded.

A few moments were devoted to conversation. All were deeply impressed with the solemnity of the occasion, and the recent sad occurrence that caused the necessity for the speedy inauguration of the President was gravely discussed.

Mr. JOHNSON is in fine health and has an earnest sense of the important trust that has been confided in him.

WM. HUNTER, Esq., the Chief Clerk of the State Department, has been appointed Acting Secretary of State.

A special meeting of the Cabinet was held at the Treasury Department, at 10 o'clock this morning.

NEWS FROM WASHINGTON.

Special Dispatches to the New-York Times.

WASHINGTON, SUNDAY, APRIL 16.

APPROPRIATE RELIGIOUS SERVICES.

Easter Sunday has been, for the most part, a cool, and fair, and sunny, and breezy day; yet the tones of all voices have been low, and the great bereavement has been the subject of all conversation. Dr. GURLEY'S Church, where Mr. LINCOLN attended, was overflowingly full at an early hour. The pulpit, the front of the choir, gallery and the vacant pew were heavily draped in mourning.

The day had been set apart for sacramental purposes, but the Rev. Doctor prefaced the services with some feeling remarks upon the death of Mr.

LINCOLN. He urged the audience to look beyond the hand of the assassin to the hand of the wise God, who overrules all things, and makes even the wrath of man to praise him. He admitted the soreness of this affliction, but doubted not that time would show God's purpose in bringing it upon us.

Most of the churches of the city are draped in mourning, and in each of them was to-day appropriate and touching remembrance of the national sorrow.

A meeting of all clergymen in the city is called at nine o'clock, to-morrow morning, to take such action as becomes a Christian community at this time. Meetings are also called for to-morrow, of a large number of State, social, literary, benevolent and religious organizations, to take action appropriate to the occasion.

THE INVESTIGATION OF THE MURDER.

The city and military authorities have been quietly pursuing investigations since yesterday morning, and persons conversant to some extent with the results thereof, are very confident that the murder of Mr. LINCOLN and the attempted murder of Mr. SEWARD, are only part of the fruits of a carefully planned conspiracy that intended the murder also of other members of the Cabinet, and the destruction of some of the public buildings, and perhaps certain sections of the city. Nothing has yet been brought to light calculated to fix the identity of the assassin of Mr. SEWARD, though various parties have been arrested and examined, and two or three are held for further examination.

RUMORS OF BOOTH'S ARREST.

Rumor has arrested BOOTH a dozen times already, and many persons will retire to-night in the confident belief that he is confined on a gunboat at the Navy-yard, but so far as can be learned from the authorities he not only has not been arrested, but very little is known as to the route he took in escaping. The aggregate reward now offered here for the arrest of these men is thirty thousand dollars.

MRS. LINCOLN.

Mrs. LINCOLN is yet much depressed, though less so than yesterday. She remains at the White House. Hon. MONTGOMERY BLAIR has tendered to her the use of his house till such time as she leaves the city, and President JOHNSON has communicated to her that he expects her to occupy the White House while she remains in Washington.

THE BODY OF MR. LINCOLN.

The body of Mr. LINCOLN, dressed in the plain black suit he wore on inauguration day, is lying in the northwest corner room of the second floor of the White House. The head lies amidst white flowers, and the features wear the calm peaceful expression of deep sleep. The corpse will be laid in state in the east room on Tuesday, and the funeral will be held on Wednesday.

Hundreds of instances of Mr. LINCOLN's personal kindness and graceful courtesy have come to light within the last two days. The *Intelligencer* says his last official act was to sign a permit allowing JACOB THOMPSON, late Secretary of the Interior, to leave the country for Europe.

LIEUT.-GEN. GRANT.

Gen. GRANT is still here and at Willard's. He has been in consultation to-day some time with the President and Cabinet. It is said that as soon as he arrived yesterday he ordered the arrest at Richmond of various prominent late rebels. . . .

INTENSE FEELING OF SORROW.

There is intense feeling in all parts of the city, and any man showing the least disrespect to the memory of the universally lamented dead, is sure to find rough treatment. One of the long-haired wandering preachers, named TOMLINSON, and hailing from Buffalo, while speaking at a soldier's camp, this afternoon, indulged in the remark that if the new President pursued Mr. LINCOLN's policy he would meet Mr. LINCOLN's fate in two weeks. He was immediately set upon by the soldiers, and only escaped severe bodily harm because he was at once arrested. In another case, a crowd of curious persons in front of the Provost-Marshal's office, on Ninety-fourth-street, where were a number of rebel soldiers and parties brought in under arrest, became incensed at the remark of one of them about Mr. LINCOLN, and set upon him in such a manner that his life was only saved by hustling him out of the back door and off to the Old Capitol, while JOHN B. HOLE and Gen. F. E. SPINNER made speeches to the crowd, and urged coolness and obedience to law.

OUR NATIONAL LOSS.

Voice of the Pulpit in New-York and Vicinity.

The Churches Put On the Habiliments of Woe.

Universal Sadness Among the Attendants.

Sketches of Some of the Sermons.

Circular of Archbishop McClosky.

It was a solemn season in the churches yesterday. The usual exultation appropriate for Easter Sunday was postponed to some extent, and everywhere the services partook largely of the popular feeling of the hour. Most of the places of worship were decorated with elaborate emblems of mourning, and not a few displayed the most elaborate resources of art and taste in these silent recognitions of grief. Our reporters have condensed below a few notes, taken in a hasty visit to the churches most accessible at morning worship.

CHURCH OF THE PURITANS.

The interior of the Church of the Puritans was put in mourning by festoons and rosettes of black and white around the pulpit, and two national flags, edged and wreathed with black, were crossed behind the speaker's desk.

Dr. CHEEVER, before the sermon, read Psalm xc. beginning, "Lord, thou hast been our dwelling place in all generations;" and Psalm xlvi., "God is our refuge and strength, a very present help in trouble." His text was Ecclesiasties iii, 14:

"I know that whatsoever God doeth it shall be forever; nothing can be put to it nor anything taken from it; and God doeth it that *men* should tear before him."

We find all our sermons to-day, said the preacher, overtaken by the voice of heaven, speaking in the awful providence of God. Since the time God spoke to the Jews from the fire and the cloud, He has never spoken to any nation as now to us. He has spoken to us in the midst of our rejoicings. The course of God's providences thus far has indicated an intention to complete the redemption of our nation. This crime seems, however, like the thunder of God's wrath. It is the culmination of the rebellion—a final expression and demonstration of the utterly demonic character of the rebellion from the beginning. It is the last spasm of the demon. It is the most remarkable and the most terrible event of centuries. One most noticeable feature of the occurrence is, that God should have caused it to take place close at the end of the week, so that the sermons to-day may the better instruct the nation in the appropriate moral.

Not more than two or three events of a character like this can be remembered in the whole records of history. Such are the assassination of JULIUS CAESAR; of HENRY IV, of France; of WILLIAM, Prince of Orange. This deed, coming at such a time, among victories and surrenders, and the labors of reconstruction, is like a repetition of God's utterance to Job out of the whirlwind:

"Who is this that darkeneth counsel by words without knowledge? Be still and know that I am God."

It is like a supernatural judgment upon the nation for not sufficiently acknowledging God in our national affairs, a direct interposition for punishment. It is, however, a judgment in mercy, to prevent us from our peculiar sins of vanity and pride; already some sinning in this way, had even begun to assert that this nation could now do without God, and some had begun to exhort to the sending out of our armies against other nations to punish them for insulting us. One of the great evils of the present day is pantheistic and atheistic denial of God's personal presence and control of the events of every day. In the midst of prevailing insensibility and folly such as this, God's judgment came forth to teach us his personal presence and overseeing power. Similar cases are those of God's threats against the Nine vices, and those in the fourth chapter of Amos, which, moreover, were made and executed substantially in vain. It is accustoming ourselves to the consciousness of God's constant personal presence and nearness which is the necessary and first preparation for dying in Christian peace. And this is the lesson meant to be taught by the occurrence spoken of to-day. There remains to be mentioned one other personal lesson—God doeth all this that men should fear before him—to bring us to repentance. This is the lesson of death, and the special lesson of the death of the President. It brings strongly before us the overwhelming solemnity of the last hour. Yesterday, Mr. LINCOLN was the ruler of a vast empire, the commander of great armies, recognized with fear and reverence and homage, holding in his hands the destinies of thirty millions of beings; full of health and strength and vigor; to-day, at the touch of the finger of a fiend, he is struck dead. And this takes place in the sight as it were of the whole nation, in the midst of their rejoicings; such circumstances fit the occurrence for an eminently impressive and ethical lesson for each person to seek his own personal salvation. At present, we feel ourselves safe as individuals; but we need to remember that if our nation does not now do justice to the loyal blacks, the present rebellion will soon be followed by another conflict which will enter into all the intricacies of social life, and in which no person will be able to consider himself safe. The speaker ended with a brief repetition of his appeal, to regard, above all, the lesson of personal repentance for sin, and preparation for death, taught by the death of the

President. The discourse was interspersed with many passages from Scripture, and was listened to with the most profound attention.

ALL SOULS CHURCH.

At the services on Sabbath morning at All Souls Church, corner of Fourth-avenue and Twentieth street, Rev. Dr. BELLOWS officiated. Half an hour before the opening services, the beautiful edifice was filled, and shortly after it was crowded with a fashionable but mourning congregation. In the middle aisle, conspicuous above those who surrounded him, was Maj.-Gen BURNSIDE. The altar was almost entirely covered by two American banners, festooned in such a manner that the blue field of stars was exhibited at either end of the pulpit, while they were fastened together by mourning rosettes and black crape tastefully thrown around the whole. Heavy mourning draperies depended from the two galleries, entirely covering the front, fastened together also with rosettes. After the usual opening exercises, Rev. BELLOWS have as his text, John xvi, verse 7:

"Sorrow hath filled your hearts. Nevertheless, I tell you the truth. it is expedient for you that I go away, for if I go not away, the Comforter will not come unto you; but if I depart I will send him unto you."

After eloquently explaining these words that Christ uttered to his disciples, the reverend gentleman added that with hearts almost withered, and brains almost paralyzed by the shock which the nation had sustained, we turn in vain for consolation to any other than the Divine Comforter. Just as we were weaving the laurels of our victories and the chaplets of peace around the emptied sepulchre of our ascended Lord; and when the four years of conflict were fully rounded, and quiet was again visiting this afflicted country, there comes out from the clear heaven the thunderbolt that misses every head but the sacred one we were ready to crown with a nation's blessings, while trusting to its wisdom, its gentleness and faithfulness to close up the country's wounds. Our prudent, firm, humble, reverential, God-fearing President is dead! He was belted round with a nation's devotion, and commanded a million of soldiers. Panoplied in honesty and sincerity of purpose, too well disposed to believe in danger to his person, he has left himself open to the malice and murderous chances of domestic foes. He has gone! ABRAHAM LINCOLN, the wise conductor of our policy through a crisis such as no other people ever had to pass; successful summoner of a million and a quarter of Americans to arms in behalf of their insulted flag and their imperiled Union; author of the Proclamation of Emancipation for four million slaves—the people's President—the heir of WASHINGTON in the homes and prayers of the land—the legitimate idol of the negro race—the perfect type of American democracy—the astute adviser of our Generals in the field—the careful student of their strategy—their personal friend, comforter and inspirer—the head of his Cabinet, prevailing by the passionless simplicity of his integrity and unselfish patriotism over the larger experience and more brilliant gifts, and more vigorous purpose of his constitutional advisers. He shed his blood for his country, and his life and career have held the martyr's palm, added to the statesman's, chief magistrate's and patriot's crown. His name shall go with WASHINGTON's down to the remotest posterity. The sickle-knife of the slaveholder has even assaulted our beloved Secretary of State; the blood-hound had sprung at the throat of him who had defied the [word illegible] to spring at the neck of the slave himself. He who to-day rose from the dead fulfills His blessed promise for "he who believes in Me shall never die; and though he were dead, yet shall he live."

DR. CHAPIN'S CHURCH

Yesterday morning, at an early hour, Dr. Chapin's Church was thronged, and long before divine service commenced numbers had to leave for want of accommodations. On the sad and subdued features of a dense congregation the dim religious light poured through the stained-glass windows, while the emblems of sorrow and mourning fell in waving folds around fretted arch and rising column. The national colors covered the reading-desk, and these in turn were overlaid with crape. The occasion of this solemnity and grief all know. The services were appropriate to this time of a nation's desolation. The jubilant strains in which the Christian Church commemorates Easter Sunday were set aside, and music—vocal and instrumental, well executed—of a character more subdued was performed. Dr. CHAPIN offered an impressive prayer, in which he alluded to the decease of the President, and invoked a blessing on him who has been so unexpectedly called to fill his place. The sermon was on the text

"I am the Resurrection and the Life."

At the conclusion, he alluded in pathetic and deeply-excited tones to the awful tragedy enacted at Washington; characterized in scathing terms the murderous assault, and, amid the applause of his hearers, said that no one North would be found dastard enough, however we act in the open field, to steal behind the back of Mr. DAVIS in an unguarded hour and plunge the knife in his heart. But ABRAHAM LINCOLN would stand forth in history as a great and a good man. There was great excitement in the church, many being moved to tears.

THE CATHOLIC CHURCHES.

At the request of Archbishop MCCLOSKY, the death of the President called forth appropriate and feeling remarks from the pastors of all the Catholic Churches in this city yesterday. At the close of all the high masses which were sung in the various temples of that faith, the sad event was announced, and its peerless atrocity as an act of gigantic wickedness, was represented before the tens of thousands who attended the various services. The clergy also read from their altars the following letter, which was addressed to the clergy:

CIRCULAR OF THE MOST
REV. ARCHBISHOP M'CLOSKY.

REV. DEAR SIR: We hereby request that to-morrow you will announce to our people, in words expressive of our common sorrow, the melancholy tidings which have come so suddenly, amid the first rejoicing of the Easter festival, to shock the heart of the nation, and plunge it into the deepest distress and mourning. A life most precious to all—the life of the honored President of these United States—has been brought to a sad and startling close by the violent hand of an assassin. The life, too, of the Secretary of State, and of his son, have been assailed by a similar act of wickedness, and both are now lying in critical condition.

While bowing down in humble fear and tearful submission to the inscrutable dispensation of Divine Providence, let us all unite in pouring forth our prayers and supplications with renewed earnestness for our beloved country in this mournful and, perilous crisis.

Given in New-York, on the 15th of April, 1865.

† JOHN, Archbishop of New-York.

In St. Joseph's Church, Sixth-avenue, the Rev. Father O'FARRELL, in alluding to the murder of the President, said all his hearers were doubtless aware of the great calamity which had befallen this great nation. Within twenty-four hours, the President of these United States was murdered by the hand of an assassin. The Secretary of State was, while on a sick bed, stabbed almost to death—and the lives of his children were assailed before his eyes. It was a dreadful calamity, and when he alluded to it, he did so in the christian spirit which the sad event demanded. The clergy had been permitted to refer to the subject by the Archbishop of the Diocese, who had requested them to call for prayers for the country from their congregations. Let them, then, beseech God, that this nation—the greatest and noblest on the earth, may be spared from any further calamity, and that it may never be dismembered. The Rev. Father FARRELL, of this church also referred to the subject in fitting terms.

In St. Ann's Church, Eighth-street, the Rev. Dr. PRESTON read the circular of Archbishop McCLOSKEY, and delivered some remarks on the untimely death of Mr. LINCOLN, in which he rebuked the spirit of the assassination and wickedness which prompted the murder, and which if allowed to prevail, would destroy the Republic. He asked the prayers of all his hearers, that God would guide the nation in this hour of its affliction, and that the bright prospects of peace which had been followed by the sad news of assassination of the Chief Magistrate be realized.

In St. Andrew's Church, the pastor, Rev. Father CURRAN, in a feeling address, commented on the murder, and the gross wickedness of the assassin who deprived the Chief Magistrate of his life.

In St. Bridget's, St. Peter's, and St. Francis Xavier's Churches there was also appropriate remarks made on the subject. . . .

THE UNION LEAGUE CLUB.

A special meeting of the club, held on Saturday evening, was very fully attended by the members and included Gens. BURNSIDE, FRANKLIN and PECK, and many other distinguished officers of the army and the navy. The chair was occupied by the President, Mr. CHARLES H. MARSHALL, who briefly referred to the solemn event that had befallen the nation.

Mr. JAY, on the part of the Executive Committee, then read the following resolutions:

Resolved, That in the great calamity which has so suddenly befallen not alone this nation but the world, stricken with awe and overwhelmed with grief we recognize the hand and bow submissively to the will of God, who has taught us by His word and by His providence, as exemplified in this war, that His wisdom is unfathomable and His ways past finding out. In the midst of our sorrow, we humbly thank Him for having preserved the life of ABRAHAM LINCOLN, so early and repeatedly threatened, until he had accomplished the work appointed him and completed the measure of his deathless fame; until he had, as the head of the nation, again "held, occupied and possessed" the seaports which had been wrested from the national control, and the rebel capital, so obstinately defended; and we remember with emotion that his last setting sun shone upon the old flag of Sumter, as it yesterday rose above the ruined fortress where four years since it was humbled by traitors.

2. That the attempted assassination at the same time of the Secretary of

State, while stretched helplessly upon a sick bed and of assistant Secretary SEWARD while attempting to protect his Father, present a series of crimes heretofore unknown, and hardly possible in the darkest ages of the past, whose blackest features are reproduced in the barbarism of rebels, who when their armies conquered in the field in fair combat were being treated magnanimously by a generous people, have resorted to the bullet and the knife, and struck at those chiefs of our government, who in the performance of their official duties, have astonished the world by the gentleness of their tone—their readiness to forgive and their persistent efforts at conciliation.

3. That the blow thus foully struck at the nation should unite loyal citizens of every shade of party, as did the first shot fired at Sumter; and that this new development of the fiendish spirit engendered by a rebellion in the interest of slavery, and of the weapons with which it is waged—starvation of Union prisoners—the attempted burning at night of crowded hotels and theatres—and now these atrocious assassinations—will richly intensify the solemn conviction of the American people that the rebellion, and slavery its cause, must be terminated by the stern arm of the law, without delay, hesitation or compromise, instantly, absolutely and forever. [Prolonged applause.]

3. That in view of the utter failure of the secession movement—of the truth it has developed that State Rights and personal freedom so sacredly guarded by the National Constitution have perished under the assertion of State Sovereignty, which has begotten despotism without a parallel and crimes without a name, there is no shadow of apology left for the slightest sympathy at the North with this expiring and infamous treason.

4. That we call upon our countrymen to rally with fresh determination around the newly-inaugurated President of the United States—himself a Southern man—who knows the value of the Union and the wickedness of the Rebellion, and we reverently invoke for him the favor of Heaven; that sustained, as he will be by a Congress of undoubted loyalty, recently elected by the people, he may have wisdom and strength to keep the solemn oath he has this day taken, and that in seeking to restore peace speedily to our afflicted country he may emulate the virtues of the great statesman whom we deplore, and profit by the lessons taught to the country by the life and by the death of ABRAHAM LINCOLN.

7. That this Club will, in accordance with their own feelings, with the grief of the nation, and with what they trust may be the universal practice, wear the usual badge of mourning for thirty days, and that a committee of thirteen, with the President of the Club, be appointed to represent the association at the funeral services in Washington.

7. That this Club propose, on some early occasion, to appoint one of its members to commemorate in a suitable discourse the Christian character and eminent service of the late President of the United States.

Mr. BANCROFT and Rev. J. P. THOMPSON moved the adoption of the resolution in eloquent and impressive addresses, copies of which were requested for publication. The resolutions were unanimously adopted, and the Club thereupon adjourned.

TAMMANY HALL GENERAL COMMITTEE

The Tammany Hall General Committee held a large meeting last evening, Supervisor TWEED in the Chair, and WM. HITCHMAN Secretary.

On motion of CHAS. G. CORNELL, the reporters were allowed to attend.

Supervisor TWEED said that is was scarcely necessary for him to say that he had called the committee together to take appropriate action in relation to the tragic death of the President. Called away at a time when it appeared that he was the only person who could safely carry the nation through its perils, he had felt it his duty to call together the committee, to express their sympathy with the loss of the nation and the bereaved family of the deceased.

On motion of CHARLES G. CORNELL, a committee of nine was appointed on resolutions. The chair appointed the following gentlemen: Chas. G. Cornell, E. J. Purdy, D. E. Delavan, P. B. Sweeny, Judge Hearne, Judge Wm. Dodge, Wm. Hutchinson and John E. Burrell.

The committee reported the following resolutions which were unanimously adopted:

Whereas, Tammany Hall, profoundly realizing the great calamity which has overtaken the nation in the heartrending death of ABRAHAM LINCOLN, President of the United States, at the hands of an assassin, deem it fitting to place on record their estimate of the character, and service of the illustrious deceased, and their conviction of the duty which this solemn event devolves upon our citizens.

Resolved, That believing ABRAHAM LINCOLN as a ruler to have been governed by patriotic motives, honesty of purpose, and an elevated appreciation of the grave and responsible duties imposed upon him in the greatest crisis of our country's history, commanding in so great a degree the confidence of the loyal people of the nation, and exhibiting in the recent events which had culminated in the downfall of the rebellion, a wise, forbearing and magnanimous statesmanship, the exercise of which gave such promise of a speedy and perfect restoration of the National Union, and the spirit and on the principles upon which it was founded, we cannot but regard his sad and untimely decease as a great misfortune to the nation at this critical period.

Resolved, That Tammany Hall pledges its unwavering support to the Federal Government in this hour of national tribulation and grief, and in the future, as in the past, will deem it a lasting obligation to discharge those duties which are incumbent upon it as the head of the great Democratic party, in such a manner as will best tend to a restoration of the national authority throughout the entire area of our country.

Resolved, That the building of Tammany Hall and the rooms of the committee be draped in mourning, as a testimonial of respect to the memory of the deceased, for the space of thirty days, and that the members of this General Committee will attend the solemnities connected with the obsequies of the deceased under the direction of the city authorities in a body.

The committee then adjourned. . . .

COLORED PEOPLE'S CELEBRATION POSTPONED.

The committee having in charge preparation for a celebration of Union victories by the colored people of this city, have suspended operations, and the jubilee stands indefinitely postponed.

FROM RICHMOND.

Order from Maj.-Gen. Ord to the People of Richmond—The Citizens Resuming their Avocations—The Army of Northern Virginia—Johnston's Army will Probably Disband—Farewell Letter of Gen. Lee.

WASHINGTON, SUNDAY, APRIL 16.

Maj.-Gen. ORD has issued an order addressed to the people of Richmond and its vicinity, that no difficulty will be made in admitting them with market-wares to that city. They are invited to commence their ordinary traffic at once, and assured of protection in passing to and fro within the lines of the United States forces. The citizens of Richmond, and shopkeepers and others, are also requested to resume their ordinary avocations as speedily as possible. It is the wish and intention of the military authorities to protect all good and peaceable citizens and to restore in as great a measure as may be practicable the former prosperity of the city.

No molestation by soldiers or others will be allowed, if possible, to any who are engaged in peaceful pursuits.

Gentlemen who arrived here from Richmond, this morning, say that this order has already had the most happy effect, the citizens being encouraged to resume their avocations with full assurance of protection.

Another order has been issued by Gen. ORD, as follows:

"All officers and soldiers of the Army of Northern Virginia who were not present at the surrender of that army by Gen. ROBERT E. LEE, at Appomattox Court-house, on the 9th of April, 1865, are hereby informed that the terms of capitulation are extended to them, and that they can at once avail themselves of the same by coming within the lines of the United States forces, at or near Richmond, laying down their arms and receiving their paroles."

The gentlemen who communicate the above information say that Gen. LEE did not, after the surrender, repair to North Carolina, but has been remaining at Appomattox Court-house, to carry out the terms of the capitulation. It is supposed that by this time he is in Richmond, Gen. GRANT having extended to him the courtesy of an escort of 100 cavalrymen. The best possible feeling exists between these two Generals.

The people of Virginia are gradually resuming their former business relations, and all regard the war as practically at an end.

Nothing definite has recently been heard in Richmond respecting JOHNSTON'S army, but it is the general impression that it will either be disbanded or melt away by desertion, provided a spirit to conciliate the discordant elements be manifested. A wise policy to win back the people generally as loyal fellow citizens is regarded as of utmost importance in this juncture of our affairs; hence the tone of the Northern press is highly appreciated by all calm and reflecting Southern citizens.

The Richmond *Whig,* of Saturday, says that Col. LOOMIS, Assistant Special Treasury Agent, is expected in that city every day with instructions, and that until he arrives and confers with Gen. GRANT, no captured property, coming under the act of Congress authorizing the Treasury to take charge of it, will be permitted to be removed from its present place of depot.

Libby prison contained yesterday upward of 3,000 Confederate prisoners, military, political and civil; but they are being released as fast as the papers necessary to their conditions of release can be made out. . . .

GEN. LEE'S FAREWELL ADDRESS TO HIS ARMY.

The following is Gen. LEE's farewell address to the army of Northern Virginia:

HEADQUARTERS ARMY NORTHERN VIRGINIA,
APRIL 10, 1865.

GENERAL ORDER, No. 9—After four years of arduous service, marked by unsurpassed courage and fortitude, the Army of Northern Virginia has been compelled to yield to overwhelming numbers and resources. I need not tell the survivors of so many hard-fought battles, who have remained steadfast to the last, that I have consented to this result from no distrust of them, but holding that valor and devotion could accomplish nothing that could compensate for the loss that would have attended the continuation of the contest, I have determined to avoid the useless sacrifice of those whose past vigor has endeared them to their countrymen.

By the terms of agreement, officers and men can return to their homes and remain there until exchanged. You will take with you the satisfaction that proceeds from the consequences of duty faithfully performed, and I earnestly pray that a merciful God will extend you his blessing and protection. With an increasing admiration of your constancy and devotion to your country, and a grateful remembrance of your kind and generous consideration of myself, I bid you an affectionate farewell,

(Signed)   R. E. LEE, General

The Nation's Bereavement.

Death, as the Northmen imagined him, is no dart-brandishing skeleton, but a gigantic shape, that inwraps mortals within the massive folds of its dark garment. Long has it been since those dread robes closed upon a mightier victim than President LINCOLN. It is like the earth's opening and swallowing up a city. The public loss is so great, the chasm made in our national councils so tremendous, that the mind, not knowing how to adjust itself to such a change, shrinks back appalled. It comes home to every bosom with the force of a personal affliction. There is not a loyal family in the land that does not mourn. It is as when there "was a great cry in Egypt, for there was not a house where there was not one dead."

No public man has ever died in America invested with such responsibilities, and the mark of so much attention, as ABRAHAM LINCOLN. The unprecedented manner of his death has shocked inexpressibly; but it is not that which most harrows the anguish. It is the loss of the man himself—the privation of him when he seemed peculiarly necessary to the country, and when the heart of the people was bound to him more than ever. Had he been taken by a natural death, the public grief would have been just as profound, though unaccompanied with the other emotions which his assassination has excited. All true men feel that they have lost a man of wondrous fitness for the task he had to execute. Few Americans have lived who has such a faculty of discovering the real relations of things, and shaping his thoughts and actions strictly upon them without external bias. In his own independent, and perhaps we may say very peculiar way, he invariably got at the needed truths of the time. Without anything like brilliancy of genius, without any great breadth of information or literary accomplishment, he still had that perfect balance of thoroughly sound faculties which gives an almost infallible judgment. This, combined with great calmness of temper, great firmness of purpose, supreme moral principle, and intense patriotism, made up just that character which fitted him, as the same qualities fitted WASHINGTON, for a wise and safe conduct of public affairs in a season of great peril.

Political opponents have sometimes denied that Mr. LINCOLN was a great man. But if he had not great faculties and great qualities, how happens it that he has met the greatest emergencies that ever befell a nation in a manner that so gained for him the confidence of the people? No man ever had greater responsibilities, and yet never were responsibilities discharged with greater acceptance. All disparagement sinks powerless before this one fact, that the more ABRAHAM LINCOLN was tried, the more he was trusted. Nobody can be so foolish as to impute this to the arts and delusions which sometimes give success to the intriguer and demagogue of the hour. It would be the worst insult to the American people to suppose them capable of being so cajoled when the very life of their country was at stake. Nor was it in the nature of Mr. LINCOLN to act a part. He was the least pretentious of men. He never sought to win confidence by any high professions. He never even protested his determination to do his duty. Nor, after he had done his duty, did he go about seeking glory for his exploits, or asking thanks for his presence for the great benefits he had conferred. Sampson-like, he could rend a lion and tell neither father nor mother of it. He was a true hero of the silent sort, who spoke mostly by his actions, and whose action-speech was altogether of the highest kind, and best in its kind. He was not an adventurer, aiming at great things for himself and courting the chances of fortune; nor was he a great artist in any sense, undergoing passions and reflecting them; but he was a great power, fulfilling his way independently of art and passion, and simple, as all great powers are. No thought of self—no concern for his own repute—none of the prudish sensitiveness for his own good name, which is the form selfishness often assumes in able and honorable men, ever seemed to enter his mind. To him it was but the ordinary course of life to do that which has made him illustrious. He had a habit of greatness. An intense, all-comprehensive patriotism, was a constant stimulus of all his public exertions. It grew into the very constitution of his soul, and operated, like a natural function, continuously, spontaneously and almost as it were unconsciously. It pervaded and vivified all that he said, and formed the prime incentive of all that he did. If he had ambition, it was to serve his country, and in that sphere where he might do it most effectually. In no way did he ever fail his country in the time of need. He was independent, self-poised, steadfast. You always knew where to find him; you could calculate him like a planet. A public trust was to him a sacred thing. Sublimer moral courage, more resolute devotion to duty, cannot be found in the history of man than he has displayed for the salvation of the American Union. It was the sublime performance of sublime duties that made him so trusted, and which has given him a fame as solid as justice, and as genuine as truth.

ABRAHAM LINCOLN had a heart full of all gentle and pure affections—a heart not prone to strong passion or tumultuous emotion, but ever glowing with a steady, warm, all-comprehensive sympathy. It was a large, equable, genial, tender heart, none the less delicately strung because its chords were deeply laid. It was a heart that could not retain a single bitter or vindictive feeling. Public life has a tendency to chill the kindly and generous affections, and blight the sweet charities of life; but of President LINCOLN it may be said as was said of Mr. Fox, that his heart was a little hardened as if he had lived and died in a farm-house. No public power, no public care, no public applause could spoil him; he remained ever the same plain man of the people. It was this which peculiarly endeared him to the people, and makes the sorrow for him so tender as a personal feeling, apart from the sense of a national calamity. It is not simply because "he hath been so clear in his great office," but because "he hath borne his faculties so meek"

"that his virtues
Will plead like angles, trumpet-tongued, against
The deep damnation of his taking off."

The Effect of President Lincoln's Death on National Affairs.

The death of President LINCOLN naturally excites universal and profound solicitude as to the immediate future of the country. He has been so marked a figure in the terrible events of the last four years, the action of the government in its contest with the rebellion has been so stamped by the impress of his personal character, and he had come to have so strong a hold upon the confidence and love of the whole people, without distinction of party, that his sudden removal from the stage of events naturally excites anxiety and apprehension in the public mind. He does, indeed, seem to have been needed to close the great work of pacification which he had so well begun.

Nevertheless, it is well to remember that the peculiar nature of our institutions makes it impossible that any one man should be absolutely indispensable to their preservation and successful working. Our government is of the people. They not only elect our rulers, but their spirit, their temper, their will pervade and control all the acts and all the measures of the government.

Whoever dies, the people live, and the government lives also. If the Emperor NAPOLEON had been assassinated, all France would have been in revolution before twenty-four hours had passed away. President LINCOLN's death, sudden and awful as it was—though it removes him in an instant from the most important and conspicuous position held by any living man,—does not interrupt for an instant the grand movement of our republican government. So far from exciting revolution, it only unites the whole people, more thoroughly than ever, in a common sentiment of devotion to the country and of profound grief for the great calamity that has fallen upon it. All party rancor is hushed. Political strife has ceased. All men of all parties, feeling a common interest and a common grief, stand together in support of the nation and of the man thus suddenly charged with the execution of the people's will.

The current of events will continue to dictate the policy of the government, as it has done hitherto. The rebellion is already substantially crushed. The war, to all intents and purposes, is closed. There is nothing in the death of Mr. LINCOLN which can raise new armies for the rebel service or inspire new hopes for the rebel cause. No portion of the Southern people will be stimulated by it to renew the struggle. The same great Generals who have given our flag victory are still at the head of our armies and the act of an assassin has so fired the loyal heart of the nation, that those armies can be doubled in number if necessity should arise. But it will not arise. The blow which has aroused the North will paralyze the South. The rebels will see in it nothing encouraging to their cause, nothing inciting them to new exertions on its behalf.

In President JOHNSON, moreover, the country has a man of courage, of sound judgment and of a patriotism which has stood the test of the most terrible trials. His sympathies are with the people, and all his action will be for their good. He will respond to their sentiments and will execute their will. Nor will he be unmindful of the fact that the general line of policy which ABRAHAM LINCOLN was carrying out, when arrested by the murderer's blow, commanded the hearty and universal approbation of the great mass of the American people. No man ever came suddenly to power with a plainer path before him than that which lies before the new President. And no one need fear for a moment that the rebellion is to gain anything by the death of President LINCOLN or by the accession to power of ANDREW JOHNSON as his successor.

The Last Address of the President to the Country.

Probably all men in all quarters of the world, who read President LINCOLN's last Inaugural Address, were impressed by the evident tone of solemnity in it, and the want of any expression of personal exultation. There he stood, after four years of such trial, and exposed to such hate and obloquy as no other great leader in modern history has experienced, successful, reëlected, his policy approved by the people and by the greater test of events, the terrible rebellion evidently coming to its end, and he himself now certain of his grand position in the eyes of history—and yet not a word escaped him of triumph, or personal glory, or even of much hopefulness. We all expected more confidence—words promising the close of the war and speaking of the end of our difficulties. Many hoped for some definite line of policy to be laid out in this address. But instead, we heard a voice as if from some prophet, looking with solemn gaze down over the centuries, seeing that both sides in the great contest had their errors and sins, that no speedy victory could be looked for, and yet that the great Judge of the world would certainly give success to right and justice. The feeling for the bondmen and the sense of the great wrong done to them, with its inevitable punishment, seemed to rest with such solemn earnestness on his soul, that to the surprise of all and the derision of the flippant, an official speech became clothed in the language of the Bible. The English and French critics all observed this peculiar religious tone of the Inaugural, and nearly all sensible persons felt if not unsuited to the grandeur and momentous character of the events accompanying it. Many pronounced it a Cromwellian speech; but it had one peculiarity, which CROMWELL's speeches never possessed—a tone of perfect kindness and good-will to all, whether enemies or political opponents.

"With charity to all and malice for none," President LINCOLN made his last speech to the world. Men will reperuse that solemn address with ever increasing interest and emotion, as if the shadow of his own tragic fate and the near and unseen dangers to the country, rested unconsciously on its words. It will seem natural that no expression of exultation or personal triumph escaped the great leader of this revolution, but that his mind was filled with the impressive religious lessons of the times. It will be thought characteristic of his sense of justice and his sincere humanity, that his last public address to the country was most of all occupied by the wrongs done to the helpless race, whose friend and emancipator he had been. And it will seem but a part of his wonderful spirit of good-will to all, that not a syllable of bitterness toward the enemies of his country, to the traitors at home, or his personal revilers, passed his lips.

It is such a speech to the world as a Christian statesman would gladly have his last—earnest, humane, truly but no technically religious, filled with forgiveness and good will.

When generations have passed away, and the unhappy wounds of this war are healed, and the whole nation is united on a basis of universal liberty, our posterity will read the dying words of the great Emancipator and leader of the people with new sympathy and reverence, thanking God that so honest and so pure a man, so true a friend of the oppressed, and so genuine a patriot, guided the nation in the time of its trial, and prepared the final triumph which he was never allowed to see. . . .

THE REBELLION.—Every possible atrocity appertains to this rebellion. There is nothing whatever that its leaders have scrupled at. Wholesale massacres and torturings, wholesale starvation of prisoners, firing of great cities, piracies of the cruelest kind, persecution of the most hideous character and of vast extent, and finally assassination in high places— whatever is inhuman, whatever is brutal, whatever is fiendish, these men have resorted to. They will leave behind names so black, and the memory of deeds so infamous, that the execration of the slaveholders' rebellion will be eternal.

PART FIVE

A NATION IN MOURNING
1865–1867

Mind of an Assassin

*F*our days after Booth fired the fatal shot, the assassin remained at large, and federal officials announced a $30,000 reward for his capture.

The "wicked malefactor," as The Times called him, was no better than the "chief of a gang of pimps and gamblers . . . an armed ruffian," whose name should be handed down to "perpetual infamy." Even Booth's final act of bravado—leaping from Ford's Theatre's state box to the stage after shooting the president—was dismissed as "the vulgarest and lowest piece of stage gymnastics that an unattached supernumerary would care to enact at a county fair."

In the wake of such condemnation, little space was devoted in any Northern newspapers to what had motivated the onetime matinee idol to discard his theatrical career and devote the last eleven months of his life in planning to kidnap, then murdering, Abraham Lincoln.

The son and brother of celebrated actors, Maryland-born John Wilkes Booth developed a passionate attachment to the most meretricious cultural myths of the Old South, including the alleged benefits of slavery and the inferiority of the black race. Abandoning the stage in May 1864, he declared, "The South wants justice" and "will wait no longer."

Convinced that Lincoln would soon declare himself king, and make African-Americans the equals of whites, Booth intensified his growing associations with the Confederate secret service and soon organized—or was enlisted to pilot—a scheme to seize Lincoln and hold him for the ransom of rebel prisoners of war. Booth was never able to consummate the unlikely plan.

Once Lee surrendered to Grant, however, Booth decided instead to murder the president, Vice President Andrew Johnson, and Secretary of State William H. Seward, with or without the approval of the defeated Confederate government. In the end, the conspirator assigned to Johnson lost his nerve, and the agent sent to attack a bedridden Seward wounded, but did not kill, him.

Though the White House had received dozens of death threats during the war, once the fighting ended, the presidential security—minimal by today's standards—all but evaporated. Lincoln did not even take his regular guard to Ford's Theatre on the fatal night of April 14.

—H. H.

THE ASSASSINATION.

Condition of Secretary Seward Improving.

New Facts About the Murderers.

Preparations for the President's Funeral.

Official Directions from Heads of Departments.

Description of the Assassins.

Reward of Thirty Thousand Dollars Offered for Their Apprehension.

Additional Details of the Conspiracy.

APPEARANCE OF THE CITY.

WASHINGTON, D.C.,
Tuesday, April 17—9:20 P.M.

The city has to some extent resumed its wonted appearance, though the great grief is still uppermost in all hearts, and its signs are apparent on every hand. Every yard of black fabric in the city on Saturday, was brought up at an early hour on that day, and hundreds of persons who wished to testify their grief by draping the residences were unable to do so. This morning, however, further supplies arrived here, and this afternoon many more houses have been draped in mourning.

Business has been partially resumed, though large numbers of stores have simply contented themselves with opening their doors and not taking down their shutters. In the Public Departments some work has been done during the day, but business generally will not be resumed therein until after the funeral.

THE NEWS IN RICHMOND.

The news of the murder of the President was received in Richmond during the evening of Saturday by special telegram to Gen. ORD's headquarters. It created a great alarm and consternation, and the first feeling among the officers who learned it Saturday evening was, that swift justice should be meted out to the authors.

THE NEWS AT FORTRESS MONROE.

One of your correspondents with the army, who came up to-day, furnishes the following paragraphs respecting the feeling on the reception of the news at Fortress Monroe, City Point and Norfolk:

"At Fortress Monroe the sad news of the assassination of President LINCOLN, and the attempted murder of Secretary SEWARD and his two sons, was received at first with incredulity; but at length the terrible news was authenticated. One cannot describe the utter feeling of poignant sorrow with which the news was received. The naval vessels in the harbor displayed their colors at half-mast, and the example was followed by nearly all the shipping. For so small a community the excitement was immense, and in the absence of any definite news the most woeful forebodings were indulged in. On the arrival of the City Point boat, from up the River James, the passengers were strangely startled by being informed of the awful calamity that had befallen the country. They had at first imagined that the drooping flags, half-masted on the shipping, was indicative of the death of Secretary Seward, he being reported injured, but their horror and indignation knew no bounds on learning who it was that the nation's ships thus mourned. Among the passengers the greatest feeling was exhibited, and several ladies on board evinced much distress. Brave men, with wounds received in battle, friends of soldiers, visiting their disabled brethren, all evinced a degree of feeling that has rarely been shown."

FEELING OF PASSENGERS.

The state of suspense among the passengers on their way up to Washington was indeed terrible. Owing to orders to search boats and many often and imperfectly-understood dispatches, progress was somewhat impeded, and one boat had to return to Newport's News to land prisoners of war, and only reached Washington at noon on Monday, having been on the route forty-eight hours.

TREACHERY AMONG REBEL DESERTERS.

At Norfolk, on Saturday, soon after the news of the death of the President arrived, some incipient signs of a rebellion exhibited themselves among two "whitewashed" regiments of rebel deserters, who have taken the oath of allegiance and been enlisted in the service of the United States. The mutinous signs and turbulent acts of the proposed insurgents were quickly quelled and their arms taken from them. On an examination of their cartridge-boxes, ammunition was found therein that had never been issued to them by the government, and it was not at all suited to the arms in their possession. It is currently reported and generally believed that guns were concealed in Norfolk or vicinity for which the mysterious cartridges would come in use. Several paroled rebel prisoners were seized on suspicion of being connected with the mutiny that has been so effectually crushed by the prompt action of the authorities. . . .

CONDITION OF SECRETARY SEWARD AND SON.

The condition of Secretary SEWARD and son Frederick, at the hour of nine o'clock this evening, is so far improved as to encourage the hope of the speedy recovery of both. Secretary SEWARD has slept well to-day, and his condition generally is much easier. The Assistant Secretary is so far improved that the hope of his recovery strengthens with every hour. The others of the injured are doing well.

ARRESTS OF SUSPECTED PERSONS.

Several arrests of parties suspected of being connected with murder of Mr. LINCOLN and the attempted assassination of Secretary SEWARD and sons have been made. Yesterday four men dressed in female attire were arrested in Georgetown and committed to the Old Capitol. Investigations by the civil and military authorities are still in progress, and the testimony of a large number of witnesses has already been taken. These investigations are proceeding quietly, however, as it is deemed best for the ends of justice that no publicity should be given at present to the facts elicited.

EFFECT ON THE FINANCES OF THE COUNTRY.

The effect of the late tragedy upon the finances of the country is most strikingly illustrated by the subscriptions to the popular Seven-thirty loan, which for Friday and Saturday last amounted to the enormous aggregate of *nine million one hundred and thirty-four thousand seven hundred dollars.* This sum was composed entirely of small subscriptions and does not include those made by heavy holders of government vouchers, who by the Loan Act of the last Congress can receive these bonds in payment of their claims. If any evidence was wanted of the determination of the people to sustain the government finances against all attempts of traitors of every dye. This is conclusive.

Dispatches to the Associated Press.

WASHINGTON, Monday, April 17.

The deep interest felt in Secretary SEWARD has thronged his residence with visitors, among them the members of the Cabinet, foreign ministers, and a large number of others.

He was informed yesterday, for the first time, of the assassination of President LINCOLN, and of the attempted assassination of himself and of the Assistant Secretary, and to some extent of the condition in which the latter lay.

Mr. SEWARD, though moved with the most intense sorrow and horror at the recital of the awful facts, nevertheless bore it with considerable firmness and composure, his strength having so far returned as to enable him to undergo the trying ordeal.

Every effort that ingenuity, excited by fervor, can make, is being put forth by all the proper authorities to capture or trace the assassin of Mr. LINCOLN and the would-be assassin of Mr. SEWARD.

The Common Council have offered a reward of $20,000 for the arrest and conviction of the assassins, and to this sum another of $10,000 is added by Col L. C. BAKER, Agent of the War Department, making a total of $30,000.

To this announcement are added the following descriptions of the individuals accused:

Description of J. WILKES BOOTH, who assassinated the President on the evening of April 14, 1865:

Height, five feet eight inches; weight, 160 pounds; compact built; hair jet black. inclined to curl, of medium length, and parted behind; eyes black, and heavy, dark eyebrows; wears a large seal ring on his little finger; when talking inclines his head forward and looks down. . . .

CONDITION OF SECRETARY SEWARD AND SON.

At 10:30 o'clock to-day, Secretary SEWARD was represented to be in an improving condition, though he rested rather uncomfortably last night from mental excitement, caused by conversation with friends in relation to recent events.

His son FREDERICK has partially recovered consciousness, and his symptoms are otherwise somewhat favorable. . . .

BOOTH'S RECENT BEHAVIOR.

The *Evening Star* says on Friday last, BOOTH was about the National Hotel, as usual, and strolled up and down the avenue several times. During one of these strolls he stopped at the Kirkwood House, and sent to Vice-President JOHNSON a card, upon which was written:

"I do not wish to disturb you. Are you in?   J. WILKES BOOTH."

A gentleman of BOOTH's acquaintance at this time met him in front of the Kirkwood House, and in the conversation which followed, made some allusion to BOOTH's business, and, in a jesting way, asked: "What makes you so gloomy? Have you lost another thousand in oil?" BOOTH replied he had been hard at work that day, and was about to leave Washington never to return. Just then a boy came out and said to BOOTH: "Yes, he is in his room." Upon which the gentleman walked on, supposing BOOTH would enter the hotel. About 7 o'clock Friday evening he came down from his room at the National and was spoken to by several concerning his paleness, which, he said, proceeded from indisposition. Just before leaving, he asked the clerk if he was not going to Ford's Theatre, and added: "There will be some very fine acting there to-night." The door-keeper at the theatre noticed BOOTH as he passed in, and shortly after the latter entered the restaurant and in a hurried manner, called for "Brandy, brandy, brandy," rapping at the same time on the bar. . . .

THE ASSASSINATION OF MR. LINCOLN.

Interesting Particulars of the Tragedy.

Correspondence of the New-York Times.

WASHINGTON, Saturday, April 15.

Through the kindness of Capt. JAS. M. McCAWLY, Ninth Regiment V.K.C., now in charge of the scene of the fearful tragedy which has stilled with horror every loyal heart in our land, I am enabled to give some particulars, which may, perhaps, have escaped the notice of other correspondents, and, for the truth of which, eye-witnesses and men familiar with both the murder and the theatre can vouch.

First of all, the idea has gone abroad that the pistol-shot was fired *through* the door, the assassin standing outside. This was not the case, Upon close examination we find the hole in the door of the stage-box, which is one of the angles of the pannel, *to have been made with a bitt large-sized gimlet.* Made probably by the assassin some time before, so as to be able to ascertain the precise position of his victim before entering the box.

The life's blood of our noble President had been shed principally upon the upper part of the chair in which he had been sitting, saturating it completely through, and remaining still moist and undried up to a late hour this (Saturday) night. Some few drops had spurted upon the jam of the door, and as the murderer stood when he fired the fatal shot, must have sprinkled his knees. There was likewise blood upon the floor.

At a late hour last night, Mr. JAMES B. FERGUSON, who keeps a restaurant adjoining the theatre, was summoned to appear and give his testimony before the Hon. Secretary of War, Gen. AUGUR and Chief Justice CHASE, which testimony has not yet been made public, but which I am able to furnish here in brief. Mr. FERGUSON was sitting upon the opposite side of the theatre to the President, and directly opposite, thus being able to see every motion made by Mr. LINCOLN or those about him, and had been talking with Booth but a short time before.

At the moment of the fearful deed the President was seated in a large and comfortable crimson velvet patent rocking-chair, his right elbow upon the arm of the chair, and his head resting upon his hand. The left hand was extended to pull gently aside the flag (belonging to the Treasury Guard) which draped the side of the box nearest him. His eyes were directed toward the orchestra, a kindly smile upon his face. At this instant the assassin burst open the door immediately behind the President, and deliberately shot him, as stated in the accounts of the press. It was all the work of a moment! The flash of the pistol, the curling of the smoke, were scarce noticed, when the murderer was seen to spring from the box upon the stage beneath, some twelve feet distant.

The box occupied by the President was a large double upper one, upon the first tier, and was tastefully decorated with our national colors and a magnificent State flag, bearing the coat of arms of the State of New-York. The "stars and stripes" were to his left, the State flag, with its rich emblazonry and silken fringe, to his right.

Mrs. Lincoln was sitting facing the President, and as the assassin advanced between them, he cried loud enough to be heard all over the house: "The South is avenged!" He then rested his left hand upon the velvet cushion which ran across the front of the box, and leaped easily to the floor of the stage. Before this Capt. RATHBONE, a step-son of Secretary HARRIS of New-York, attempted to seize the assassin; but the wretch turned as quick as lightning, and drawing a knife, dealt him a severe blow.

This slight detention, however, had the effect to cause the spur of the murderer to catch in the fringe of the State flag alluded to, and he fell, striking his right knee and thigh, and dragging the flag from its fastening down upon the stage with him, and detaching the spur, which he left behind him. As he arose, he exclaimed *"Sic Semper Tyrannis!"* and staggering across the stage in a tragic manner, and brandishing the large knife which he had drawn, cried again: "I have done it," or "It is I who did it!"

In the meantime, Mrs. LINCOLN had thrown her arms around her loved husband, and the cry resounding throughout the house that the President had been assassinated, and a wail of mingled agony and rage went up from the hearts of all there, which had the subdued ferocity of a wild beast in its breath.

In the midst of this terrible commotion Miss LAURA KEENE came forward to the foot-lights and implored the public to calm themselves. At first, the majority of the audience believed that the lady was about to inform them of the happy capture of the fiend in human shape, assisted in gaining quiet, but that the assassin had made good his escape—having but about fifty or sixty feet to traverse, to reach the stage door, at the back of the theatre, where his horse was awaiting him, ready saddled and bridled.

Since the dread tragedy, the theatre has been in the hands of the military authorities, and we have heard, incidentally, of some mysterious acts which would seem at least to require explanation.

Upon taking possession, one of Capt. McCAWLY's orderlies asked a subordinate of the establishment whether or not any civilian beside himself was then in the house? His answer was a decided "No." Soon afterward a stranger was seen to steal across the stage and enter a small room. Soon afterward this subordinate was seen with another man crossing the stage. He had black hair, (very little showing,) and beside a black moustache, a red beard, which had every appearance of being artificial. Although immediately followed, the under officer could not track them. *They* were familiar with the intricacies of the scenery, and all that rubbish and glitter that it takes to represent a mimic world behind the scenes. When taxed with this fact the subordinate stoutly denied, and, when cross-examined, declared that he had gone out but a few minutes through the front door. The guard who was stationed there, however, as stoutly denied that any living soul had passed. Immediate and thorough search was made, but the mysterious stranger was not found; and soon after, as we understand, the subordinate in question disappeared as mysteriously.

There can be but little doubt that JOHN WILKES BOOTH was the willing agent of Satan in this matter. A thousand incidents point to this conclusion, apart from the pronounced recognition of many prominent witnesses.

When the President arrived, he is said to have been waiting on the pavement in front of the theatre, and to have received a kind word and bow from Mr. LINCOLN, who knew him. Later, he appeared behind the scenes, and inquired if Gen. GRANT had come. It is supposed that he would have assassinated the President as he left his carriage, but was waiting for Gen. GRANT. He then went around to the front part of the theatre, and entering by the front door, lounged for a short time about in the lobby, holding his hat in his hand. The next time he was seen was when he jumped upon the stage. . . .

Mrs. Surratt Captured

Stunned by the news of Lincoln's assassination, the public avidly followed the search for John Wilkes Booth and his fellow conspirators. Within hours of the shooting, police searched Mary Surratt's boarding house, where Booth had frequently stayed. They were correct in believing that Mrs. Surratt had some knowledge of Booth's earlier plot to kidnap President Lincoln, in which her son, John Surratt, was deeply involved, but they found little evidence to connect her with the assassination. Then the unannounced arrival of Lewis Payne (or Paine, the alias of Lewis T. Powell), one of Booth's co-conspirators, at the boarding house confirmed police suspicions and Mrs. Surratt was hauled off to jail.

Tried before a military commission, she was convicted on slight evidence and was sentenced to be hanged. Pleas to President Johnson were rejected; he remarked that she "kept the nest that hatched the rotten egg." She was hanged, along with the other conspirators, on July 7, 1865.

Meanwhile, newspaper readers closely followed details of the arrangements for the funeral, since the death of no other president had aroused such universal grief. Throngs of mourners came to the White House to pay their final tribute. Perhaps 25,000 gained entrance, but at least as many were turned away. In the end it was decided that the president's body would lie in state in the rotunda of the Capitol.

297

—D. H. D.

THE ASSASSINATION.

The Last Marks of Respect to Our Late President.

Immense Throng to Visit the Remains.

Preparations for the Funeral.

Arrest of the would-be Murderer of Mr. Seward.

Special Dispatches to the New-York Times.

WASHINGTON, Tuesday, April 18—10 P.M.

There arrived here this evening two committees from New-York, to be present at the obsequies to-morrow. One committee represents the great meeting in Wall-street of last Saturday, and is composed of Messrs. James Brown, Charles H. Russell, Moses Taylor, Moses H. Grinnell, W. E. Dodge, Samuel Sloan, J. J. Astor, W. M. Evarts, Edwards Pierrepont, E. B. Cutting and R. M. Blatchford. They called on the President this evening at the Treasury Department, and were presented by Secretary McCULLOCH. A very pleasant hour was spent by the committee, who all seemed well pleased with President JOHNSON. Subsequently the Union League Committee proceeded to the department and were also presented to the President. This committee consists of John Jay, Jonathan Sturges, Col. Frank E. Howe, John A. Weeks, Theodore Roosevelt, George Cabot Ward, James W. Beekman, C. E. Detmold, Samuel Westmore, Charles Butler, Parker Handy and Otis D. Swan. This committee will represent the League at the funeral to-morrow, and will remain long enough to formally present their respects to the President.

A committee of the Common Council of New-York are expected here to-morrow morning.

TRIBUTE TO THE MEMORY OF MR. LINCOLN.

Many other distinguished civilians from New-York are here, among them Hon. W. A. DARLING and Collector DRAPER. Among the most beautiful tribute to the memory of the late President is a beautiful floral design, forwarded by Col. STETSON, of New-York, through N. D. SPERRY, Esq., Secretary of the National Union Committee. It is in the shape of an anchor, and composed of Japonicas and other exotics, most

298

beautifully arranged. It has been placed on the centre of the President's coffin.

ARRANGEMENTS FOR THE FUNERAL.

The arrangements for the funeral to-morrow are being closed to-night by Secretary HARRINGTON, who has been prominent and efficient in the matter. The services will take place in the great east room, and admission thereto will only be had by ticket, which will be issued only to members of Congress, Cabinet members, Ministers, prominent committees, &c., to a sufficient number to fill the room.

Rev. Dr. GURLEY will officiate, assisted by several other clergymen of different denominations.

THE REMOVAL OF THE REMAINS.

It has been decided to-night that the remains will leave the city on Friday morning by way of Baltimore, and Harrisburgh, and Philadelphia, reaching Philadelphia in the afternoon, and lying in state over night at Independence Hall, thence to New-York on Saturday, remaining there over Sunday, proceeding on Monday by way of Albany to Buffalo, Cleveland and Chicago.

INTERVIEW WITH THE PRESIDENT.

The Illinois delegation, headed by Gov. OGLESBY, called on the President this morning to exchange greetings. The several gentlemen were introduced, when the Governor addressed President JOHNSON in a brief but pertinent and feeling speech. The President replied in a speech of some length, the importance of which justified the full report which has been sent forward. The interview was of an exceedingly pleasant character and very encouraging to the delegation and to the President.

THE KENTUCKIANS AND THE PRESIDENT.

At 7 o'clock, this evening, the Kentucky delegation, headed by GREEN CLAY SMITH, paid their respects to the President. Mr. SMITH addressed Mr. JOHNSON, in behalf of the delegation and the Union men of Kentucky, assuring him of their cordial support. The President responded in happy and appropriate terms. The new President is rapidly growing in popular estimation.

ARREST OF THE SURRATT FAMILY.

As you were informed early this morning, the wretch who attempted the lives of the SEWARD family is now in the hands of the officers of the law, with such a conclusive record of both positive and circumstantial evidence against him, that he cannot possibly escape the punishment he so richly deserves.

Col. WELLS, Provost-Marshal-General of this department, was yesterday pursuing investigation into the recent assassinations. He had decided to arrest Mrs. Surratt, who resides in this city, at No. 543 11-street, but subsequently decided to arrest the whole family, including her daughter KATE, two young ladies, whom she calls her nieces, and two colored servants. Col. H. S. ALCOTT, Special Commissioner of the War Department, was called upon for requisite forces, and he detailed his deputy, R. C. MORGAN, Esq., with Officers SAMPSON, DEVOE, MERMERSKIRCH and RASH of the New-York Detective force, who, with Major SMITH, Assistant-Adjutant on Gen. AUGUR's staff, proceeded to the house about 11 o'clock.

Major SMITH proceeded up the steps alone, the house being a three-story brick, with high stoop, and rapped. A woman raised a window, and asked who is there? The reply was "I'm an officer, let me in." The door was opened and the Major entered. Immediately afterward the rest of the party entered one by one, until all were in. The purpose of the visit was announced and the inmates seemed somewhat surprised; the daughter especially being frightened, but the mother took it as calmly as though she had been expecting it.

They were all assembled in the parlor, and not allowed to communicate with each other while the officers hunted up the bonnets, shawls and shoes of the ladies, preparatory to conveying them to Col. INGRAHAM's office. This took some little time, during which Miss KATE SURRATT broke out into sobs, seeming deeply affected, while her mother chided her for such an exhibition of her feelings.

Just as the ladies were ready to proceed, Officer DEVOE having brought up the carriage, a loud rap was heard on the door. Mr. MORGAN stepped into the hall, followed by Maj. SMITH and Officer MERMERSKIRCH, who were each armed with a pistol. MORGAN opened the door, and a man stepped in and the door was at once locked by Morgan, who handed the key to MERMERSKIRCH. The man seemed rather surprised, and said, "I guess I've made a mistake." When asked what he wanted, he said he was looking for Mrs. SURRATT. He was assured that he had made no mistake, and told to sit down in the parlor.

The women being now ready to depart, they were at once put in the carriage, with Officer DEVOE, who conducted them to the office of the Provost-Marshal, whence they were subsequently sent to the Old Capitol Prison.

The man who thus had entered the house bore evidence at once of having assumed a partial disguise. He had a heavy pickaxe on his shoulder, wore a cap made from the bottom part of the leg of a pair of drawers, which fitted closely to his head, and hung down behind, gray coat and vest, black or dark colored pants, a light pair of boots. Both boots and pants were completely covered with mud up to his knees. When he sat down he was asked by MORGAN: Who are you? What do you want here at this time of night?" He pulled out of his pocket a copy of the oath of allegiance, and said: "Stop, I will show you who I am," remarking that he got it in Baltimore last June. On examination it proved to the an oath of allegiance administered to LOUIS PAINE, of Fauquier County, Va., dated Baltimore, March 14, 1865. He was further interrogated by Mr. MORGAN as to his business at that house at that time of night with a pickaxe on his shoulder. He said he had come to dig a gutter for Mrs. SURRATT, and wanted to know what time he should begin in the morning. He also stated he was but 20 years old, that he had no money, that he obtained his living by working as a laborer with that pickaxe, to which he seemed to cling with peculiar tenacity. He stated he could neither read nor write, that he had been obliged to work on his father's farm in Fauquier County for a living for the last four years, and could not go to school; that he was down on the rebels, and much more of the same kind of stuff, which only convinced the officers that they were in the presence of a party connected with the murderous assault on Mr. SEWARD.

He was subsequently interrogated by Major SMITH and Officers SAMPSON and MERMERSKIRCH, to whom he made various replied, some of them conflicting with the stories he had told MORGAN. When asked where he intended to sleep that night, he said he did not know, as he had no money, and the night before he had slept on the railroad track.

The man was then conducted to the carriage by Officer SAMPSON, who took him to Gen. AUGUR's office, where he underwent a search and another examination, when $25 in money was discovered on his person, also a pocket compass, with a comb and brush, and several minor articles. Here he told other stories as to his whereabouts for the last three days, and as to his means of support.

A close examination and scrutiny of his person revealed a man of good physique, about twenty-five years of age, six feet high, very good form, dark rich black hair, dyed, light complexion, and a refinement of person which gave the lie to his profession of hard labor. His dress was much soiled, from evident exposure, but was of very good material. Had he been really well dressed he would have presented the appearance of a stylish gentleman.

The colored servant, who admitted the murderer to Mr. SEWARD's on Friday night, was now sent for. The room was darkened when he came in, the gas was turned on, when the boy was told to pick out the man. As soon as his eyes fell on the prisoner, he threw up his hands and exclaimed, *"There he is; I know him, I don't want to see him no more."* The only impression produced upon the man by this development was an apparent nervousness, but otherwise he seemed to master his feelings completely.

Without further conversation, at about 4 o'clock A.M. he was heavily ironed and sent off to a safe spot, where he can never escape from his captor and where public violence cannot reach him.

While Mr. MORGAN was interrogating PAINE at the house, Major SMITH and Officer SAMPSON were instituting a search of the dwelling, which was continued by SMITH, MORGAN and MERMERSKIRCH after the departure of Officer SAMPSON with the prisoner. Much evidence was found, showing it to have been a regular treason-brewing nest. Letters were found containing expressions of diabolic hate toward the President, and in Miss KATE SURRATT's portfolio Major SMITH found an envelope addressed to J. WILKES BOOTH, National Hotel. A card about half as large as a playing card was found, which was certainly emblematical of the hate which Secessionists have fostered toward the President. On the top was this line: *"Thus will it ever be with tyrants."* Their shield, in the colors of red, white and red, and the original thirteen States. This was surmounted with the small rebel flags, between which was the State coat of arms of Virginia, with the motto, *"Sic Semper Tyrannis."* Beneath this, in large, red letters, "Virginia, the Mighty," and at the bottom of the card, in circular shape, another copy of Virginia's coat of arms and motto.

The house was found in a very disorderly condition, beds all unmade, the clothes piled on chairs, and everything in confusion, showing very plainly that the inmates had other business on hand than the usual business of housekeeping. Two colored servants, a man and a girl—the first of whom was found sleeping on the back parlor floor—were also apprehended and locked up.

Mrs. SURRATT is a large-sized woman, about forty years of age, and of coarse expression. She was rather shabbily dressed. Her daughter was far more genteel in appearance and dress. Young SURRATT, who has been in the city up to the assassination, has, it is believed, fled to Canada. He is being pursued.

THE EVIDENCE AGAINST PAINE CONCLUSIVE.

Later—10 P.M.—The evidence against PAINE is now conclusive beyond doubt. He was this afternoon confronted by Major SEWARD, Miss FANNY SEWARD, the nurse who was so severely wounded and another colored servant, who saw him, and they all promptly recognized him as the assassin. His clothing has been taken off and is undergoing examination. It will be remembered that the villain left a slouch hat behind at Mr. SEWARD's on Friday night, which explains the precise cap he wore. . . .

THE BODY LYING IN STATE.

No more suggestive sight was ever seen than that around the White House to-day. It was publicly known that the doors would not be opened till 10 o'clock this morning, but the crowd began to gather at the gates by 8:30, and by 9:30 the line, four and six persons deep, was nearly a quarter of a mile long. The arrangements at the house for entrance and exit were the same as usual on New-Year's reception days, viz., entrance at the main door, thence to the Great Room, thence to the East Room, and out the window by the customary steps. It is scarcely an exaggeration to say that 25,000 persons passed through the rooms, and that half as many more, seeing the immense throng, left without trying to get in.

The approaches were guarded by a battalion of veteran reserves. The east room, in which the remains were laid, was tastefully decorated in mourning, the work being done under the supervision of Mr. JOHN ALEXANDER. The windows at either end of the room were draped with black barrage, the frames of the mirrors between the windows, as well as those over the marble mantles, being heavily draped with the same material. The heavy gildings of the frames were thus entirely enshrouded, while the plates of the mirrors were covered with white crape. The chandeliers at the western and southern ends of the room were also draped with mourning—the central chandelier having been removed to make room for the catafalque. This was a very handsome affair—the dais or platform, on which the coffin rested, being raised some three feet from the floor, and being covered with evergreens and japonicas.

The corpse was in charge of several army and navy officers, among whom were Gen. HITCHCOOK and Gen. EATON, and Lieut.-Commander STONE, of the monitor *Montauk*.

But a limited number of persons were admitted to the house at a time, and these were required to pass through as rapidly as was consistent with decency and propriety. The expressions and appearance of the people, as they looked for the last time on the face of the honored dead, were conclusive, if further proof were needed, that the great majority regard the President's death as a personal and individual loss, as well as a national calamity. Hundreds addressed words of farewell to the cold inanimate body; and thousands passed from the platform with weeping eyes. Every class, race and condition of society was represented in the throng of mourners, and the sad tears of farewells of whites and blacks were mingled by the coffin of him to whom humanity was everywhere the same. The most touching exhibitions of sorrow were made by the many whose dress marked them as the poorer classes of society. "He was the poor man's friend," was a very common remark.

The vast throng outside, as well as inside, was quiet, orderly and reverent, all day, though two to three hours was the average period of waiting for admission, and many persons waited even five and six hours. The clerks of each of the public departments were marshaled at 11 o'clock, under their respective heads of bureaus and marched in grand and solemn procession into the White House and past the body in the east room.

Such intense anxiety was manifested to-day to see the loved face once more, and so many persons were unable to get an opportunity to do so, that it is proposed now to let the body lie in state during Thursday in the rotunda of the Capitol and not start westward with it before Friday. Preparations to this effect are making this evening, with the consent of Mrs. LINCOLN and her friends from Illinois.

The features of Mr. LINCOLN retain their sweet, placid, natural expression, and the discoloration caused by the wound is so slight as not to amount to a disfigurement. . . .

THE FEELING IN CANADA

**Opinion of the Leading Canadian Journal—The Deep Regard
and Affection Felt for the President—The Secessionists
Carousing in Honor of the Assassin—A Plea for the
Murderer—His Crime Justified.**

From the Toronto Globe.

ABRAHAM LINCOLN.

At twenty-two minutes after seven o'clock, on Saturday morning, about nine hours after he had received the shot of the assassin, ABRAHAM

LINCOLN drew his last breath, surrounded by members of his family, his Cabinet, and leading political and personal friends. His death would, under any circumstances, have produced an extraordinary sensation, but accompanied by murderous violence, the feeling which has been created has been the most intense. No single event of the present century in America can at all compare with it in effect on the popular mind, and we think that in England the shock will be nearly as deeply felt. The grief which is being expressed has two very distinct origins, the stronger of which seems to arise from personal sympathy and regard for the deceased. We hear in all quarters the strongest expressions of admiration of the character of Mr. LINCOLN, and deep sorrow that his noble career should have been brought to an untimely end. His simplicity of character, his straightforward honesty, his kindness, even his bluntness of manner, seem to have won the popular heart, even among a foreign, and, in matter of opinion, a hostile nation. We may judge by that fact of his popularity among the citizens of the Northern States. Almost all of us feel as if we had suffered a personal loss. Mr. LINCOLN is spoken of in the same terms as are used toward a familiar friend. All mourn his untimely fate. He had risen by industry, ability and integrity to the great position of Chief Magistrate of his country. He found it in the most imminent danger, and his power to control the elements which were sweeping over the land were far from generally acknowledged. He was regarded with fear and trembling by the friends of his government, and with contempt by his opponents. But steadily he made his way. He was not the best man who could have been imagined for the post of Chief Magistrate in a great civil war. He had not the commanding force which infuses energy into all around him, and his public appearances were often lacking in dignity. But he was sagacious, patient, prudent, courageous, honest and candid. If he did not inspire the great General, he gave every man in the army an opportunity of developing the talents within him. He recognized merit and rewarded it. He placed confidence, as a rule, where it was due, and he had his reward in great military successes. Some say that he has been cut off at a favorable moment for his reputation, but we cannot accept this view. It seems to us that he had gone through his worst trials, that his patience, sagacity and honesty would have borne even better fruits for the settlement of the affairs of the South than during the wild commotion of the war. He has been cut off at a time when, certainly, he had accomplished a great deal, but leaving much undone which he was very qualified to do. A naturally strong man, of only fifty-six, he might have hoped to live many years after finishing his work as President, in the enjoyment of the respect and admiration justly due to one who had saved the life of his country. He will be held, we think, by Americans, if not equal to WASHINGTON, second to none but he. But he had not the gratification of his great predecessor, of seeing his work completed and enjoying for a long period the gratitude of his countrymen and the admiration of strangers. There are few so hard of heart as to not shed a tear over the sudden and bloody termination of so bright a career. As great as Washington in many moral and mental qualities, his genial character was calculated to win far more popular sympathy than his predecessor. Ability and honesty all admire, but when to them are added kindness, simplicity, and freedom from selfishness, haughtiness and pride in high position, they win love as well as respect.

The Murder Justified.

From the Toronto Leader.

A man may, on the spur of the moment, be so maddened with rage as to strike another down to the earth; but if the accounts which come to us of this distressing affair are correct, the attack upon Mr. LINCOLN's and Mr., SEWARD's lives were concocted some time prior to the inauguration ceremony on the 4th of March, and only failed of accomplishment because one of the parties in the plot lost heart to carry out the scheme at that time. Would that he had never found it again! The act was not committed without due time for reflection as to its awful nature. For over a month the plan remained unacted upon in the bosom of its author, and time seems but to have added to the burning desire to carry it out. There must have been a strong feeling on the part of the person who committed the crime that a grievous wrong had been done, either to himself or to his country, by the President or the government he represented. Had a Southern man, during the four years of the war, taken the life of the President, there would be no difficulty in tracing it to a cause. We cannot so soon forget the numberless acts of wickedness committed in the South by the servants and emissaries of the Northern Government; the beautiful homesteads leveled to the ground with demonical fury; the fair women violated by a ribald soldiery; the brave men shot down in coldest blood in the insane plea of retaliation—all this and much more is still fresh in our memories, and serve to remind us that if the assassination had been committed in the heat of the war by a Southern man, who had so much more to drive him to desperation, a reason for his conduct could readily be found. In the present instance these considerations do not help us to discover the cause of the assassination. That the deed was committed by JOHN WILKES BOOTH, a brother of EDWIN BOOTH, the celebrated actor of the present day, there seems to be little doubt. But why should he make himself the champion of the Southern people or the Southern cause? He must have been goaded almost to the verge of madness. No man of ordinary nerve or trivial impulse could have jumped into a private box at the theatre, as he did, calmly shoot down the object of his wrath, then spring on the stage uttering words which serve to give a clue to the act of assassination, and ultimately find his way through the theatre to a place of escape. The man who could have done all this, must have considered that his chances of escape were very few indeed, and that, if need were, he was ready to give up his own life for that which he had taken. There is desperation in such a thought—such a desperation as is caused by a deep consciousness of wrong-doing on the part of the person against whom it is conceived. . . .

Booth's Letter

Meanwhile, the public eagerly sought to learn more about the perpetrator of this mad act. They received some information when Booth's brother-in-law, John S. Clarke, turned over to authorities a letter Booth had entrusted to his keeping the previous year. Written when he was planning the kidnapping, not the murder, of the president, it told little about the assassination plot but revealed a great deal about the disordered state of Booth's mind.

Much of the letter is disingenuous. Booth probably never earned $20,000 a year as an actor. To assert that "the South have never bestowed upon me one kind word," ignored the fact that he received his warmest reception as an actor in Richmond. His claim that Southerners "are not, and nor have they been fighting" for the continuance of slavery was a flagrant misreading of history.

But the letter makes it clear that Booth had come to see the Civil War as a struggle between freedom and tyranny, personified in Abraham Lincoln. His own brother judged that he was insane on this one point.

—D. H. D.

THE MURDERER OF MR. LINCOLN.

Extraordinary Letter of John Wilkes Booth—Proof that He Meditated His Crime Months Ago—His Excuses for the Contemplated Act—His Participation in the Execution of John Brown.

From the Philadelphia Inquirer.

The following verbatim copy of a letter, in writing which is the hand-writing of JOHN WILKES BOOTH, the murderer of President LINCOLN, has been furnished us by the Hon. Wm. MILLWARD, United States Marshal of the Eastern District of Pennsylvania. It was handed over to that officer by JOHN S. CLARKE, who is a brother-in-law of Mr. BOOTH. The history connected with it is somewhat peculiar. In November, 1864, the paper was deposited with Mr. CLARKE by BOOTH, in a sealed envelope, "for safe keeping," Mr. CLARKE being ignorant of the contents. In January last BOOTH called at Mr. CLARKE's house, asked for the package and it was given up to him. It is now supposed that at that time he took out the paper and added to it his signature, which appears to be in different ink from that used in the body of the letter, and also from the language employed could not have been put to it originally. Afterward he returned the package to Mr. CLARKE again for safe keeping, sealed and bearing the superscription, J. WILKES BOOTH.

The inclosure was preserved by the family without suspicion of its nature. After the afflicting information of the assassination of the President, which came upon the family of Mr. CLARKE with crushing force, it was considered proper to open the envelope.

There was found in it the following paper, with some 7:30 United States bonds, and a certificate of shares in oil companies. Mr. CLARKE promptly handed over the paper to Marshal MILLWARD, in whose custody it now remains. From a perusal of this paper it seems to have been prepared by BOOTH as a vindication of some desperate act which he had in contemplation; and, from the language, used, it is probable that it was a plot to abduct the President and carry him off to Virginia. If this was meditated it failed, and from making a prisoner of the President to his assassination was an easy step for a man of perverted principles. It also appears that BOOTH was one of the party who was engaged in the capture and execution of JOHN BROWN, of Osawatomie, at which time he doubtless imbibed from WISE and his associates those detestable sentiments of cruelty which have culminated in an infamous crime. The letter is as follows:

—.—. 1864

MY DEAR SIR,—You may use this as you think best. But as *some* may wish to know *when, who* and *why,* and as I know not *how* to direct, I give it (in the words of your master)

"TO WHOM IT MAY CONCERN":

Right or wrong, God judge me, not man. For be my motive good or bad, of one thing I am sure, the lasting condemnation of the North.

I love peace more than life. Have loved the Union beyond expression.

For four years have I waited, hoped and prayed for the dark clouds to break, and for a restoration of our former sunshine. To wait longer would be a crime. All hope for peace is dead. My prayers have proved as idle as my hopes. God's will be done. I go to see and share the bitter end.

I have ever held the South were right. The very nomination of ABRAHAM LINCOLN, four years ago, spoke plainly, war—war upon Southern rights and institutions. His election proved it. "Await an overt act." Yes, till you are bound and plundered. What folly! The South was wise. Who thinks of argument or patience when the finger of his enemy presses on the trigger? In a *foreign war* I, too, could say, "country, right or wrong." But in a struggle *such as ours,* (where the brother tries to pierce his brother's heart,) for God's sake, choose the right. When a country like this spurns justice from her side she forfeits the allegiance of every honest freeman, and should leave him, untrammeled by any fealty soever, to act as his conscience may approve.

People of the North, to hate tyranny, to love liberty and justice, to strike at wrong and oppression, was the teaching of our fathers. The study of our early history will not let *me* forget it, and may it never.

This country was formed for the *white,* not for the black man. And looking upon *African Slavery* from the same stand-point held by the noble framers of our constitution, I for one, have ever considered it one of the greatest blessings (both for themselves and us,) that God has ever bestowed upon a favored nation. Witness heretofore our wealth and power; witness their elevation and enlightenment above their race elsewhere. I have lived among it most of my life, and have seen *less* harsh treatment from master to man than I have beheld in the North from father to son. Yet, Heaven knows, *no one* would be willing to do *more* for the negro race than I, could I but see a way to *still better* their condition.

But LINCOLN's policy is only preparing the way for their total annihilation. The South are *not, nor have they been fighting* for the continuance of slavery. The first battle of Bull Run did away with that idea. Their causes *since* for *war* have been as *noble and greater far than those that urged our fathers on. Even* should we allow they were wrong at the beginning of this contest, *cruelty and injustice* have made the wrong become the *right,* and they stand now (before the wonder and admiration of the world) as a noble band of patriotic heroes. Hereafter, reading of *their deeds,* Thermopylæa will be forgotten.

When I aided in the capture and execution of JOHN BROWN (who was a murderer on our Western border, and who was fairly *tried and convicted,* before an impartial judge and jury, of treason, and who, by the way, has since been made a god), I was proud of my little share in the transaction, for I deemed it my duty, and that I was helping our common country to perform an act of justice. But what was a crime in poor JOHN BROWN is now considered (by themselves) as the greatest and only virtue of the whole Republican party. Strange transmigration! *Vice* to become a *virtue,* simply because *more* indulge in it.

I thought then, as *now,* that the Abolitionists *were the only traitors* in the land, and that the entire party deserved the same fate of poor old Brown, not because they wish to abolish slavery but on account of the means they have ever endeavored to use to effect that abolition. If Brown were living I doubt whether he *himself* would set slavery against the Union. Most or many in the North do, and openly curse the Union, if the South are to return and retain a *single right* guaranteed to them by every tie which we once *revered as sacred.* The South can make no choice. It is either extermination or slavery for *themselves* (worse than death) to draw from. I know my choice.

I have also studied hard to discover upon what grounds the right of a State to secede has been denied, when our very name, United States, and the Declaration of Independence, *both* provide for secession. But there is no time for words. I write in haste. I know how foolish I shall be deemed for undertaking such a step as this, where, on the one side, I have many friends, and everything to make me happy, where my profession *alone* has gained me an income of more than twenty thousand dollars a year, and where my great personal ambition in my profession has such a great field for labor. On the other hand, the South have never bestowed upon me one kind word; a place now where I have no friends, except beneath the sod; a place where I must either become a private soldier or a beggar. To give up all of the *former* for the *latter,* besides my mother and sisters whom I love so dearly, (although they so widely differ with me in opinion,) seems insane; but God is my judge. I love *justice* more than I do a country that disowns it; more than fame and wealth; more (Heaven pardon me if wrong,) more than a happy home. I have never been upon a battle-field; but O, my countrymen, could you all but see the *reality* or effects of this horrid war, as I have seen them, (in *every State* save Virginia,) I know you would think like me, and would pray the Almighty to create in the Northern mind a sense of *right* and *justice,* (even should it possess no seasoning of mercy,) and that he would dry up this sea of blood between us, which is daily growing wider. Alas! poor country, is she to meet her threatened doom? Four years ago I would have given a thousand lives to see her remain (as I had always known her) powerful and unbroken. And even now, I would hold my life as naught to see her what she was. O, my friends, if the fearful scenes of the past four years had never been enacted, or if what has been had been but a frightful dream, from which we could now awake, with what overflowing hearts could we bless our God and pray for his continued favor. How I have loved the *old flag,* can never now be known. A few years since and the entire world could boast of *none* so pure and spotless. But I have of late been seeing and hearing of the *bloody deeds* of which she has *been made the emblem,* and would shudder to think how changed she had grown. O, how I have longed to see her break from the mist of blood and death that circles round her folds, spoiling her beauty and tarnishing her honor. But no, day by day has she been dragged deeper and deeper into cruelty and oppression, till now (in my eyes) her once bright red stripes look like bloody gashes on the face of Heaven. I look now upon my early admiration of her glories as a dream. My love (as things stand to-day) is for the South alone. Nor do I deem it a dishonor in attempting to make for her a prisoner of this man, to whom she owes so much of misery. If success attends me, I go penniless to her side. They say she has found that "last ditch" which the North have so long derided, and been endeavoring to force her in, forgetting they are our brothers, and that it's impolite to goad an enemy to madness. Should I reach her in safety and find it true, I will proudly beg permission to triumph or die in that same "ditch" by her side.

A Confederate doing duty upon his own responsibility.
J. WILKES BOOTH. . . .

United in Mourning

The arrival of Lincoln's remains in New York City, following huge public funerals in Washington, Baltimore, Harrisburg and Philadelphia, drew hundreds of thousands of spectators as the cortege moved slowly downtown to City Hall. There, his body was carried into the same building where Lincoln, then president-elect only four years earlier, had been greeted so coolly by municipal dignitaries.

Placed in an open coffin on the second floor above the Rotunda, Lincoln's body went on public view for twenty-four hours, and tens of thousands of mourners filed patiently up the stairs and past the catafalque through the night and into the next day. Women who tried to kiss the dead president's face were held back by guards, but many admirers reached out to touch the body.

One particularly audacious woman managed to have her son place a huge floral bouquet in the shape of Lincoln's initials—"A. L."—on the late president's chest before policemen could stop her. Not quite sure what to do next, the guards ushered the mother and child away but left the flowers where they rested. When a local photographer, Jeremiah Gurney, later aimed his camera at the scene to capture the only known pictorial record of Lincoln in death, the initials were still clearly visible, as if they were needed to identify the body. Secretary of War Edwin Stanton ordered the photograph confiscated, but fortunately for history, did not destroy it. Ninety years later, the picture was discovered among the papers of Lincoln's private secretary.

The mercurial Stanton could be generous as well. When he learned that African-Americans had been denied permission to march in the gigantic New York funeral procession, he overruled Tammany Hall and ordered that they be allowed to participate. "It is the desire of the Secretary of War," his telegram made clear, "that no discrimination respecting color should be exercised in admitting persons to the funeral procession."

In the end, 300 black mourners joined some 11,000 soldiers along the route, holding aloft a banner that declared: "Two Million of Bondsmen He Liberty Gave." On a day notable for the absolute silence of the vast throng, their appearance elicited the only applause during the days of mourning in the city.

Five years earlier, on the day he delivered his Cooper Union address, Lincoln had met the acclaimed historian George Bancroft at Mathew Brady's photography gallery on Broadway. Eyewitnesses were amused by the contrast between the elegant scholar and the unpolished politician; Bancroft, a Democrat, seemed decidedly unimpressed. Not now. Of the man who had saved the Union, Bancroft declared: "His enduring memory will assist during countless ages to bind the States together, and to incite to the love of our one undivided, indivisible country."

On April 26, Lincoln's funeral train slowly left New York and began retracing the route that had carried him from Springfield to Washington for his first inauguration in 1861. Crowds lined the tracks all the way up the Hudson River valley through Yonkers, Hastings, Irvington, and points north. In Albany, city fathers postponed a long-scheduled traveling menagerie—a street parade featuring giraffes, bears, tigers, leopards, lions, deer and, for good measure, an ostrich—so that the presidential funeral procession could march in dignity up the steep hill on State Street toward the capitol building.

"The hearse, with the coffin," The Times *noted, was borne on "an elegant and elaborately finished catafalque, which was trimmed with white silk, adorned richly with silver mountings, and surmounted by the eagle." Again placed on public display, Lincoln's remains were viewed by thousands more before being returned to the depot to resume the trip west toward Illinois.*

Back downstate, the New-York Historical Society organized a public meeting featuring tributes, eulogies, and personal memories. Rising to speak, William M. Evarts, who headed a special mission to Britain and would be a U.S. Attorney General, eloquently summed up the overpowering grief still clinging to New York: "We have so vast and intense a sorrow, that there is a great cry as if one were dead in every house."

—H. H.

THE OBSEQUIES

President Lincoln's Murder Planned in Canada.

One of the Seward Assassins a St. Albans Robber.

Official Day of Mourning Appointed.

Progress of the Federal Cortege from Philadelphia.

Demonstrations of the People of New-Jersey.

Reception of the Remains in this City.

Arrival at the City Hall.

Immense Turn Out of the People.

Appearance of the Corpse.

Forty Thousand Persons Visit the Hall up to 2 A.M.

Midnight Dirges by German Societies.

Order from the Secretary of War.

Full Particulars and Details of the Arrangements of Yesterday and To-day.

The Murder of the President Planned in Canada.

[Official]

313

WAR DEPARTMENT, WASHINGTON, April 24, 1865.

To Maj.-Gen. Dix:

This department has information that the President's murder was planned in Canada and approved in Richmond.

One of the assassins, now in prison, who attempted to kill Mr. SE-WARD, is believed to be one of the St. Albans raiders.

EDWIN STANTON
Secretary of War.

A Day of Mourning for President Lincoln.

[Official.]

By the President of the United States of America:

A PROCLAMATION.

Whereas, by my direction, the Acting Secretary of State, in a notice to the publication on the 17th of April, requested the various religious denominations to assemble on the 19th of April on the occasion of the obsequies of ABRAHAM LINCOLN, late President of the United States, and to observe the same with appropriate ceremonies; and whereas, our country has become one great house of mourning, where the head of the family has been taken away, and believing that special period should be assigned for again humbling ourselves before Almighty God, in order that the bereavement may be sanctified to the nation; now, therefore, in order to mitigate that grief on earth which can only be assuaged by communion with the father in Heaven, and in compliance with the wishes of Senators and Representatives in Congress, communicated to me by a resolution adopted at the national capital, I, ANDREW JOHNSON, President of the United States, do hereby appoint Thursday, the 25th day of May next, to be observed wherever in the United States the flag of the country may be respected, as a day of humiliation and mourning, and I recommend my fellow-citizens then to assemble in their respective places of worship, there to unite in solemn service to Almighty God in memory of the good man who has been removed, so that all shall be occupied at the same time in contemplation of his virtue, and sorrow for his sudden and violent end.

In witness whereof, I have hereunder set my hand and caused the seal of the United States to be affixed.

Done at the City of Washington, the 25th day of April, in the year of our Lord 1865, and on the independence of the United States the eighty-ninth.

ANDREW JOHNSON
By the President:
W. HUNTER, Acting Secretary of State.

THE FUNERAL CORTEGE.

From Philadelphia to New-York.

PHILADELPHIA, MONDAY, APRIL 24.

The funeral party started from the Continental Hotel at 2 o'clock this morning, and halted before the State House until the coffin was conveyed to the hearse.

The transparency which adorned the front of the building, namely, the portrait of the late President, with a dark border representing a coffin, afforded a relief to the surrounding gloom of the morning—the words "Rest in Peace" still blazing from the gas-jets.

The Invincibles, a city organization, with torches, composed a part of the procession, and the City Guard acted as the escort. A band of music played dirges on the march.

The procession reached Kensington Station at 4 o'clock. Thousands of men, women and children were still in the streets, and not a few half-dressed residents in that neighborhood, who, apparently, had just hurried from their beds, ran forward to join the already large crowds waiting at the depot. The funeral party with difficulty pressed their way to the cars.

At a few minutes after 4 o'clock the train started. A locomotive preceded it by ten minutes. The engine is trimmed with the national flag draped with mourning, and there is a telegraph and two signal men accompanying it to guard against accidents.

The train consisted of nine elegant cars, provided by the Camden and Amboy Railroad, all tastefully trimmed.

The funeral car last night was additionally decorated, heavy silver fringe being placed at the end of the black coverings of the several panels, and the festoon being fastened with stars and tassels of similar material. First Lieut. JAMES A. DURKEN, Lieut. MURPHY and Sergeants C. ROWHART, S. CARPENTER, A. C. CROMWELL and J. McINTOSH, spent the entire of last night thus improving the exterior of the car, and clothing the interior with additional drapery. The materials were contributed by citizens of Philadelphia.

Mr. HALL STANTON, Chairman of the Philadelphia Councils, who accompanied us, with marked courtesy and constant attention and efficiency, carried into effect the liberal spirit of Philadelphia Councils in the extension of the hospitalities of the city to its guest.

There was on board the cars a committee from Newark, consisting of the Mayor of that city, JOSEPH P. BRADLEY, Esq., and the President and other members of the Councils, together with eight additional citizens.

These and the Mayor of Washington and other civilians, occupied seats in the front cars. Next in order were Senators and members of the House of Representatives, with their respective officers. Then followed the Iowa and Illinois delegations and representatives of the several States and Territories.

The Guard of Honor occupied the next car, and after this was that containing the remains of the late President and his little son WILLIE. . . .

PHILADELPHIA, Monday, April 24.

The body of President LINCOLN remained in state till 1 o'clock this morning, when the entrances were closed, all the throng having had an opportunity of viewing the remains.

Dr. BROWN, the embalmer, removed the dust that had settled on the face, and preparations were made for the departure of the body. At 3 o'clock the body was placed in the hearse, and the line of march taken for the Trenton Railroad Depot.

The escort consisted of the One Hundred and Eighty-seventh Pennsylvania Infantry, the city troops, guard of honor, and a detachment of soldiers to guard the body, Perseverance Hose Company, and the Republican Invincibles.

The train started for New-York at 4 o'clock A.M.

At a few minutes past 4 o'clock the train left the Kensington station, and soon reached Bristol, where several hundred persons had assembled.

The sun was now rising in its full glory, beautifully illuminating the rural scenes.

Gov. PARKER came on board at the State line—at Morrisville—with his staff consisting of Adj.-Gen. R. F. STOCKTON, Quartermaster General PERRINE and others of his staff.

They were accompanied by United States Senator JOHN. P. STOCKTON, REV. D. HENRY MILLER and Col. MURPHY, and were received by Gov. CURTIN, of Pennsylvania, who had joined the funeral party at Harrisburgh.

The Delaware River, which separates the State of Pennsylvania from that of New-Jersey, was crossed at 5½ o'clock; and as the train passed through Trenton, the bells of the city were tolled. Immense throngs of spectators had here gathered. Every hilltop and the line of the road, and other advantageous points, were largely occupied. The train proceeded onward until it reached the station, where it stopped for thirty minutes. The population here had assembled in much larger numbers, for this was the more attractive point.

The station was elaborately festooned, and the national banner draped with crape was a prominent feature. There was a detachment of the Reserved Veterans and Invalid Corps drawn up in line on the platform, giving the customary funeral honors. Music was performed by an instrumental band, minute guns were fired, the bells continuing to toll.

A number of persons rushed from various directions toward the car containing the body of the President, but the masses generally retained their standing positions, evidently showing they were satisfied to restrain their impatience for a few minutes until the car could pass before them.

Absorbed in the general interest of the scene, it did not occur to the male part of the throng that a general lifting of the hat would have been a silent but becoming mark of respect to the dead. Everywhere, however, the emblems of mourning were prominent, showing that the people of Trenton, like all other true patriots, were not unmindful of the great loss which has befallen the nation in the violent death of our beloved and honored President.

Leaving Trenton, the train arrived at New-Brunswick at about 7½ o'clock, where it halted for perhaps half an hour, to afford the residents an opportunity to examine the funeral car and its treasured but inanimate contents. Crowds, accordingly, hurried in that direction. Meantime, minute guns were fired and the bells tolled. At 8 o'clock the train was again in motion.

Twenty-five minutes past 8 o'clock, and we were at Rahway, and at fifteen minutes to nine arrived at Elizabeth.

At both these places the emblems of mourning were numerously seen, and flags draped, as at the cities and other places previously passed. The tolling of bells and the firing of cannon were repeated.

Near the latter town a party of young men displayed, on differently colored banners, the words, separately, of "Victory," "Peace," "Union," GRANT, SHERMAN, with the usual crape attachments.

As we move on the crowds begin to largely increase, for we are in the sight of Newark, a city of 80,00 inhabitants.

The private residences and public buildings and stores and workshops are, some of them, elaborately draped, flags at half-mast, and other evidence of sorrow exhibited.

Arrived at Newark, and the train for a few minutes at rest, a fine opportunity is afforded from the car window to view the animated scene.

Guns are fired and the bells toll. All Newark, with the exception of those in the windows, seem to be out of doors. Trees and house-tops, and door-steps, and car-tracks, in fact, all the highest attainable positions and points where an unobstructed view can be had, were occupied. Throngs of people from various parts of New-Jersey might here be measured for miles.

And here it should be stated that as the funeral train passed, nearly every man lifted his hat as a mark of respect, and many women removed their bonnets, animated by a feeling similar to that which governed the opposite sex.

Among the more prominent features was the United States Hospital, suitably decorated. In front were a large number of soldiers, some of them on crutches.

All the patients, who could move themselves, were drawn up in double file. Every one of them stood uncovered, and seemed to be deeply affected by the touching spectacle of the hearse bearing the remains of the assassinated President.

The train is again in motion, and soon reaches—at 10 o'clock—Jersey City.

Here the arrangements seemed to be perfect, and that nothing had been neglected which could give due effect to the ceremonies of the occasion.

The coffin was removed from the hearse-car by eight soldiers. It was partially covered with the American flag, and with flowers not yet entirely withered.

The Remains in New-York.

The funeral train conveying the remains of President LINCOLN, left Newark at 9:07 yesterday morning, in charge of Mr. COULTER, the senior conductor of the road, the same officer who was conductor of the train in which Mr. LINCOLN went on to Washington.

While the cars were passing onward toward Jersey City, the people of that place were gathering at windows and roofs, filling the streets, and occupying all possible points of view around the great station-house at the ferry way.

THE SCENE WITHIN THE STATION-HOUSE

was very quiet, but very impressive. The train was due about 10 o'clock. Much before 9 the balcony that runs round the interior of the station-house began to be occupied by ladies and their escorts. Along the front of the balcony, around the whole vast interior, hung one single broad band of black cloth, relieved with white stripes crossed diagonally. At the eastern end was a large national flag draped and festooned in mourning, with the impressive motto, "Be still, and know that I am God," and at the opposite extremity, the station clock was heavily draped in black and stopped at the hour of the President's death, with the motto, "A nation's heart is struck," and the date of the deed.

ARRIVAL.

A guard of two hundred regulars from the Second and Sixth United States Infantry, under Capt. LIVINGSTON and Maj. McLAUGHLIN, is posted in and around the station. As the hour for the arrival of the funeral train approaches, the squad within the station-house, standing at ease, with stacked arms, is suddenly ordered into line. They form and march, the words of command sounding out clearly in the great empty, quiet, vaulted room; and a line of sentinels is posted at short distances along the midmost of the five tracks that run lengthwise through the house. The galleries are slowly filling up; the spacious floor of the great room is almost empty. A low murmur of conversation comes from the balcony; the noise and bustle of the ferry passengers sounds loudly from without, and every minute or two the brazen clash of an engine-bell breaks suddenly in from the tracks outside of the western gates; the long line of sentinels, with bayonets fixed, moves waveringly hither and thither; the rest of the squad stand at ease, with arms stacked; the representatives of the press are conversing together in a group; all the faces are grave; there is a hush in the whole feeling of the place, enhanced by the vast empty space of the station-house, so silently awaiting the entrance of the corpse of the dead ruler of the land.

Mr. Secretary of State DEPEW, and Mr. Police Commissioner ACTON, quietly enter the building; a little afterward, the delegation from the municipalities of Jersey City, Hoboken, and Bergen, file in; then the Saengerbund, or united German Singing Societies of Hoboken, come in and take their place. Brig. Gen. HATFIELD, commanding the Hudson brigade of New-Jersey State troops, Brig.-Gen. HUNT, commanding the troops of the harbor and defences of New-York, and a few other officers, enter. Beyond the gates, glimpses can be seen of silent crowds plied like drifts of light snow on roofs, cars, and other elevated places.

The train is approaching. The line of sentinels is extended, quite cutting off the area within which the cars are to enter. Mr. WOODRUFF, the polite Superintendent of the railroad, is just in season to secure the reporters their professional immunities from military command.

Almost unheard, the nine cars of the funeral train, all draped with black, glide steadily in through the western gates of the station. Now the guards present arms; a battery of the Hudson County Artillery, at a little distance, fires minute guns; and the Saengerbund chants, in a great volume of strong and manly voices, with much feeling and good execution, an impressive *Grabesruhe,* or Requiem.

THE TRANSIT.

The last car of the train, the gorgeous and highly finished one built for President LINCOLN's use while he was alive, is detached. That immediately in front of it, its somber, almost black, paneling contrasting strongly with the strong crimson of the other, was finished expressly for its present sad purpose. The civic and military delegation who have escorted the body of the dead from Washington, gather to the door of this funeral car. All heads are uncovered, and the coffin is reverently borne forth by soldiers of the Veteran Reserves, and carried to the hearse. As it leaves the station-house the deep voices of the Germans are silent, and the various delegations, forming into line, march slowly from the building by its western exit, pass down Exchange-place towards the ferry-boat; the Washington escort first, the Mayor and Common Councils of New-York next, and the military and other civic bodies following.

Above the entrance to the ferry way appears the inscription: "WASHINGTON, the Father; LINCOLN, the Savior of his country." A strong line of guards keeps clear a broad and ample space for the procession. Outside their line a great and dense but serious and silent crowd is gathered. All are quickly on board the boat, and moving at once out of the slip, she crosses without delay or accident to the foot of Debrosses-street.

THE PROCESSION TO THE CITY HALL.

The Seventh Regiment and the police maintained a perfectly clear area throughout the whole space of Debrosses-street, from end to end. As the boat entered the slip the singers again took their places near the hearse. The procession took order as it passed from the boat. The Seventh Regiment, already formed, took the right of line, the hearse moving within a hollow square formed by its ranks. Next moved three lines of coaches, conveying the Washington escort, and the line was closed by the civic deputations.

Along the whole distance from the ferry the excellent police arrangements of the day maintained clear roadway. But the sidewalks, windows, roofs, posts, trees, all imaginable points for advantageous view, were crowded to their utmost capacity, and there was, it is believed, not one building without its signs of mourning.

Passing through this immense, almost soundless, but intensely interested and deeply sympathetic crowd by Debrosses-street to Canal, by Canal to Broadway, down Broadway to the Astor House, up Park-row to the eastern side of the Park at Printing House-square, the procession moved slowly into the open space before the City Hall, and the gray lines of the Seventh Regiment marked the margin of the broad area already kept clear by the police. Within inner lines of soldiers, while the great audience in reverent silence uncovered their heads, the hearse halted before the main entrance of the City Hall.

The City Hall.

At an early hour yesterday morning, the people began to gather about the Park. By 8 o'clock several thousands had assembled, and seemed determined to stand their ground at any inconvenience, so that an early view might be had of the remains. The City Hall was barred and locked; around the front, and guarding every side, stood lines of uniformed police, keeping perfect order, and strictly enforcing the rule that no one should enter. Invitations extended by the courtesy of Alderman J. D. OTTIWELL secured the admission of the press to the rotunda, and subsequently to the Governor's Room, where, in spite of the singular opposition of a man named LEWIS CARPENTER, a mechanic, who seemed to be temporarily in charge, they remained during the exhibition. The sound of hammers mingled with the voice of authority, while the decorations were being completed and arrangements made by the committee. Gen. HALL, with his aids and assistants, were in one room, receiving messages and sending dispatches; Alderman OTTIWELL, and the other members of the committee, were in another room, winding up the ends of their programme for the day; the builder and decorator of the velvet-carpeted resting-room of the Martyr-President were smoothing out wrinkles, adjusting folds and driving the last tack; Col. HAMILTON, of Gen. SANDFORD's staff, and Maj. RATHBUN, of the army, were making arrangements for the accommodation of the many military gentlemen expected; Gen. BURNSIDE, with several elegant ladies, waited for the arrival of the body with floral testimonials of regard; the half-dozen members of the press, after arguing with one door keeper, parleying with another, escaping the machinations of CARPENTER, who followed them like a second old man of the mountain, noted the appearance of the hall and the Governor's Room, and viewed from the balcony the sight of all others, the great massing of people. All around the pillars in the rotunda and in front of the hall wound gracefully folds of cloth and crape, black as night; about the walls hung great masses of somber bunting; CARPENTER's "Study of Lincoln" rested quietly with sad expression opposite the entrance to the Governor's Room, and the exponents of our city's pomp and power—her colors—draped the walls on either side. The hours wore on and the multitude deepened; far up Chatham-street waited thousands of men, women and children, whose impatience burst forth in occasional and periodical push-ings, which only the sharp rap of the policemen's club could quiet; Printing-house-square was full, the Park was held by very many who hugged close to the line of the police, contenting themselves with the sight of the City Hall and the sound of the tolling bells; boys and men mounted the trees, and Washington's monstrosity in the park, dark sashed, was the involuntary support of half a score of adventurous youths who neither feared the police nor regarded the Father of his Country.

The scene at the east side of the Park was most interesting. At first it was determined to keep the people double lined, in which order they could pass in and out of the Hall, but this was not only impracticable but impossible. It is no easy task to count the heads in a crowd, but time and patience combined with a little arithmetic will do wonders, and by the ju-dicious exercise of this combination, we estimated the numerical force of the crowd, at half after ten, at ten thousand; three times as many gathering there at half past three. To keep this tired, waiting multitude quiet and or-derly, was no light duty; pushing and hauling, scrounging and elbowing, talking and scolding, were the order of the day. The officers did well at first, but policemen should be relieved often, or else made superhuman patient. No mere humanity could stand such an amount of annoyance long, and soon the locusts were taken in hand, and the stern direction was enforced by the sterner blow. So far as we could observe, no person was seriously injured, but the amount of headache induced by these delicate attentions of the Metropolitans must have been fearful.

Several incidents occurred before the arrival of the procession, which served to break the monotony of the occasion. In the first place, and ad-venturous band of men and boys attempted to break the lines in front of the Hall; they partially succeeded, but were soon routed ignominiously by the force in charge, and after a few moments' disgrace, were released on promise of good behavior; then a short line of venerable men, under es-cort of Officer McWATERS, drew near the Hall—each man faltered some-what in step, and seemed broken in post; still the tear-dimmed eye and the crape-bound arm betokened the presence of feeling and the beating of a national heart—they were the remnant of the war of 1812, and as they filed behind the pointed iron railing on which they leaned for support, they were recognized by the crowd, and welcomed with a cheer. Presently a break was noticed in the dense crowds about the TIMES building, then a wider opening, from which marched, headed by a brass band, a great number of foreign-born citizens, singers, members of the several Ger-man singing societies of our city and vicinity, who united on this occa-sion in friendly harmony, to do honor and homage to the mortal remains of their former President. The singers comprised the membership of the

Saengerbund, Liederkranz and Arion Societies, some two thousand in all, under the baton of Mr. POWELL.

Three bearded men entered the east gate of the Park, passed the thousands who wondered who they were, and were marshaled quietly and quickly as though familiar with military order, on either side of a passage through which the coffin and its escort were to pass. Armed with the proper passes, His Honor Recorder HOFFMAN and the clerks of his court appeared upon the balcony overlooking the assemblage. Superintendent KENNEDY, with official cape and business air, stood on the esplanade. The handsome figure and courteous bearing of Gen. VAN VLIET, of the army, marked him conspicuous among the noted people waiting the arrival of the procession. GURNEY & SON were preparing to photograph the interior of the building, its decorations, and subsequently the body.

SCENE FROM THE BALCONY.

At precisely 11:30 o'clock the head of the procession entered the gate east of the park. The scene from the balcony of this moment was one never to be forgotten. Far off and near waved mournfully in the bright, balmy air, the draped colors of a sorrow-stricken nation. From every possible point of exhibition were flung to the view of scores of thousands, clean against the blue horizon, the red, white and blue emblem of liberty, sabled with the somber tone of mourning. On the right marched, with singular precision and rare exactness, the famous Seventh, to whose reputation for efficiency and readiness at home will ever be added its willingness to fight when ordered. All around the hemisphere, to the minor harmonies of their celebrated band, stretched the full ranks of our soldiers. In front, reaching from the line of the police to the further verge of the park, resting literally against the iron railings, stood an army of interested, anxious men and women, whose uncovered heads and upturned countenances resembled a quiet sea of expectancy; the double force of singers, bareheaded and ready for the dirge; the short line, fifteen in all, of venerable men who fought and bled in their country's cause half a century ago, lifted from their bald heads their hats, banded with weeds; the strong sun in mid-heaven sent down a Summer heat, and the wind, which a few moments before whistled wildly along, burdened with clouds of dust, hushed into a whisper, and breathed balmily on every spot. From distant batteries the cannon belched at each minute a thunder tone of woe. From all the steeples came forth the wailing of bells, while from the spire of old Trinity floated upon the breeze the tuneful chimings of "Old Hundred."

The band, preceded by a detachment of police, entered the Park with stirring music, and the gallant Seventh, Col. EMMONS CLARK at its head, took possession of the place. On, on until the right rested at the west end, they marched, and in due time, conducted with all fitting ceremony the hearse to its assigned position.

Borne on the sturdy shoulders of the Veteran Reserve Corps, the coffin, with its sacred dust, was taken into the hall rotunda, preceded by Maj.-Gen. SANDFORD and Superintendent KENNEDY, and flanked by Maj.-Gens. Dix, Hunter and Barnard, Brig.-Gens. Van Vliet, Townsend, Ramsay, Howe, Caldwell and McCallum, Col. D. T. Van Buren, Lieut. Col. O'Bierne and Capt. Barstow. Following were a long line of dignitaries, of whom we will speak as they appear in the Governor's Room.

THE ROTUNDA.

The coffin, a massive combination of wood, lead, black velvet and silver adornments was carried into the rotunda, while the eight hundred choristers without, led by their band and conducted by Mr. POWER, their head, chanted with fine effect and in perfect harmony the magnificent "Pilgrim's Chorus," from TAUHAUSER [sic], and afterward as the solemn procession wound slowly along the spiral stairway, the singers gave the startling "Chorus of the Spirits," by SCHUBERT, a composition as popular as it is weird and effective. The interior of the rotunda presented at this moment a beautiful though mournful spectacle. The entire circle was covered up, representing a marque, the walls were formed of National, State and city flags, extending from dome to level. Across these flags ran a winding chain of black paramatio, which formed a deep hem as it were, bordering the partitions made by the flags. At the rear of the rotunda, fronting the catafalque was CARPENTER's portrait of the late Mr. LINCOLN. This was studded with silver stars and edged around with black. The skylight was covered with black, causing a splendid light to pervade the interior, which was mellowed by the lights from two chandeliers on each side of an inclined plane at the head of the stairs, through which the light permeated by means of ground glass globes.

On this plane, which formed a portion of the catafalque, the coffin was placed; after which the troops retired, policemen were stationed at the head of either stairway, and sentries stood at all the doors.

The coffin resting on the plane formed a base line for the magnificent catafalque, which fronted on the rotunda, opening also into the Governor's Room, where were the distinguished and invited quests. The catafalque is worthy of description, and seen through the medium of the embarrassed light struggling through the dusky corridors from the park, or feebly peering through the thick grounding of the chandelier globes, it is at once impressive and mystic in its appearance. The front of the canopy presents the appearance of a dark square on which rests an elliptical gothic arch extending across the whole width of the square or parallelogram at the base of the arch. The dimension of this can be conceived by the statement of its height from the peak of the arch to the base of the structure, which is twenty feet. The width is ten feet and the depth is twelve feet. The exterior adornments are plain, elegant and proper. The summit or peak of the arch is topped by an eagle, in silver, which slightly relieves the somber aspect of all. The wings are folded, the head or beak slightly drooped. In the centre, under the eagle, is a bust of Mr. LINCOLN, also in silver. These, with a number of stars and a margin of silver fringes and tassels placed on a ground of fine black cloth and velvet, which covers the entire receptacle, conveys a clear idea, bearing in mind the dimension already given, of the exterior appearance of the catafalque. The base of the arch of the canopy is done in fine cloth, honeycombed. The two sides of the canopy are adorned with two urns covered with black cloth. The drapery in front of the arch, inside, is lined with white silk of superior texture. Inside the catafalque the black is unrelieved, save by the dots of silver stars here and there through the surface, and four marble statues underneath, standing at the four angles, being busts of WASHINGTON, WEBSTER, JACKSON and CLAY. The interior covering is in the inevitable black cloth and velvet, the canopy overhead being lined with fluted cloth, radiating in folds from the middle to the sides. The rest is all plain black cloth or black velvet. The two pillars of the City Hall, standing on each side of the catafalque, are wrapped in the national colors, heavily draped with crape and black silk, and have drapery of black profusely bound around them in spiral folds.

THE GOVERNOR'S ROOM.

Admission to the Governor's Room was a privilege extended by note to many distinguished citizens, official and lay, to certain members of the press, to the escorting Guard of Honor, and to friends of the Common Council. When the procession arrived at the hall and the coffin was placed in position, Maj.-Gen. DIX, Maj.-Gen. SANFORD, Maj.-Gen. PECK and Maj.-Gen. BARNARD stepped from the catafalque into the room, while others entered by the door. . . .

Judge DAVIS, of the Supreme Court, and a few of the male relatives of Mrs. LINCOLN accompanied the delegation, as did an embalmer and undertaker.

The coffin was given in charge of the embalmer, who opened it, and prepared the body for exhibition, dressing it in clean under-clothing and collar, and arranging it for the photographer. So soon as all was ready Mrs.

CHARLES E. STRONG, of No. 38 East Twenty-second-street, accompanied by Gen. BURNSIDE, entered the catafalque, and placed in the coffin one of the most beautiful arrangements of flowers we have ever seen. On a ground, shield-shaped, of scarlet azalias and double nasturtiums, was a cross of pure white of japonicas and orange blossoms—an offering as rich and beautiful, as it was chaste and [word illegible] "Master GEORGE WASHINGTON IRVING [word illegible] BISHOP," led by his mother, placed, also, on the coffin white flowers arranged as "A. L." and [word illegible]. These done, Mr. GURNEY, Jr., to whom had been granted the exclusive right of taking pictures of the body and the scene, took possession of the hall and retained it for over half an hour, during which time he succeeded in assuring material for a photograph as interesting as it will be historic. . . .

Hastily and reverently the people approached, and with uncovered head, bent forward to seize an impression of the honored features. To those who had not seen Mr. Lincoln in life, the view may be satisfactory; but to those who were familiar with his features, it is far otherwise. The color is leaden, almost brown; the forehead recedes sharp and clearly marked; the eyes deep sunk and close held upon the sockets; the cheek bones, always high, are unusually prominent; the cheeks hollowed and deep pitted; the unnaturally thin lips shut tight and firm as if glued together; and the small chin, covered with slight beard, seemed pointed and sharp. The body is dressed in black, the white turned-over collar and the clean white gloves making a strong contrast to the black velvet cloth and the leaden-hued features. This is all that remains of the man whom goodness made great and whose rest in the hearts of the people is forever and abiding. It will not be possible, despite the effection of the embalming, to continue much longer the exhibition, as the constant shaking of the body aided by the exposure to the air, and the increasing of dust, has already undone much of the [word illegible] workmanship, and it is doubtful if it will be decreed wise to tempt dissolution much further.

The glittering tinsel of the coffin's decorations, the brilliant uniforms of the officers, and the simple beauty of the fragrant flowers sink into utter insignificance before the awful reality of the stern, gaunt corpse that rests, dressed with faultless nicety, in that narrow box. The people seem to think so, for as they filed singly with timid step past the head of the coffin, the eye rested not on the gallant O'BIERNE, the dark-browed HUNTER, the floral wonders, the magnificent embroidery, the galaxy of uniformed officers, whose starred shoulder straps have elicited many cheers in the heat and front of battle, nor the gorgeous trappings of the velvet canopy, but singly and alone upon the face of the dead, whose words, once law, are now passed into history.

Guided by the sentries and the police, the crowd pushed on—at the rate, now of fifty, now of thirty, a minute, averaging, perhaps, during the first watch, thirty-five a minute. Few words were spoken, few tears shed, but over all and pervading was a deep tone of sympathy, of regret, of respectful regard for the President who had gone. A noticeable feature was the preponderance, at first, of young girls—[word illegible] girls, apparently, between the ages of sixteen and twenty. It is doubtful if, in the eighteen hundred people who passed during the first hour, there were two hundred young men. There were old men, middle-aged men, laborers and craftsmen—women of every age, children of tender years, and not a few colored people; but the youth of the city were all there.

At 2 o'clock the second watch came on duty. . . .

During this watch, matters were somewhat changed in regard to admittance to the Governor's Room, and those desiring to enter were obliged to obtain passes from Gen. DIX. This was peculiarly annoying to those who could not find the General, and who relied upon passes obtained from the committee. To Col. RIBLET, who was authorized by Col. D. T. VAN BUREN, Adjutant-General of the department of the East, the reporters were under obligations, as he kindly countersigned their permits, which insured free access and egress, as the Colonel was officer of the day, and his men guarded the entire place. All this was soon arranged, as the civic and military officials agreed that mutual accommodation was the best policy, and all passes, from whatever source, were thenceforth respected. The details soon became monotonous. Out doors the vast crowd surged against the Metropolitan rock, and roared with anger as they were clubbed back between the lines or laughed with glee if one of their number succeeded in eluding the vigilance of the officer. Struggling with strong and sturdy men, selfish in the anxiety to get into line, delicate women, young girls, mothers with children, babies, and, in some cases, families, stood, or tussled, or swayed violently with the current of people. Of the thousands there but few could get in. The coffin, perched at the head of a narrow passage, is reached by perhaps eighteen hundred an hour, while it might have been placed where three or five times as many could have seen it. . . .

THE OBSEQUIES

Sombre Grandeur of the Funeral Pageant.

Imposing Demonstrations of the People's Respect.

Tremendous Crush and Pressure in the Streets.

Suburban, Metropolitan, and Miscellaneous Crowds.

Sixty Thousand Citizens in the Funeral Procession.

The Closing Scenes About the Coffin and in the Streets.

Mr. Bancroft's Oration at Union Square.

Departure of the Funeral Train.

The coffin in which was deposited the dead body of our deceased President was kept open from 12 o'clock Monday noon, until 12 o'clock Tuesday noon. From the earliest moment to the latest, every facility compatible with the narrow arrangements of the committees, was afforded the public for viewing the remains. The Guard of Honor, divided into twelve watches, did duty until the lid was fastened on the casket, relieving each other every two hours.

THE EIGHTH WATCH

took charge at 2 o'clock Tuesday morning, down to which time the TIMES account of yesterday was complete. . . .

These gentlemen stood patiently and quietly until 4 o'clock in the morning. Doubtless they had anticipated a season of reflection rather than action; they knew that at such hours honest men were asleep and that rogues were watched by the police. For once they were mistaken. The crowds that filed through the Hall exceeded those which but two hours before preceded them. A glance from the balcony toward Chatham-street revealed not only a broad line of pilgrims wending slowly their way to the bier of the martyr, but far beyond stood the dense masses of immovable people, with but one apparent thought, one determination; turning to the west end of the Park a still greater force of men and women, and not a few children, who, provided by the courtesy of the members of the committee, had passed the sentinels and now stood silent and glum in vain expectancy of success. But these vast hosts were only the exponents of the civic multitudes which were massed solid in the streets. One could go neither up nor down the street; crossing was perilous, as it involved an encounter with scores of hundreds of irate citizens, some of whom would like no better sport by which to relieve the tedium of the hour than a tossing and whipping of any such offender, and a passage from point to point by persons who had no desire even to visit the Hall was a simple impossibility. Of course these people did not get into the Hall; many of them stood there for hours in the hot sun, exposed to the wind and dust; some came early in the evening and braved the long weariness of time between 8 and 2, and then from excess of faintness gave up their places and trudged, provoked and out of temper, homeward. Others, however, held on, and many of them were so fortunate as to get foothold upon the City Hall basement steps, but their difficulties were but then commenced. From the bottom step to the top, thence along the corridor to the second flight, and thence again to the Governor's Room, stood in every place a man, or what was worse, a woman. Little by little, the fagged-out men and the toilworn women, and the pallid, sleepy children, moved toward the desired point; a step at a time, and a very little step at that, was all they could even think of, and this was taken with fear and trembling, for on each side, in front and behind, stepped likewise a neighbor—an unpleasant eager neighbor, one of the anxious, imperative sort, who push and haul, elbow and knuckle violently at every opportunity, but with no good result to himself. If graciously permitted to enter the Governor's Room, how short was the stay, how unsatisfactory the look on the dead man's face, how instantly the police moved them on—on and out of the door at the other end of the room, around the rotunda and back again in the dense crowd, with long flight of stairs before them, up which came the eager ones, as the disappointed and weary went down. To the public, the exhibition of the discolored face of the President was not desirable. Sympathy and love for the deceased led many doubtless to the side of the coffin, but if we may judge from the effect produced upon them by the sight, by their subsequent action, curiosity had a still greater power over them, and took them through troubles and over difficulties, which, under ordinary circumstances, would have been deemed insurmountable. The features were so very unnatural, the color so thoroughly turned, and the general appearance so unpleasant, that none could regard the remains with even a melancholy pleasure.

Among those who availed themselves of this opportunity were the compositors of the TIMES newspaper, who, kindly favored by Superintendent KENNEDY and Capt. BRACKETT, of the Twenty-sixth Precinct, were speedily passed through the crowd and granted the melancholic satisfaction of viewing the remains.

The still night was occasionally broken upon by a sob; the monotony of the scene was varied now and then by an incidental remark, the dropping of a flower or a tear, the harsh voice of a policeman "passing on" the crowd, or the "hurry up there" of some impatient lingerer in the corridor beyond.

At 4 o'clock commenced the

which lasted until 6. . . .

During these hours the pressure very sensibly diminished—the successful people had gone home disappointed, and the unsuccessful had gone provoked. Their places, in the main vacant, were filled partially by new comers, men who had slept all night, risen early, taken breakfast, and were prepared with vigor for the race set before them. These were gradually reinforced by a crowd from the adjoining cities and the country round about. The Fulton and other ferries, more particularly the former, had been patronized to an incredible extent all day, but their receipts at night doubtless exceeded those of any other occasion. Gentlemen with ladies, thinking the early morning hours the best, had gone over at 1 or 2 o'clock, only to find the streets blockaded and the passage to the Hall an impossibility. Disliking to give it up so, they would hang about the place an hour or two and then retrace their steps, meeting on their homeward route as many more, who preferred the experience of the moment to the wisdom of its predecessors. Fulton-street, Beekman-street, and Park-row were alive with inhabitants of the City of Churches; and while New-York was filling up from the other direction, Brooklyn can boast of her full share in the turn-out of the day.

At a little after 5 Mr. BROWN, the embalmer, who, skilled and competent as he is, could not be expected to perform a miracle on short notice, looked at the corpse. He detected with an experienced eye the change in color and the slight falling of the lower jaw. The dusty hue of the face, which, by the way, had become painfully perceptible, was in part attributable to the dust brought in by the crowd, which settled on it as well as on everything else. The rarely beautiful flowers, for instance, had become soiled to such an extent that it was difficult to make out what they were, while the cloth upon the coffin and the various trappings of the catafalque were dingy and dusty, and will need much refurbishing before they can be cut into coats or cloaks. A brush with the handkerchief removed a portion of the dirt, leaving the face distinct. The jaw was likewise arranged and the collar cleaned, the coat brushed and the neckcloth dusted. After this we looked again upon the features of him who so short a time since stood head and shoulder above his country-men. Alas, that it was deemed wise to show them. In life about the saddened countenance played gleams of wit and humor; the eye, though mournful at times and in rest, was fired with keen appreciation of the great and good, as it was powerful in indignation; the mouth, large and tight drawn, was ever ready to speak kind words or smile pleasantly; the dear face, homely and peculiar as we all knew it, was radiant ever with love to man, and expressive always of a desire for the right. How changed in death. Those thousands who crowded zealously in the street, pushed vigorously on the stairs, strove earnestly in the corridor, glanced hastily at the face and passed hurriedly from the room, saw no ABRAHAM LINCOLN. The flurry of the crush was yet upon them when they found themselves in the presence of the dead; curiously they looked at him and instantly were gone. In this brief period philosophical reason had no sway, the physical eye saw and reported to the mind—what? A face dark to blackness, features sharp to a miracle, an expression almost horrible in its un-nature, a stiff, starched countenance resembling none they knew of and expressive of nothing familiar. Such a sight revealed nothing of ABRAHAM LINCOLN.

From 6 o'clock until 8 the tenth watch guarded the remains. . . .

Nothing of peculiar interest transpired during this watch. The visitors did not average above twenty a minute, of whom the vast majority were young men and boys. At this time the hundreds of people from Brooklyn, who had tried themselves beyond endurance during the tedious hours of the seventh and eighth watches, waiting in the streets, might with ease have obtained entrance and a good view of the corpse, but they had gone home, and those who took their places were men of better calculation. The Jersey City boats now began to pour forth a flood of people, who, converging at that place from the many railway points about, united in a steady phalanx and marched toward Broadway. The consequence was that, by 8 o'clock, the street from the west end gate to Barnum's Museum was blocked by thousands, who stood there, not because they were so directed, but because their fellow-citizens were with them. They had no expectations of seeing the remains; they came over to see the procession, which was advertised to move at 1 o'clock, some five hours ahead. It was curious to look at these. With the fact before them that five mortal hours must elapse before even the advertised hour should arrive they stood patiently, good humouredly, and apparently content.

At 8 o'clock the Eleventh watch relieved the Tenth. . . .

Now began the closing scenes of the funeral occasion. From this time on an immensity of detail transpired, repetitious in nature, but eminently intrusting in feature. Outside the pressure was tremendous. The line on the west side of the Park extended to John-street unbroken and impassible. The mass on the Chatham-street side reached to Pearl, dense, close-packed, and momentarily denser and closer packed. The Brooklyn folks for some reason known only to themselves, formed in procession in Fulton-street, extending from the ferry to the *Herald* office, but at this time making no progress in any direction, and apparently intending none. To all of these departments constant additions were made, and the few who passed into the City Hall made no perceptible difference in the crowd for two good reasons: In the first place they were immediately succeeded by new comers, and in the second, when they left the Hall they became part and parcel of the crowd on the other side. At either end of the Hall the processional visitors passed in. Those entering at the east going up and down the rotunda steps, those entering at the west going to the rear of the catafalque by way of the Governor's room, passing out at the further door, and forming a descending line on the right of the steps, on which others were advancing. And concerning this west entrance it is fit to mention that at first the Common Council intended to have their families and friends visit the remains at night, entering by means of a special permit by the west gate. There could have been no objection to this if the detail had been properly attended to. But every Alderman and every official found that he not only had a family and a few friends, but that he was the happy possessor of the friendship of the entire ward. Such brotherly love as seems to exist between the members of the City Government and their constituents and their constituents' country cousins, is wonderful to a degree and most creditable to all concerned. It is not well, however, to prejudice the rights of an entire community, even to maintain the relatives of so very happy a family; and when it was ascertained that the families and "few friends" of the officials were rushing through the Governor's Room at the rate of three thousand an hour, and that there were many thousands yet to come, it was deemed wise to stop it. This was done for a time, but after deliberation, it was concluded that if three thousand could go through doing no damage, other thousands might do the same, and word was given to admit any and all who could get to the door. The result of this was that by 9 o'clock there were two steady currents of people— one by the rotunda, averaging perhaps forty per minute, and a second by the Governor's Room, at the rate of fifty a minute.

The Seventh Regiment was still on duty. As escort to the remains their labor began when the body reached the city, on Monday at noon, and terminated only when the farewell whistle was blown from the locomotive boiler. The Council chambers were used by the members who were not on guard, and presented a scene of chaotic regimentalism. The weary men lay in every conceivable position, on table, desk, and floor; guns were stacked, swords placed on chairs, pitchers, tumblers, bottles and cigars were handy and confusion apparent, but order in reality reigned throughout the place. During this watch, however, all were up and at work preparing for the grand parade of the day. Col. CLARK and Adjutant J. HARRY LABINEAU were busily engaged with the officers of the day. The sentries paced their from lonely posts. The men burnished their guns, selected clean gloves and made themselves trim. Capt. E. P. ROGERS, of Company

K, was stationed at the east gate, and his men had their hands full to manage the persistent and pertinacious crowd which continually tried their patience. To Capt. ROGERS we are under obligations for a rescue from the midst of an unaccommodating crowd, who failed to recognize the right of newspaper men to go where *they* were forbidden. From Adjutant LABINEAU we learned that the entire "Music Guard" was composed of veteran members of the Seventh who had passed into higher rank in actual service, among them being a Colonel, a Lieutenant-Colonel, a Major, three Captains and an Adjutant.

At 10 o'clock the twelfth and last watch went on guard. . . .

Just at this moment some one on the roof or at one of the upper windows of the Hall, threw a lighted cigar away; falling on the drapery just below the inscription, "The Nation Mourns," it set fire to it, but luckily it was at once extinguished, and but little damage done.

The police then took possession of the Park, although the square was still guarded by the Seventh Regiment. So tremendous had become the pressure that it was found necessary to extend chains across, by means of which the crowds were kept back. To the members of the force, from the Commission down, the public are under great obligations for the excellent discipline maintained by the men in a time of general disorganization, and for the singular good order of the city, in a time of unprecedented excitement. . . .

At a little after eleven, the sergeants of the Veteran Corps, who came to carry the coffin to the hearse, filed into the room, taking position at the side of the hall. The embalmer and the undertaker then proceeded to close up the casket. . . . Nothing was said. What should be? The sightless eye, the speechless lips, the harsh, unmeaning lines, cold and dark—if eloquence was needed, surely these supplied it. One look more—the dust was brushed away from the high forehead, the collar somewhat arranged; the lid was put on, the screws turned, the cold, collapsed figure emboxed, and the men whose commissions he had signed and issued could see him no more forever.

Strange contrast to this scene was the next. The door opened, and in walked the highly decorated representatives of Great Britain, Russia and France—scarlet, gilt, silver-laced, costly trappings, high coat-collars, bearing embroidered cocked hats under their arms, birth and breeding in every gesture, desirous of seeing the corpse. They were too late. The dead was given over to the hand of him who does the final apparelling, and the time had passed when to ABRAHAM LINCOLN the call of Kings or Emperors meant more than that of the humblest boor. . . .

The square in front of the TIMES office was cleared by the police, but up to the lines it was crowded full. The flags of all buildings round about were at half-mast and draped, the windows were filled with ladies, and the roofs held up greater burdens than ever before. The same scene was presented on Broadway and on the east side—everywhere the people filled the streets, and flags waved peacefully in the air.

At a little after 12½ o'clock a stir was made at the west end of the Park, and there, drawn by sixteen magnificent gray horses, led each by a colored groom, came

THE FUNERAL CAR.

It was drawn slowly down the line to the east gate, then turned back and nearly up to the centre of the esplanade, leaving a line of march of, perhaps, forty feet from the precise center, to the car. The reader will picture it thus: Imagine a box twelve or fifteen feet long, by six feet wide, on wheels; the box covered with black broadcloth, which falls to the ground, entirely concealing the wheels; on this, silver lace and fringe are elaborately and effectively displayed, embroidered in the shape of shields and stars, and fringing delicately yet richly the entire crape; above this box is reared a pavilion, American flags decorating each pillar, and it in turn covered with cloth ornamented like the other, and surmounted by a temple of liberty with a gilded dome, from which floats the national colors; heavy mourning plumes from every available point, and the elegance and costliness of the arrangement are only equaled by the entire beauty and symmetry of its shape and its perfect adaptation to the service for which is was intended. It is pleasant to find anything done under the supervision of the authorities worthy of commendation. This deserves it, and we but echo the universal comment of "well done, beautiful, perfect." After steps had been placed at the side of the car, for the convenience of the soldiers who were to carry the coffin, Gen. HALL was notified that all was ready. The Seventh then formed in order of march—the funeral car being guarded by a parallelogram of troops, and the signal was given for the

REMOVAL OF THE COFFIN.

On the sturdy shoulders of the Veteran Reserves the casket was tenderly taken from the dusty catafalque, borne down the winding stairs and brought to the City Hall steps. Here a halt for a few minutes occurred, when the procession moved forward to the car, the troops presented arms, the drum rolled, the colors drooped, and thirty thousand men in front bared every one his head. It was a memorable scene. . . .

Had the procession moved at once, the programme would have been excellent, but as on all other occasions of the sort, there was

A VEXATIOUS DELAY.

Gen. DIX and Staff, accompanied by Gen. BUTTERFIELD and HUNT, were mounted and took position in front of the horses of the car; the others walked behind it. For an hour and a half Gen DIX sat like a monument upon his horse, waiting for the procession to move; for an hour and a half the gallant veterans forming the "guard of honor," whose word for years has been law, to whose "go" or "come" immediate heed was paid, now stood in the hot sun, weary and worn with watching and fatigue, while the head of the procession moved far up Broadway. The people are patient in this city. They had waited, thousands of them, for hours, literally without a morsel of food, to see the car with its beloved load pass on, and now another hour and a half was added by the lack of head in the management of the affair.

The Governor's Room was deserted when the body was removed. Curious people picked up pieces of silver lace and fringe as mementoes, and some carried off portions of a broken bust of WASHINGTON which had fallen, smashed upon the velvet carpet of the catafalque; on the balcony were gathered a few notables, several ladies and the press—all that was of interest was resting, unconscious of delay, in the gorgeous box upon the car. Presently a bugle sounded, Gen. SANDFORD had moved, the superb band of the Seventh struck up, and slowly, mournfully, wearily the funeral car, with its precious burden, rolled from in front of the City Hall, and out upon the stony pavement of hushed Broadway.

The Procession.

Even during all the night before yesterday, preliminaries for the great funeral procession had been going forward at many points in the city. Before dawn, the stir increased. Almost as soon as it was light, the vast mass of our great metropolitan population began to move perceptibly toward the sadly magnificent ceremony of the day. At first, solitary soldiers, uniformed and armed, or single civilians, in decent black, were gathering to a thousand rendezvous of regiment, society, club or association, as to centers of crystallization sprinkled over the extensive city map. And while uniform and civic costume varied in their respective many ways, two universal marks, distinguishable, indeed, in almost every citizen, whether to be participant or spectator of the somber pageant—the crape band on the arm, and the countenance serious and often sad—silently witnessed that the vast city arose in oneness of heart to offer a last testimony of grief and love at the death of the liberator, the patriot, the honest man and wise ruler. . . .

were to form. These streets may be sufficiently well represented by a fan wide open, the handle at the City Hall park, and the eight sticks, (the divisions) spreading out North, East and South, from Broadway around eastwardly to Nassau-street. The First Division standing in line for a mile and three quarters on Broadway from the park to Fourteenth-street, could thus be conveniently followed by each of the others in its order, all crossing the park and wheeling to the right into Broadway.

THE SPECTATORS.

As the time of starting approached, a tremendous crowd of spectators lined the whole of the appointed route, standing often in a dense human hedge twelve or fifteen feet deep along the curb-stones. Another almost equally numerous body occupied the steps, gratings and inner border of the walk; while all windows were filled with men, women and children— occupancy being often sold for money, and advertised by handbills posted up outside. Thousands and thousands of these lookers-on were too young to know their right hands from their left—and were doubtless brought in order that, in old age, they might say they saw the funeral procession of ABRAHAM LINCOLN. Eaves, roofs, trees, posts, were edged or tipt or fructified with men or women. Along the middle of each sidewalk crept in either direction a sluggish, narrow stream of passengers, like the slow snow-broth of a half-frozen stream creeping between wide edgings of fixed ice. And between two such triple living borders, the watchful and peremptory policemen—their active efforts seconded by the desire of all to comply with the regulations of the day—easily secured an empty roadway, perfectly clear from curbstone to curbstone.

THE START.

It is 1 o'clock, and with prompt good faith the great procession gets forward. The right of the first or military division resting on Fourteenth-street, it was of course at that point that the actual movement began. . . .

336 Down the whole long line of the great thorough-fare, clear to the Park, the regiments are standing at ease, facing eastward. One after another, in quick succession, they now break into column of sections, and now a bird's eye view would show the whole distance from Union park to the City Hall, one long track of stony gray, bordered with the heavy black masses along each sidewalk, and from end to end, transversely striated

with the sections, deliberately gliding northward in common time, the swords and bayonets sparkling and glinting in the perfect sunlight. But to us on the earth, this impressive effect is invisible except in imagination; we count the soldiers and the guns; we can scarcely perfectly apprehend at one glance the twenty sections of one full regiment. As we look, however, section after section, regiment after regiment, brigade after brigade, marches steadily by. They may be called our house-hold troops. They are our own city regiments, and though most of their members have the pale face that tells of recent indoor life, yet many of them have once, at least, been embrowned by the Southern sun in actual service. In close lines, marching true and even, they pass and pass, until seemingly a whole army has gone by already, and still the long vista of the street is blue with the troops coming up from the South, nor can any sign of the funeral car yet be seen. . . .

THE FUNERAL CAR.

Only two blocks away can now be seen the gray uniforms of the Seventh Regiment, acting as guard of honor; and within its hollow square, rolling slowly nearer and nearer, comes the funeral car, a gloomy and imposing structure, its heavy plumes nodding and waving to and fro. Before the guard of honor marches a strong platoon of policemen, sweeping once more every inch of the street from curb to curb. There has, however been scarcely the least infringement of the orders in this matter. Here and there some weary old lady or careless boy sits down with feet in the gutter; but the crowd, though dense and massed to a degree even far beyond that of the remarkable occasion just after the Inauguration Day, keeps heedfully to the sidewalk.

THE GUARD OF HONOR,

the Seventh Regiment, Col. EMMONS CLARK, with reversed arms: its mathematically accurate marching and thoroughly soldierlike array justifying its employment in this melancholy but honorable duty.

The car itself rolls slowly and gloomily before us. Its sixteen gray horses are shrouded in black, and led each by a colored groom. Immediately about it march the faithful squad of soldiers of the Veteran Reserves who have accompanied the remains from Washington. The car itself consists of a broad platform fourteen feet by eight, on which is a stage or dais where the coffin lies. Over this is a rich canopy upon four columns, having planted at the foot of each column three national flags festooned and craped. Above the four corners of the canopy are four great shadowing and waving masses of sable plumes, and at the top is a small model of a circular temple, unwalled, open, empty. Thus—so would teach this little emblem—was the nation, the house of freedom, bereft of its representative man. Or, perhaps—thus empty of its former tenant, is the body of the dead, the temple of life, within the car is lined with white satin, and above the coffin hangs a large eagle, his wings outspread as if he hovered there, and carrying in his talons a wreath of laurel. All around the black draperies hung almost to the earth. Up on the surface of the dais and platform, beautiful white flowers were reposed in graceful, plenteous wreaths and bouquets and the deep blackness of the draperies is moreover somewhat relieved by festoons and spangles of silver bullion.

THE DOG MOURNER.

Under the car there is walking a dog, though invisible from the outside. It is "Bruno," the great Saint Bernard dog belonging to Edward H. MOSTLY, Esq. He was standing with his master at the corner of Broadway and Chambers-street, as the car passed by, when suddenly, without warning, and in spite of his master's call to him to return, he sprang into the street, passed beneath the car, followed its motions, and is still there. By what instinct was this? For "Bruno" was a friend and acquaintance of Mr. LINCOLN's, and had passed some time with him only a few days before his death.

The long impressive array of the first division is now closed by the Grand Marshal of the day, Gen. HALL, and his aids.

THE CIVILIAN PROCESSION.

The military portion of the procession is thus concluded, with a few small exceptions. With similar exceptions, the remainder of it, in place of the rich effects of the uniforms, the order of march, and the glitter and gleam of weapons, presented a monotonous, although impressive, column of civilians, in black clothes and hats. In several respects this portion of the procession was to the thoughtful observer more significant than the military part; but it was by virtue of implications and associated ideas, not by considerations of color and arrangements.

DETAILS AS TO CIVILIANS.

The immense number of organizations, political, benevolent, municipal and others, renders it impossible to give details in full and connectedly, of its parts. It was, however, a very interesting observation, that of all the high dignitaries, national, State and city, only a very small number could possibly have been distinguished from their companions, except by knowledge of their persons. Governors, Judges, officials of every grade and kind, walked quietly by, in the same ranks of twenty each, with private citizens, and the utter absence of signs of rank was even an inconvenience to the inquisitive beholder.

FOREIGN UNIFORMS.

Among the occupants of the carriages near the head of the Second Division were a few foreign officers, in full dress uniform. Most conspicuous of these was an Englishman in white trowsers and red coat. One or two of these gentlemen were all ablaze with gold lace. Probably few noticed them without considering whether the sight of this tremendous crowd in one city might not tend toward a more adequate conception of our real national strength and unity.

A VIOLATION OF RULE.

In glaring violation of the rule of the day against political inscriptions, one strong force of citizens, in the Second Division, marched as "The Democracy General Committee of Tammany Hall." No other such case was visible.

THE CALIFORNIA HUNTER.

Much attention was attracted to Mr. KINMAN, the Californian, who walked in a full hunting suit of buckskin and fur, rifle on shoulder. Mr. KINMAN, it will be remembered, presented to Mr. LINCOLN some time ago a chair made of California elk-horn, and continuing his acquaintance with him, had, it is said, enjoyed quite a long conversation with him the very day before the murder.

NATIONALITIES.

The numerical strength and watchful nationalities of the Irish among us was once more shown by the fact that one whole division, the Fifth, consisted entirely of Irish associations—and a large division it was. Among them marched, as in the Inauguration procession, a number of companies of boys, in green blouses, and hand in hand. The little fellows looked well and marched finely.

The athletic German turners, in their plain linen coats, looked strong, ready and sensible.

A long array of mechanics' protective and provident associations continued the latter part of the civilians' procession, a very few among them here and there, disgracefully enough, showing the influence of liquor.

The Brooklyn delegation constituted the Eighth Division, and after it, bringing up the rear, with a strong double rank of policemen before and behind, came a body of about two hundred colored men. Part of them were freedmen recently from slavery, and these bore a banner with two inscriptions: "ABRAHAM LINCOLN, our Emancipator," and "To Millions of Freemen he Liberty gave." This was the only portion of the procession which was received with any demonstrations of applause. For them a just and kindly enthusiasm overrode the street proprieties of the occasion, and handkerchiefs waved and voices cheered all along as they marched.

THE END.

The head of the procession had reached the railroad station at 2:10. The rear of it had not reached Fourteenth-street at 5. It must have contained full sixty thousand men. After the delivery of the remains to the charge of the railroad authorities, it was hours before the rear of the procession ceased marching. The allotted route having been passed over, the various component parts quickly dispersed to their respective rendezvous.

The deep sobriety of this ceremony gave it a profound and weighty character, far more impressive than the festal pomp of most pageants. And the wailing notes of the dirge played by the bands greatly increased this effect. The streets were in remarkably good condition. The air and sky were perfect; the arrangements for the occasion very good indeed; and in grandeur of form, as well as in ethical and political meaning, the great funeral pageant given by the City of New-York to the remains of President LINCOLN was entirely successful. . . .

––––––––

Lingering Questions

On April 26, 1865, John Wilkes Booth was cornered inside a barn near Port Royal, Virginia, and shot by an overzealous soldier. Dragged to the porch of an adjacent farmhouse to die, Booth's final words were: "Useless . . . useless."

Booth's death made front-page news in all the papers. The New York Times *carried two long articles by its own correspondent but, so eager was the desire for details, it also ran long dispatches from the Associated Press and from* The Evening Post.

In general, the accounts were accurate and quite similar, though each had different details. All, however, left unanswered some questions that would continue to bedevil students of the assassination. Were Richard Garrett and his sons, who harbored Booth on their Virginia farm, really unaware of his identity? Was David E. Herrold, the pharmacist's clerk who accompanied Booth, so light and trifling—as he was often described—as to be stupidly unaware of the plot in which he had been engaged? Did Boston Corbett, who fired the bullet that killed Booth, act without authority and without necessity? And, of course, for assassination buffs, there is always the main question: Was it really John Wilkes Booth who was killed on the Garretts' farm?

—D. H. D.

BOOTH KILLED.

Full Account of the Pursuit and its Result.

He is Traced into St. Mary's County, Maryland.

Harrold and Booth Discovered in a Barn.

Booth Declares He will not be Taken Alive.

The Barn Set on Fire to Force Them Out.

Sergt. Boston Corbett Fires at Booth

He is Shot Through the Neck and Dies in Three Hours.

His Body and Harrold Brought to Washington.

[Official.]

WAR DEPARTMENT,
WASHINGTON, APRIL 27, 1865—9:20 A.M.

Maj.-Gen. John A. Dix, New-York:

J. WILKES BOOTH and HARROLD were chased from the swamp in St. Mary's County, Maryland, to Garrett's farm, near Port Royal, on the Rappahannock, by Col. BAKER's force.

The barn in which they took refuge was fired.

BOOTH, in making his escape, was shot through the head and killed, lingering about three hours, and HARROLD was captured. BOOTH's body and HARROLD are now here.

EDWIN M. STANTON,
Secretary of War.

Details of the Capture of Booth.

Special Dispatch to the New-York Times.

WASHINGTON, Thursday, April 27.

About 8 o'clock last evening we received the intelligence of the capture of J. WILKES BOOTH, the assassin of ABRAHAM LINCOLN, and one of his accomplices in the murder, DAVID C. HARROLD. The following are such of the particulars as we were enabled to gather, which, with the exception of the precise locality where the occurrence took place, we give as being reliable and correct. It having been pretty clearly ascertained that BOOTH and his accomplice had crossed the Potomac River at or near Aquia Creek, our cavalry scouts in that vicinity have been in consequence unusually active in their endeavors to get on their trail. Early yesterday morning a squad of about twelve men, belonging to the Sixteenth New-York Cavalry, under command of a Lieutenant, whose name we did not learn, succeeded in discovering the fugitives in a barn on the road leading from Port Royal to Bowling Green in Caroline County, Va. As soon as they were discovered, the place was surrounded and the assassins ordered to surrender. This they both refused to do, BOOTH declaring that he would not be taken alive, and offering to fight the whole squad if he would be permitted to place himself twenty yards distant from them. His proposition was not, however, acceded to, and as they persisted in their refusal to surrender, the Lieutenant determined to burn them out, and accordingly set fire to the barn, shortly after which HARROLD came out and gave himself up. BOOTH remained in the burning building for some time, and until driven out by the fire, when he rushed out and was immediately shot through the neck by the sergeant of the squad.

Since the above we have had an interview with two of the cavalrymen engaged in the capture of the assassins. From them we learn that the whole party consisted of twenty-eight, including two detectives. The first information respecting BOOTH's crossing the river, and his probable whereabouts, was obtained from disbanded rebel soldiers who were met with in all directions in that part of the country. From one and another of these the clue to BOOTH's movements was gathered and held until just at

daybreak they came upon the barn, where he and HARROLD were secreted. A parley was held, and BOOTH manifested the most desperate determination not to be taken alive, and to take as many of the lives of the
party as possible. Lieut. EDWARD P. DOUGHERTY, who commanded the
scouting party, determined to make short work of him. When HARROLD
saw the preparations for firing the barn, he declared his willingness to
surrender, and said he would not fight if they would let him out. BOOTH,
on the contrary, was impudently defiant, offering at first to fight the whole
squad at one hundred yards, and subsequently at fifty yards. He was hob-
bling on crutches, apparently very lame. He swore he would die like a
man, etc. HARROLD having been secured, as soon as the burning hay
lighted the interior of the barn sufficiently to rend the scowling face of
BOOTH, the assassin, visible, Sergeant BOSTON CORBETT fired upon him
and he fell. The ball passed through his neck. He was pulled out of the
barn, and one of his crutches, and carbine and revolvers secured; the
wretch lived about two hours, whispering blasphemes against the government, and messages to his mother, desiring her to be informed that he
died for his country. At the time BOOTH was shot he was leaning upon one
crutch and preparing to shoot his captors. Only one shot was fired in the
entire affair—that which killed the assassin.

Lieut. DOUGHERTY is one of the bravest fellows in the cavalry service,
having distinguished himself in a sharp affair at Culpepper Court-house
and on other occasions. The Sixteenth New-York Cavalry is commanded
by Col. NELSON SWELTZER; and has been doing duty in Fairfax County.
This regiment formed part of the cavalry escort on the day of the President's obsequies in Washington. The body of BOOTH and the assassin's
accomplice, HARROLD, were placed on board the *Ida* and sent to Washington, arriving here about 1 o'clock this morning.

Accurate Account of the Pursuit and Capture of Booth.

Special Dispatch to the New-York Times.

WASHINGTON, Thursday, April 27.
Without recurring to the circumstances that brought together and put to
work a large body of detectives in pursuit of the assassin BOOTH and his
accessories in crime, I propose to state briefly and consecutively the incidents in the pursuit from the time the detachment started from this city
until their arrival here this morning with the corpse of BOOTH and the
body of HARROLD. The following facts I obtained from Col. BAKER and
the other persons engaged with him.

From the time the Secretary of War telegraphed Col L. C. BAKER at

New-York, twelve days ago, to come here immediately and take charge of the matter of ferreting out the facts, and arresting the criminals in the assassination, up to last Sunday, but little progress was made in the right direction. All the lower counties of Maryland were scoured by a large force consisting of 1,600 cavalry and 500 detectives and citizens. On Sunday last Col. BAKER learned of a little boy in Maryland some facts which satisfied him that BOOTH and HARROLD had crossed the river about 11 o'clock A.M. and had gone into Virginia. A telegraph operator with a small body of soldiers was sent down the river to tap the wires at a given place and make certain inquiries. This party returned on Monday morning last, bringing with them a negro man whom they picked up at Swan Point, who, on being closely interrogated, disclosed that he had seen parties cross in a boat, and the description of these parties assured Col. BAKER that BOOTH and HARROLD were the men. No examination or search had yet been made by official authority in Virginia. Demand was made upon Gen. HANCOCK for a detachment of cavalry, and twenty-eight of the Sixteenth New-York were immediately sent to Col. BAKER, under command of Lieut. DOHERTY, one of this detachment being BOSTON CORBETT. The whole party were put in charge of Lieut. L. B. BAKER and Lieut.-Col. E. J. CONGOR [*sic*]. They were instructed to go immediately to Port Royal; that BOOTH had crossed the river, and had had time to reach that point; that he could not ride on horseback, and must therefore have traveled slowly.

At twenty-five minutes past four o'clock on Monday afternoon, this force left the Sixth-street wharf in the steamer *Ida.* They were directed that when they arrived at the land place—Belle Plain—they should shove or swim their horses to shore, if they could not make a landing, for they must have the horses on land. That night the party went down the river four miles, but heard nothing satisfactory. They finally, at daylight, brought up below Port Royal some miles. They returned, finding no trace of the criminals till they got to Port Royal Ferry. Lieut. BAKER rode up, found the ferryman, and made inquiries. The ferryman stoutly denied having seen any such persons as those described. Lieut. BAKER throttled him and threatened him, yet he denied any knowledge of the persons sought. By the side of the ferryman a negro was sitting. Lieut. BAKER presented a likeness of BOOTH and HARROLD. The negro upon looking at these exclaimed, "Why, Massa, them's the gentlemen we brought cross the river yesterday." The ferryman then admitted that he had brought BOOTH and HARROLD over the river in his boat. The cavalry was started off and went fourteen miles beyond GARRETT's place. There they met a negro who said he saw two men sitting on GARRETT's porch that afternoon. The description of one accorded with that of BOOTH. Lieut. BAKER and his party returned to GARRETT's house. GARRETT denied that the two men had been there. BAKER threatened to shoot him if he did not tell the truth. GARRETT'S son thereupon came out of the house and said the two men were in the barn. The barn was at once surrounded. This was about 2 A.M. BAKER went up and rapped at the door. BOOTH asked "Who are you, friends or foes? Are you Confederates? I have got five men in here, and we can protect ourselves." Col. BAKER replied, "I have fifty men out here; you are surrounded, and you may as well come out and surrender." BOOTH answered, "I shall never give up; I'll not be taken alive." The instructions were that every means possible must be taken to arrest BOOTH alive, and BAKER, CONGER AND DOHERTY held a consultation a few feet from the barn. In the meantime BOOTH was cursing HARROLD for his cowardice, charging him with a desire to meanly surrender, etc.

Col. BAKER and his party returned and held a parley with BOOTH, thus consuming about an hour and a quarter. Another consultation of officers was held, and it was determined that, in view of the probability of an attack from a tolerably large force of rebel cavalry, which they had learned were in the neighborhood, the barn should be fired, and BOOTH thus forced to come out.

CONGER gathered a lot of brush, and placed it against and under the barn, and pulled some hay out of the cracks, in the mean time holding a lighted candle in his hand. BOOTH could now see through the openings of the barn all their movements. The lighted candle was applied to the hay and brush, and directly the flames caught the hay inside the barn. BOOTH rushed forward towards the burning hay and tried to put out the fire. Failing in this, he ran back to the middle of the floor, gathered up his arms and stood still pondering for a moment. While BOOTH was standing in this position Sergt. BOSTON CORBETT ran up to the barn door and fired. Col. BAKER, not perceiving where the shot came from, exclaimed "he has shot himself," and rushed into the barn and found BOOTH yet standing with a carbine in hand. BAKER clasped BOOTH around the arms and breast; the balance of the party had also, in the mean time, got inside. CORBETT then exclaimed "I shot him." BOOTH fell upon the floor apparently paralyzed. Water was sent for and the wound bathed. It was now just 3:15 o'clock. The ball had apparently passed through the neck and the spine. In a few moments BOOTH revived. He made an effort to lift his hands up before his eyes. In this he was assisted, and upon seeing them he exclaimed somewhat incoherently. "Useless!—useless!—useless!—blood!—blood! ! and swooned away. He revived from time to time, and expressed himself entirely satisfied with what he had done. He expired at 7:10 yesterday morning.

The body was placed in a cart and conveyed to the steamer *Ida,* and brought upon that vessel to the navy-yard, where the boat arrived at 5:20 o'clock this morning.

While the barn was burning, HARROLD rushed out and was grappled by Lieut. BAKER, thrown to the ground and secured.

CORBETT says he fired with the intention of wounding BOOTH in the shoulder, and did not intend to kill him.

BOOTH had in his possession a diary, in which he had noted events of each day since the assassination of Mr. LINCOLN. This diary is in possession of the War Department. He had also a Spencer carbine, a seven-shooter, a revolver, a pocket pistol and a knife. The latter is supposed to be the one with which he stabbed Mayor RATHBURNE. His clothing was of dark blue, not Confederate gray, as has been stated.

CORBETT, who shot BOOTH, was born in England, and is about 33 years old. He came to this country some years since, and resided for several years in Troy, N. Y. He resided for a time in Boston, where he became a member of a Methodist Church, and took in baptism the name of "Boston." He is a man of small stature, slight form, mild countenance and quiet deportment.

Surgeon-Gen. BARNES says the ball did not enter the brain. The body, when he examined it this afternoon, was not in a rapid state of decomposition, but was considerably bruised by jolting about in the cart. It is placed in charge of Col. BAKER, in the attire in which he died, with instructions not to allow any one to approach it, nor to take from it any part of apparel, or thing for exhibition hereafter; in brief, it is necessary for the satisfaction of the people that two points shall be positively ascertained: first, that the person killed in GARRETT's barn, and whose body was brought to this city, was J. WILKES BOOTH; secondly, that the said J. WILKES BOOTH was positively killed. The first point was to-day confirmed by overwhelming testimony, such as no jury would hesitate to accept. The substantial one of the second point is shown in the report of Surgeon-General BARNES, which will be officially announced.

BOOTH's leg was not broken by falling from his horse, but the bone was injured by the fall upon the stage at the theatre.

Besides the articles heretofore mentioned, BOOTH had on his person a draft for sixty pounds drawn by the Ontario Bank of Canada on a London banker. The draft was dated in October last.

DISPATCH TO THE EVENING POST.

WASHINGTON, THURSDAY, APRIL 27.

On Monday, April 24, the Sixteenth New-York Calvary detachment started out on the south side of the Potomac in chase of Booth. They crossed the Rappahannock River at Fredericksburgh, and moved down on the west fork of that stream to the vicinity of Port Royal, a distance of some twenty-five miles. They had with them a photograph of Booth and an accurate personal description.

While riding along the road toward an old barn they discovered fresh horse tracks, which were immediately followed to the barn, where BOOTH and HARROLD lay concealed.

The cavalry came up to the barn about 3 o'clock yesterday (Wednesday) morning. HARROLD was secured soon after the barn had been surrounded; but BOOTH was concealed behind some boards, so that the troops could not see him—yet they heard him. He said that it was no use to try to take him alive; that he had a shot for every man who approached the crack in the boards behind which he lay.

At first BOOTH denied that that was his name, or that he had killed the President. HARROLD, also, at first called him some other name.

When it became evident that every man who approached him would be killed, the moment daylight came Sergt. CORBETT fired, BOOTH evidently not expecting a shot. The ball of a navy revolver entered his neck, and he fell over, with his own revolver grasped tightly in his hands.

GARRETT, the owner of the barn, denies having secreted HARROLD and BOOTH, and declares that he refused them admittance to his own house, and did not know that they were in his barn.

Negroes and rebel deserters furnished such evidence to the cavalry as to lead to the belief that the two men were somewhere in that section.

Later accounts show that every effort was made to take Booth alive. The troops parleyed with him for nearly an hour. HARROLD begged him to surrender, but he persistently refused, stating that he would never be taken alive, and that he would fight all of them, and intended to die for his country then and there.

During the conversation in which all present begged him to give up, he said that he fractured his leg when jumping from the stage-box on the stage. His last words were, "Tell my mother I died for my country."

On his person were found two Colt's revolvers, each a six-shooter, and the dagger with blood on it, which he had used on Maj. RATHBONE.

In his pockets were found a few greenbacks and a sixty pound note on the Bank of Montreal.

WASHINGTON, Thursday, April 27—3:30 P.M.

The body of BOOTH has just been formally identified by prominent surgeons. From long exposure it has changed very much.

A surgical operation performed upon him several weeks ago rendered identification easy.

The left leg was broken, and appearances indicate that this injury was sustained when BOOTH jumped from the President's box to the stage of Ford's Theatre.

The bullet which killed BOOTH struck the spinal column, paralyzing the body.

———

Dispatches to the Associated Press.

WASHINGTON, Thursday, April 27.

Yesterday morning a squadron of the Sixteenth New-York Cavalry traced Booth and HARROLD to a barn between Bowling-green and Port Royal, near Fredericksburgh, Va.

The barn was surrounded, and a demand made for their surrender, which HARROLD was in favor of doing, but upon BOOTH calling him a coward he refused to do so.

The barn was then set on fire and upon its getting too hot HARROLD again presented himself and put his hands through the door to be hand-cuffed.

While this was going on BOOTH fired upon the soldiers, upon which a Sergeant fired at him.

The ball of the Sergeant took effect in the head of BOOTH, killing him.

HARROLD was taken alone, and he and BOOTH's body were brought to the Washington Navy-yard last night.

BOOTH was discovered in the barn by the cavalry.

He declared his intention never to surrender, and said he would fight the whole squad, consisting of twenty-eight men, if they would permit him to place himself twenty yards distant.

The scouting party was under the command of Lieut. EDWARD DOUGHERTY.

BOOTH was on a crutch and was lame.

He lived two hours after he was shot, whispering blasphemies against the government and sending a farewell message to his mother.

At the time he was shot it is said he was leaning on his crutch and preparing to fire again upon his captors.

WASHINGTON, Thursday, April 27.

The *Star* has the following particulars of the capture of BOOTH:

To Lieut.-Col. L. C. BAKER, special detective of the War Department and his admirably trained detective force, and to the Sixteenth New-York Cavalry, active participators in the seizures of the criminals, the country owes a dept of gratitude for this timely service. It seems that a detachment of the Sixteenth New-York Cavalry, numbering about twenty five men, was dispatched from this city on Monday, under the direction of

Col. L. C. BAKER, Special Detective of the War Department, in command of Lieut. DOUGHERTY, accompanied by some of Col. BAKER's officers, captured and killed BOOTH, and captured HARROLD, one of his accomplices, alive.

The cavalry after leaving here landed at Belle Plain in the night and immediately started out in pursuit of BOOTH and HARROLD, having previously ascertained from a colored man that they had crossed the river into Virginia at Swan Point in a small canoe hired by BOOTH from a man for three hundred dollars.

Proceeding on toward Bowling Green, some three miles from Port Royal, Lieut. DOUGHERTY, who was in command of the cavalry, discovered that BOOTH and HARROLD were secreted in a large barn owned by a man named GARRETT, and were well armed.

The cavalry then surrounded the barn, and summoned BOOTH and his accomplices to surrender.

HARROLD was inclined at first to accede to the request, but BOOTH accused him of cowardice. Then both peremptorily refused to surrender, and made preparations to defend themselves.

In order to take the conspirators alive, the barn was fired, and the flames getting too hot for HARROLD, he approached the door of the barn, and signified his willingness to be taken prisoner.

The door was then opened sufficiently to allow HARROLD to put his arms through that he might be handcuffed.

As an officer was about placing the irons upon HARROLD's wrists, BOOTH fired upon the party from the barn, which was returned by a Sergeant of the sixteenth New-York, the ball striking BOOTH in the neck, from the effects of which he died in about four hours.

BOOTH, before breathing his last, was asked if he had anything to say, when he replied, "Tell my mother that I died for my country."

HARROLD and the body of BOOTH were brought into Belle Plain at 8 o'clock last night, and reached the Navy-yard here at 1 o'clock this morning, on board of the steamer *John S. Ides,* Capt. HENRY WILSON.

The statement heretofore published that BOOTH had injured one of his legs by the falling of his horse has proved to be correct. After he was shot it was discovered that one of his legs was badly injured, and that he was compelled to wear an old shoe and use crutches, which he had with him in the barn.

BOOTH was shot about 4 o'clock in the morning, and died about 7 o'clock.

BOOTH had upon his person some bills of exchange, but only $175 in Treasury Notes.

It appears that BOOTH and HARROLD left Washington together on the night of the murder of President Lincoln, and passed through Leonardstown, Md., concealed themselves in the vicinity until an opportunity was afforded them to cross the river at Swan Point, which they did as above stated.

The man who hired BOOTH and his accomplice the boat in which he crossed the river was captured, we understand, but afterward made his escape.

HARROLD has been lodged in a secure place.

Bowling Green, near which place BOOTH was killed, is a post village and the capital of Caroline County, Virginia, on the road from Richmond to Fredericksburgh, forty-five miles north of the former place, and is situated in a fertile and healthy region. It contains two churches, three stores, two mills, and about three hundred inhabitants.

Port Royal is a post village in Caroline County, Virginia, on the right bank of the Rappahannock River, twenty-two miles below Fredericksburgh. It has a population of 600 and has a good steamboat landing near the place.

WASHINGTON, Thursday, April 27

The *Star,* in a later edition, has the following of BOOTH:

BOOTH and HARROLD reached Garrett's some days ago, BOOTH walking on crutches. A party of four or five accompanied them, who spoke of BOOTH as a wounded Marylander on his way home, and that they wished to leave him there a short time, and would take him away by the 26th (yesterday.) BOOTH limped somewhat, and walked on crutches about the place, complaining of his ankle. He and HARROLD regularly took their meals at the house, and both kept up appearances well.

One day, at the dinner table, the conversation turned on the assassination of the President, when BOOTH denounced the assassination in the severest terms, saying that there was no punishment severe enough for the perpetrator. At another time some one said in BOOTH's presence, that rewards amounting to two hundred thousand dollars had been offered for BOOTH, and that he would like to catch him, when BOOTH replied: "Yes; it would be a good haul, but the amount would, doubtless, soon be increased to five hundred thousand dollars."

The two Garretts, who lived on the place, allege that they had no idea that these parties—BOOTH and HARROLD—were any other than what their friends represented them, *i. e.,* paroled Confederate soldiers on their way home. They also say that when the cavalry appeared in that neighborhood, and they heard that they were looking for the assassins, that they sent word to them that these two men were on the place. In other words, they assert that they are entirely innocent of giving the assassins any aid and comfort, knowing them to be such.

The *Ida,* tugboat, reached here about 2 o'clock last night with HARROLD and the two men above referred to as well as the body of BOOTH. HARROLD was immediately put in a safe place. He, thus far, it is stated, has manifested no dispositions to speak of the affair, but as he was known as a very talkative young man, he may soon resume the use of his tongue.

BOOTH and HARROLD were dressed in Confederate gray new uniforms. HARROLD was, otherwise not disguised much. BOOTH's moustache had been cut off, apparently with a scissors, and his beard allowed to grow, changing his appearance considerably. His hair has been cut somewhat shorter than he usually wore it.

BOOTH's body, which we have above described, was at once laid out on a bench, and a guard placed over it. The lips of the corpse are tightly compressed, and the blood has settled in the lower part of the face and neck. Otherwise the face is pale, and wears a wild, haggard look, indicating exposure to the elements, and a rough time generally, in his skulking flight. His hair is disarranged and dirty, and apparently had not been combed since he took his flight.

The head and breast are alone exposed to view, the lower portion of the body, including the hands and feet, being covered with a tarpaulin. The shot which terminated his accursed life, entered on the left side, at the back of the neck; a point, curiously enough, not far distant from that in which his victim—our lamented President—was shot.

No orders have yet been given as to what disposition will be made of the body. Large numbers of persons have been seeking admission to the Navy yard to-day, to get a sight of the body and to hear the particulars; but none excepting the workmen, the officers of the yard, and those holding orders from the department are allowed to enter.

A Spencer carbine, which BOOTH had with him in the barn at the time he was shot by Sergt. CORBETT, and a large knife with blood on it, supposed to be the one with which BOOTH cut Major RATHBONE, in the theater box, on the night of the murder of President LINCOLN, and which was found on BOOTH's body have been brought to the city. The carbine and knife are now in the possession of Col. BAKER at his office.

The bills of exchange, which were for a considerable amount, found on BOOTH's person, were drawn on banks in Canada, in October last. About that time BOOTH was known to have been in Canada. It is now thought that BOOTH's leg was fractured in jumping from the box in Ford's Theatre upon the stage, and not by the falling of his horse while endeavoring to make his escape, as was at first supposed.

The fourth edition of the *Star* has the following additional details of the capture of HARROLD and the killing of BOOTH:

The detachment of the Sixteenth New-York Cavalry under Lieut. DOUGHERTY, numbering twenty-eight men, and accompanied by two of Col. BAKER's detective force, which went down the river on Monday, obtained the first news of BOOTH at Port Royal on Tuesday evening from an old man, who stated that four men, in company with a rebel Captain, had crossed the Rappahannock a short time previous, going in the direction of Bowling-green; and he added that the Captain would probably be found in that place, as he was courting a lady there. On pushing on to Bowling-green, the Captain was found at a hotel and taken into custody.

From him it was ascertained that BOOTH and HARROLD were at the house of John and William Garrett, three miles back toward Port Royal, and about a quarter of a mile from the road passed over by the cavalry,

In the meantime it appears that BOOTH and HARROLD applied to GARRETT for horses to ride to Louisa Court-house; but the latter, fearing the horses would not be returned, refused to hire them, notwithstanding the large sums offered. These circumstances, together with the recriminations of BOOTH and HARROLD, each charging the other with the responsibility of their difficulties, had aroused the suspicions of the GARRETT brothers, who urged BOOTH and HARROLD to leave, lest they (the GARRETT's) should get into trouble with our cavalry. This BOOTH refused to do without a horse, and the two men retired to a barn, the door of which, after they had entered, GARRETT locked and remained himself on guard in a neighboring corn crib; as he alleged, to prevent their horses from being taken and ridden off in the night by BOOTH and HARROLD.

Upon the approach of our cavalry from Bowling Green about 3 o'clock on Wednesday morning, the GARRETT's came out of the corn-crib to meet them, and in answer to their inquiries directed them to the barn.

BOOTH was at once summoned to surrender but refused. HARROLD expressed his willingness to give himself up, but was overruled by BOOTH for some time, but he finally surrendered, leaving BOOTH in the barn. The latter, then, assuming a defiant air, called out to know the commanding officer, and proposed to him that his men should be drawn up at fifty yards distance, when he would come out and fight them.

352

After the barn had been burning three-quarters of an hour, and when the roof was about to fall in, BOOTH, who had been standing with a revolver in one hand and a carbine resting on the floor, made a demonstration as if to break through the guard and escape. To prevent this, Sergt. CORBETT fired, intending to hit BOOTH in the shoulder, so as to cripple him. The ball, however, struck a little too high and entered the neck, resulting fatally, as above stated.

BOOTH had in his possession the short, heavy bowie-knife with which he struck Maj. Rathburn, a Spencer carbine, a seven-shooter of Massachusetts manufacture, three revolvers, and a pocket pistol. He wore, beside his suit of gray, an ordinary cloth cap, a heavy high-topped cavalry boot on his right foot, with the top turned down, and a government shoe on his left foot.

No clue could be obtained of the other two men; and taking the two Garretts into custody the command immediately set out for Washington, after releasing the Captain.

Lieut. Dougherty, who commanded the squadron, entered the service with the Seventy-first New York Militia.

Sergt. CORBETT, who shot Booth, was baptized in Boston about seven years ago, at which time he assumed the name of BOSTON CORBETT. To-day he has been greatly lionized and on the street was repeatedly surrounded by citizens who occasionally manifested their appreciation by cheers.

The two GARRETTS are dressed in rebel gray, having belonged to LEE'S army and just returned home on parole. They profess to have been entirely ignorant of the character of BOOTH and HARROLD, and manifest great uneasiness concerning their connection with the affair.

BOOTH and Harrold narrowly escaped capture on this side of the Potomac Marshal MURRAY and a posse of New York detectives tracked them to within a short distance of Swan Point, but the Marshal being unacquainted with the country and with out a guide during the darkness of the night, took the wrong road, and before he could regain the trail, BOOTH and HARROLD succeeded in crossing the river to Virginia.

The report that BOOTH attempted to shoot himself while in the barn is incorrect. He, however, in his parley with his besiegers, indicated that he would not be taken alive. His manner throughout was that of hardened desperation. Knowing that his doom was sealed, and preferring to meet it there, in that shape, to the more ignominious death awaiting him, if captured, he appeared to pay little attention to the fire raging about him, until the roof began to fall in, when he made a movement indicating a purpose to make the desperate attempt to cut his way out, and perhaps really hoped to succeed amid the smoke and confusion. It was this movement on his part that seems to have caused CORBETT to fire the fatal shot. HARROLD, before leaving the barn, laid down his pistol, which was immediately picked up by BOOTH, who had it in his hand at the time he was shot.

BOSTON CORBETT, who killed BOOTH, is said to be a man of deep, religious feeling, who has at prayer meetings lately prayed fervently that the assassin of the late President might be brought to justice. It is said also, that in pulling the trigger upon BOOTH, he sent up an audible petition for the soul of the criminal.

The pistol used by Corbett was the regular large-sized cavalry pistol. He was offered $1,000 this morning for the pistol with its five undischarged loads.

This afternoon Surgeon-General BARNES, with an assistant, held an autopsy on the body of BOOTH.

It now appears that BOOTH and HARROLD had on clothes, which were originally some other color than the Confederate gray, but being faded and dusty presented that appearance.

Booth's Body in Washington

WASHINGTON, Thursday April 27

The greatest curiosity is manifested here to view the body of the murderer, BOOTH, which yet remains on the gunboat, in the stream off the Navy-yard. Thousands of persons visited the yard, to-day, in the hope of getting a glimpse at the murder's remains, but none not connected with the yard were allowed to enter.

The wildest excitement has existed here all day and the greatest regrets are expressed that BOOTH, was not taken alive. The news of BOOTH's death reached the ears of his mistress while she was in a street car, which caused her to weep aloud, and drawing a photograph likeness of BOOTH from her pocket, kissed it fondly several times.

HARROLD, thus far, has evaded every effort to be drawn into conversation by those who have necessarily come in contact with him since his capture; but outward appearances indicate that he begins to realize the position in which he is placed. There is no hope for his escape from the awful doom that certainly awaits him. His relatives and friends in this city are in the greatest distress over the disgrace that he has brought upon themselves.

SKETCH OF SERGT. CORBETT.

BOSTON CORBETT, who shot the assassin BOOTH, is a native of England. He came to this country when quite a lad, and learning the trade of a hatter, was for some years employed by Mr. ESPENCHEID, of No. 118 Nassau–street. On the 12th of April, 1861, he enlisted in the Twelfth New-York Militia, returned to the seat of war with his regiment three times, and was taken prisoner at Harper's Ferry, when MILES surrendered to STONEWALL JACKSON. He was soon afterward exchanged, joined the Sixteenth New-York Cavalry, and was captured by MOSBY at Fairfax Court-house. CORBETT was deserted by his companions when MOSBY's cavalry came down upon them. He refused to surrender, and setting his back against a tree, he used his pistols so well that he kept twenty-six of the rebels at bay for more than hour. His ammunition being expended, he advanced upon them, sword in hand, and MOSBY, admiring his gallantry, ordered his men not to fire upon him but to take him alive. He was sent to Andersonville, where he saw his comrades die around him by thousands, and contracted a disease from which he is even yet suffering.

CORBETT is a member of the Attorney-street Methodist Church, in this city. He is said to be an earnest Christian, reading the Scriptures to his fellow soldiers and preaching the word whenever opportunity offers. His comrades relate that on one occasion he was sent to the guard-house for reproving his Colonel for using profane language on parade. In person he is slightly made, is about five feet six inches in height, and has a mild and intelligent countenance. He is about twenty-six years of age and a widower.

THE CAPTURE OF BOOTH.

The Feeling in the City—Satisfaction at the Result.

Considerable excitement was manifested in the city yesterday on the receipt of the intelligence that the assassin BOOTH had been captured, together with his accomplice, HARROLD. The meager details which were first made public, seemed only to whet the people's appetite for more news as to the how, where and when the captures took place, what had been done with the prisoners, how they behaved and what they said. When it became known that BOOTH had been shot, and that the government were only in possession of his dead body, some dissatisfaction was at first expressed, but subsequently public opinion appeared to undergo a change upon this point. The more sensible ones saw that the excitement which has prevailed since the first news of the assassination reached us would only have been increased by BOOTH's trial and execution, and that it was better that he should have been shot dead than that this excitement should continue.

The comments on the capture were, of course, various. "I wish," said one individual, "that he had been taken alive, so that he might have confessed, and given the names of his accomplices." "Yes," answered another; "but I don't think it would have been easy to get any confession out of him. He seems to have been a determined fellow." "Ah!" said another man, "I'd have had him broke on the wheel, but what I'd make him confess." He was reminded that "breaking on the wheel" is not in vogue at the present day even in case of such gigantic crimes as that of BOOTH's. "I always told you," said a returned soldier, "that he'd escape to those swamps. I know those swamps, and I could point out just the spot where they took him. It's as lonesome a place as you might wish to see. Why, a man might hide there a year and you couldn't find him." "But they did find him," said a small boy. "Why, of course they did," said the soldier, "because they'd tracked him all the way. Don't you remember the newspapers said as BOOTH fell from his horse and broke his leg; and sure enough, when he was shot it was found he'd been using a crutch." "That's so," said another man, "If he hadn't been lamed he'd got clear away." "What will they do with HARROLD?" asked one of the group; "he didn't kill anybody?" "No; but he's supposed to have been the man that unscrewed the lock on he President's box at the theatre, and he's just as bad as BOOTH," said one of the crowd. "Oh! They must have had no end of confederates," said one man, "else how could they have kept out of reach so long? Some one must have helped 'em along. They have got sympathizers in Maryland, yet, depend on it." "But they were taken in Virginia," said another man. "Ah, yes; but only after they were hunted out of the Maryland swamps that this soldier's been talking about," said the first man. "Well," was the general exclamation, "we're glad they've got him anyhow." "Those as captured him'll get a pretty snug sum for their trouble, too," remarked on person; "$114,000 they say they're to get for the two, alive or dead." "Nothing like offering a good reward for capturing criminals," said one man. "It brightens the eyes of those who are looking after 'em amazingly." "Well," said another man, "I am glad all the excitement's cooling down. W'eve had enough of it lately to last for a year or two to come. Why there was a boy, the other day, cut his throat all through this excitement, and there'l be others doing the same thing if one don't take care. New-York's been turned topsy turvy for the last two or three days."

Judging from the casual expressions which were let fall yesterday, there is but little doubt that the public are glad that the affair of BOOTH's capture ended as it did.

Superintendent KENNEDY entered the court-room while the police trials were progressing, yesterday morning, and announced the capture of BOOTH and his companion, HARROLD. The news was received by the officers and men who filled the room with the most uproarious cheering, clapping of hands, &c., and it was some minutes before quiet could be restored. . . .

THE ASSASSINS.

Important Proclamation by President Johnson.

Mr. Lincoln's Murder Planned by Leading Traitors.

Most of these Traitors Are Harbored in Canada.

Jefferson Davis is the Head of the Assassins.

He is Aided by Jacob Thompson, Clement C. Clay, Beverly Tucker and George N. Sanders.

One Hundred Thousand Dollars Reward for Davis

Twenty-five Thousand for Each of the Others.

Ten Thousand for Wm. C. Cleary, Mr. Clay's Clerk.

A Description of the Conspirators to be Published.

By the President of the United States of America.

A PROCLAMATION

Whereas, It appears, *from evidence* in the Bureau of Military Justice, that the atrocious *murder of the late President,* ABRAHAM LINCOLN, and the attempted assassination of Hon. WM. H. SEWARD, Secretary of State, were incited, concerted and procured by and between

JEFFERSON DAVIS, late of Richmond, Va., and
JACOB THOMPSON,
CLEMENT C. CLAY,
BEVERLY TUCKER,
GEORGE N. SANDERS,
W. C. CLEARY,

And other rebels and traitors against the Government of the United States, *harbored in Canada;*

Now, therefore, to the end that justice may be done, I, ANDREW JOHNSON, President of the United States, do offer and promise for the arrest of said persons, or either of them, within the limits of the United States, so that they can be brought to trial, the following rewards:

One Hundred thousand dollars for the arrest of JEFFERSON DAVIS.

Twenty-five thousand dollars for the arrest of CLEMENT C. CLAY.

Twenty-five thousand dollars for the arrest of JACOB THOMPSON, late of Mississippi.

Twenty-five thousand dollars for the arrest of GEORGE N. SANDERS.

Twenty-five thousand dollars for the arrest of BEVERLY TUCKER, and

Ten thousand dollars for the arrest of WILLIAM C. CLEARY, late clerk of CLEMENT C. CLAY.

The Provost-Marshal-General of the United States is directed to cause a description of said persons, with notice of the above rewards, to be published.

In testimony whereof I have hereunto [L. S.] set my hand and caused the seal of the

United States to be affixed. Done at the City of Washington, the second day of May, in the year of our Lord one thousand eight hundred and sixty-five, and of the independence of the United States of America the eighty-ninth.

ANDREW JOHNSON.

By the President:

W. HUNTER, Acting Secretary of State.

The Flight of Jeff. Davis.

A NARROW ESCAPE FOR THE REBEL CHIEF—STONEMAN'S CAVALRY ON THE WATCH.

KNOXVILLE, TENN., Tuesday, May 2.

A man who was on one of the railroad trains captured by STONEMAN'S cavalry, between Greensburgh and Salisbury, says that JEFF. DAVIS was on the same train, on his way to Charlottesville. Learning that the railroad was cut above and below, DAVIS, with the other passengers, escaped and returned to Greensburgh.

Stoneman's cavalry is now in the valley of the Saluda River, with its headquarters at Anderson, S.C., and the cavalry are scouting from there toward Augusta, Ga., with instructions, if they can hear of JEFF. and his treasure, to follow him as long as there is a horse left.

The infantry portion of STONEMAN'S command is engaged in clearing the mountains of bushwackers, guerrillas and horse thieves, and they are making clean work.

Jefferson Davis Almost Within the Reach of Stoneman's Cavalry.

Information from STONEMAN's cavalry states that JEFF. DAVIS was at Yorkville, S. C., on the 28th ult., and that STONEMAN's forces came in on the following day. DAVIS has one day's start of STONEMAN. Jeff. is escorted by 2,000 cavalry, well mounted and commanded by Gen. DRIBBRELL. He is accompanied by BENJAMIN BRECKINRIDGE and other notorious characters, and will probably be joined by all the desperadoes fleeing from justice and the vengeance of the United States Government. It is hoped that Gen. STONEMAN's forces will overtake and capture DAVIS, as he is burdened with eleven wagons supposed to be loaded with specie.

THE PRESIDENT'S OBSEQUIES.

Mr. Lincoln again at Home

The Journey from Chicago to Springfield—Demonstrations Along the Route—Immense Gathering at Springfield— Reception and Ceremonies—Preparations for the Burial

SPRINGFIELD, ILL., Wednesday, May 3.

The funeral train arrived here at 9 o'clock this morning. All the way from Chicago persons were gathered on the road, and funeral arches were erected and mourning emblems everywhere displayed.

An immense crowd was assembled at the principal depot here. The remains were conveyed to the capitol, where the apartments were decorated in a most elaborate and beautiful manner. Deep solemnity prevailed. Bells were tolled and minute guns fired. Thousands of people are here from the adjoining States, all contributing to swell the vast multitude which has assembled to honor the lamented and illustrious dead.

An Address by Hon. Schuyler Colfax.

Correspondence of the New-York Times.

CHICAGO, Sunday, April 30—Evening.

A cold drizzling rain has prevailed all day, and we are fearful that it may continue through the morrow, and thus interfere with the great demonstration for which arrangements have been made. At this writing— 10 o'clock—there is no appearance of a breaking away of the clouds.

Hon. Schuyler Colfax has spoken twice in this city to-day, upon the death of the President, in the afternoon to a dense crowd, more than filling Bryan Hall, notwithstanding the rain. His address was a feeling and eloquent tribute to the memory of Mr. Lincoln, and was listened to with tearful attention. In the evening he repeated it in the Second Baptist Church, in the West Division, one of the largest houses in the city, to a packed audience. At the same time Dr. Patton was speaking to a full audience in Crosby's Opera House, and Dr. Ryder in St. Paul's Church, both of whom had just returned from Richmond. The people never tire of hearing about our noble President. On Thursday afternoon, while the funeral services are in progress at Springfield, a discourse is to be delivered in Bryan Hall by Rev. C. H. Fowler. Several of our ministers, by request of their congregations, repeated to-day, the sermons they preached by them upon the death of the President on the previous Sabbath.

The Great Demonstration.

Correspondence of the New-York Times.

CHICAGO, Monday Evening, May 1.

I do not propose to give a detailed or even a graphic description of the great demonstration in Chicago to-day on the reception of the remains of our late President. It was of such gigantic proportions that columns would fail to do justice to it in all parts; and then it was but a repetition of the events of the past week, which have attended the passage of the funeral cortège through the country, only on a larger scale than has been witnessed west of New-York.

At an early hour the whole population of the city was in motion. The people poured into and thronged the streets. At about nine o'clock the different sections of the grand procession began to move into place, although the funeral train was not expected to arrive until eleven. All along the route, which was a mile and a half in length, including our magnificent Michigan-avenue, emblems of mourning were plentifully displayed from all the buildings. The innumerable banners borne in the procession were appropriately draped, and there was deep and subdued solemnity pervading the multitude.

At the point where the remains were received from the railroad, among other things, thirty-six young girls, clothed in white, representing the States, were stationed, who strewed flowers upon the coffin as it passed beneath a mourning arch.

It was a late hour before the immense procession got in motion—the funeral cortege and escort passing through the long line, which was formed in open order—each section falling in as it was passed.

The procession passed through the great hall of the court-house, where the body is to remain in state, and which is beautifully and appropriately draped. Upon the second landing of the hall was placed some two hundred of the best vocalists of the city, who sang dirges and requiems as the immense multitude was moving along. The effect was sublime.

Such is the general outline of the great demonstration. It was a tribute of the people to the memory of our loved and murdered President, such as was never before witnessed in the West. It was not a vain show—an empty pageant—for I saw many tears fall to-day, as the mortal remains of ABRAHAM LINCOLN passed by. It was a heartfelt tribute of a grateful people, for great services rendered them and their common country, in the hour of its need.

The body is to lie in state until to-morrow evening. It was exposed to public view from a late hour this afternoon, and has already been visited by thousands.

The military display was fine and a large number of distinguished general officers, with their respective staffs, wore in the processions. All the arrangements were well considered and admirably carried out.

Contrary to our anticipations, last evening, we have been favored with a pleasant day, through there is considerable mud left over in the streets.

To-morrow evening the funeral party will depart for Springfield. A large delegation will accompany it from here, and remain over until the closing funeral services on Thursday. A monument will be erected at Springfield, for which purpose an organization has already been formed.

I have just been reading over an account of the death of Washington, and the services attending thereupon throughout the country, in an old Ulster County paper. Although the nation mourned the death of the "Father of his Country," the expression seems weak and feeble in comparison with that which has followed the death of Mr. LINCOLN—"The Savior of his country," as some have termed him. Verily, "the people mourn when the good man dies."

The Journey from Chicago.

Dispatch to the Associated Press.

CHICAGO, Wednesday, May 3

The streets for several miles are densely filled with people to witness the passage of the funeral procession to the Chicago and Alton Railroad Station, from which the remains are to be conveyed to Springfield. The crowds seem to be as large, if not larger, than those assembled yesterday morning when the funeral party arrived at the Lake Shore. The coffin is solemnly transferred from the hearse to the car especially designed for its reception, amid the thousands who accompanied it in procession. The glare of hundreds of torches light the way. Multitudes of human beings are in the immediate vicinity, and many male voices singing a dirge: the bells are tolled, and before the music of an instrumental band has ceased, we leave Chicago on our mournful errand to Springfield, with the remains of the beloved and honored President.

Mr. BLACKSTONE, the President, and ROBERT HALL, the Superintendent of the Railroad Company, together with many other accessions, are on board, and Mr. PULLMAN, the proprietor of the sleeping cars, has provided a sufficient number of them for the entire party, giving his personal attention to these truly desirable accommodations.

Speaker COLFAX, on leaving Chicago, was made the medium for delivering to the President, ANDREW JOHNSON, a brief address from the Independent Order of Odd Fellows of Canada, sympathizing with the nation in its affliction, tendering their well-wishes to the President for a successful and beneficent administration of the government, while expressing their friendship for him personally. The address is written in old English text on parchment. Speaker COLFAX was selected as the medium on account of his being a distinguished member of the Order.

We soon reach Bridgeport. The people here have lighted bonfires, and with torches light the way as the train slowly moves along. Passing by Summit, Joyes and Lennox, where we also see crowds of spectators, we reach Lockport at 11:33. At this place minute guns are fired. Many persons line the track holding torches, and in the background is an immense bonfire. Many of the houses are draped in mourning, and some are illuminated. One of the mottoes is: "Come Home." Hundreds of persons are here congregated, the men intently gazing with uncovered heads. The train passed all the stations slowly, at which times the bells of the locomotives are tolled.

JOLIET — Midnight.

Minute guns are fired and the bells tolled, and a brass band plays a funeral air. Many ladies and gentlemen, arranged on a heavily draped platform sung a hymn. It is said that 12,000 persons are gathered. The depot here, as at the preceding stations, bears an illuminated portrait of the late President, with the motto: "Champion, Defender and Martyr of Liberty." Bonfires light up this interesting scene. Draped national flags are waved by the color-bearers. It is raining, but this does not prevent even women and children from a participation in these outward marks of respect. The train moves beneath an arch which spans the track. It is constructed of immense timbers, decked with flags, mottoes and a profusion of evergreens, and surmounted by a figure of the Genius of America. "There is rest for thee in Heaven," was sung by male and female voices as we slowly left this interesting locality.

At Elwood and Hampton the people had kindled immense bonfires. . . .

[L]arge and small flags, mourning drapery and evergreens. Of the latter is formed a cross intertwined with black, bearing the motto: "Ours the Cross; thine the Crown."

ARRIVAL AT SPRINGFIELD.

We have now reached the city, where is to be deposited all that is mortal of ABRAHAM LINCOLN. Since leaving Washington, on Friday, the 21st of April, to this time, the 3d of May, (twelve days,) we have traveled by a circuitous route, seventeen or eighteen hundred miles. The funeral cars with which we started from Washington, have been brought all the way hither by rail. No accident, even of a trivial character, has happened, so perfect have been the arrangements of Brevet Brig. Gen. MCCALLUM, who has given to the movements his personal attention. Mr. DAKEHART, of the Baltimore and Ohio Railroad, has acted as an aid, and been efficient in that capacity. Col. ROBINSON, who is connected with the military railroads, now composes one of our party.

The fatigue of the journey has been relieved by kind attentions everywhere, and hospitalities profusely bestowed.

The remains of President Lincoln were received at the Chicago, Alton and St. Louis Station. The procession formed in the following order: Brig. Gen. COOK and staff; military escort; Maj.-Gen. HOOKER and staff; the guard of honor; relatives and friends in carriages; the Illinois delegation from Washington; Senators and Representatives of the Congress of the United States, including their Sergeant-at-Arms and Speaker COLFAX; the Illinois State Legislature; the Governors of different States; delegations from Kentucky; the Chicago Committee of Reception; the Springfield Committee of Reception; the Judges of the different courts; the reverend clergy; officers of the army and navy; firemen of the city; citizens generally; colored citizens, &c.

While the procession was moving, the law office of ABRAHAM LINCOLN, in a block of three-story brick buildings, was pointed out. The entrance was draped in mourning, and at the door hung a portrait of the deceased.

The hearse which carried the coffin was splendidly adorned. It was brought from St. Louis especially for the purpose, and cost over $5,000. It was drawn by six black horses. All the trappings were in accordance with the purpose for which it was used. The procession moved to the funeral music of an instrumental band. The houses on the streets through which it passed, all bore portraits and emblems of woe, with appropriate mottoes.

The Illinois and Mississippi Telegraph office was ornamented with a side view of an obelisk of pure white on a black ground. About midway up the shaft is the word "LINCOLN." Enclosed in a wreath of immortelle, and on the base is inscribed a sentiment from his last inaugural, namely: "With malice towards none; with charity for all. The windows are also tastefully adorned, including a bust of the late President standing on a black velvet pedestal, trimmed with silver fringe.

The remains were deposited in the State House with the usual solemn formalities.

SPRINGFIELD. Wednesday, May 3.

The outside of the dome of the capitol is deep black, and this, together with the cornice and pillars on which it rests are elaborately festooned with white and black. Similar drapery falls from the eves and the columns; the pediments, both on the north and south entrances, are corrugated with evergreens, and the capitol draped with white and black muslin. All the windows are partially curtined with black-white trimmings at the top and black falling at the base; from the crown of the dome is a staff on which is the national flag at half-mast with black streamers. The general arrangement is artistic and appropriate. The entrance to the capitol and the rotunda is heavily draped, and festoons of evergreens hang from the dome. The body lies in the Representatives' Hall, the galleries of which are supported by twelve columns, and, together with the panels, are covered with black velvet, trimmed with silver fringe. In the centre of each panel is a representation of a sprig of myrtle made of silver. On each column, under the gas jets, is an evergreen wreath, dotted with silk ribbons. On the west side of the hall is a painted blue ground, with white stars and alternate white and red, somewhat representing the national flag, with a black cloud above, as typical of the nation's gloom. Immediately in front of this is the catafalque. From the corners rise pillars, which are surmounted by black plumes, and covered with velvet, bordered with silver fringe. The ceiling is lined with white lace, dotted with golden stars, which glitter in the light of numerous gas jets. The effect is solemnly impressive. The coffin is placed on a platform, approached by steps. It is surrounded by evergreens and flowers. The walls are adorned by the following inscriptions: "Sooner than surrender this principle, I would be assassinated on this spot." "Washington the Father, Lincoln the Saviour."

The remains were, soon after their being placed in the State House, exposed to public view.

SPRINGFIELD, Wednesday, May, 3.

Thousands of persons have to-day visited the remains of the President, which have very much changed since they left Washington. To-night the stream continues. The appearance of the Hall of Representatives is worthy of a full description. The general arrangement was to make the decorations correspond with the room, which is a semicircular colonnade of eleven Corinthian columns, supporting a half-dome, the straight side being toward the west, the centre of which was the speaker's chair, which had been removed for the occasion. At the apex of the dome is a rising sun, radiant to the circumference. On the floor a dais was erected, ascended by three steps. On the dais a hexagon canopy, supported on columns twelve feet high, the shaft covered with black velvet; the capitals wrought in white velvet, with silver bands, and fills the canopy, tent-shaped, rising seven feet in the centre, covered with heavy black broadcloth in radiating stack folds, surmounted at the apex and at each angle with black plumes having white centers. A draped eagle is perched on the middle of each crown-mould. The cornice is of Egyptian pattern, corresponding with the captols covered with black velvet; the bands and mouldings are of silver; the lining of the canopy is of white crepe in radiating folds over blue, thickly set with stars of silver, and terminating at the cornice inside in a band of black velvet with silver fillets. Between the columns a rich valance in folds, with heavy silver fringe, from under which depend velvet curtains extending from each column two-thirds of the distance from the capitols to the centre of the cornice, looped with silver band—the whole so disposed as to exhibit both columns and capitols inside and out. The effect of the canopy and its supports and the drapery is very imposing, the whole being unique and elegant, combining lightness with massiveness with good harmony. Twelve brilliant jets of gas burning in ground globes spring from the columns, lighted the interior and reflected from the folds of double lining an opulent atmosphere to the whole.

The catafalque is covered with black velvet, trimmed with silver and satin, and adorned with thirty-six burnished silver stars, twelve at the head and twelve on each side, and was built after drawings made by Col. SCHWARTZ. The floor of the dais was covered with evergreens and white flowers. The steps of the dais were spread with broadcloth drapery, banded with silver lace.

The columns of the room are hung with black crape and the capitals festooned and entwined with the same, so as to display the architecture to good advantage, without detriment to the effect. The cornice is appropriately draped, and in large antique letters, on a black ground, are the words of President LINCOLN at Independence Hall, Philadelphia, Feb. 22 1861: "Sooner than surrender these principles, I would be assassinated on the spot." In front of the gallery are black panels nine feet by two and a half, having silver bands and centers of crossed olive-branches; above the gallery looped curtains of black crape extending around the semi-circle; below the gallery white crape curtains overhung with black crape festoons. Each column is ornamented with a beautiful wreath of evergreens and white flowers, the gift of Mrs. GEHLMAN, of Springfield. On the top of the gallery, extending the entire length, is a festoon of evergreens. The Corinthian cornice is festooned on the west at each side, twenty-four feet forward the center, supported by pilasters of the same order, the space between being surmounted by an obtuse arch reaching within one foot of the apex, and projecting six inches, leaving, after the removal of the speaker's chair, a depression resembling a panel, thirty-three feet wide by thirty-seven feet high. At the extreme height, in the upper portion of this was placed a blue semi-circle field, sixteen feet across, studded with thirty-six stars, six inches in diameter, and from which radiated the thirteen stripes on the American flag in delicate crape, two feet wide at the circumference of the blue field, increasing to the extreme lower angle, breaking on the dais below and the pilasters on either side, the whole crowned with blue and black crape, and so disposed as to correspond with the blue field, the stars and radiated panels of the ceiling. The central red stripe falls opposite the opening in the curtains at the head of the catafalque. On the cornice, each side of the flag work are placed two mottoes, corresponding with that on the semicircular freese, forming together these words; "WASHINGTON, the Father, and LINCOLN, the Savior." A life-sized portrait of Washington; the frame draped in blue crape stands at the head of the dais. . . .

. . . Capt. ROBERT LINCOLN and J. G. NICOLAY, the private secretary of the late President, arrived here to-night. During the day upward of five thousand persons have visited the former residence of President LINCOLN. It is a plain frame house, about thirty six feet front and eighteen high; two stories, with a heavy bracket-cornice, painted drab, and finished with green blinds. The rear of the building is in the form of an L, and sits several feet right from the street, and is approached by steps. The lady of the house was very kind, giving such information as was desired by the visitors.

To-Morrow there will be a grand military and civic procession to escort the remains of the late President to their last resting-place.

The horse formerly owned by ABRAHAM LINCOLN, is announced as one of the features of the programme. . . .

Long Journey Home

Leaving Springfield for Washington four years earlier, Lincoln had admitted to his neighbors that he did not know "when or whether ever I may return." Now he was back. On May 4, 1865, the bodies of the late president and his son, Willie, were laid to rest in a temporary receiving vault at Oak Ridge Cemetery just outside his home town. (Not for years was a monument built atop the hill to house the family permanently.) It was the closing act, The Times acknowledged, to "the grandest funeral procession in history."

As the cortege rolled slowly to Oak Ridge, it passed the large sign hanging over the windows of his old law office: "He Lives in the Hearts of His People." Nearby stood his brother-in-law's former store, above which Lincoln had composed his first inaugural address. Only a few blocks to the east was the only home he ever owned, now draped in black and crowded outside with neighbors and sightseers waiting to have their pictures taken there. At the graveyard ceremonies, Lincoln's eldest son, Robert, stood close to the vault. Mourners sang hymns, and ministers offered prayers.

The official sermon was delivered by Bishop Matthew Simpson of Springfield's Methodist Church, who struck a chord when he wondered aloud why so many people had thronged to cities across the nation to pay their respects. Simpson thought he knew the answer: "He made all men feel a sense of himself." And people, in turn, "saw in him a man who they believed would do what is right." Then the mourners joined in a final prayer. When the last verse echoed over the grassy hills, the tomb was sealed. Lincoln's long, fateful journey from Springfield to Washington and back to Springfield was over.

—H. H.

THE BURIAL.

President Lincoln Again at His Western Home.

The Mortal, Four Years Absent, Returns Immortal.

Close of the Grandest Funeral Procession in History.

Two Weeks' Solemn March Among Millions of Mourners.

The Place of Sepulture and the Last Ceremonies.

Eloquent Funeral Oration by Bishop Simpson.

Touching Manifestations by Mr. Lincoln's Neighbors.

SPRINGFIELD, ILL., Thursday, May 4.

The already large number of visitors who have been called here to view the remains of the late President Lincoln, was increased last night and this morning by numerous arrivals from all quarters.

The remains will be accompanied to the vault by a military and civic procession.

The ground selected for the burial is exceedingly beautiful.

The weather is clear and calm.

Second Dispatch

SPRINGFIELD, ILL., Thursday, May 4

Large numbers have continued to visit the former residence of the late President, on the corner of Eighth and Jefferson streets. It is hung with mourning without, and tastefully decorated within.

Large delegations from the adjoining States and neighboring settlements arrived through the night and this morning the hotels are overflowing. Some of the visitors are being entertained by the citizens, while thousands of others are unable to find accommodations.

The weather is warm and the sun unclouded. Everybody in Springfield are on the streets. The State House continued to be visited. At 11 o'clock last night, the ladies of the Soldier's Aid Society laid upon the coffin a beautiful cross of evergreens, studded with rare flowers. Other similar tokens have been contributed to-day.

At noon, twenty-one guns were fired, and afterward, single guns at intervals of ten minutes. About noon, the remains were brought from the State House and placed in the hearse, which was from St. Louis, and was used at the funerals of Hon. THOMAS H. BENTON, Gen. LYON and Gov. GAMBLE. The hearse was surmounted by a magnificent crown of flowers. Meanwhile, a chorus of hundreds of voices, accompanied by a brass band, sang the hymn,

> "Children of the heavenly King,
> Let us journey as we sing."

from the portico of the Capitol. . . .

The long line of civilians was closed by the Free Masons, Odd Fellows and citizens at large, including colored persons. The hearse was immediately followed by the horse formerly belonging to Mr. LINCOLN. His body was covered with black cloth trimmed with silver fringe.

Never before was there so large a military and civic display in Springfield. There were immense crowds of people in the immediate vicinity of the Capitol to see the procession as it passed, and the people for several miles occupied the sidewalks.

The procession arrived at Oakwood Cemetery at 1 o'clock. On the left of the vault in which the remains of the President and his son were deposited immediately on their arrival, was a platform, on which singers and an instrumental band were in place, and these united in the chanting and singing of appropriate music, including a burial hymn by the deceased President's Pastor, Rev. Dr. GURLEY. On the right was the speaker's stand, appropriately draped with mourning.

A short time ago, a piece of property containing eight acres, and located in the heart of the city, was purchased by the citizens for $53,000. The ground is improved with several substantial houses, and trees and shrubbery. It was designed to render the site additionally beautiful and attractive, and to erect thereon a monument to the illustrious dead. A vault has been completed for the reception of the remains, but owing to the wishes of ROBERT LINCOLN, the remains were deposited in Oak Ridge Cemetery nearly two miles from the city. The vault at this place is erected at the foot of a knoll in a beautiful part of the grounds, which contains forest trees of all varieties. It has a Doric gable resting on pilasters, the main wall being rustic. The vault is fifteen feet high and about the same in width, with semi-circular wings of bricks projecting from the hillsides. The material is limestone, procured at Joilet, Illinois. Directly inside of the ponderous doors is an iron grating. The interior walls are covered with black velvet, dotted with evergreens. In the centre of the velvet is a foundation of brick, capped with a marble slab, on which the coffin rests. The front of the vault is trimmed with evergreens. The "Dead March" in Saul was sung, accompanied by the band as the remains were deposited.

Thousands of persons were assembled at the cemetery before the arrival of the procession, occupying the succession of green hills. The scene was one of solemnly intense interest. The landscape was beautiful in the light of an unclouded sun.

The religious exercises were commenced by the singing of a dirge.
Then followed the reading of appropriate portions of the Scriptures and a prayer. After a hymn by the choir, Rev. Mr. HUBBARD read the last inaugural of President LINCOLN. Next a dirge was sung by the choir, when Bishop SIMPSON delivered the funeral oration. It was in the highest degree eloquent, and the patriotic portions of it was applauded. Then followed

another hymn, when benediction was pronounced by Rev. Dr. GURLEY. The procession then returned to the city.

We have followed the remains of President Lincoln from Washington, the scene of his assassination, to Springfield, his former home, and now to be his final resting-place. He had been absent from this city ever since he left it in February, 1861, for the national Capital, to be inaugurated as President of the United States. We have seen him lying in state in the executive mansion, where the obsequies were attended by numerous mourners, some of them clothed with the highest public honors and responsibilities which our republican institutions can bestow, and by the diplomatic representatives of foreign governments. We have followed the remains from Washington through Baltimore, Harrisburgh, Philadelphia, New-York, Albany, Buffalo, Cleveland, Columbus, Indianapolis and Chicago to Springfield, a distance in circuit of 1,500 or 1,800 miles. On the route millions of people have appeared to manifest by every means of which they are capable, their deep sense of the public loss, and their appreciation of the many virtues which adorned he life of ABRAHAM LINCOLN. All classes, without distinction of politics or creeds, spontaneously united in the posthumous honors. All hearts seemed to beat as one at the bereavement, and, now funeral processions are ended, our mournful duty of escorting the mortal remains of ABRAHAM LINCOLN hither is performed. We have seen them deposited in the tomb. The bereaved friends, with subdued and grief-stricken hearts, have taken their adieu and turn their faces homeward, ever to remember the affecting and impressive scenes which they have witnessed. The injunction, so often repeated on the way, "Bear him gently to his rest," has been obeyed, and the great heart of the nation throbs heavily at the portals of the tomb.

Bishop Simpson's Address.

Fellow-citizens of Illinois and of Many Parts of our Entire Union: Near the capital of this large and growing state of Illinois, in the midst of this beautiful grove and at the open mouth of the vault which has just received the remains of our fallen Chieftain, we gather to pay tribute of respect and drop the tears of sorrow around the ashes of the mighty dead. . . . Three weeks have passed. The nation has scarcely breathed easily yet. A mournful silence is abroad upon the land. Nor is this mourning confined to any class or to any district of the country. Men of all political parties and of all religious creeds seem united in paying this mournful tribute. . . . Here and there, too, are tears, as sincere and warm as any that drop, which come from the eyes of those whose kindred and whose race have been freed from their chains by him whom they mourn as their deliverer.

Far more have gazed on the face of the departed than ever looked upon the face of any other departed man. More eyes have looked upon the procession for sixteen hundred miles or more, by night and by day, by sunlight, dawn, twilight and by torchlight, than ever before watched the progress of a procession. . . .

Just in the midst of the wildest joy, in one hour—nay, in one moment—the tiding rang throughout the land that ABRAHAM LINCOLN, the best of Presidents, had perished by the hands of an assassin. And then all that feeling which had been gathering for four years in forms of excitement, grief, honor and joy, turned into one wall of woe—a sadness inexpressible; anguish unutterable. But it is not the time, merely, which caused this mourning: the mode of his death must be taken into account. Had he died on a bed of illness with kind friends around him; had the sweat of death been wiped from his brow by gentle hands while he was yet conscious; could he have had the power to speak words of affection to his stricken widow; words of counsel to us like those which we heard in his parting for Washington, in his inaugural, which shall now be immortal—how it would have softened or assuaged something of that grief! There might at least have been preparation for the event. But no moment of warning was given to him or to us. He was stricken down when his hopes for the need of the rebellion were bright and the prospects of a joyous life were before him. . . .

[The report is unfinished in consequences of the bad working of the wires.]

Swift Justice

Since Lincoln was, at the time of his murder, commander-in-chief in time of war, authorities ruled that the assassination had been a military crime. The surviving conspirators were denied a trial by civilian jury, and placed before a military tribunal. Their fate was never much in doubt. Before any evidence was offered, Secretary of War, Edwin M. Stanton declared, "The stain of innocent blood must be removed from the land."

From May 9 to June 30, the nine-man court heard an avalanche of testimony, a good deal of it irrelevant, from more than 300 witnesses. The accused sat on a platform at the front of a sweltering hearing room inside Washington's Old Penitentiary, separated by guards so they could not communicate with each other. None ever offered a word in their own defense. To no one's surprise, they were all found guilty.

Three of the defendants, Samuel Arnold, Michael O'Laughlen, and Dr. Samuel Mudd, the Maryland physician who had treated Booth's broken leg after the assassination, were sentenced to life in prison at the disease-

infested Fort Jefferson prison off the coast of Florida. Ned Spangler was or-
dered there for a term of six years. The other four—Lewis Powell, David
Herold, George Atzerodt, and Mary Surratt—were sentenced to death.

No woman had ever before been executed by the federal government,
and Mrs. Surratt—whose conspirator son, John, had not only escaped but
failed to return when his mother was captured—won considerable sympa-
thy. But President Andrew Johnson, though urged by many to pardon her,
showed no mercy.

On July 7, a day so hot that guards held umbrellas over the condemned
to shield them from the sun on the gallows, the four were hanged in the
prison yard. Seldom had justice worked so swiftly. Abraham Lincoln had
been dead for less than three months.

The controversy over the trial and sentencing has raged ever since.
Some historians have argued that Mrs. Surratt should have been spared
and that Dr. Mudd was railroaded. But the most recent scholarship makes
a convincing case for the guilt of both—while suggesting that the govern-
ment erred inexcusably by not granting a civilian trial to the men and
woman accused in the crime of the century.

—H. H.

THE CONSPIRATORS.

Finding of the Court.

Herrold, Payne, Atzeroth and Mrs. Surratt to be Hung.

The Execution to Take Place This Morning.

Dr. Mudd, Arnold and O'Laughlin to be Imprisoned for Life.

Spangler to be Confined in the Penitentiary at Albany for Six Years.

Delivery of the Death Warrants to the Condemned.

A Resume of the Testimony in Each Case.

WASHINGTON, Thursday, July 6.
In accordance with the finding and sentences of the Military Commission, which President JOHNSON approved yesterday, DAVID E. HERROLD,

LEWIS PAYNE, Mrs. MARY E. SURRATT and GEORGE A. ATZEROTH, are to be hung to-morrow, by the proper military authorities.

Dr. MUDD, SAMUEL ARNOLD and O'LAUGHLIN, are to be imprisoned for life.

SPANGLER is sentenced to six years' imprisonment at hard labor in the penitentiary at Albany.

The Executive Order.

WASHINGTON, Thursday, July 6.
The following important order has just been issued:

WAR DEPARTMENT, ADJUTANT-GENERAL'S OFFICE,
WASHINGTON, July 5, 1865.

To Maj.-Gen. W. S. Hancock, United States Volunteers, Commanding Middle Military Division, Washington, D. C.:

Whereas, by the Military Commission appointed in paragraph four, Special Orders No. 211, dated, War Department, Adjutant-General's Office, May 6, 1865, and of which Maj.-Gen. DAVID HUNTER, United States Volunteers, is President, the following persons were tried and sentenced as hereinafter stated, as follows:

First—DAVID E. HERROLD.

Finding—Of the specification "Guilty," except combining, confederating and conspiring with EDWARD SPANGLER, as to which part thereof, "Not guilty." Of the charge "Guilty," except the words of the charge that "he combined, confederated and conspired with EDWARD SPANGLER," as to which part of the charge, "Not guilty."

Sentence—And the commission therefore sentence him, the said DAVID E. HERROLD, to be hanged by the neck until he be dead, at such time and place as the President of the United States shall direct, two-thirds of the members of the commission concurring therein.

Second—GEORGE A. ATZEROTH.

Finding—Of the specification "guilty," except combining, confederating and conspiring with EDWARD SPANGLER. Of this "not guilty."

Sentence—And the commission does therefore sentence him, the said GEORGE A. ATZEROTH, to be hung by the neck until he be dead, at such time and place as the President of the United States shall direct, two-thirds of the members of the commission concurring therein.

Third—LEWIS PAYNE.

Finding—Of the specification "guilty," except combining, confederating and conspiring with EDWARD SPANGLER—of this not guilty. Of the charge "guilty," except combining, confederating and conspiring with EDWARD SPANGLER—of this not guilty.

Sentence—And the Commission does therefore sentence him, the said LEWIS PAYNE, to be hung until he be dead, at such time and place as the President of the United States shall direct, two-thirds of the members of the commission concurring therein.

Fouth—MARY E. SURRATT.

Finding—Of the specification "guilty," except as to the receiving, entertaining, harboring and counseling SAMUEL ARNOLD and MICHAEL O'LAUGHLIN, and except as to combining, confederating and conspiring with EDWARD SPANGLER. Of this not guilty. Of the charge "guilty," except as to combining, confederating and conspiring with EDWARD SPANGLER. Of this not guilty.

Sentence—And the commission does, therefore, sentence her, the said MARY E. SURRATT, to be hung by the neck until she be dead, at such time and place as the President of the United States shall direct, two-thirds of the members of the commission concurring therein.

And whereas the President of the United States has approved the foregoing sentences in the following order, to wit:

EXECUTIVE MANSION, July 5, 1865.

The foregoing sentences in the cases of DAVID E. HERROLD, GEORGE A. ATZEROTH, LEWIS PAYNE and MARY E. SURRATT are hereby approved, and it is ordered that the sentences in the cases of DAVID E. HERROLD, GEO. A. ATZEROTH, LEWIS PAYNE and MARY E. SURRATT, be carried into execution by the proper military authority, under the direction of the Secretary of War, on the 7th day of July, 1865, between the hours of 10 o'clock A. M., and two o'clock, P. M., of that day.

ANDREW JOHNSON,
President.

Therefore, you are hereby commanded to cause the foregoing sentences in the cases of DAVID E. HERROLD, G. A. ATZEROTH, LEWIS PAYNE and MARY E. SURRATT to be duly executed in accordance with the President's order.

By command of the President of the United States.

E. D. TOWNSEND,
Assistant Adjutant-General.

In the remaining cases of O'LAUGHLIN, SPANGLER, ARNOLD and MUDD, the findings and sentences are as follows:

Fifth—MICHAEL O'LAUGHLIN.

Finding—Of the specification "guilty," except the words thereof as follows: "And in the further prosecution of the conspiracy aforesaid, and its murderous and treasonable purposes aforesaid, on the nights of the 13th and 14th of April, A. D. 1865, at Washington City, and within the military department and military lines aforesaid, the said MICHAEL O'LAUGHLIN did then and there lie in wait for ULYSSES S. GRANT, then Lieutenant-General and Commander of the Armies of the United States, with the intent then and there to kill and murder the said ULYSSES S. GRANT." Of said words "not guilty; and except "combining, confederating and conspiring with EDWARD SPANGLER." Of this "not guilty." Of the charge "guilty," except combing, confederating and conspiring with Edward Spangler. Of this "not guilty."

Sentence—The commission does, therefore, sentence MICHAEL O'LAUGHLIN to be imprisoned at hard labor for life.

Sixth—EDWARD SPANGLER.

Finding—Of the specification, "not guilty," except as to the words "The said EDWARD SPANGLER, on said 14th day of April, A. D., 1865, at about the same hour of that day as aforesaid, within said military department and military lines aforesaid, did aid and abet him," meaning JOHN WILKES BOOTH, "in making his escape," after the said ABRAHAM LINCOLN had been murdered in the manner aforesaid, and of these words, "guilty." Of the charge, not guilty, but guilty of having feloniously and traitorously aided and abetted JOHN WILKES BOOTH in making his escape; after having killed and murdered ABRAHAM LINCOLN, President of the United States, he, the said EDWARD SPANGLER, at the time of aiding and abetting as aforesaid, well knowing that the said ABRAHAM LINCOLN, President as aforesaid, had been murdered by the said JOHN WILKES BOOTH, as aforesaid.

The commission sentenced SPANGLER to be confined at hard labor for six years.

Seventh—SAMUEL ARNOLD.

Of the specifications:

"Guilty," except combining, confederating and conspiring with EDWARD SPANGLER; of this "not guilty."

Of the charge:

"Guilty," except combining, confederating and conspiring with EDWARD SPANGLER; of this "not guilty."

The commission sentenced him to imprisonment at hard labor for life.

Eighth—SAML. A. MUDD.

Of the specifications:

"Guilty," except combining, confederating and conspiring with EDWARD SPANGLER; of this "Not guilty;" and excepting, receiving, and entertaining and harboring, and concealing said LEWIS PAYNE, JOHN W. SURRATT, MICHAEL O'LAUGHLIN, GEORGE A. AZTEROTH, MARY E. SURRATT, and SML. ARNOLD; of this "not guilty."

Of the charge:

"Guilty," except combining, confederating and conspiring with EDWARD SPANGLER; of this "not guilty."

Sentence.—The commission sentence Dr. MUDD to be imprisoned at hard labor for life.

The President's order in these cases, is as follows:

It is further ordered that the prisoners SAMUEL ARNOLD, SAMUEL A. MUDD, EDWARD SPANGLER and MICHAEL O'LAUGHLIN, be confined at hard labor in the penitentiary at Albany, New-York, during the period designated in their respective sentences.

ANDREW JOHNSON, President.

Visit to the Prisoners—Preparations for the Execution.

Special Dispatch to the New-York Times.

WASHINGTON, Thursday, July 6.

At 11 o'clock to-night we visited the Arsenal, in which the condemned prisoners are confined. The grounds and buildings are more strictly guarded than heretofore.

A double guard is on duty, the first of the sentinels being out at the gate, about a quarter of a mile north of the prison. About half-way between the gate and the building another body of armed soldiers halted us, and after making the required showing, we passed on to the prison. Here the greatest care is observed as to who pass in or out of the building.

Gen. HANCOCK arrived just as we alighted, and held a short consultation with Gen. HARTRANFT, who has charge of the prisoners, and Rev. Mr. BUTLER, of the Lutheran Church of this city, passed in at the same moment to the cell of ATZEROTH, who was sitting in close conversation with his brother, the latter preparing to take a final leave of the unhappy culprit.

The regular physician of the arsenal had just made his report of the condition of the prisoners. Mrs. SURRATT was, and had been since the sentence was read to her, dangerously prostrated, and the physician had prescribed wine of valerian. ATZEROTH was also equally prostrated, and for him brandy was ordered. The other prisoners were about as usual.

The spiritual advisors of Mrs. SURRATT were with her. The other prisoners were alone. PAYNE expresses no hope of life beyond the hour of execution to-morrow. Nor does he talk much to-night. He says JOHN SURRATT is acting cowardly, most villainously, in failing to appear and be with his mother. Being asked if he had any direction to give as to the disposition of his body, he answered that he had no friends within reach or immediate communication, and therefore his body must be subject to such disposal as the officers shall direct. He maintains that his relatives are all in Florida, and that his real name is POWELL. He expresses the deepest regret that Mrs. SURRATT is to be a sufferer by reason of any act of his, and evinces a solicitude for her not unlike that of a tender child for its parent, seemingly thinking only of her fate and the suffering she is about to undergo.

HERROLD is as he has been all through the trial, apparently inappreciative of his fearful position, and is scarcely more serious to-night than he has been at any time since the trial commenced. He has been visited several times to-day by his sisters, who are bowed in the most painful grief. He, too, expects no mercy, and makes no request other than that his body may be delivered to his family.

ATZEROTH is, characteristically, weighed down, and in fear and trembling. He is bewildered, stunned, and only appears to consider the bodily pain he is condemned to suffer. For his soul he has manifested no care. He was a coward when the time arrived for him to fulfill his part in the horrible drama on the night of the 14th of April. He is a greater coward now that he is to face death. He is devoid of sensibility other than to bodily harm.

The findings and sentences were read to the condemned separately, to-day, about 12 o'clock, by Gen. HARTRANFT, in the presence of Gen. HANCOCK, to whom the warrant for execution is directed, and of several officers of Gen. HARTRANFT'S staff. At the moment of reading the warrant no outward signs of emotion were visible on the part of the prisoners, save Mrs. SURRATT and AZTEROTH, each of whom trembled and grew deathly pale. Mrs. SURRATT faintly uttered a few words, saying: "I had no hand in the murder of the President."

In a few moments after the reading, however, all except PAYNE and HERROLD were deeply moved, though none had much to say, and their emotions being generally discoverable from their demeanor.

Soon after the promulgation of the sentences the friends and relatives of the prisoners began to arrive at the arsenal. Miss SURRATT, the daughter of the wretched woman of that name, was among the first to visit the prison.

The meeting of the criminal mother and sorrow-stricken daughter was most heart-rending. Soon, however, the former rallied, and straightway visited the President, to plead for a commutation of the sentence to an imprisonment for life.

She was joined by two Catholic priests and her mother's attorneys, who urged that the sentence and findings be set aside upon the ground that new and important evidence has been discovered which will exculpate their client.

The President was too ill to give them an audience, and referred them to Judge HOLT. The latter after hearing Miss SURRATT promised to present the subject to the President, but as yet nothing further is known to have transpired in the matter.

The sisters of HERROLD, five in number, called also in a body at the Executive Mansion to ask for a commutation, and they, too, were referred to Judge HOLT. There is no reason to believe that the President will pardon or commute the sentence of any, unless it may be in the case of Mrs. SURRATT.

As to whom it is understood that all the members of the Commission added to the sentence of a recommendation to the President, that in the exercise of his clemency it might be advisable to commute her sentence to imprisonment for life.

A scaffold is prepared and will be erected early in the morning, in the enclosed lot south of the arsenal, upon which the four prisoners condemned to death will be executed.

They will all be hung at the same moment. One o'clock is the hour at which the execution will take place. The lot in which the scaffold is to be erected is about one hundred and fifty by two hundred feet.

Surprise is expressed, almost unanimously, that the execution should be fixed for a day so immediate after the promulgation of the sentence. A week or ten days, it is thought, should have intervened between the announcement of the judgment and the day of execution.

It is believed that Mrs. SURRATT's sentence will be commuted to imprisonment for life. Such appears to be the general desire so far as can be determined this evening.

———

Dispatch to the Associated Press.

WASHINGTON, Wednesday, July 6.

Major-Gen. HANCOCK repaired to the arsenal at noon to-day, and delivered the death-warrants of PAYNE, HERROLD, Mrs. SURRATT and ATZEROTH, to Major-Gen. HARTSRAUFT, who is in charge of the prisoners, when they together visited the condemned to inform them of the sentences pronounced, and the time fixed for their execution. PAYNE was the first to whom the intelligence was communicated. It did not seem to take him by surprise, as doubtless he anticipated no other sentence, and had nerved himself accordingly. The other prisoners were naturally more or less affected. Mrs. SURRATT, particularly, sank under the dread announcement, and pleaded for four days' additional time to prepare herself for death.

All the prisoners will be attended by clergymen of their own designation. The scaffold has been erected in the South yard of the old Penitentiary building which is enclosed by a high brick wall. The coffins and burial clothes have already been prepared. Only a limited number of persons will be admitted to the scene. The sentences of the conspirators who are to be imprisoned will be carried into immediate effect.

Resume of the Evidence, and Personal Description of the Prisoners.

DAVID E. HERROLD.

The evidence against HERROLD of having assisted BOOTH in the assassination, and aided him to escape, was clear. As early as February last he was found to have been in confidential relations with the assassin, and was proved to have been present on several occasions at secret meetings with BOOTH, ATZEROTH and others of the conspirators. Once he was at Mrs. SURRATT'S in company with them. He called with SURRATT and ATZEROTH at the tavern in Surattsville, and left the two carbines and ammunition which were taken away from the tavern by him and BOOTH on the night of the assassination. During their flight he acknowledged to WILLIE JETT and other rebel soldiers that he and BOOTH were the assassins of Mr. LINCOLN, and he was captured in the barn with BOOTH. There can be no doubt whatever of his guilt. His personal appearance during the trial was described as that of a boy of nineteen, dressed in a faded blue suit, in height about five feet four inches, dusky black, neglected hair, lively, dark hazel eyes, slight tufts of hair along the chin and jaws and faintly surrounding the mouth, rather round face, full but not prominent nose, full lips, foolish, weak, confiding countenance indicating but little intelligence, and not the faintest trace of ferocity. HERROLD seemed to live but in the smile of BOOTH, following him devotedly in his flight, and sharing his privations, perils and capture.

GEORGE A. ATZEROTH.

It was shown beyond doubt that ATZEROTH was a co-conspirator in the assassination plot. He, like HERROLD, made his first appearance at Mrs. SURRATT'S house in the early part of February, inquiring for John H. SUR-

RATT or Mrs. SURRATT, and was thereafter frequently found in secret communication with BOOTH and his confederates. To him was assigned the murder of President JOHNSON at the Kirkwood House; but, notwithstanding it appears that there was no obstacle in the way of its performance, he does not seem to have made any effort to get access to his intended victim on the evening of the 11th of April. On the afternoon of the 11th he was apparently in flight, after he should have performed the task which he had voluntarily undertaken. He was traced to the Kirkwood House on horseback, about 9 o'clock in the evening, but did not remain there long, and was not seen near the house after that hour. He proved false to his confederates no doubt for want of pluck to do the murder, but is proved to have been in active cooperation with them throughout the night, and to have absconded at daylight the next morning, first throwing away the knife with which he was to have assassinated Mr. JOHNSON, and disposing of a pistol which belonged to HERROLD. During the trial ATZEROTH looked rather unconcernedly on, and at no time evinced a high sensibility of his almost inevitable doom. He is a man of small stature, Dutch face, sallow complexion, dull dark blue eye, rather light-colored hair, bushy and unkempt.

LEWIS PAYNE.

This prisoner is shown to have been the confederate of BOOTH, and to have been intimate with JOHN H. SURRATT. There has never been the slightest intimation on the part of himself or his counsel to deny his guilt. He went to Secretary SEWARD's house with the intent to kill him, representing to the servant, as he hurriedly passed him by, that he had brought medicine from Dr. VERDI, the family physician. Before he left the house, he not only stabbed Secretary SEWARD, but also nearly succeeded in killing Mr. FREDERICK W. SEWARD, and inflicted serious wounds upon Mr. AUGUSTUS H. SEWARD, Mr. FREDERICK W. HANSELL and Mr. GEO. F. ROBINSON, Secretary Seward's nurse. PAYNE is a native of Florida, and served some time in the rebel army, from which he deserted. He made his appearance at Mrs. SURRATT's in the early part of March, when he stated that his name was Wood, and afterward was a frequent visitor at the house, staying there on one occasion two or three days, and participating with JOHN H. SURRATT, ATZEROTH and BOOTH in the secret consultations. He and SURRATT were discovered in the bed-room of the latter, playing with bowie-knives. In this room were also found two revolvers and four sets of spurs, of the same kind as the spurs and revolvers found in ATZEROTH's room in the Kirkwood House. After doing his bloody work, PAYNE made his escape from Washington, whither he returned on the evening of the 17th, when he presented himself at Mrs. SURRATT's house, dressed as a laboring man, and carrying a pick-ax on his shoulder, saying that he had been engaged to dig a gutter. He was then arrested. In appearance, PAYNE is described as a wild and savage-looking man, showing no marks of culture or refinement—the most perfect type of the in-grain, hardened criminal. He is fully six feet high; of slender, bony, angular form, square and narrow across the shoulders, hollow breasted, hair black, straight, irregularly cut, and hanging indifferently about his forehead, which is rather low and narrow; blue eyes, large, staring, and at times wild; square face, angular nose, thin at the top, but expanding abruptly at the nostrils, thin lips and a slightly twisted mouth, curved un-symmetrically a little to the left of the middle line of the face.

MARY E. SURRATT.

This woman appears to have been cognizant of the intended crime al-most from its inception, even if she were not its instigator. Her house had been a refuge for blockade runners, and she was an active participant in overt acts. Her character appears to have been that of general manager. She received and entertained all the prisoners except Dr. MUDD, O'LAUGHLIN and ARNOLD. With Dr. MUDD she planned the means and assistance for the escape of the assassins. She visited Surrattville at 5 o'clock on the day of the assassination to see that the carbines, &c., should be in readiness, and informed LLOYD, the tavern-keeper, that they would be called for that night. BOOTH frequently called at her house and held long and confidential talks with her. He was in her company a few minutes on the afternoon of the 14th. When confronted with PAYNE on the night of his arrest, when he went to her house in disguise, she protested that she had never seen him, and added, "I did not hire him; I don't know him." It was proved that she knew Payne well, and that he had lodged at her house. She is described as a large woman of the Amazonian style, aged about fifty years. Her form is square built, her hands mascu-line, her face full, her eyes dark gray and lifeless, her hair not decidedly dark, and her complexion swarthy. During the trial she bore up strongly against the weight of crushing testimony against her, only once seeming to be at all disturbed.

MICHAEL O'LAUGHLIN.

To this prisoner appears to have been assigned the murder of Gen. GRANT; but whether he failed to make the attempt from lack of courage, from disinclination or from missing the opportunity, does not appear.

Gen. GRANT was announced to visit the theatre, but suddenly and unexpectedly took the cars to Philadelphia. ATZEROTH made the remark the next day when it was reported that Gen. GRANT had been shot, that "probably it is the fact, if he was followed by the man that was to do it." O'LAUGHLIN was clearly shown to have been in conspiracy with BOOTH. He was found lurking in the hall of Secretary STANTON's house on the night of the 13th of April, evidently watching the movements of Gen. GRANT, who was Secretary STANTON's guest, that he might be able with certainty to identify him. During the day and night before, he had been visiting BOOTH, and on the night and at the very hour of the assassination was in position at a convenient distance to aid and protect BOOTH in his flight, as well as to execute his own part of the conspiracy by inflicting death upon Gen. GRANT, who, happily, was not at the theatre nor in the city, having left the city that day. MC LAUGHLIN is an ordinary looking individual, about five feet five inches in height, bushy black hair, of luxuriant growth, pale face, black eyes, slight black whiskers, delicate silky moustache and thin goatee; weight about 130 pounds.

EDWARD SPANGLER.

The prisoner does not appear to have been in the conspiracy at an earlier period than a few hours before the commission of the crime. He was recognized as being one of three men in company with BOOTH in front of the theatre, and was heard that day to promise BOOTH assistance. His participation appears to have been in preparing the means of escape by keeping the passage-way clear on the stage, and by closing the door after BOOTH had passed through, so as to retard the movements of pursuers. Standing at the door after BOOTH had passed out, he exclaimed, "Hush, don't say anything about it!" He appears to have been BOOTH's drudge, sometimes taking care of and feeding his horse. During the progress of the trial his bearing was somewhat stolid. He is of short, thick stature, full face, showing indications of excessive drink, dull, gray eyes, unsymmetrical head, and light hair, closely cut.

SAMUEL ARNOLD.

ARNOLD was proven to have been at one time in full communion with the conspirators. His counsel claimed that at this time the plot was simply to abduct the President, and that ARNOLD and BOOTH quarreled, and the former withdrew from the conspiracy. The prisoner afterward went to

Fortress Monroe, and took a situation as clerk in a sutler's store, where he remained till his arrest, two days after the assassination. ARNOLD was at one time in the rebel service. He is about thirty years of age, five feet eight inches in height, dark hair and eyes, clear light complexion, and an intelligent and prepossessing countenance.

SAMUEL A. MUDD.

Dr. MUDD was shown to have been in the full confidence of BOOTH as long ago as last November. He had a suspicious meeting with SURRATT and BOOTH at the National Hotel in January. He introduced BOOTH to SURRATT. Visited him at his room in the Pennsylvania Hotel. BOOTH and HERROLD fled to his house directly after committing the murder. He dressed BOOTH's broken leg, and assisted the escape into Lower Maryland, of the latter and HERROLD. Three days afterwards, when called upon by the officers, he denied that he knew other of the criminals. When arrested on the Friday following, he prevaricated, lied outright, and finally admitted that he knew BOOTH. He said that he first heard of the assassination on Saturday at church, and it was shown by abundant proof that he was at Bryantown on the day preceding, (Saturday,) at an hour when the populace was all excitement, the town guarded by and full of soldiers, and every man, woman and child in the place had not only heard of the murder, but knew the name of the assassin. Of Dr. MUDD's being an accomplice in the assassination there can be no shadow of doubt. In appearance Mudd is described as being five feet ten inches in height, slender in form, hair red and sandy, and of thin growth, pale oval intelligent face, blue eyes, high forehead, rather prominent nose, thin lips, and a red tuft of hair upon his chin. . . .

END OF THE ASSASSINS

—

Execution of Mrs. Surratt, Payne, Herrold and Atzeroth.

—

Their Demeanor on Thursday Night and Friday Morning.

—

Attempt to Release Mrs. Surratt on a Writ of Habeas Corpus.

—

Argument of Counsel—Order of the President.

—

Scenes at the Scaffold.

—

The Four Hang Together and Die Simultaneously.

Interesting Incidents—Excitement in Washington—Order and Quiet in the City.

Special Dispatch to the New-York Times.

WASHINGTON, Friday, July 7, 1865.

The conspirators have gone to their long home, the swift hand of justice has smitten them, and they stand before the judgment seat. Electrified—saddened as the country was by the terrible calamity brought upon it by the damnable deeds of these deep-dyed villains, astounded as it has been by the daily revelations of the trial of the criminals, it was doubtless unprepared, as were all here, for the quick flash of the sword of power, whose blade to-day fell upon the guilty heads of the assassins of our lamented President.

Tried, convicted and sentenced, they stood this morning upon the threshold of the house of death, all covered with the great sin whose pall fell darkly upon the land. Young and old, equal in crime, they spent the night as is told hereafter, and when the first grey pencillings of the early morning traced the dawning day upon the sky, the city was all agog for the coming scene of retribution and of justice.

The Habeas Corpus.

Mrs. SURRATT's friends have been constant and faithful. They have manipulated presses and created public sentiment. The papers received here to-day were singularly unanimous in the supposition that the President would commute the sentence of Mrs. SURRATT to imprisonment for life. Such a sentiment found no echo here. It was well known that the counsel, family and friends of the culprit were determined to make every exertion, to strain every nerve in a strong pull and tug at the tender heart of the President in her behalf. She was a woman, and a sick woman at that. Her daughter was with her, and her cowardly son, with secrets in his possession that might mitigate her guilt—these and like arguments, it was said, would be brought to bear upon the President, backed with certain political strength which could not fail to succeed. But such talk has seemed idle from the first. Woman as she was, she knew her business well; sick as she was, she had strength sufficient for her fearful purpose, and stern as the sentence was, its justice was absolute, its execution certain. We have heard many express the desire that the woman's life might be spared and its weary hours passed in the quiet of the prison, but no one

384

who knew the President and his unmoveable nature supposed for an instant that the sentence would be changed in jot or tittle.

The hotels were thronged on Thursday. The streets were filled with restless, impatient people. The headquarters were surrounded by crowds of anxious men, who desired above all things to witness the execution, and who were willing to spend hundreds of dollars for that poor privilege. All day long the trains came in loaded with people from the North; all night long the country roads were lined with pedestrians, with parties hurrying on to the city, where they might at least participate in the excitements of the occasion.

Officials of every grade and name, with or without influence, were pestered by applications for tickets; the subordinate officers of the department were approached in every conceivable way, and by every possible avenue, by those whose idle or morbid curiosity impelled them to come to this hot and sweltering city in search of food for gossip and remembrance. Of course all endeavor was futile. Major-Gen. Hancock, who had charge of everything, had carefully prepared the list of people entitled to admission, and beyond those therein named, no one was permitted to be present. The

SCENES AT THE OLD CAPITOL

Prison on Thursday night were by no means so harrowing in intensity as the public doubtless imagine. So far as the authorities were concerned, there was possibly an increased vigilance, and extra precautions were taken with Mrs. SURRATT; but beyond that, matters went along quite in accordance with the general custom.

MRS. SURRATT,

about whose fearful participation in the murder of the President there has been thrown so much mystery, was a very remarkable woman, and, like most remarkable women, had an undertone of superstition which served her in place of true religion, and enabled her to sleep peacefully even while cognizant of such a crime as that for which she has now suffered. She was fifty years of age, but, although since her illness of the past two weeks she has grown old and looked pale and thin, she would be called rather forty-two or three. Firmness and decision were part and parcel of her nature. A cold eye, that would quail at no scene of torture; a close, shut mouth, whence no word of sympathy with suffering would pass; a firm chin, indicative of fixedness of resolve; a square, solid figure, whose proportions were never disfigured by remorse or marred by loss of sleep—these have ever marked the *personnel* of MARY SURRATT—these, her neighbors say, were correct indices of her every-day and every-year life.

Those who have watched her through the whole of this protracted trial have noticed her utter indifference to anything and everything said or suggested about her. The most terrible flagellation produced no effect upon her rocky countenance, stolid, quiet, entirely self-possessed, calm as a May morning, she sat, uninterested from the opening to the close.

Her guardians say she anticipated an acquittal, she alone knew why. When, therefore, she was informed of the finding of the court, the sentence, and its near execution, she might well be roused from the state of utter listlessness she had thitherto maintained. Weakened by continued illness, with head stunned by the sudden blow, she for a moment forgot the SURRATT in the woman, and felt the keenness of her position. Fainting, she cried aloud in the bitterness of her woe, wailing forth great waves of sorrow, she fell upon the floor and gave vent to a paroxysm of grief, partially hysterical, and wholly nervous. This was so unlike her, so entirely different from any conduct previously noticed, that the officer and her attendants were alarmed for her life. They sent at once for the regular physician of the arsenal, who pronounced her system deranged and dangerously prostrated. Wine of valerian and other quieting drink was given to her, and she revived, but no longer was she the Mrs. SURRATT of the court-room. She desired to see her spiritual advisers, and they were sent for. The sacred vail of ghostly comfort should not be rudely rent nor lightly lifted, but we may state with entire propriety that the miserable woman expressed the most emphatic desire for prayer and holy consolation. Desirous of clearing her mind first of all worldly affairs, she indicated the disposition she wished made of her property, and talked long and earnestly of her children and their future prospects. Toward her cowardly son JOHN she quite naturally entertained feelings of deep-seated bitterness. This she in a measure overcame after having relieved her mind about him and his conduct, and finally appeared reconciled to his desertion. What the feelings of the scoundrel must be to-day we cannot well imagine. If, as Mrs. SURRATT's friends more than intimated, his testimony would save her, if, as his own offer proved, his revelations would keep her from a death of infamy, we cannot believe he will dare survive her. Suicide and the unknown possibilities of the future, would seem preferable to life and the certain remorse and disgrace attending it here.

As the night wore on Mrs. SURRATT, who had been removed from the larger room where she has been confined since her illness, began to toss uneasily on her narrow bed. She was really ill and the kind offices of the physician were frequently needed. Conscious of the approach of day, she betook herself again to the preparation of her soul for its infinite journey. She rallied mentally and physically and determined evidently to bear and brave the scaffold. Her daughter, whose faithful service has been most touching in its constancy, had done all she could. The President had been seen, Judge HOLT had been visited. To both of them the most fervent appeals, inspired by a filial love as devoted as it was disinterested, had been presented, but in vain. Five of the members of the court had joined in a recommendation for commutation to imprisonment for life, and it was understood that the entire court concurred in the same, but this too was in vain. These facts the heartbroken daughter had communicated to her sentenced mother, and as she bent her head upon her neck she bathed her shoulders with tears of unfeigned grief and sympathy.

Seemingly convinced of the utter hopelessness of her situation, and apparently desirous of quieting the exceedingly demonstrative outbursts of her daughter, Mrs. Surratt rose from her bed and again betook herself to her devotional exercises. It may seem strange that this woman, who was proven to know all about the projected assassination, who kept open house for the scoundrels who planned and the villains who did the deed, who insisted that she had never seen and never knew Payne, and who said, when informed of her sentence, "I had no hand in the murder of the President," should seem so calm and consistent in her preparation for death. Nevertheless the fact is that after turning her back upon hope, she gave herself with apparent sincerity and with heartiness to prayer and communion, the effect of which it is not for us to judge.

This morning, however, the counsel of Mrs. SURRATT, Messrs. AIKEN and CLAMPITT, who had determined to leave no stone unturned to effect her release, if not that of detention in the execution of sentence, went at an early hour before Judge WYLIE, of the Supreme Court of this city, and applied for a writ of habeas corpus, directed to Maj.-Gen. Hancock, who had charge of the prison and control of the prisoners, commanding him to bring into Court the body of Mary E. SURRATT. . . .

After hearing the argument, the Judge indorsed upon the petition:

Let the writ issued as prayed, returnable before the Criminal Court of the District of Columbia, now sitting, at the hour of ten o'clock A.M., this seventh day of July, 1865.

(Signed,)   ANDREW WYLIE

A Justice of the Supreme Court of the District of Columbia.

JULY 7, 1865, AT 3 O'CLOCK A.M.

The writ was then formally issued, and the marshal of the District was directed to serve it. The news spread like wildfire, and all sorts of reports were circulated throughout the city. The hotels swarmed with talkative people, every one of whom had the latest news, and was only too ready to communicate it to his neighbor. "Mrs. SURRATT is pardoned," "She is not expected to live," "Her sentence has been commuted." Every one had his pet theory, but it concerned Mrs. SURRATT alone—the fate of the others seemed certain.

THE RETURN

was ordered at 10 o'clock, and at that hour the court room was thronged with people interested to know the result. The Marshal, in response to a question by the court, stated that Major-Gen. HANCOCK had not yet appeared, although it was past the hour.

After sundry criticism and objections to the proceedings by the District-Attorney, the counsel for Mrs. SURRATT stated that if his client was guilty of any crime, she was amenable to this court, a court which was competent to take cognizance of the same, and not to a military tribunal.

The District Attorney Mr. CARRINGTON, after reading the certificate of the Marshal, stating that he had served the writ on Gen. HANCOCK, at 8:30 o'clock, said that he appeared to defend the action of the Marshal by direction of the court, and he desired to report to the court, that the Marshal had done his duty.

The Court:

". . . The court acknowledges that its powers are inadequate to meet the military power possessed by Gen. HANCOCK. If the court were to decide at this moment that Gen. HANCOCK was in contempt, the only process which it would issue, would be an attachment for the disregard of its authority; but why issue a statement against the whole military power of the United States? This Court acknowledges that the laws are silent, and that it is without power in the premises, and therefore declines to make any order whatever. If there be a disposition on the part of the military power to respect the authority of the civil courts, they will respect the writ which has already been served; if on the other hand it is their determination to treat the authority of this court with contempt, in this matter they have the power, and will treat with equal contempt any other process which the court might order. The court therefore must submit to the supreme physical power which now holds the custody of the petitioner, and declines to issue an attachment to make any other order in this case." . . .

PRESIDENT'S INDORSEMENT.

EXECUTIVE OFFICE, July 7, 1865 — 1 O'CLOCK A.M.

To Major-Gen. W. S. Hancock, Commander, &c:

I, ANDREW JOHNSON, President of the United States, do hereby declare that the writ of habeas corpus has been heretofore suspended in such cases as this, and I do hereby especially suspend the writ, and direct that you proceed to execute the order heretofore given upon the judgment of the Military Commission, and you will give this order in return to this writ.

Signed,   ANDREW JOHNSON, President.

THE COURT—This court finds itself powerless to take any further action in the premises, and therefore declines to make orders which would be in vain for any practical purpose. . . .

This settled the case, so far as Mrs. SURRATT was concerned, and word was at once sent to her that all hope was gone.

Concerning PAYNE or POWELL, as he called himself, there has been a great deal of unnecessary mystery and foolish surmisings. His name, as far as the public is concerned, is

LEWIS PAYNE,

and if behind that he hid the honest name of a respectable family, the fact is one to his credit; but of that no one cares. He is dead; gone before the bar of a higher tribunal than that which last judged him, and with his future we have naught to do. The cool villainy, the absolute savagery of the fellow, has been consistent with the atrocity of his crime, until, with singular emotion, he became the apologist for his fellow-criminal, and the assailer of her son. By no means handsome, or of the romantic scoundrel stamp, PAYNE seems to have been a very common kind of person, with an exceedingly hard head and apparently no heart. No mere man would or could have deliberately cut and slashed the face of a sick and dying sufferer; it required the instinct of a demon and the temper of a brute to suggest and execute such a project. He was a species of idiot, an intelligent beast, with wit enough to understand his duty, sense enough to do it thoroughly, but unable to talk or maneuver himself out of such a scrape as he fell into at the door of Mrs. SURRATT'S house.

Throughout the trial he has been unmoved. Never sullen nor morose, he kept his eyes about him, seeing everybody and everything, but never for an instant admitting by sign or gesture that he recognized anything.

389

The confinement didn't annoy him at all. Quite likely he would have enjoyed a night in the town, and been as ready for a spree or a murder as ever; but he rarely opened his mouth, and as rarely closed his eyes, which wandered around and around, as if in continual search for an object of rest.

In his cell, PAYNE manifested no different appearance. His conduct was the same everywhere and at all times. He was a fit tool for the hand that used him—a reliable blade for a bloody purpose. At night he slept; in the morning he awoke early; his appetite was always good, and when the time for the meeting of the court was announced, he went along quietly as a lamb, as docile as an ox in yoke. When, therefore, his sentence was read to him, it was to be expected that his don't-care-ativeness, or stupidity, or *sang froid,* or whatever it may be termed, would still characterize him. He neither appeared surprised nor disappointed. Had he been pronounced "not guilty," it would have been the same—until he was freed; then he might have developed differently, though that is more conjecture, baseable upon no reliable data.

Doubly ironed, doubly guarded, PAYNE spent the day and night before his death. No future presented aught of hope or fear for him; no God or devil stared him in the face with searching scrutiny or tantalizing punishment. He simply felt nothing, and yet in the midst of apathy and indifference, we find him explaining that Mrs. SURRATT had nothing to do with the murder, inveighing against John SURRATT as a coward and scoundrel who had deserted his mother, leaving her to die when he should fill her place, and expressing tenderest regret that any set of his should have brought her into trouble and put her life in jeopardy. It is difficult to reconcile these two phases of character, so entirely different. Common sense forbids the belief that he feigned stupidity and was in reality a man of birth and breeding, and it likewise scouts the theory that he was entitled to sympathy on account of idiocy. Declining to participate in any religious mummery, and wholly averse to any religious reality, he passed his last hours in quiet stupidity, exerting himself to please no one, caring apparently nothing, either for the people here or the probabilities of the hereafter. His body was a source of no earthly considerations. Until he died it was not his—his keepers had it; after his death it was not his, and he did not care who had it. His friends, he said, lived in Florida. Before they could come, if they would, he would be gone, and the senseless clod which tenemented his scared soul would be en route to corruption. Why should he care? He didn't care.

One redeeming feature stood prominent. Noticing the kind consideration of Miss SURRATT toward her mother, PAYNE expressed regret that they should be compelled to part. He said he would do anything, say anything which could help Mrs. SURRATT, who was an innocent woman. He emerged from his brutism and became humane; he left his carelessness behind him and asserted the case of the mother against her recreant son; he forgot the idiot and resumed for the moment the attitude and intelligence of a man. With the clergymen he had but little to say. He seemed entirely careless as to his future, and down to the very last maintained his stolid, indifferent, hang-dog manner.

Perhaps there was more sympathy expressed for

DAVID E. HERROLD

than for any of the prisoners. He was young, thoughtless, light and trivial. He probably had never known a serious moment nor a sober thought. His following of BOOTH was very much such a companionship as a dog affords, and it seemed as if he might have been so thoroughly under the influence of that fascinating fiend as to be entirely *non compos*. The legal evidence against him was, however, clear and conclusive. As early as February last he was found to have been in confidential relations with the assassin, and was proved to have been present on several occasions at secret meetings with BOOTH, ATZEROTH and others of the conspirators. Once he was at Mrs. SURRATT'S in company with them. He called with SURRATT and ATZEROTH at the tavern in Surattville, and left the two carbines and ammunition which were taken away from the tavern by him and BOOTH on the night of the assassination. During their flight he acknowledged to WILLIE JETT and other rebel soldiers that he and BOOTH were the assassins of Mr. LINCOLN, and he was captured in the barn with BOOTH. His personal appearance was that of a boy of nineteen, dressed in a faded blue suit, in height about five feet four inches, dusky black, neglected hair, lively, dark hazel eyes, slight tufts of beard along the chin and jaws, and faintly surrounding the mouth, rather round face, full but not prominent nose, full lips, foolish, weak, confiding countenance, indicating but little intelligence, and not the faintest trace of ferocity. His sisters, who are apparently very estimable young women, labored with him, hoping to make some serious impression upon him, but in vain. He was full of levity almost to the very hour of his death. At the announcement of the finding of the court, HERROLD was unmoved. Indeed, none of the prisoners at first manifested any great concern—HERROLD and PAYNE least of any. PAYNE was sullen and indifferent, HERROLD careless and free. After a little, when the later hours of the night were passing silently by, he became more tractable and for the time left his habit of joking and gossiping, and when asked if he had any requests to make, desired that his body might be given to his family. With the clergyman he was ever respectful, but beyond a routine representation of words and phrases seemed to know and care little more about the coming than the present world. Impressible to a remarkable degree, but equally elastic, he talked and wept with the ministers, but was as ready for a quib or joke immediately after as ever. It is difficult to say that he was not a responsible person, and yet he seemed more like a butterfly than a man. He was at no time manly in deportment, and his exit from this world, was in accordance with his variable temperament while in it.

GEORGE A. ATZEROTH

was a coward, mentally, morally and physically. He failed to grasp the magnitude of the conspiracy as unfolded to him by the leaders; he failed to accomplish his part of the assassination scheme, and he failed to make any one care a rap whether he lived or died. During the trial he was unconcerned; since his imprisonment, was peevish and full of complaints, and on the night before his death he was restless and uneasy. He couldn't sleep at all, and, unlike PAYNE, had no appetite. He was a poor, miserable fellow, and his death amounted to no more than did his life.

THE MORNING OF THE DAY

appeared, and with it came thousands of people from afar to witness the execution. They might as well have come to see GEORGE WASHINGTON, the one was easy as the other. As above stated, every person in any way connected with the government, was tortured and annoyed by applications for passes to the prison. This morning the crowd of besiegers again appeared before 7 o'clock, and most of them failing to receive the desired pass, the curious wended their way to the arsenal grounds, two miles distant, in the hot sun, there to renew their importunities. When we arrived at the latter place, about 10 o'clock, the streets and avenues were blocked up by hundreds of vehicles, and probably 2,000 lookers-on, whose only reward for their exposure and labor was a peep at the prison walls in the distance. Four and One-half-street, the thoroughfare leading directly to the arsenal, was strongly and thickly guarded from Pennsylvania-avenue to the arsenal lot, and at the entrance to the latter, and completely surrounding it, were numerous soldiers on guard. Entering the enclosure, we found several regiments on duty—in all, two brigades of HANCOCK's corps—scattered here and there between the gates and the prison.

Pedestrians were flocking rapidly toward the building, and when we entered the latter, we found already several hundred persons—a mixed assembly of civilians and military men. We learned that none of the prisoners had slept during the past night save PAYNE and HERROLD, both of whom had a sound, quiet rest of about two hours. None of them had eaten anything scarcely except PAYNE, who partook heartily of breakfast. During the night opiates had been given Mrs. SURRATT to produce rest, but without avail. The spiritual advisers and friends of the condemned left the prison shortly after 11 o'clock last night, and none returned until this morning, except Miss SURRATT, who remained with her mother from about midnight until 5 o'clock A.M. No confessions had been made. None, indeed, could have been expected from either PAYNE, HERROLD or ATZEROTH, who had already from time to time, given in the main, probably, the truthful account of their relations to the bloody tragedy in which they were participants. Mrs. SURRATT was the only one remaining who had not acknowledged the full measure of her guilt. She, it was rumored, had made a full confession to her confessor, but on inquiry we found her confession in preparation for receiving the sacrament, was confounded with an acknowledgement of guilt for publicity. She had hope up to almost the hour of her execution that her sentence would be respited, if not commuted, and she had apparently lost sight of her own interest in deep solitude for her daughter, of whom she constantly talked, and repeatedly, frantically and with wringing of hands asked: "What will become of her—what will be ANNA's fate?"

STATEMENTS OF PAYNE.

PAYNE, last evening, informed Col. DODD, who has special charge of the prisoners, that so far as he knew, Mrs. SURRATT had nothing to do with the plot for assassination. Certainly she had never said a word to him on the subject, nor had any of his co-conspirators mentioned her in connection with the matter. She may have known what was going on, but to him she never disclosed her knowledge by word or act. That immediately after he had made the murderous attack upon Mr. SEWARD, he felt he had done wrong, and he had wandered around and slept in the woods that night, frequently feeling inclined to come to the city and give himself up. That when, finally, he was by hunger and loss of rest driven to Mrs. SURATT's house he had doubts about his reception there and whether she would not deliver him to the officers of the law for punishment. Col. DODD, who has been constantly in conversation with PAYNE, recently says the latter has never varied from one straightforward, consistent story, claiming at all times that he was informed and believed that he was acting

393

under an order from the rebel authorities, and did not, therefore, originally view his act as a murderous one. HERROLD says in the original plot to him was assigned the duty of shutting off the gas in the theatre, and he had once rehearsed the work with BOOTH; that, however, on the night of the assassination, he was only required to be in waiting near the Navy-yard Bridge to assist BOOTH in his escape.

These statements embrace substantially all the prisoners have given in the nature of confessions, other than what is found in the proofs and admissions on the trial.

DEMEANOR OF THE CONDEMNED.

We were permitted to look in upon the cells on several occasions during the forenoon, and up to a few minutes before the execution. The four prisoners condemned to death were removed yesterday from the upper floor of the prison to a tier of cells on the first floor South. ATZEROTH occupied the eastern apartment, No. 151, Mrs. SURRATT the next West, No. 153, HERROLD, No. 155, and PAYNE, No. 157, thus leaving a vacant cell between each of the prisoners.

Our first observation of ATZEROTH, found him in company with the Rev. Mr. BUTLER, a Lutheran minister of the gospel. The prisoner was lying upon his bed an intent and quiet listener to the whisperings of the minister. At another time ATZEROTH seemed utterly unnerved and tossed about, frequently clasping his hands together and wringing them as in hopelessness and despair. At noon and thereafter he became calmer and scarcely spoke or moved.

Mrs. SURRATT throughout the day continued in physical prostration, but grew calmer as the hour approached for execution. The parting between herself and daughter was borne with more fortitude than was expected of her, and whilst the latter swooned away, and was carried to an adjoining apartment senseless, Mrs. SURRATT appeared to rally in strength for the moment. Soon again, however, she lost strength, and when taken from her cell to the scaffold, she had to be almost literally lifted and borne along by the officers.

HERROLD's demeanor was somewhat after the manner he has shown from the commencement of the trial—listlessness and lack of appreciation of his fearful position, with alternatives of serious reflection.

PAYNE was, throughout the day, quiet and firm, occasionally joining the Rev. Dr. GILLETTE in earnest prayer.

THE SCAFFOLD.

In the lot south of the prison, and surrounded by a wall thirty feet high, the scaffold was erected. This structure is about seventy feet from the prison nearby, say thirty feet distant, were four freshly dug graves, and beside them four large pine coffins coarsely constructed.

The scaffold was so arranged that the four condemned could be hung at the same time.

The enclosure was much larger than was stated in my dispatch of last night, and there must have been present within the lot and upon the top of the wall, which was literally packed with soldiers, quite 3,000 spectators, three-fourths of whom were soldiers.

About 12:30 o'clock, Gen. HANCOCK arrived, and remained personally inspecting all the official acts.

THE PROCESSION OF DEATH.

At 1:15 the procession proceeded from the prison to the scaffold in the following order, preceded by Gen. HARTRANFT:

Mrs. SURRATT, supported by an officer and a noncommissioned officer, and attended by Rev. Fathers WALTER and WIGETT.

AZTEROTH, attended by an officer, with whom walked his spiritual advisers, Rev. J. G. BUTLER, of the Lutheran Church, and Chaplain WINCHESTER.

HERROLD came next, attended by Rev. Dr. OLDS, of Christ Church; Episcopal.

PAYNE, attended by Rev. Dr. GILLETTE, of the First Baptist Church, of this city, and Rev. Dr. STRIKER, of Baltimore.

Mrs. SURRATT, attended by two soldiers. Her waist and ankles were ironed; she was attired in a plain black alpacca dress, with black bonnet and thin veil. Her face could be easily seen. She gazed up at the horrid instrument of death, and her lips were moving rapidly as in prayer. She was assisted upon the scaffold and seated in a chair near the drop. She gazed upon the noose, which dangled in the wind before her face, and again her lips moved as if in prayer.

ATZEROTH followed, with a glaring, haggard look. He seemed to have changed in appearance greatly since his incarceration. He, also, was assisted by two soldiers, and seemed very feeble, but appeared to rally when on the scaffold, and took an evident interest in the proceedings.

HERROLD came next, supported on each side. He seemed very feeble, but revived a little subsequently. He realized his position now, if he never did before. He was very pale and careworn. He examined the scaffold closely, upon approaching it, and especially the drop.

PAYNE came next, with his usual bold, straight attitude, looking with seeming indifference upon the instrument of death. He wore a blue shirt and straw hat. There was not firmness in his step as he marched to the scaffold. . . .

THE LAST PAINFUL SCENE.

Gen. HARTRANFT read the order of the War Department, embracing the President's Executive Order, for the execution.

The limbs of each of the prisoners were now pinioned. The caps were drawn over their heads, Mrs. SURRATT exclaiming in a faint voice, "Don't let me fall; hold on!"

ATZEROTH exclaimed in a loud tone: "Gentlemen, take warning;" then, after an interval of about two minutes he said: "Good-by, gentlemen who are before me; may we all meet in the other world."

It was now twenty-five minutes past 1 o'clock. The officer in charge of the scaffold here made some preconcerted motions to the attendant soldiers to step back from the drop, and then, with a motion of his hand, the drop fell and the bodies of the criminals were suspended in the air.

The bodies fell simultaneously, and swayed backward and forward for a few minutes. Mrs. SURRATT, appeared to suffer very little. PAYNE and HARROLD, on the contrary, writhed in apparent agony, the first for about two minutes, and the latter for about five minutes. The muscles of their feet and hands were visibly contracted. Payne's hands, which were more exposed than the others, became purpled, as did his neck near where the rope was fastened. ATZEROTH's agony seemed, like Mrs. SURRATT's, to be of but very short duration.

After the lapse of ten minutes, the medical officers, Surgeon WOOD- WARD, U.S.A., Dr. OTIS, U.S.V., and Dr. PORTER, U.S.A., and Surgeon of the post examined severally the bodies, and pronounced life extinct. The ropes were cut, the bodies lowered, stretched upon the tops of the coffins, and a further and more minute examination was made by the Surgeons, who state that the necks of each were instantly broken.

At about 4 o'clock the bodies were placed in the coffins and buried.

The soldiers who were required to let fall the trap of the scaffold, are of Company F, Fourteenth Veteran Reserves. They were chosen by the Commander of that regiment who, without making known what was his purpose, required four able bodied men of the regiment to be selected from the left of the line, to perform a special and important duty. The selection was accordingly made before the service to be performed became known to the members of the regiment.

MUDD, ARNOLD, O'LAUGHLIN and SPANGLER will probably be sent to the Penitentiary to-morrow.

"Oh Captain! My Captain!"

Few contemporaries had felt a greater affinity for Lincoln than the poet Walt Whitman. Whether the future sixteenth president was genuinely influenced by the bracing literary style that Whitman introduced years earlier in "Leaves of Grass"—as one modern scholar recently argued—there is no question Whitman worshipped Lincoln.

As a wartime nurse in Washington, Whitman often saw Lincoln riding through the streets, bowed to him, and on occasion imagined that his acknowledgment was reciprocated. Lincoln "had faults," the poet later wrote, "and show'd them in the Presidency." But he remained in Whitman's opinion, "the greatest, best, most characteristic, artistic, moral personality" in American history.

Whitman demonstrated his reverence in the best way he knew: by paying tribute in verse. His deeply felt, and unusually complex lamentation, "When Lilacs Last in the Door-yard Bloom'd," reflected a passionate mourning for his hero.

> O powerful, western, fallen star!
> O shades of night! O moody, tearful night!
> O great star disappear'd! O the black murk
>   that hides the star!
> O cruel hands that hold me powerless! O
>   helpless soul of me!
> O harsh surrounding cloud, that will not free
>   my soul!

But by the time Whitman marked the twenty-second anniversary of Lincoln's assassination with a lecture at New York's Madison Theatre— *"an old man bent with years" as a* Times *reporter described him—he had earned his greatest fame with a far simpler poem about the assassination. From 1866 until his own death, Whitman could rarely get through a lecture or reading without someone from the audience calling for:*

O Captain! my Captain! Our fearful trip is done;
The ship has weather'd every rack, the prize we sought is won. . . .

—*H. H.*

A TRIBUTE FROM A POET

Walt Whitman Tells of Lincoln's Death.
TWO NOTABLE ASSEMBALGES PAY HONOR TO THE DAY AND THE
WORDS OF THE GRAY-HAIRED ORATOR.

Yesterday was the anniversary of the death of this country's greatest President. There was no public evidence of the fact, however. The majority of men in the pressure of personal affairs forgot it entirely. But a poet, an old man bent with years and tottering through the sunset of life to the twilight and the dark, came feebly forth from his retirement to lay his wreath upon the grave of his friend. The Poet was Walt Whitman and the President was ABRAHAM LINCOLN.

And a notable gathering came forth to listen to his words. At the Madison-Square Theatre were many whose names are national and many representatives of the highest literary circles of the city. There were James Russell Lowell, John Burroughs, Mrs. Frances Hodgson Burnett, John Hay, Augustus St. Gaudens, the sculptor; E. C. Stedman, Richard Watson Gilder; President D. C. Gilman, of Johns Hopkins University; Mary Mapes Dodge, Roswell P. Smith, Harry Edwards and Mrs. Edwards, Andrew Carnegie, A. M. Palmer, and others filling up the auditorium. The curtain rose at 4 o'clock upon a drawing room scene with a table in front. At the left was a handsome wreath of laurel with depending ribbons in red, white, and blue.

A moment later an old man, his hair and beard snow white, entered from the right. He leaned on the arm of a young man, supporting himself with a cane. He came slowly to the table, sat in the chair beside it, and laid his cane on the floor. The audience gave him the greeting of friends to a friend. He fumbled a little as his hands sought his glasses and adjusted them. Then he took up his manuscript and read. His voice was somewhat high-keyed, but clear, firm, and audible. His manner and pose were those of a venerable patriarch in his study talking to the friends who had gathered around. His lecture was a compilation of various memoranda which he has printed from time to time. He began:

"How often since that dark and dripping Saturday, that chilly April day now 22 years agone, my heart has entertained the dream, the wish to give Abraham Lincoln's death its own special thought and memorial. Yet, now the sought-for opportunity offers, I find my notes incompetent, and the fitting tribute I dreamed of seems as unprepared as ever. As oft, however, as the rolling years bring back the hour, I would that it might be briefly dwelt upon. And it is for this, my friends, that I have called you together. For my own part, I hope and intend, to my dying day, whenever the 14th of April comes, to gather a few friends and recall its tragic reminiscence."

He proceeded to generally describe the circumstances antecedent to the memorable tragedy. He spoke of his first sight of Lincoln. It was in front of the Astor House when Lincoln stopped here for a day on his way to Washington to be inaugurated for the first time. A crowd of many thousands had gathered in front of the hotel. He was not their choice as President. There was enmity to him in the throng. It had even been agreed that his few friends should make no laudatory outcry whatever, since it might excite an opposing manifestation of dislike. Accordingly, when Lincoln left his barouche and mounted the steps there was a dead silence. He turned and looked over the sea of faces with calm curiosity. With equal curiosity they stared at him. Amid perfect silence he then left them and entered the hotel.

The reader passed over the event that followed with light and general touches, and finally came down to the description of the tragedy, of which he was almost a witness, having been at Ford's Theatre that night. As he told the story slowly and clearly the effect was peculiar. He made no gesture, but as his words touched any part of the theatre he would look up at it in a way that was better than any gesture and impressive in the extreme. He said:

"The deed hastens. The popular afternoon paper of Washington, the little *Evening Star,* had scattered all over the third page divided among the advertisements, in a sensational manner, in a hundred different places, 'The President and his lady will be at the theatre this evening.' Lincoln was fond of the theatre. I have myself seen him there several times. I remember thinking how funny it was that he, in some respects, the leading actor in the stormiest drama known to real history's stage, should be there and be so completely interested and absorbed in those imaginary doings.

"On this occasion the theatre was crowded. There were many ladies in rich and gay costumes, officers in their uniforms, many well known citizens, young folks, the usual clusters of gaslights, the usual magnetism of so many people, cheerful and talkative, with perfumes and the music of violins and flutes in the air. And over all, and saturating all, that vast, vague, yet realistic wonder, victory, the Nation's victory, the triumph of the Union, filling the air, the thought, and the senses with exhilaration more than all the music and perfumes.

"The President came betimes, and with his wife witnessed the play from the large stage boxes of the second tier, two boxes thrown into one, and profusely draped with the national colors. The acts and scenes of the piece, ('Our American Cousin') one of those singularly written compositions which have at least the merit of giving entire relief to an audience engaged in mental action or business excitements and cares during the day, as it makes not the slightest call on either the moral, emotional, aesthetic, or spiritual nature, had progressed through, perhaps a couple of its acts, when in the midst of it came a scene not really or exactly to be described at all, for on the many hundreds who were there it seems to this hour to have left little but a passing blur in which two ladies are informed by an impossible Yankee that he is not a man of fortune. The dramatic trio made their exit, leaving the stage clear for a moment. At this period came the murder of Abraham Lincoln.

"Great as that was, with all its manifold train circling round it, and stretching it into the future for many a century in the politics, history, and art of the New World, the main thing, the actual murder, transpired with the quiet and simplicity of any common occurrence—the bursting of a pod in the growth of vegetation, for instance. Through the general hum following the stage pause, with the change of positions came the muffled sound of a pistol shot, which not one hundredth part of the audience heard at the time. There was a moment's hush, a vague, startled thrill, and then, through the ornamented, draperied, starred and striped spaceway of the President's box, a man raises himself with hands and feet, stands a moment on the railing, leaps below to the stage, a distance of perhaps 14 or 15 feet, falls out of position, catching his boot heel in the drapery of the American flag, but quickly rises and recovers himself as if nothing had happened, Booth, the murderer, dressed in plain black broadcloth, bareheaded, with raven glossy hair and eyes like some mad animal, flashing with light and resolution, yet with a certain calmness, holds aloft a large knife. He walks along, not much back from the footlights, turns fully toward the audience his face of statuesque beauty, lit by those basilisk eyes flashing with desperation, perhaps insanity, and launches out in a firm and steady voice these words: "Sic Temper Tyrannis." Then he walks with pace neither slow nor rapid diagonally across the back of the stage and disappears.

"A moment's hush—a scream—a cry of "Murder!" and Mrs. Lincoln leans out of the box with ashy cheeks and lips, and pointing to the retreating figure, cries: 'He has killed the President.'

"There is a moment's strange, incredulous suspense, and then—the deluge. The mixture of horror and uncertainty, a rising hum, upon which the clatter of hoofs intruded, and then the people burst through the chairs and railings, and break them up. There is inextricable confusion and terror. Women faint, feeble persons fall and are trampled on, cries of agony are heard, the broad stage suddenly fills to suffocation with a dense and motley crowd, and the audience rush madly anywhere. The actors and actresses are all there in the play costumes and painted faces, with mortal fright showing through the rouge. The screams and confused talk redouble, treble; two or three manage to pass up water from the stage to the President's box; others try to clamber up, and all is chaos. In the midst of it all the soldiers of the President's guard, with others, burst in. They scour the house through all the tiers inflamed with fury, literally charging the audience with fixed bayonets crying, 'Clear out, you—.' Such was the wild scene in that playhouse on that night.

"Outside, too, in the atmosphere of shock and craze, crowds of people come near in several places to committing murder upon innocent people. In one such case they got started against one man, either for words he uttered or perhaps without any cause, and hurried him to the nearest lamp-post. They were actually proceeding to hang him when he was rescued by a few heroic policemen, who placed him in their midst and then fought their way through great peril toward the State House. Through the pale-faced eddying and frenzied crowd they slowly progressed, but finally reached the haven and a second murder was avoided."

From this the reading took the turn of philosophy and panegyric. He talked of the influence of great men and their death. He wondered what the Greeks would have done with such a Lincoln and such a man as was ours in pæan and history and romance and their sad, sad farewell to them whom he called "unspeakably precious to the Union and the Democracy, their first martyr Chief!" by reading his poem, "Oh, Captain, My Captain," which ended with—

> "*Exult, oh shores, and ring, oh bells,*
> *But I with mournful tread*
> *Walk the deck, my Captain lies*
> *Fallen, cold and dead.*"

And then a beautiful incident occurred. Mr. Whitman had mentioned in his lecture that on the day of the murder the lilacs were blooming richly, and he never had since seen them in their season without having the memory of Lincoln recalled. Forth on the stage came a beautiful basket of lilac blossoms, and behind it was a little bit of a maiden in a white Normandy cap and a little suit of Quaker gray, her eyes beaming and her face deeply impressed with the gravity of the occasion. She walked to where he sat and held out her gift without a word. He stared, took them, and then took her. It was December frost and Maytime blossom at their prettiest contrast as the little pink cheek bone shone against the snow-white beard, for the old man told his appreciation mutely by kissing her and kissing her again.

INDEX

Abbott, E. W., 253
Action (police commissioner), 319
Adams, John Quincy, 4
agricultural colleges, 167
Aiken (lawyer), 387
Alcott, H. S., 300
Alexander, John, 303
Allston, Charles, 96
American Colonization Society, 139
amnesty oath, 192–197
Anderson, Robert, 95, 96, 97, 98, 99, 100, 101–102, 103, 104, 133
Andrews (Mass. senator), 40
Andrews, R. F. (surveyor), 253, 260
Arnold (representative), 266
Arnold, Benedict, 92
Arnold, Samuel, 371, 373, 375, .376, 381, 382–383, 397
articles of Confederation, 83–84
Ashmun (Massachusetts representative), 265–266
Aspinwall (businessman), 50

Associated Press, 38–42, 80–81, 199–206, 293–294, 348, 378–379
Astor, J. J., 298
Atlantic Monthly (magazine), 11
Atzerodt, George, 372, 373, 374, 376, 378, 379–380, 382, 391, 392, 393.394, 395, 396
Augur, Christopher (Gen.), 251, 254, 257, 261, 266, 295, 300

Baker, Edward D., 78, 137
Baker, Lafayette ("L. C."), 293, 343–344, 348–349, 352
Baker, Luther ("L. B."), 341, 344–345
Baldwin, Abraham, 20, 21, 22, 23
Bancroft, George, 280, 312
banking system, 131–132, 158–161, 293
Banks (governor), 45
Banks, N. P., 143, 238
Barnard (Gen.), 324, 325
Barnes (surgeon general), 243, 255, 267, 354

Barstow (Capt.), 324

Bassett, Richard, 21

Bates, Edward, 138

Baxter (commodore), 53

Beauregard, P. G. T., 95, 96, 98, 99, 100, 101, 102

Beecher, Henry Ward, 18

Beekman, James W., 298

Bell, John, 46, 47

Bellows (minister), 275

Belmont, August, 60

Benton, Thomas H., 368

Bigler (senator), 69

Bigslow (Newark mayor), 61

Birgfield (band musician), 187

black recruitment, 181, 183–185

Blackstone (railroad president), 362

Blair, F. P., 39, 40

Blair, J. P., Sr., 258

Blair, Montgomery, 138, 211, 220, 258, 271

Blatchford, R. M., 298

Bonaparte, Louis Napoleon, 31

Booth, Edwin, 306–307

Booth, John Wilkes, 235–236, 240, 248, 249, 251–252, 255–256, 263, 271, 289–290, 293–294, 296, 302, 306–311, 340–356, 375, 379, 380, 382, 383, 391, 394

Border States, 121

Bount, William, 20

Brackett (Capt.), 329

Bradley, Joseph P., 315

Brady (New York politician), 48

Brady, Matthew, 312

Brainard, Cephas, 43

Breckinridge, Benjamin, 359

Breckinridge, John C., 45, 46, 76, 172, 228

Briggs, J. A., 19

Brooks, Noah, 11

Brown (doctor; embalmer), 316, 330

Brown (Missouri delegate), 41

Brown, James, 298

Brown, John, 29–30, 31, 307–311

Browning (Illinois delegate), 40

Bryant, William Cullen, 19

Buchanan, Franklin, 172

Buchanan, James, 1, 4, 68, 75, 76–77, 78, 79, 89, 91, 166

Buckner, Simon B., 172

Buell (Gen.), 143

Burnett, Mrs. Frances Hodgson, 398

Burnside, Ambrose (Gen.), 154, 155, 197, 278, 321

Burrell, John E., 280

Burroughs, John, 398

Bushnell (Connecticut delegate), 210

Butler, Charles, 298

Butler, J. G. (Rev), 376, 394, 395

Butler, Pieter, 21

Butterfield (Gen.), 335

Button (Gen.), 227

Caesar, Julius, 274

Caldwell (Brig. Gen.), 324

Cameron, Simon, 4, 135, 136–137

Campbell, A. J., 213, 214, 218

Canada, 257, 304–307, 313–314, 351, 357

Candy (Capt.), 203

Carnegie, Andrew, 398

Carpenter (artist), 324

Carpenter (deputy), 56

Carpenter, Lewis, 321

Carpenter, S. (Sgt.), 315

Carrington (district attorney), 388

Carroll, Daniel, 21

Centar (Young Men's Republican Union), 43

Chandler, Zachariah, 4

Chapin (minister), 276

Charleston Mercury (newspaper), 65

Chase, Salmon P., 3–4, 8, 77, 78, 129, 131, 138, 158–159, 160–161, 207, 222, 223, 250, 253, 258, 262, 269, 295

Cheever (minister), 273

Chestnut (ex-senator), 98, 100

Chicago Daily Mail (newspaper), 15

Chicago Press and Tribune (newspaper), 10

Chicago Tribune (newspaper), 106

civil liberties, 167–176

Clampitt (lawyer), 387

Clark (Col.), 332

Clark, Emmons, 323–324, 337

Clarke, John S., 307, 308

Clay, Cassius M., 37, 135, 136

Clay, Clement C., 357, 358

Clay, Henry, 42, 325

Cleary, William C., 357, 358

Clymer, George, 21

Cochrane, John, 68

Colfax, Schuyler, 243–244, 265–266, 359–360, 362, 363

Confederate States of America, 4, 91

Conger, E. J., 344, 345

Conklin (congressman), 212

Conkling, F. A., 131

Conkling, James C., 7, 183–185

conscription, 161–166, 176–181, 210–211. *See also* draft riots

Constitution (U.S.), 5, 19, 20, 21, 22–23, 24, 31–32, 65, 73–74, 79, 83, 168–176, 193, 208

Constitutional Amendment, 217

Cooper Union Address, 10, 18–35, 312

Corbett, Boston, 341, 343, 346, 351, 352–355

Corn Exchange, 114, 115

Cornell, Charles G., 50, 280

Corning, Erastus, 168–176

Corse (Gen.), 227

Couch (Maj.-Gen.), 186

Coulter (senior railroad conductor), 316

Craig, D. H., 202, 204

Crane (doctor), 267

Crawford (doctor), 101

Crawford (sculptor), 228

Crew, R. S., 219

Cromwell, A. C. (Sgt.), 315

Curran (minister), 278

Curtin (governor), 316

Curtis (doctor), 267

Curtis (judge), 243

Cutting, E. B., 298

Daily Journal (newspaper), 102

Darling, W. A., 212, 298

Datton, Jonathan, 22

Davis, David (judge), 3, 69, 325

Davis, Jefferson, 91, 116, 161, 226, 228, 229, 240, 276, 357, 358–359

Dayton, W. L., 57–58

DeBare (Gen.), 227

Declaration of Independence, 65, 83

Delano (Ohio delegate), 39

Delavan, D. E., 280

Democratic Party, 4, 7, 9.16–18, 11

Dennison, William, 208, 253, 269

DePew, Chauncey (secretary of state), 319

Detmold, C. E., 298
Devins (Gen.), 228
Devoe (New York City detective), 300–301
Dewey, H., 54
Dittenhoff (Republican), 44
Dix, John A. (Maj. Gen.), 203, 205, 231, 241, 249, 250, 313–314, 324, 325, 327, 335, 341–342
Dodd (Col.), 393
Dodge, Mary Mapes, 398
Dodge, William E., 212, 280, 298
Doherty (Lieut.), 344
Dougherty, Edward P., 343, 348, 349, 352
Douglas, Stephen A., 9, 10, 15–18, 19, 20, 24–25, 34, 36, 37, 43, 44, 45, 46, 78, 79
Douglass, Frederick, 156, 211
draft. See conscription
draft riots, 176–181
Draper (New York City collector), 298
Dribbrell (Gen.), 359
Durken, James A., 315

Eaton (Gen.), 304
Eckert (Maj.), 219, 260
education system, 166–167
Edwards, Harry, 398
Edwards, Harry, Mrs., 398
Ellsworth (army officer), 62
emancipation, 138–140
Emancipation Proclamation, 3, 7, 12, 145–146, 147–149, 155–158, 182, 184, 190–192, 211, 218, 237
Emerson, Ralph Waldo, 2
Etheridge, Emerson, 118
Evarts, William M., 38, 40, 41, 50, 298, 313

Evening Post (newspaper), 44
Everett, Edward, 185–186, 187, 188
Ewell (Gen.), 227

Farnsworth, John (Gen., congressman), 243, 253, 254, 258
Farragut, James Glasgow, 228, 266
Farrell (minister), 278
Fehrenbacher, Don E., 235
Fenton, Reuben, 212
Ferguson, James B., 295
Fessenden (congressman), 132
Few, William, 20, 21, 23
Field, David Dudley, 19
Field, M. B., 253
Field, Maunsell B., 259–262
Fillmore, Millard, 1, 89
Fish (ex–New York governor), 50
Fitzsimmons, Thomas, 21
Foot (senator), 258
Foote (Capt.), 53
Forbes (army officer), 62
Forbes, Charles, 219
Ford's Theater, 12, 240–242
forgery
    newspapers, 199–206
Fowler, C. H., 360
France, 89, 333
Franklin (Gen.), 153, 278
Frémont, John C., 8, 133–135, 141, 144, 207, 211
French (Maj.), 266
French, B. B., 81
Fry (provost-marshal-general), 210–211

Gamble (Gov.), 368
Gansevoor, (Capt.), 53

Garrett (railroad president), 112

Garrett, John, 344–345, 346, 352, 353

Garrett, William, 344–345, 346, 352, 353

Garrison, William Lloyd, 213

Gatch, C. D., 253

Germany, 339

Getty, R. P., 202

Gettysburg Address, 11–12, 185–190

Gilder, Richard Watson, 398

Gillette (minister), 394, 395

Gilman, D. C., 398

Gilman, Nicholas, 21

Grant, Ulysses S., 6, 7–8, 197–199, 213, 214–216, 220, 226, 227, 229–235, 239, 242, 243, 244, 247, 265, 266, 272, 282, 296, 317, 381–382

Greeley, Horace, 5, 12, 19, 35, 38, 145–146

Grimes, James H., 4

Grinnell, Moses H., 50, 298

Grow, G. A., 118

Gurley, P. D., 252, 261, 263, 264, 270, 299, 369

Gurney, Jeremiah, 311–312, 326

habeas corpus, 167–176, 384–385

Hale, John P., 258, 265

Hall (Gen.), 321, 334

Hall (judge), 174

Hall, Neal, 253

Hall, Robert, 362

Halleck, Henry (Gen.), 141, 143, 198, 203, 253, 261, 266

Hamilton (Col.), 321

Hamilton, Franklin Alexander, 24

Hamlin, Hannibal, 36, 37, 38, 45, 47, 76, 207

Hancock, Winfield (Gen.), 344, 373, 376, 378, 387, 388–389, 392, 395

Handy, Parker, 298

Hansell, Emrick (State Dept.), 244

Hansell, Frederick W., 380

Hardenberg, A. A., 57

Harper, James (ex–New York City mayor), 53

Harriman (Col.), 214

Harrington, George (assistant secretary of the treasury), 266, 299

Harris, Clara, 240, 241, 253, 260

Harris, Ira (senator), 260

Harrold, David C., 341–344, 346–354, 355–356, 380, 396

Hartranft, John (Gen.), 377, 378, 395, 396

Hatfield (Brig. Gen.), 319

Hawes (comptroller), 52

Hawthorne, Nathaniel, 11

Hay (Col.), 243

Hay, John, 11, 89, 253, 261, 398

Hay, Mrs. John, 252

Heintzelman, S. P., 143

Henry IV (king of France), 274

Henry, Alexander (Philadelphia mayor), 64–65

Herold, David E., 372, 373, 374, 378, 379, 383, 391–392, 393, 394, 395–396

Hickman (vice-presidential candidate), 37

Hicks (Gov.), 69, 112

Hills, A. C., 44

Hitchcock (Gen.), 304

Hitchman, William, 280

Hoffman (recorder), 323

Hole, John B., 272

Hollander (arrested by Andrew Jackson), 174

Holt (judge), 378
Holzer, Harold, 16
Hooker, Joseph (Gen.), 153, 363
Howard, Joseph, 200
Howe, Frank E., 298
Howel (Brig. Gen.), 324
Hubbard (minister), 369
Huger, B. F., 112
Humphrey, James (congressman),
    212
Humphreys, Andrew (Gen.), 227
Hunt, Lewis (Brig. Gen.), 319,
    335
Hunt, Henry Jackson (Col.), 152
Hunter, David (Gen.), 143, 324,
    326, 373
Hunter, R. M. T., 213, 214, 215,
    218
Hunter, William, 250, 267, 270,
    314, 358
Hutchinson, William, 280

Illinois State Journal (newspaper),
    9, 10
Ingalls, Rufus (Gen.), 219
Ingraham (Col.), 256, 300
Irving, George Wasington, 326

Jackson, Andrew, 2, 106, 174–175,
    207, 325
Jackson, Thomas J. ("Stonewall"),
    154, 355
Jay, John, 278, 298
Jeffers, N. L., 257
Jefferson, Thomas, 1, 30, 127, 226
Jett, Willie, 379
Johnson, Andrew, 207, 208, 212,
    249, 250, 258, 268, 269–270,
    286, 290, 294, 297, 298, 299,
    300, 314, 357–358, 362, 373,
    374, 376, 380, 386, 389
Johnson, William S., 21

Johnston, Joseph E., 172
Jones, D. R., 96
Judd, Norman (Lincoln friend),
    16, 39, 67, 69

Keene, Laura, 296
Kelly, William (New York
    gubernatorial candidate), 48
Kennedy, J. J. C., 152
Kennedy, John A. (New York City
    police superintendent), 55,
    323, 324, 329, 356
Kershal (Gen.), 227
Ketes, E. L., 143
King, Rufus, 21, 22, 23
Kinman (Californian), 339
Kinney, Miss, 253, 262
Kinney, Mrs., 253, 262
Koontz, George, 219

Labineau, J. Harry, 332
Land-Grant College Act, 166–167
Lander (Gen.), 143
Landseer (artist), 260
Langdon, John, 21, 23
Lawson, Marshall W. B., 152
Lee, Custis, 227
Lee, Robert E., 4, 96, 110, 145,
    172, 181, 226, 227, 229–235,
    242, 265, 281–283, 289–290
Letcher, Bob, 106
Lieberman (deathbed visitor), 253
Lincoln, Mary Todd, 10, 60, 67,
    71–73, 137, 240, 241,
    242–246, 253, 262, 266, 271,
    296, 325, 359, 400, 401–402
Lincoln, Robert, 4, 73, 75, 253,
    261, 262, 265, 366, 369
Lincoln, Tad, 137, 226, 228
Lincoln, Willie, 137, 138, 316
Livingstone (Capt.), 319
Loomis (Col.), 282

Louaillier (publisher), 174
Lowell, James Russell, 398
Lyon (Gen.), 368
Lyons, Lord (British minister), 110

Madison, James, 21, 159
Magrath (judge), 99
Magruder, John B., 172
Manning, J. L.(ex–South Carolina
    governor), 96, 98, 100
Marcy (Gen.), 152, 153
Marshall (Capt.), 50
Marshall, Charles H., 278
McCallum (Brig. Gen.), 324, 363
McCawly, Jas. M., 295, 296
McClellan, George Brinton,
    140–141, 142, 143, 144, 145,
    151, 152–155, 197, 208,
    211–212
McClosky (archbishop), 273, 277,
    278
McCrillis (Maine delegate), 40
McCullough, Hugh, 247, 253, 258,
    268, 298
McDowell, I., 143, 197
McHenry, James, 20
McIntosh, J. (Sgt.), 315
McLaughlin (Maj.), 319
McLean, John, 39
McWaters (officer), 322
Meade, George Gordon (Gen.), 4,
    189–190, 198
Meigs, Montgomery (Gen.), 243,
    253, 261
Meller (Treasury Dept.), 260
Merchants' Exchange, 114
Mermerskirch (New York City
    detective), 300, 301
Mifflin, Thomas, 20
Miles (surendered to Jackson),
    354–355
Miles, W. Porcher, 96, 98, 99

Miller (judge), 256
Miller, D. Henry, 316
Mills, Clark, 218
Millward, William, 308
Minturn, Robert (businessman), 50
Mitgang, Herbert, 46
Morel (lawyer), 174
Morgan, Edwin D. (New York
    governor), 47
Morgan, R. C., 300, 301, 302
Morrell, George (Gen.), 153
Morrill Act, 167
Morrill, Justin (senator), 167
Morris, Gouverneur, 24
Morris, Robert, 21
Mosby, John S. (Corbett captured
    by), 355
Mostly, Edward H., 338
Mudd, Samuel A., 371, 372, 373,
    376, 381, 383, 397
Murphy (Lieut.), 315

Napoleon Bonaparte (emperor of
    France), 2, 286
New York Herald (newspaper),
    204, 331
New-York Historical Society,
    312–313
New York Journal of Commerce
    (newspaper), 199, 200–206
New York Sun (newspaper), 204
New-York Times (newspaper), 5,
    11, 15, 16, 18, 36, 49,
    66–67, 90, 102, 110,
    152–153, 158, 162–166,
    167, 181, 200, 201, 213,
    214, 217, 240–241,
    245–246, 248, 270, 289,
    295–297, 298, 312, 333,
    340–341, 360–361, 384, 397
New York Tribune (newspaper), 5,
    10, 12, 65, 204

New York World (newspaper), 199, 200–206, 235
Nicolay, John G., 11, 90, 366
Nye (Gen.), 19, 104

O'Bierne (Col.), 324, 326
O'Farrell (minister), 277–278
O'Laughlin, Michael, 371, 373, 375, 376, 381–382, 397
Oglesby, Richard (Gen., Illinois governor), 243, 253, 265, 266, 299
Olds (minister), 395
Olin (judge), 256
Ord, Edward (Maj. Gen.), 281–282, 291
Orsini (Italian revolutionary), 31
Otis (doctor), 267, 396
Ottiwell, J. D., 321
Otto (assistant secretary of state), 253

Paine, Lewis, 301, 302, 303. *See also* Payne, Lewis; Powell, Lewis
Palmer, A. M., 398
Parker (Gov.), 316
Parker (Lieut.), 229
Patterson (Gen.), 118
Patterson, William, 21
Patton (doctor), 360
Payne, Lewis, 297, 373, 374, 376, 377, 378, 380–381, 387, 389–391, 392, 393–394, 395, 396. *See also* Paine, Lewis; Powell, Lewis
Peck (Gen.), 278, 325
Perrine (quartermaster general), 316
Phillips, Charles, 2
Pickens, Francis W. (South Carolina governor), 102

Pierce, Franklin, 1, 4, 89
Pierrepont, Edwards, 298
Pinckney, Charles, 22, 23
Polk, James Knox, 2, 89
Pope, John (Gen.), 197
Porter (doctor), 396
Porter, David Dixon (Adm.), 226, 228
Porter, Fitz-John, 152, 153
Powell (choirmaster), 323
Powell, Lewis, 235, 297, 372. *See also* Paine, Lewis; Payne, Lewis
Power (chorister), 324
Preston (minister), 278
Preston, William B. (Gen.), 172
Price (journalist), 102
Prime, William (newspaper owner), 203
Prylor, Roger, 96
Pullman, George, 362
Purdy, E. J., 280

Ramsay, George (Brig. Gen.), 324
Ramsey, Alexander (senator), 258
Rash (New York City detective), 300
Rathbone, Henry (Maj.), 240, 241, 296, 346, 347, 353
Rathbun (Maj.), 321
Raymond (Col.), 53
Raymond, Henry J., 5, 11, 208–210, 212
Read, George, 21, 22, 23
Reeder (vice-presidential candidate), 37
Republican Central Campaign Club, 44–45
Republican Party, 8, 26–30, 33, 41, 42
Reynolds (Gen.), 153

Riblet (Col.), 327
Richards (Washington police
    superintendent), 251
Robert (army officer), 62
Robinson (Col.), 363
Robinson, George F., 380
Rogers, E. P., 332–333
Roosevelt, Theodore, 298
Rowhart, C. (Sgt.), 315
Russell, Charles H., 298
Russia, 333
Rutledge, John, 24
Ryder (doctor), 360

St. Gaudens, Augustus, 398
Sackett (Col.), 152
Sacramento Daily Union
    (newspaper), 11
Sampson (NYC detective), 300,
    301, 302
Sanders, George N., 357, 358
Sandford (Gen.), 321, 325
Schubert, Franz (composer),
    324
Schurz, Carl, 39, 40
Schwartz (Col.), 365
Scott, Thomas (assistant secretary
    of war), 137
Scott, Winfield (Gen.), 69, 89
Second Bank of the United States,
    2
Selden (Col.), 77
Seward, Augustus, 380
Seward, Clarence, 247
Seward, Fanny, 303
Seward, Frederick, 242, 244, 247,
    249, 250, 254, 292, 294, 300,
    303, 380
Seward, William H., 4, 6, 18, 35,
    36, 37, 38–39, 40, 41, 42,
    44, 45, 74, 75, 90, 103, 105,
    138, 186, 187, 197, 201,
    202, 218–219, 220, 221,
    241, 244, 245, 246, 247,
    249, 250, 252, 255, 264,
    271, 290, 291, 292, 293,
    294, 300, 301, 302, 306,
    313–314, 357, 380, 393
Seymour, Horatio, 176–181, 186,
    212
Shepard, Eliot F., 43
Shepley (Gen.), 228
Sheridan, Philip Henry, 226, 227
Sherman, Roger, 20, 21, 23
Sherman, William T., 198, 211,
    317
Shields (Gen.), 143
Shields, James, 10
Shubrick (Adm.), 266
Simons (Gen.), 100
Simpson, Matthew, 367, 368,
    369–371
Sloan, Samuel, 298
Smith (Maj.), 301, 302
Smith (Maryland delegate), 39
Smith, Green Clay, 300
Smith, Roswell P., 398
Spangler, Edward, 373, 374, 375,
    376, 382, 397
Spangler, Ned, 372
Speed, James, 247, 253, 258, 269
Sperry, N. D., 299
Spinner, F. E., 272
Springfield (Mass.) *Republican*
    (newspaper), 5
Stanford (Maj. Gen.), 324
Stanton, Edwin M., 4, 135, 136,
    138, 211, 227, 231, 233, 242,
    244, 247, 249, 251, 253, 258,
    265, 269, 312, 313–314, 342,
    371, 382
Stanton, Hall, 315
Staples, John S., 162
State Register (newspaper), 9

Stedman, E. C., 398

Stephens, Alexander H. (Confederate vice president), 213, 214, 215, 217

Stetson, (Col.), 299

Stevens, Thaddeus, 106, 131

Stewart, William (senator), 258

Stock Exchange, 114

Stockton (minister) , 187, 190

Stockton, John P. (senator), 316

Stockton, R. F. (Adj. Gen.), 316

Stone (Lieut. Cmdr.), 304

Stone, Andrew (newspaper owner), 203

Stone, B. K., 253, 255, 260, 267

Stoneman, George (Gen.), 358–359

Striker (minister), 395

Strong, Charles E., 326

Sturges, Jonathan, 298

Sumner, Charles, 4, 67, 132, 243, 253, 266

Sumner, E. V., 143

Surratt, John, 255, 256, 303, 376, 379–380, 386, 390

Surratt, Kate, 300–302, 377–378, 390

Surratt, Mary, 297, 300–303, 372, 373, 374, 376–381, 383, 384–388, 389, 390–391, 392, 394, 395, 396

Swan, Otis D., 298

Sweeny, P. B., 280

Sweitzer (Col.), 152

Sweltzer, Nelson, 343

Tammany Hall General Committee, 280–281, 339

Taney, Roger B., 74, 76, 77, 78, 89

Tannhauser (composer), 324

Taylor, Frank, 260

Taylor, Moses, 298

Taylor, Zachary, 2, 37, 89

Thomas (Gen.), 215

Thompson, J. P., 280

Thompson, Jacob, 272, 357, 358

Tileston (businessman), 50

Todd (Gen.), 253, 262

Toft (doctor), 267

Tomlinson (preacher), 272

Toombs, Robert (Confederate secretary of state), 116

Topp (army officer), 62

Townsend, Edward. D. (Brig. Gen.), 324, 374

Trumbull, Lyman, 4

Tucker, Beverly, 357, 358

Tuthill, G., 203

Tweed, William M. ("Boss"; New York City politician), 280

Tyler, John, 89

Tyrell (Lieut.), 256

Ullman, Daniel, 44, 45

Union League Club, 278–280, 298

United Kingdom, 30, 89, 333, 339

Usher, J. P., 247, 253

Vallandigham, Clement L., 7, 168, 172–175

Van Buren, D. T., 324, 327

Van Buren, Martin, 1, 89, 131

Van Ranst (businessman), 56

Van Vliet (Brig. Gen.), 323, 324

Van Vorst (Jersey City mayor), 57

Verdi (doctor), 244

Wade, Benjamin F., 45, 134, 137

Wadsworth, James, 143

Walker, R. J., 161

Wallace (doctor), 62

Wallach (Maj.), 251

Wallace, James P., 203

Walter (minister), 395
Ward, George Cabot, 298
Washington, George, 1, 21, 28, 52, 70, 127, 228, 276, 325, 366, 392
Webb (businessman), 50
Webster, Daniel, 3, 37, 42, 325
Webster, E., 44–45
Weeks, John A., 298
Weitzel (Gen.), 228
Welles, Gideon (secretary of the navy), 138, 244, 247, 253, 269
Wells, Henry H. (Col.), 300
Westmore, Samuel, 298
Wharton, J. W., 44
Whig Party, 2–3, 4, 8, 9, 10, 42, 158
Whitman, Walt, 49, 397–402
Wickliffe (Kentucky delegate), 133
Wigett (minister), 395
Wigfall, (Col.), 99, 100

Wigfall, Louis T. (Confederate congressman), 116
Willcox, Orlando (Gen.), 214
William, Prince of Orange, 274
Williams (Gen.), 219
Williams, G. F., 216
Williamson, Hugh, 20
Winchester (minister), 395
Wise, Henry A. (Virginia governor), 308
Wood (army officer), 62
Wood, Fernando (New York City mayor), 50–52, 53, 55–56
Woodward (doctor), 267, 396
Wright (Gen.), 227
Wylie, Andrew, 387

Yates, Richard (senator), 254, 258, 265, 266
Young Men's Lyceum (Springfield, Illinois), 2
Young Men's Republican Union, 43–44

216